THE TWO HORIZONS OLD TESTAM[ENT COMMENTARY]

J. GORDON McCONVILLE and CRAIG BARTHOLOMEW, *General Editors*

Two features distinguish THE TWO HORIZONS OLD TESTAMENT COMMENTARY series: theological exegesis and theological reflection.

Exegesis since the Reformation era and especially in the past two hundred years emphasized careful attention to philology, grammar, syntax, and concerns of a historical nature. More recently, commentary has expanded to include social-scientific, political, or canonical questions and more.

Without slighting the significance of those sorts of questions, scholars in THE TWO HORIZONS OLD TESTAMENT COMMENTARY locate their primary interests on theological readings of texts, past and present. The result is a paragraph-by-paragraph engagement with the text that is deliberately theological in focus.

Theological reflection in THE TWO HORIZONS OLD TESTAMENT COMMENTARY takes many forms, including locating each Old Testament book in relation to the whole of Scripture — asking what the biblical book contributes to biblical theology — and in conversation with constructive theology of today. How commentators engage in the work of theological reflection will differ from book to book, depending on their particular theological tradition and how they perceive the work of biblical theology and theological hermeneutics. This heterogeneity derives as well from the relative infancy of the project of theological interpretation of Scripture in modern times and from the challenge of grappling with a book's message in its ancient context, in the canon of Scripture and history of interpretation, and for life in the admittedly diverse Western world at the beginning of the twenty-first century.

THE TWO HORIZONS OLD TESTAMENT COMMENTARY is written primarily for students, pastors, and other Christian leaders seeking to engage in theological interpretation of Scripture.

Genesis

James McKeown

WILLIAM B. EERDMANS PUBLISHING COMPANY
GRAND RAPIDS, MICHIGAN / CAMBRIDGE, U.K.

Published 2008 by

Wm. B. Eerdmans Publishing Co.

2140 Oak Industrial Drive N.E., Grand Rapids, Michigan 49505 /

P.O. Box 163, Cambridge CB3 9PU U.K.

Printed in the United States of America

14 13 12 11 10 09 08   7 6 5 4 3 2 1

Library of Congress Cataloging-in-Publication Data

McKeown, James.
   Genesis / James McKeown.
        p.   cm.   — (The two horizons Old Testament commentary)
   Includes bibliographical references and index.
   ISBN 978-0-8028-2705-0 (pbk.: alk. paper)
   1. Bible. O.T. Genesis — Commentaries.
   2. Bible. O.T. Genesis — Theology.   I. Title.

BS1235.53.M35   2008
222'.1107 — dc22

                                                              2007044628

www.eerdmans.com

Contents

Contents

Acknowledgements

While writing this book I was very dependent on the help of a number of people. I am grateful to the editor, Dr. Gordon McConville, for his encouragement, advice, and guidance throughout the project. At the beginning of the work I benefited from a semester of study leave which was kindly granted by the Board of Belfast Bible College, to whom I owe my sincere thanks. Colleagues in the Institute of Theology, Queen's University Belfast also made helpful suggestions relating to their own field of expertise. My M.Th. student, Philip Moore, took the time to read and comment on the entire work, and I am most grateful to him also. Finally, thanks to my wife Audrey for her patience, encouragement, and unstinting support.

Abbreviations

AB	*Anchor Bible*
ABD	*Anchor Bible Dictionary*, ed. D. N. Freedman
ANET	*Ancient Near Eastern Texts Relating to the Old Testament*, ed. J. B. Pritchard
BA	*Biblical Archaeologist*
BAR	*Biblical Archaeology Review*
BASOR	*Bulletin of the American Schools of Oriental Research*
BBR	*Bulletin for Biblical Research*
BJRL	*Bulletin of the John Rylands University Library of Manchester*
BSac	*Bibliotheca sacra*
BSC	Bible Student's Commentary
BSOAS	*Bulletin of the School of Oriental and African Studies*
CBQ	*Catholic Biblical Quarterly*
CC	Continental Commentaries
ConBOT	Coniectanea biblica: Old Testament Series
COS	*The Context of Scripture*, ed. W. W. Hallo
DOTP	*Dictionary of the Old Testament: Pentateuch*, ed. T. D. Alexander and D. W. Baker
DtH	Deuteronomistic History/Historian
ErIsr	*Eretz-Israel*
ESV	English Standard Version
ExpTim	*Expository Times*
FOTL	Forms of the Old Testament Literature
GKC	*Gesenius' Hebrew Grammar*, 2nd ed.
HUCA	*Hebrew Union College Annual*
ICC	International Critical Commentary
IDB	*The Interpreter's Dictionary of the Bible*, ed. G. A. Buttrick
IDBSup	*The Interpreter's Dictionary of the Bible: Supplementary Volume*, ed. K. Crim

viii

Int	*Interpretation*
JAAR	*Journal of the American Academy of Religion*
JANES	*Journal of the Ancient Near Eastern Society*
JAOS	*Journal of the American Oriental Society*
JBL	*Journal of Biblical Literature*
JPS	Jewish Publication Society
JSOT	*Journal for the Study of the Old Testament*
JSOTSup	Journal for the Study of Old Testament: Supplement Series
JTS	*Journal of Theological Studies*
JTSA	*Journal of Theology for Southern Africa*
KJV	King James Version
LXX	Septuagint
MT	Masoretic Text
NDBT	*The New Dictionary of Biblical Theology,* ed. T. Alexander and B. S. Rosner
NEB	New English Bible
NICOT	New International Commentary on the Old Testament
NIDOTTE	*New International Dictionary of Old Testament Theology and Exegesis,* ed. W. A. VanGemeren
NIV	New International Version
NJB	New Jerusalem Bible
NJPS	New Jewish Publication Society *Tanakh*
NKJV	New King James Version
NLT	New Living Translation
NRSV	New Revised Standard Version
NT	New Testament
OBT	Overtures to Biblical Theology
OT	Old Testament
OTL	Old Testament Library
PWCJS	*Proceedings of the World Council of Jewish Studies*
RSV	Revised Standard Version
RTR	*Reformed Theological Review*
SR	*Studies in Religion*
SSN	Studia semitica neerlandica
TOTC	Tyndale Old Testament Commentaries
TynBul	*Tyndale Bulletin*
VT	*Vetus Testamentum*
VTSup	Supplements to Vetus Testamentum
WBC	Word Biblical Commentary
ZAW	*Zeitschrift für die alttestamentliche Wissenschaft*

Introduction to Genesis

Genesis is an anonymous book. We are not told anywhere in the Bible who wrote it, nor are we given any clues about the date when it was completed. At an early stage in the development of the Hebrew canon, Genesis became associated with Exodus, Leviticus, Numbers, and Deuteronomy. Together these five books were known in Jewish circles as the Torah and as the "Five Books of Moses," or simply "Moses." Although this nomenclature did not necessarily mean that Moses wrote everything in these five books, a strong tradition of Mosaic authorship developed and was very widely accepted in both Jewish and Christian circles until the 18th century.

To describe Genesis as a book is misleading if we understand the term "book" in a modern sense. Genesis does not conform, nor should we expect it to conform, to the criteria that we apply to modern literature when we describe, for example, a novel or a history book as "good." Genesis does not have a single plot, but, just as there are several stories, there are several plots and their interrelatedness is not always obvious. Indeed, some of the stories in Genesis could be lifted out of their present contexts in the Genesis narrative and used independently.[1] On the other hand, Genesis is more than a collection of short stories, because even if some of them could be used independently and, at some early stage, may have been, they are unified in the book of Genesis as we now have it. The stories are not preserved as independent chapters or passages, but they all contribute in some way to the overall goal and aim of the book.

Since many of the stories in Genesis have their own individual plots, it is helpful to think of Genesis as moving towards a goal rather than as a book with a unified plot. The idea of movement captures the character of Genesis

---

1. E.g., Genesis 14 contains all the necessary information for the story to be understood without reference to the preceding chapters.

very well, since much of the book's interest and dynamic impact is made through at least five different ways of conveying movement and development. The most noticeable of these methods of conveying movement are chronological, spatial, and historical. However, the work also moves, perhaps less obviously, towards thematic and theological goals. It is the way in which the diverse materials of Genesis are all caught up in this dynamic and multifaceted matrix of development that gives Genesis its appeal as an action-packed book with a profound theological message and enables us to read it as a unity. Therefore, the reader should approach Genesis as a complex but exciting work that comprises a rich interplay of themes and plots that are caught up together in an inexorable movement towards the purpose and goal of the work.

Title and Structure

The Hebrew title of Genesis is בְּרֵאשִׁית/*bĕrē'šît*, from the first word of the book: it is usually translated "In the beginning." The title that we are familiar with in our English translations, "Genesis," is a transliteration of a Greek word meaning "origins."

Even a cursory reading of Genesis reveals that the book has two main sections: chapters 1–11 and 12–50. This division is on the basis of subject matter: the first 11 chapters are universal in content and outlook, while the remaining 39 chapters have a narrow focus on one family line. However, while this is a convenient way of dividing the material, it can mislead the reader by giving the impression that the first 11 chapters are merely introductory and unrelated to chapters 12–50. But this would be a gross underestimation of the value and function of these early chapters, since they establish principles and themes that provide a foundation and, indeed, an interpretative key for the events of chapters 12–50. For example, the way in which God deals with Adam in relation to the garden of Eden provides a useful introduction to the promise of the land of Canaan to Abraham.

However, a more complex structure is apparent when Genesis is studied in detail. Genesis is divided into 10 sections by a phrase that is often called the "Toledot Formula." This formula is a phrase that is usually translated in English as "These are the generations of . . ." or "this is the family history of . . ." The most significant Hebrew noun in this phrase is תּוֹלְדֹת/*tôlēdôt*, and hence the name. Ten times the phrase אֵלֶּה תּוֹלְדֹת/*'ēlleh tôlĕdôt* occurs (2:4; 6:9; 10:1; 11:10; 11:27; 25:12; 25:19; 36:1; 36:9;[2] 37:2). On one occasion there is a

---

2. Genesis 36:9 repeats 36:1. Verse 9 is not considered to be the beginning of a new section

similar expression: זֶה סֵפֶר תּוֹלְדֹת/*zeh sēper tôlĕdōt,* "This is the book of the generations of"(5:1). These occurrences of this formula divide Genesis into 10 main sections. The noun *tôlēdôt* is linked to the verb ילד/*yld,* which means "to bear children." This is reflected in most of the modern translations: NRSV "generations of"; NJB "descendants of." The main difficulty with such translations is that they cannot really apply to the first occurrence of the word *tôlēdôt* in 2:4 in relation to the heavens and the earth. This is probably why the NIV prefers to translate *tôlēdôt* with "account of." However, this is not entirely satisfactory, since the *tôlēdôt* sections do not introduce the account of the person named, but they usually give the history of his descendants. It is better to use a translation for the occurrence in 2:4 different from the later occurrences. The use of *tôlēdôt* in this way draws the reader's attention to the importance of birth and genealogical lines in Genesis and shows that the theme of "offspring" is an important one throughout the book.

Rhetorical and Literary Characteristics of Genesis

An understanding of the literary and rhetorical devices used in the book of Genesis is necessary if we are to distinguish between how ancient writers communicated their message and how modern authors do. One of the book's most obvious distinguishing features is the widespread use of repetition. While source critics have focused on repeated material as evidence of multiple sources, rhetoricians view repetition as a device used by the ancient writers to highlight and emphasize the most important aspects of their message.

Repetition is widely used as a rhetorical device in Genesis to an extent and with an effectiveness that is probably not evident in any other biblical book. Not only is repetition used to highlight and emphasize certain aspects of the message, it is also used to compare and contrast characters, to convey subtle nuances of meaning, and to unify the work thematically and structurally.

Verbal Repetition

This is the most obvious form of repetition in Genesis. Key names or words are repeated to convey urgency or special significance. Examples are "Abra-

---

since the information in vv. 9-43 merely expands the brief introduction to the *tôlēdôt* of Esau in vv. 1-8.

ham, Abraham" (22:11) and the fivefold repetition of the Hebrew root associated with blessing in 12:1-3.

Repetition as a structuring device is also used within smaller rhetorical units such as the genealogies, and we have seen how the repetition of the *tôlēdôt* formula acts as a structuring device to divide Genesis into 10 sections.

Thematic Repetition

The main unifying themes of the book are evident in every cycle. The most obvious themes that provide a sense of cohesion and continuity throughout Genesis are the themes of *Offspring, Blessing, and Land*. It is not just their repetition but the way in which these themes are developed that is significant. In the introduction to this chapter we observed that Genesis is a book that moves towards a goal; the material is continually taking the reader forward into ever-changing vistas with such gradual momentum that they themselves are scarcely aware of the changing scene. The themes of offspring, blessing, and land are the fundamental elements of the book's cohesion, and it is through their permeation of the material that the entire work achieves a unity of purpose and direction. It is through these themes that God reveals himself to the characters in Genesis and indeed to those who have read the book ever since.

Each unifying theme depends on God for both development and denouement, but the way in which God relates to the themes and, through them, to the characters concerned undergoes a number of staged changes until at the end of the book a transformation has taken place. God's method of choosing people for special attention, bestowing blessing, and apportioning land changes from his regular walk in the garden and direct conversation with its inhabitants to less frequent face-to-face contact with Abraham and Jacob. By the end of the book the closest encounters are through dreams while the eponymous ancestors of the tribes seem to have no direct communication with God at all. So while the same themes repeatedly occur and convey a sense of unity, they also convey development in which God seems to distance himself from the main characters. This distancing of God from people happens in tandem with a noticeable decline in the moral and religious standing of some of the main characters.

Reader Expectations

All readers approach texts with their own ideas and expectations. This personal perspective can help to illuminate the text, but it can also cause the reader to miss or filter out some of the more controversial elements of the message. For example, a person whose faith has been severely tested may derive courage from the text and understand it at a deeper level than the more casual reader. This is particularly the case with the text's presentation of the character of God and his dealings with human beings. From what we know of Israelite history, it was a turbulent experience with only short periods of comparative peace and prosperity and many examples of external pressures and internal instability both politically and theologically. Israelite experience of God had its fair share of misunderstanding and trial of faith (cf. Psalm 44). Many of those who read Genesis through the years of Israel's tribulations as a nation would come to the text with genuine questions about why the nation should have suffered so many catastrophes if they were God's people. Genesis is not a superficial book that ignores the spiritual struggles and doubts that religious people face, and it does not attempt to cover up their problems and questions. Genesis has a very relevant message for people who are struggling with life and with faith because most of the characters face such struggles. The book presents God in terms that do not avoid the hard questions that people of faith face. Facile answerers never achieve anything, as Jeremiah pointed out to those who listened to the false prophets (cf. Jeremiah 28). Therefore, the characterization of God presents him as a God who judges people very rigorously, and the world is not the cozy, idealistic world of the pietistic sort of religion that always believes that everything will go well for good people. On the contrary, good people (like Hagar and Joseph) suffer in Genesis, and so do good animals such as those who drown outside the ark. Even people of faith like Abraham must wait an inordinately long time to see the goal of their faith realized. They probably could not have identified with some of our traditional hymns; it is doubtful, for example, if Abraham's or Joseph's experiences verified that "not a doubt nor a fear, not a sigh nor a tear, can abide while we trust and obey." Genesis spurns superficial language and presents life, even for its most godly characters, as a struggle of faith. For people going through their own personal struggles Genesis offers support, not in a superficial way, but by realistically illustrating that life throws up surprises for us all and that even God does not act entirely predictably towards the faithful. In particular, people like Abraham went through periods when it appeared that God had forgotten about them and their lives showed the importance of waiting patiently for God's promises to be fulfilled.

Many come to Genesis expecting to receive answers to their scientific questions about creation. Many Jews and Christians have for centuries believed that Genesis answers questions such as "How was the world made?" and "How long did it take God to create the world?" Even before the modern era this brought some people into conflict with scientific theory since, for example, those who read Genesis literally found it difficult to believe that the moon reflects the light of the sun and does not produce light itself. Also the description of the moon as a *great* light became problematic when people realized that many of the planets are much larger than the moon. Calvin sought to obviate these difficulties by suggesting that Genesis 1 presents creation as it would have been seen by the naked eye in the days of Moses and his contemporaries.

However, further intractable problems would follow. In the 17th century the archbishop of Armagh, James Ussher, used the genealogies in Genesis to determine that the date of creation was 4004 B.C. This very influential proposition was challenged in the 19th century by the declaration of geologists that the earth was many thousands of years older than this date suggested. Biblical interpreters replied with the theory that the flood had distorted the evidence, making the earth look older than it is in reality. Furthermore, it was argued that God created mature specimens of, for example, trees and rocks, giving them the appearance of age.

When Charles Darwin published his *Origin of Species* in 1859, the idea of evolution was perceived as a direct challenge to the teaching of Genesis, since it was taken to imply that the first humans were not intelligent and were little more than animals. Evolution is still a very contentious issue among Christians, since many believe that the choice is simple — you either believe that the Bible is the Word of God or else you believe in evolution, but you can't have both. Some have sought to overcome the problems by interpreting Genesis in a way that removed any conflicts with science. One such attempt postulated gaps in the text to accommodate scientific discoveries while maintaining the scientific accuracy of Genesis. Similar motivation has led others to allege that the days of Genesis need not be 24-hour days since, as in English, the word "day" sometimes refers to a period of time. These approaches, especially the latter, are still very popular, but they face the criticism that they let modern science be the key to interpret texts that were written thousands of years ago for primarily theological reasons. Genesis was written for people who had serious challenges to their faith, and they desperately needed the reassurance that Genesis brought. If we read this ancient book to a scientific agenda only, we shall miss the message of encouragement and challenge that it brought to those who read it first.

For many, however, the Bible is God's Word for today, and the fact that it was written thousands of years ago is irrelevant. While this approach must be applauded because of the high level of respect that it affords to the text in terms of divine origin and absolute authority, it is only one dimension of the

Bible's existence. To understand the Bible we should also inquire about the world and circumstances from which it emanated. It was not written in heaven and dropped down to earth, but it developed in the rough-and-tumble of human life, reflecting human struggles and misunderstanding. Emphasis on divine authorship should not blind us to the human dimension of Scripture because God used human beings to write down the words. As we read these words, it is evident that the circumstances and background of the writers are reflected in the vocabulary used, in the literary style, and in the illustrations employed.

It is actually very exciting to remember that when we open the pages of the Bible we are reading literature that was written some three thousand years ago, and as we flick through the pages of India paper we should not forget that some of these words would have been written for the first time on a very different material.

The Mystery of Authorship

There are a number of references in this book to commentaries that use the dating system associated with the Documentary Hypothesis. A very basic and brief introduction to this hypothesis is given here to acquaint readers with the nomenclature used. However, in recent years the Documentary Hypothesis has lost the preeminent position that it once enjoyed in OT studies, since many scholars prefer to concentrate on the final form of the text and see a synchronic approach as a better way to get an overview of the books of the Pentateuch.

From 18th to the early 20th century a number of theories were postulated culminating in the Developed Documentary Hypothesis. The most influential scholar in this area was Julius Wellhausen (1844-1918). Building on the work of scholars who preceded him, Wellhausen gained widespread support for the Developed Documentary Hypothesis. He argued that the Pentateuch was composed from four originally distinct documents. These documents were labelled using the letters JEDP. The first document was labelled J because one of the main methods of identifying it was that its preferred name for God was Yahweh (Jahweh in German). This Yahwistic source was believed to be the earliest pentateuchal source, written about the 9th century. Later scholars dated it earlier still in the 10th century. The second source was labelled E because one of the main ways used to identify it was its use of the name Elohim instead of Yahweh. It was argued that this source did not use the name Yahweh until the time of Moses. The Elohist source was dated in the

7

late 9th or early 8th century and certainly earlier than the 8th-century prophets. It was argued that these two documents were combined by an editor and are now very difficult to separate. In fact, they are so difficult to separate that some influential critics such as Claus Westermann doubt whether they ever existed as separate continuous documents. The third source was labelled D because it was believed to comprise an early edition of Deuteronomy. This was added in the time of Josiah and was probably influenced by the 8th-century prophets. Finally, it was believed that during the 5th century a document was written in priestly circles with a strong emphasis on rituals and laws; for obvious reasons, it was labelled P. Eventually, the Priestly document was combined with the earlier material.

The Documentary Hypothesis rejected Mosaic authorship and replaced it with a hypothetical theory that placed the final edition of Genesis and the other books of the Pentateuch in the postexilic period. Some of the main reasons given for rejecting Mosaic authorship are as follows: a) The Pentateuch contains the record of Moses' death (Deuteronomy 34) and several other passages which Moses could not have written. For example, it is argued that reference to Moses being the most humble person on earth could not have been written by him! b) The formula "until this day" (Gen 32:32; 35:20; Deut 3:14; 34:6). c) The statement "at that time the Canaanites were dwelling in the land" (Gen 12:6; 13:7). d) Passages which mention "a king in Israel" (Gen 36:31). e) Names are given to places which they would not have had until after the time of Moses (Gen 14:14). However, these points do not preclude the possibility that Moses might have written substantial parts of the Pentateuch.

A great deal of work was done by scholars evaluating and developing the Documentary Hypothesis. In spite of all the work done, the authorship and prehistory of the Genesis text are still a mystery. The legacy of the work done is an awareness of the complexity of determining the composition and authorship of an ancient document. Although important questions remain about the origins of Genesis, source-critical studies of the book have reached an impasse and many have turned their attention to the final form of the text, since the hypothetical nature of the previous studies combined with the impossibility of proving or disproving the plethora have made further progress elusive.

The Methodological Crisis

Thus, for almost two centuries the majority of studies in Genesis concentrated on an analysis of the sources underlying the book. Comparatively little attention was focused on the final work. While there were always been a few "wilderness" voices raised in protest against this imbalance, they were scarcely audible because of the impressive unison of the vast majority. From the 1980s, however, the protests became more vociferous and effective. Meir Sternberg, for example, complained about

> over two hundred years of frenzied digging into the Bible's genesis, so senseless as to elicit either laughter or tears. Rarely has there been such a futile expense of spirit in a noble cause; rarely have such grandiose theories of origination been built and revised and pitted against one another on the evidential equivalent of the head of a pin; rarely have so many worked so long and so hard with so little to show for their trouble.[3]

So, an increasing number of scholars turned their attention to the biblical text in its final form, a change of direction that was described as "from analysis to synthesis." Most scholars would still agree that source-critical studies have a role to play. However, when it comes to understanding the message of a book such as Genesis in the form it has been handed down to us, a holistic approach provides a less fragmented picture of the work.

However, it is not a simple matter of opting for the New Literary Approach instead of the analytical approach, because a plethora of approaches have been developed under the umbrella of New Literary Approach. As Sternberg argues, "The Literary approach, with its monolithic ring, is downright misleading."[4] The description "new" was also misleading, since it is often the case that "what purports to be a newly discovered prescription for correctness of method turns out, less excitingly but perhaps more usefully, to be a serviceable description of what was happening all the time."[5]

Most synchronic studies, regardless of how the methodology is fine-tuned, tend to create an awareness of the literary qualities of the entire work in a way that source analysis could not do. In particular, holistic studies enable the researcher to highlight the recurrence of the key words, phrases, motifs, and themes that give the work its distinctiveness as a literary unity. It is this synchronic approach that is followed in this commentary.

3. Sternberg, *The Poetics of Biblical Narrative*, 13.
4. Sternberg, *Poetics*, 3.
5. Barton, *Reading the Old Testament*, 11.

Approach Taken in This Book

Although in Christian circles there is an emphasis on applying the Scriptures in a way that makes them relevant today, it is also helpful to try, at least to some extent, to identify with the ancient readers. Although we can know comparatively little about them, this is no reason to read the text as if it was written primarily for 21st-century Christians. If we imagine how the text would help ancient Israelites in their walk with God, we may understand the text at a deeper level. It is very tempting to apply a Christian hermeneutic to everything we read, but this will cause us to miss some issues that the early readers would have found interesting and important. For example, if we take the usual Christian approach to Gen 3:15 and declare that the "seed" of the woman who will bruise the serpent's head is Jesus Christ, we shall not look any further in the book of Genesis to discover what it has to say about this "promised seed." The first readers, on the other hand, who were living before the time of Christ would read Genesis with this promise in view. They would expect Genesis to give them information about the line of descent through which this "seed" would come.

In order to identify with the issues that may have faced early readers of Genesis and indeed of the Pentateuch, the commentary which follows draws attention to passages that may have been helpful to readers who were in exile or who had recently returned from exile. I have chosen the exilic readers because this avoids most objections about the date of authorship, and it also relates well to the subject matter of Genesis. The concepts of exile and homecoming are very prominent throughout Genesis. Thus Adam, Cain, and the temple-builders experience exile in chapters 1–11. Abram must leave his home country and accept voluntary exile, and the book records several examples of exile from Canaan to Egypt or Aram involving Abram, Jacob, and Joseph. Returning from exile is a particularly prominent theme in the story of Jacob. Since these concepts of exile and return are so prominent in Genesis, it seems a good method of contextualizing the material to ask what sort of help exiles would receive from it. The issues facing the exiles such as national identity, future hope, patience in the light of apparent divine indifference, and relationships with foreign nations are issues that the main characters in Genesis also face. Therefore, in the commentary I seek to show how Genesis would have encouraged exilic and postexilic readers. By reading Genesis from the perspective of exiles, we may be enabled to understand it from a fresh perspective and gain something of the excitement of people who were reading these rich and evocative texts over two and half thousand years ago. This approach not only helps us to contextualize Genesis, but it also allows us to appropriate these texts and see their relevance in a world where exile is still an all too common experience.

Literary Context of Genesis

Genesis should also be read as a component of a much larger work. It is immediately obvious that it is part of the Pentateuch, but we should also note that the Pentateuch is part of what Martin Noth referred to as the "Deuteronomistic History." Noth argued that Joshua to 2 Kings was the work of a single author/ compiler tracing Israel's story to the exile. The description *Deuteronomistic* History reflects Noth's thesis that the compiler of this work used Deuteronomy (or an early version of it) as the introduction to his work. Noth's thesis was successful in showing that the books from Deuteronomy to Kings were a unified work rather than simply a collection of books. J. Gordon McConville helpfully explains why most scholars accept that the Deuteronomistic History is a unified work.[6] He outlines the story line of the DtH and shows how smoothly the story flows from one book to the next. McConville also draws attention to the theological themes that recur consistently. On the other hand, he also suggests that individual books have theological concerns of their own.

T. Desmond Alexander has shown that the corollary of seeing the Pentateuch as a unified work and also the Deuteronomistic History as a unity is that the entire group of books from Genesis to Kings should be viewed as a unity.

> The idea that the books of Genesis to Kings were brought together to provide an account of Israel's history seems an obvious explanation for their redactional unity. Beginning in Genesis we trace the growth of Israel from the initial call of Abraham through to the establishment of his descendants as a nation in the land of Canaan. Years of struggle and frustration eventually give way to a time of stability and splendour during the reigns of David and Solomon. Thereafter, the nation's history is marked by decline, leading eventually to the overthrow of the kingdom of Judah at the hands of the Babylonians.[7]

Therefore, Genesis is not to be viewed as a single isolated book but is part of a much wider literary corpus. This means that our reflection on the themes and messages of Genesis must not treat them in isolation but see them as part of the overall theme and message of both the Pentateuch and the Deuterono-

6. McConville, *Grace in the End*, 73-78.
7. Alexander, *From Paradise to the Promised Land*, 83.

11

mistic History. Moreover, since these books are also part of the canon of Scripture, their relationship to the entire biblical message must also be considered. At this level the message of Genesis should be seen in the light of both the Old Testament and the New Testament. So, whereas our starting point for the understanding of the book of Genesis as we now have it should be Jewish readers in the context of the history of Israel, the book must be seen in its wider context in the Christian church. From this perspective we will show the book to have a message that is just as relevant today as it was for the Israelites returning from exile.

Genesis in the Literary and Cultural Context of the Ancient Near East

Genesis was written for people who lived in a world dominated by superpowers such as Egypt and Babylon. Yet the influence of these powers was not limited to military and economic matters, but also impacted the realm of philosophy and religion. Israel was not an isolated unit in the world at that time, and even in matters as important as building the temple the expertise of neighboring nations was used.[8] Similarities in language and content suggest a relationship between Genesis and other writings of the ancient world that were written centuries before the biblical material. It is clear that this relationship was not one of slavish dependence since, although the points of contact cannot be denied, the theological teaching of Genesis is fundamentally different from anything else that has been discovered. It is in this distinctive theological message that we should look for the motivation behind the writing of this material. Although in the life and worship of the church today we look to Genesis as the divinely inspired word for us, we must also remember that a human being laboriously wrote these words down on carefully prepared clay tablets or parchment and believed that they had an important role to play in the world of that time. At least part of the motivation of Genesis must surely have been to combat what the writer saw as the errors of other religions. A comprehensive view of what people in the ancient Near East believed three thousand years ago is not available to us, but the texts we have provide some indication of the world of faith and ideas into which Genesis was launched.

A work known as *Enuma Elish,* written on seven tablets, is the most complete Babylonian creation account. The title repeats the first two words of

---

8. Hiram king of Tyre was an important ally of both David and Solomon, and his workmen played an important role in providing both materials and expertise for Solomon's most important buildings.

the work and means "when on high." This mythological work traces the beginning of creation back to Tiamat (goddess of the sea waters) and to Apsu (god of the fresh waters). The period before creation is described as a time when nothing had a name. Likewise in Genesis, the pronouncement of names is significant throughout the book, from God naming the "night" and "day" to the patriarchs giving names to their children and to sacred places such as Bethel. Thus things that exist must have a name.

> When skies above were not yet named
> Nor earth below pronounced by name,
> Apsu, the first one, their begetter
> And maker Tiamat, who bore them all,
> Had mixed their waters together,
> But had not formed pastures, nor discovered reed-beds;
> When yet no gods were manifest,
> Nor names pronounced, nor destinies decreed,
> Then gods were born within them.[9]

Other generations of gods appear, culminating in the birth of Marduk, whose superiority is praised from his birth.

> Proud was his form, piercing his stare,
> Mature his emergence, he was powerful from the start. . . .
> Elevated far above them, he was superior in every way.
> His limbs were ingeniously made beyond comprehension,
> Impossible to understand, too difficult to perceive.
> Four were his eyes, four were his ears;
> When his lips moved, fire blazed forth.
> The four ears were enormous
> And likewise the eyes; they perceived everything.
> Highest among the gods, his form was outstanding.[10]

Marduk, according to the epic, supports the younger gods in their conflict with the dragonlike Tiamat, eventually slaying her. Marduk creates the heavens and the earth from Tiamat's split body, and he then proceeds to create stars and planets. Last of all he creates human beings from the blood of the rebel god Qingu so that they could relieve the gods from some of the hard work that they had done previously. Marduk founded the city of Babylon and

9. Dalley, *Myths from Mesopotamia*, 233.
10. Dalley, *Myths from Mesopotamia*, 235-36.

its temple, the height of which is emphasized in a way reminiscent of the tower of Babel story in Genesis. The gods held a great feast in Marduk's honor and listed 50 names to show his greatness.

While the differences between *Enuma Elish* and Genesis are obvious, it is also important to note the points of contact between the two works while at the same time avoiding the temptation to exaggerate the similarities. Both accounts relate creation to the separation of the chaotic waters. Both record primeval darkness but, also in both, light comes before the creation of the sun, moon, and stars. Another theme common to both *Enuma Elish* and Genesis is that of rest, but the subject is dealt with in very different ways. The Babylonian literature places an almost comical emphasis on the need of the gods to rest and to sleep. Some of the main conflicts arise because their sleep has been disturbed. The theme of rest is very prominent in Genesis, but with no reference to God requiring sleep; here rest is simply a cessation from the program of creating, and it becomes a model for human beings.

The main difference is that *Enuma Elish* is unashamedly polytheistic while Genesis is not only monotheistic but is actually anti-polytheistic. Genesis takes every opportunity to deny divinity to heavenly bodies, referring to them as simply lights. In the same way, the account denies divinity to sea monsters, listing them as creatures God created in the same category as ordinary fish and fowl. Further evidence of the apologetic and polemic nature of the Genesis account is found when we compare it with the other Old Testament references to creation. Psalms, Job, and Isaiah include references to creation that use mythical language and refer to mythical forces that Yahweh subdued such as "Rahab" and "Leviathan," whom he crushed and slew (Ps 89:9-12; Job 9:13-14; 26:12-13; Isa 27:1). In contrast to these references, Genesis leaves not a vestige of mythical language or thought; Genesis is a complete denial of the polytheistic and mythological worldview. No doubt the other biblical creation passages also attacked these views, but they employed a different strategy. Isaiah and Job asserted the superiority of Yahweh over the hypothetical mythological creatures and over every putative supernatural power, while in Genesis their very existence was denied.

The importance of these points of contact is that they highlight the differences between the accounts, giving the impression that the Genesis narrative was probably written with the Babylonian epic in mind and with the intention of refuting it. *Enuma Elish* begins with the existence of the watery chaos in the form of two deities, but Genesis begins with no preexistent matter at all and God creates from nothing. The chaotic waters are not deities in Genesis but material that God made and also controlled.

The Mesopotamian flood story — the Gilgamesh Epic — is a mythological work with a basis in history. The hero, Gilgamesh, was a king of Uruk (ca. 2500 B.C.). The epic describes him as two thirds divine and one third human. This mixture of human and divine, which seems so incredible to us, was common in ancient mythology. The ancients would probably have had much less difficulty with passages such as Gen 6:1-4 because the idea of divine beings and humans marrying and having children was not unfamiliar.[11]

According to the epic, Gilgamesh is a proud, powerful, and violent man without equal. The goddess Aruru makes a combatant for him (Enkidu) from a piece of clay. Enkidu and Gilgamesh become good friends and carry out many exploits together, such as slaying the evil monster Humbaba. Enkidu dies, and this impresses upon Gilgamesh that he too is mortal and must die. Thus begins the quest of Gilgamesh to receive eternal life. He crosses the sea to meet a man named Utnapishtim, who is the only mortal who has become immortal. Utnapishtim relates how the gods have secretly decided to send a flood. One of the gods whispers the secret to Utnapishtim's reed house, and in this way advises him to build a boat to save himself, his family, and the animals. The storm that rages on the earth for seven days and seven nights is so violent that the gods themselves are terrified and they "cowered like dogs." The gods regret sending the flood and sit weeping. The following section graphically describes the end of the flood and has striking resemblances to Genesis:

> The sea became calm, the *imhullu*-wind grew quiet,
>   the flood held back.
> I looked at the weather; silence reigned,
> For all mankind had returned to clay.
> The flood-plain was flat as a roof.
> I opened a porthole and light fell on my cheeks.
> I bent down, then sat. I wept.
> My tears ran down my cheeks.
> I looked for banks, for limits to the sea.
> Areas of land were emerging everywhere (?).
> The boat had come to rest on Mount Nimush . . .
>
> When the seventh day arrived,
> I put out and released a dove.
> The dove went; it came back,
> For no perching place was visible to it, and it turned round.
> I put out and released a raven.

11. The commentary on Gen 6:1-4 presents a number of possible interpretations, but it is likely that the ancient readers would have found a literal reading less problematic than we do.

> The raven went, and saw the waters receding.
> And it ate, preened (?), lifted its tail and did not turn round.[12]

Like the biblical Noah, when Utnapishtim leaves the boat his first action is to offer sacrifices which are arranged "seven and seven." Smelling the pleasant fragrance of the sacrifice, the gods swarm over it like flies! One of the main differences from the Genesis account is that the gods receive nourishment from the sacrifices, but in Genesis God simply smells the sacrifice and does not require it for his nourishment.

The god Enlil then confers divinity on Utnapishtim. This is a special case, but before he leaves Utnapishtim reveals to Gilgamesh that there is a secret plant with thorns that will spike the hand. This plant will bring rejuvenation to anyone who partakes of it. Before Gilgamesh can restore his youth, a serpent silently steals the plant; Gilgamesh watches as the plant takes effect and the serpent sheds its old skin. Thus his quest for immortality fails.

An earlier version of the flood story from Babylonia is known as the Atrahasis Epic, and the flood account in Gilgamesh may have been based on it. The Atrahasis story begins with an explanation of why the world was created and then describes its destruction by the flood. According to this myth, originally the gods do all the manual work, including digging out the canals and riverbeds. The Tigris and the Euphrates are credited to this early work of the gods. However, far from rejoicing in their achievements, the gods rebel against the more senior gods who compel them to do this hard work.

> Every single one of us gods declared war!
> We have put [a stop] to the digging,
> The load is excessive, it is killing us!
> Our work is too hard, the trouble too much!
> So every single one of us gods
> Has agreed to complain to Ellil.[13]

The solution to this problem is the creation of humans, who are made from the flesh and blood of a slaughtered god mixed with clay. This plan works well for a time, and the humans do the work previously performed by the gods. However, after a period of 600 years overpopulation becomes a problem because of the excessive noise; the country is "as noisy as a bellowing bull."[14] The god Elil complains that he is losing sleep because of the racket. Various

12. Dalley, *Myths from Mesopotamia*, 114.
13. Dalley, *Myths from Mesopotamia*, 12.
14. Dalley, *Myths from Mesopotamia*, 18.

measures are taken to counteract the overpopulation, including disease and drought, but they are largely ineffective because of the wise counsel of Atrahasis and his special relationship with the god Enki. Eventually the gods decide to send a flood and, although Enki cannot directly advise Atrahasis what to do because he has sworn an oath, he speaks instead to the reed hut of Atrahasis and makes known the plan.

> Wall, listen constantly to me!
> Reed hut, make sure you attend all my words!
> Dismantle the house, build a boat,
> Reject possessions, and save living things.[15]

Atrahasis with the help of his neighbors builds the boat with upper and lower decks. The main building materials seem to have been reeds and bitumen. Taking his family and selected birds and animals on board, Atrahasis seals the door with bitumen. For seven days and seven nights, rain falls and the storms rage. It is not just the humans who suffer but also the gods who, deprived of the sacrifices that feed them, become hungry and thirsty. Unfortunately about 58 lines are missing, presumably those that tell of the sending out of the birds and the end of the flood. However, these details are covered in the Gilgamesh Epic. After the flood, Atrahasis offers sacrifices and the gods gather over the offering like flies to partake of it. In the aftermath of the flood the life span of the human beings is limited to avoid overpopulation, but before the flood primeval mankind had lived for centuries.

The OT creation account has little in common with these myths. Some scholars think that there are indications that the biblical creation developed from earlier mythological accounts. However, they admit that if this is the case, the biblical account has completely demythologized the earlier accounts. Thus some see an echo of the chaos monster (Tehom) in the Bible, but he is no longer a personal being or an independent force. Yahweh's creation of the world takes place without opposition.

As in the accounts of creation produced by other nations, Israel made her national God the central figure in the creation event. But the difference was that Israel saw Yahweh as not only unrivalled and unequalled but as the only one who existed. The account is unquestionably monotheistic. Unlike other accounts, the OT gives no details of events in heaven such as conflict among the gods which gave rise to creation. The creation was an event brought about by God as the outworking of his own will and not something forced upon him because of circumstances beyond his control.

15. Dalley, *Myths from Mesopotamia*, 29-30.

Commentary on Genesis

1:1–2:3 Creation

Genesis opens with an account of creation that is carefully structured and designed (1:1–2:3). Although this opening chapter is not formal poetry, it uses poetic language and symmetric structuring to evoke the imagery and grandeur of the creation event. This is more than a piece of prose narrative; it is literary choreography in which every word has been carefully chosen and precisely positioned. Such careful structuring, together with the rhetorical devices employed, enhances the impact and contributes to the meaning of the chapter. The majesty and impeccable design of the account are highly appropriate vehicles to convey the message about the creation and design of the universe.

The opening words of Genesis are dramatic and dynamic: a fitting introduction to the book that describes the origins of the universe and of God's dealings with humankind. It introduces God as the main character of the book and lays a good foundation for understanding the remainder of Genesis; even when the other characters are not aware of him, this divine presence pervades every narrative.

Grammatically, we could translate the first sentence as a temporal clause, "When God began to create." Comparisons with 2:4 and 5:1 show that this is possible, and it is the translation preferred by the NEB. However, the familiar translation of "In the beginning God created" has much to commend it. As Derek Kidner points out, it is "supported by all the ancient versions, and affirms unequivocally the truth laid down elsewhere (e.g., Heb 11:3) that until God spoke, nothing existed."[1] This interpretation presents God as unencum-

---

1. Kidner, *Genesis*, 43.

bered and unlimited by time or space, both of which, as Nahum Sarna observes, "He proceeds to create."[2]

The word translated "God" is אֱלֹהִים/*'ĕlōhîm*. This is a general Hebrew term for deity, and the context determines whether it refers to God or to a plurality of pagan gods. Although the word is plural, when it refers to Yahweh singular verbs are used. Perhaps, this is "a plural of majesty," but we cannot be certain.[3]

The verb בָּרָא/*bārā'*, translated "to create," is never used with human beings as the subject.[4] This highlights the very special nature of the events in this chapter, and it emphasizes the power and transcendence of God. These creative events are not repeatable by anyone else. Furthermore, God is not one of a number of deities competing with each other; he alone creates, and he has neither equal nor rival.

The phrase "the heavens and the earth" may be described as a "merism," a phrase that refers to two extremes to convey a sense of totality. An example of a merism that occurs frequently in the Bible is the reference to "those who go out and those who come in," which, since theoretically all people are either going out or coming in, refers to everyone. Similarly, the reference to "the heavens and the earth" embraces the entire created order; God creates everything.

The description of the earth as "formless and empty" (1:2 NIV) or "without form and void" (KJV and ESV) has led to the "Gap Theory." Advocates of this theory ask, "Would God have created a world 'without form and void'?" They argue that God created a perfect world that later suffered a catastrophe which left it in chaos. This theory seeks to take Genesis literally while at the same time accounting for scientific discoveries. It identifies an age of unknown duration during which dinosaurs and other prehistoric creatures could have existed. However, the "Gap Theory" presents two main problems. First, the Hebrew expression תֹהוּ וָבֹהוּ/*tōhû wābōhû* means "unformed and empty"; it is not inappropriate to attribute a formless and empty creation to God since this was just the first stage in the creative process.[5] Second, the Bible gives no indication of a gap, and early Jewish commentators saw no hint of it. The corollary of the Gap Theory is that the text was so unclear that it misled all its readers until the modern era. If the original author was aware of

2. Sarna, *Genesis*, 5.

3. A popular Christian reading of Genesis interprets this plural as a reference to the Trinity.

4. Another Hebrew word is spelled the same as the verb "to create," but it means "to cut." For example, it is used to describe clearing a forest (Josh 17:15).

5. The expression also appears in Jer 4:23, where an enemy invasion leaves the land desolate and bereft of both plant and animal life.

a gap between the first two verses of Genesis, this could have been made clear in the text. The text makes good sense without this hypothetical gap and declares that God created the raw material from which he would form the world; he then proceeded to shape and order this raw material before furnishing and filling it with living creatures.

Darkness is mentioned without any suggestion about its origin, but according to Isaiah, God creates darkness (Isa 45:7).

The NEB translates רוּחַ אֱלֹהִים/*rûaḥ ʾĕlōhîm* as "a mighty wind" rather than the more familiar translation "the Spirit of God" (NIV). Some scholars support this, including Westermann, von Rad, Speiser, and Sarna, on the basis that Hebrew *rûaḥ* means "wind" or "spirit" and that *ʾĕlōhîm* sometimes represents the superlative.[6] However, others argue that the traditional translation "Spirit of God" is probably correct.[7] One way of deciding between these interpretations is to ascertain the action of the *rûaḥ ʾĕlōhîm* and then to consider whether spirit or wind is the most appropriate subject of this action. The action predicated of the *rûaḥ ʾĕlōhîm* is conveyed by a verb used in Deut 32:11, where it relates to a bird hovering over its young, and in Jer 23:9, where it refers to bones shaking or trembling. Movement is involved in both cases, but neither indicates the violent action of a mighty wind. This supports the traditional translation with its evocative imagery of the Spirit hovering above the water like a bird.

1:3-5 Day One

Creation commences with divine speech (cf. Ps 33:9). With words that are powerful and effective, the Creator calls light into existence.[8] God does not destroy all darkness, but he separates it from the light and defines the boundaries of day and night.

It is significant that light was the first thing that God made in the six days of creation and that it is mentioned before the sun and the moon. Astral bodies were worshipped as the source of light and heat, but Genesis shows that light existed before they were formed; God is the real source of light. Sarna comments,

---

6. E.g., in Jonah 3:3 the city of Nineveh is described as "a great city of/to God," which the NIV translates as "a very large city."

7. E.g., Skinner, Cassuto, Kidner, and Wenham prefer the traditional translation.

8. The Latin translation of the phrase "Let there be light" is *fiat lux,* which has led to the expression "creation by Divine Fiat."

21

The source of this supernal, nonsolar light of creation became a subject of rabbinic and mystical speculation. Genesis Rabba 3:4 expresses the view that this light is the effulgent splendor of the Divine Presence. Psalm 104:2, with its theme of creation, describes God as "wrapped in a robe of light."[9]

God gives names to the things he creates. Today, people take great care about the names they give to all sorts of things ranging from boats and houses to hurricanes, but our love for appropriate names does not compare with the significance of names in the ancient world. Names were an essential corollary of existence: to have no name was the equivalent of nonexistence. Sarna refers to an Egyptian text that describes the period before creation as the time when "no name of anything had yet been named."[10] God gives names to day, night, earth, sky, and sea. The combination of this twofold process, creating and naming, demonstrates that God is unrivalled as the ultimate authority over everything that exists.

With the passing of evening and morning, the end of the first day is announced. The reference to "evening and morning," rather than the other way round, may reflect the custom of regarding a day as beginning and ending with sunset. God's activities are placed in the framework of a working week representing the ideal work pattern of human beings. No indication is given about the length of these days, and since the first three were without sun or moon, some argue that each day could represent an age of unknown duration. This suggestion about creation in six "ages" allows its advocates to reconcile Genesis with scientific theories. It is a popular approach because it enables the modern reader to accept the text as literal while also accepting scientific discoveries about the age of the earth. This theory will be discussed in more detail in the section "Genesis and Science."

Following the creation of the first day, God pronounces it "good." This is the first of seven references to creation being good in God's sight. Clare Amos suggests that this is an important point and one that should affect our approach to creation and our understanding of our own responsibility towards it:

> If the world is created as *good* it is important that humanity continues to keep it so: concern for justice, peace and the integrity of creation ultimately stems from this chapter. In the New Testament we are reminded of God's intentions by Peter's words on the Mount of Transfiguration. *It is good, Lord, to be here* (Mark 9:5).

9. Sarna, *Genesis*, 7.
10. Sarna, *Genesis*, 7.

Amos argues that Peter's statement suggests that "on that mountain for a brief moment creation was restored to its intended harmony."[11]

1:6-8 Day Two

On the first day, God had separated light from darkness. Now, on the second day, this work of separating continues with the division of the waters above from the waters below. God effects this division by making a רָקִיעַ/*rāqîaʿ*, something that has been stamped or hammered out, like a sheet of metal. The Latin, *firmamentum,* has come to us through the KJV translation "firmament." The NIV renders it as "expanse" and the NRSV as "dome." In Ps 19:1 the same word is translated "the skies" (NIV). The word also occurs in Ezek 1:22-26 and 10:1, where it refers to a platform above the heads of the living creatures, on which Yahweh's throne rests. In Genesis, this expanse or dome separates the waters below it from the waters above. Thus, one of the main functions of creation is to separate and control.

1:9-13 Day Three

Water, regarded as powerful, unpredictable, and dangerous in the ancient world, is clearly subject to the Creator's will in Genesis. The waters are gathered to the place appointed for them; the dry land appears and obediently bursts into vegetative life in response to the divine command. The water and the land are not gods, but objects that God has made. Fertility cults, which deified nature, were prevalent in ancient religions and were a constant temptation to the Israelites.[12] Genesis leaves no room at all for the personification or deification of nature.

The emphasis on day three is not just on creation but also on its continuance; the regeneration of plant life is ensured by the production of "seed" from which new plants of the same kind will grow. This early focus on the concept of seed is significant, because throughout Genesis this same word is used to describe the offspring of animals and human beings. Genesis focuses on a line of seed that traces its origin to Abraham. By analogy, the faithful Abraham should produce seed who would replicate his qualities of obedience and faith. However, this analogy breaks down in Genesis because Abraham's

---

11. Amos, *The Book of Genesis,* 7-8.

12. Fertility cults were polytheistic religions that worshipped a mother goddess and personified natural phenomena. Seasonal changes, e.g., were attributed to activities of the gods.

seed do not bear much resemblance to him, especially in the realms of faith and obedience to God. Sadly, Genesis reflects the reality that plants are more likely to bear the image of their parent plants than humans are to replicate the better qualities of their forbears.

Within the carefully controlled structure of Genesis, God pronounces each day of creation "good," but on the third day this pronouncement occurs twice (1:10, 12). Apparently, this is why Tuesday is a popular day for Jewish weddings!

1:14-19 Day Four

By declaring "God made two great lights," Genesis avoids mentioning the names "sun" and "moon," probably because these had been adopted as the names of celestial deities. Judging from their content, the purpose of these verses is to show that all the objects in the sky have been made and placed in position by the Creator: a) he brought them into existence by his authoritative word (1:14-15); b) he formed them (1:16); c) he set them in place (1:17).

The succinct reference to the stars at the end of 1:16 contrasts with the respect and devotion that the ancient world usually paid to the stars. Commenting on this passage, von Rad speaks of the

> diligence with which every form of independent godlike astral power here is disputed. To comprehend the significance of these statements, one must remember that they were formulated in a cultural and religious atmosphere that was saturated with all kinds of astrological false belief. All ancient Oriental (not Old Testament!) thinking with regard to time was determined by the cyclical course of the stars.[13]

This relegation of the heavenly bodies from the status of deity, afforded to them in the ancient world, to the inventory of objects created by God is one of the clearest indications that one of the main purposes of Genesis is to combat the beliefs that were prevalent when the material was first written and read.

1:20-23 Day Five

On the fifth day, at the Creator's command, the waters teem with life and birds fly in the skies. "God created the great sea monsters" (1:21 NRSV). It is signifi-

13. Von Rad, *Genesis*, 55.

cant that God does not simply "make" sea creatures but he "creates" them. This is the second appearance of the verb בָּרָא/*bārā'*, "to create." Since the narrator chooses this verb for the opening sentence of the book of Genesis and then uses it sparingly at highly significant points in the account,[14] its use in relation to "sea creatures" is fascinating. It highlights the significance of this aspect of creation and shows that an important message is being communicated.

Why, however, is the creation of sea creatures significant enough to merit special emphasis? The Hebrew word for sea creature is תַּנִּין/*tannîn* (cf. Ps 148:7). The KJV often translates it as "dragon" (Ps 74:13). In Isa 27:1 the *tannîn* is identified as God's enemy, and he will slay it. Some ancient myths regarded these monsters as divine, and perhaps Genesis highlights their creation to show that they are creatures that God made and not gods that people should worship or fear. Many readers of Genesis lived in a polytheistic society, and it was important to reassure them that there was only one God. As Sarna observes, by mentioning the creation of the *tannîn* so late in the creative process, "the narrative at once strips them of divinity."[15]

On the fifth day God pronounces blessing for the first time (1:22). Blessing is a prominent concept in Genesis. The term does not usually appear in this book as an isolated self-explanatory term; rather, it is often accompanied by a definition of what it means in a particular context. In other words, "blessing" is understood as "beneficial power," the purpose of which is either defined or understood from the context. Here the three explanatory terms, "be fruitful," "multiply," and "fill," make it clear that the purpose of this first pronouncement of blessing is procreation in abundant measure. Through the efficacy of God's powerful creation words, life has begun, and now he speaks again to continue the process using words of blessing. Living creatures in both sea and air receive blessing on the fifth day.

1:24-31 *Day Six*

The record of God's creative activity on day six is more detailed than the record of the previous days. This reflects the importance of the sixth day as the completion of God's creative program.

God calls on the land to produce living creatures (1:24). The role of the land exhibits a subtle difference in comparison with that of the waters (1:20). The role given to land, "to produce" actively, involves it in the process of cre-

---

14. Note that on the third occasion that the verb is used in Genesis 1, it is repeated three times in one verse (1:27). A fourth occurrence of the verb in 2:3 rounds off the account.

15. Sarna, *Genesis*, 10.

ation, whereas the sky is simply a place where the birds fly and the water is merely the place where the fish swim. This clearly discouraged superstitious belief in the mythical power of water, which was prevalent in the ancient world. In contrast to water, the earth is not passive in the created order, and its unique productive powers give it a special status. However, the earth is not deified and its productive powers are bestowed by God.

The high point of creation arrives in 1:26, "Let us make man." This plural form is difficult to explain. It may be a plural of majesty, but whereas there are examples of nouns being used in this way,[16] we cannot be sure that it was applied to verbs or pronouns.[17] One possible explanation is that God was speaking to heavenly beings whom he had already created, but this would imply that humans were created not only in the image of God but also in the image of these other creatures. A Christian interpretation may discern "the first glimmerings of a trinitarian revelation."[18] Although Christians are familiar with Trinitarian concepts, the earliest readers and listeners of the Hebrew text would not have understood this. It is also unlikely that the writer of Genesis, who is so clearly committed to monotheism, would have written something that was ambiguous enough to give any room for polytheistic interpretations. On the other hand, Genesis refers to God's Spirit having a role in creation, and the idea of God addressing himself or his Spirit is not polytheistic, nor is it a fully developed doctrine of the Trinity (1:2). As Clines points out, in a number of OT passages, apart from Genesis 1, "the Spirit is the agent of creation."[19] Clines draws attention to the "vivid personification of Yahweh's wisdom in Proverbs 8 as His partner in creation" and suggests that "it is perhaps not inconceivable that the Spirit could have been similarly thought of by the author of Genesis 1 as another 'person' within the divine Being."[20]

None of these explanations of the plural in Genesis 1:26 has gained overall approval and the matter must, for the moment, remain open.

God creates the human beings "in our image, in our likeness." While these terms "image" and "likeness" are interchangeable in the OT, they provide slightly different nuances. As Bray points out, the former term "refers primarily to a concrete image, a definite shape; the latter is more abstract — a

16. The word frequently used for "God" is plural and is possibly a plural of majesty: אֱלֹהִים/*'ĕlōhîm.*

17. Cf. Clines, "The Image of God in Man," 65.

18. Blocher, *In the Beginning,* 84.

19. Clines, "The Image of God in Man," 69. The examples he gives are Job 33:4; Ps 104:30; and Ezekiel 37.

20. Clines, "The Image of God in Man," 69.

21. Bray, "The Significance of God's Image in Man," 196.

resemblance, or a likeness."²¹ The use of these two synonyms in this phrase probably refers to the same reality and provides emphasis through repetition. Although it is difficult to ascertain the meaning of the "image," it is closely associated with the uniqueness and distinctiveness of humans in the created order; the image of God sets humans apart from all other creatures. The corollary of this is that God can have a closer relationship with humans than with the animals. To put it another way, if God was to appear on earth, it would be inconceivable for him to appear as an animal but perfectly appropriate for him to appear in human form.²²

This is the third occurrence of the term *bārā'*, "to create," but now it appears three times in one verse (1:27). As in 1:22, the concept of blessing is closely associated with *bārā'* (1:28). Although God addresses the same imperative of procreation to both animals and humans in their respective blessings, a slight difference occurs in the description of the blessing of human beings. This is the addition of the words "God said to them" (1:28 RSV). Most commentators agree that this addition is both intentional and significant. Wenham describes its purpose as to draw "attention to the personal relationship between God and man."²³ Humanity is elevated to a superior and responsible relationship with God. God has a unique relationship with the creatures made in his image, and this is the ideal context for blessing.

God gives the humans authority over the rest of creation, to subdue (כָּבַשׁ/*kābaš*) the earth and rule (רָדָה/*rādâ*) over its creatures. The word translated "subdue" usually refers to hostile action and may connote "rape" (Esth 7:8) or the conquest of enemies (Num 32:22). The majority of the occurrences of *rādâ* ("to rule") in the OT are in the context of ruling over reluctant subjects. For example, it refers to being ruled by one's enemies (Lev 26:17); Ezekiel uses the same verb when he reprimands those who rule over Israel harshly and brutally (Ezek 34:4). Yet, rather than implying empowerment to exercise dictatorial rule over the rest of creation,²⁴ the verbs in this context of creation and blessing should be understood as indicating a supremacy that is harmonious and mutually beneficial.²⁵

---

22. A more detailed discussion of the "image of God" is included below in the section, "Key Theological Teaching of Genesis."

23. Wenham, *Genesis 1–15*, 33.

24. Vawter, *On Genesis*, 60.

25. Lohfink, *Great Themes from the Old Testament*, 177, 179.

2:1-3 Day Seven

The statement that "God rested from all his work" is not intended to evoke the image of an exhausted deity who must rest from his labors. Such an interpretation is compatible with ancient myths that assume that the gods require rest and sleep, but it is not feasible within the first creation account where the emphasis is on the transcendence and majesty of the Creator.[26] The verb used, שָׁבַת/*šābat,* means "to cease, desist," and as Westermann observes, "to cease from" is a more accurate translation than "to rest."[27] The use of the verb elsewhere supports this view, thus "Day and night shall not cease" (8:22 ESV) and, "then shall the offspring of Israel cease from being a nation" (Jer 31:36 ESV).[28] Although the noun "Sabbath" is not used in relation to this period of rest, the use of the cognate verb *šābat* means that the idea of Sabbath is clearly implicit. God keeps a Sabbath to set an example to human beings and to provide a model that they should follow.

For the third time the concept of blessing appears. Since the first two pronouncements of blessing relate to living creatures and, in particular, to their fertility (1:22, 28), it is surprising to find that the beneficiary of the third benediction is the seventh day.[29] It may mean that the day is empowered to be a source of blessing to people.[30] If this interpretation is correct, the blessing on the seventh day gives it the power to be beneficial for human beings in permitting them to desist from their labors and enabling them to follow the pattern set by the Creator and through the hallowing of the day enter into a closer relationship with him. In this sense, the seventh day could be fertile or fruitful through its beneficial effects on human beings and animals.

It is possible that the blessing of the seventh day belongs to a second category of blessing that is an acknowledgement of one party's blessedness by another. This appears frequently in the context of human beings blessing God (14:20) or showing respect for each other (14:19). In these passages, blessing is not bestowed but acknowledged; the person addressed is honored and praised as one characterized by blessing. Thus the common phrase "blessed

---

26. During his confrontation with the prophets of Baal on Carmel, Elijah taunts his opponents with the suggestion that their god Baal may be asleep (1 Kgs 18:27).

27. Westermann, *Genesis 1–11,* 173.

28. Cassuto prefers the translation "He abstained from work"; *A Commentary on the Book of Genesis,* 1:63.

29. Wenham observes that, since the blessing on animals and man is closely connected with reproduction, it is "paradoxical that the day on which God refrains from creative activity is pronounced blessed"; *Genesis 1–15,* 36.

30. Westermann, *Genesis 1–11,* 172.

be God" means that he is worthy of praise. To say that God blessed the day is confusing because it is not clear how a day can be blessed since it is not alive (2:3); but if we classify the blessing as belonging to this second category, the meaning becomes clear. God acknowledges the benefits received from the seventh day and honors it. He then sanctifies it and sets it apart so that people may receive blessing from it and benefit from a cessation of labor.

2:4a The Account of the Heavens and the Earth

This is one of the 10 occurrences in Genesis of the phrase אֵלֶּה תוֹלְדוֹת/'ēlleh *tôlĕdôt*.[1] These occurrences divide Genesis into 10 main sections and provide a framework for the book. English versions translate the phrase in various ways:

1. "These are the generations of . . ." (KJV, NRSV, ESV)
2. "This is the account of . . ." (NLT, NIV)
3. "Such was the story of . . ." (NJB)

The associated verb means "to bear children." With the exception of this first occurrence, the phrase is linked to a person's name and family history. Its use here relates to the heavens and the earth, and therefore in this context the idea of bearing children is figurative.

It is difficult to decide whether this occurrence of the phrase is a conclusion to the creation account in 1:1–2:3 or whether it is an introduction to what follows, marking the beginning of a more intimate and detailed description of the creation of the human beings.[2] While the later occurrences of the *tôlĕdôt* clause seem to begin a section, this first occurrence acts very effectively as a conclusion to the creation of the heavens and the earth (1:1–2:3) and would be less appropriate as an introduction to the next section, in which the heavens are not prominent.

---

1. The phrase אֵלֶּה תוֹלְדוֹת/'ēlleh *tôlĕdôt* occurs in 2:4; 6:9; 10:1; 11:10; 11:27; 25:12; 25:19; 36:1; 36:9; 37:2. A similar expression is also found in 5:1.

2. P. J. Wiseman argued that this phrase is a colophon and that it always concludes a section in Genesis; *Clues to Creation in Genesis*, 34-45. Most commentators think that it refers to the material that follows; this seems satisfactory for the majority of its occurrences but not for the first.

2:4b-7 The Creation of the First Human

Verse 4b introduces a more detailed account of creation that focuses on human beings and their immediate environment. The change of perspective and focus is introduced in 2:4b by the phrase "the earth and the heavens." Previously the order has been "heavens and earth" (1:1; 2:4a). By inverting the usual order, this phrase prepares the reader for the detailed accounts of the first human beings and the earth that they inhabit. This change of perspective is from an emphasis on the transcendence and power of the Creator who brings order out of chaos to an emphasis on the involvement of the Creator with his creatures and especially with the human beings.

Genesis gives us two complementary portrayals of creation (1:1–2:3; 2:4-25). Taken together these two perspectives present God as transcendent and separate while, at the same time, caring and involved. Unlike the Synoptic Gospels, which present the reader with different perspectives on the ministry of Jesus, these first two chapters of Genesis are not parallel accounts of creation. Chapter 1 is a majestic overview, while ch. 2 selects certain aspects of creation and deals with them in more detail. Furthermore, the subjects covered are not the same, since ch. 2 continues into ch. 3 and deals with the crisis brought about by the serpent's seductive act.

One very significant change introduced in 2:4b is the use of the name "Yahweh" for the first time in Genesis. Throughout 1:1–2:3 the generic term for God identifies the Creator. Now God's personal name is also used — the name by which he revealed himself to Moses (Exod 6:2-3). This name is indicated by the four Hebrew consonants, יהוה/*YHWH*, and is usually translated in English versions as LORD, written in capitals. The anglicized form is "Jehovah," but "Yahweh" is closer to the Hebrew.[1] Scholars still debate how this term could appear in Genesis since Moses was, apparently, the first to learn its meaning and significance.[2]

This passage does not repeat everything that has happened in ch. 1, but it deals mainly with the details necessary to set the context for the garden of Eden. It begins with an empty earth devoid of plants and animals. In the absence of rain, mists provide the moisture necessary for growth, and the hu-

1. The word Jehovah is formed by combining the consonants YHWH with the vowels of another word meaning "lord" (אֲדֹנָי/*'ādônāy*).
2. In *Targum Onkelos*, the name Yahweh is used from the first verse of Genesis, presumably in order to avoid any confusion that might arise from the plural form of the word, אֱלֹהִים/*'ĕlōhîm*. If those producing the Targum believed it was necessary to change the names in order to make it clear that the creator God was Yahweh, the God of Israel, it is possible that they were continuing a practice that had begun earlier in the Hebrew text.

man being is brought into existence to work the ground. God is intimately involved in the creation of human beings; he forms the first "man" as a potter would make a pot from clay (cf. Ps 139:13-15). By using terminology reminiscent of pottery production, the text emphasizes the dependence of the human being on his Creator and the sovereignty of God over human beings who are his handiwork. The idea of humans rebelling against their Creator is just as foolish and ridiculous as a pot rebelling against the potter (cf. Isa 29:16).

God's special concern for the first human being is emphasized by the intimate act of breathing the breath of life into the clay body that he had produced; this happened to no other creature. Kidner draws a parallel here with John 20:22, "where Jesus bestows the Holy Spirit as the animating breath of the new creation, the church. Even at our making, then, the pattern 'God so loved . . . that he gave . . .' is already visible."[3]

There is an unmistakable emphasis on the close relationship between the first human and the ground. This relationship is highlighted by an interesting wordplay between the name "Adam" (אָדָם/*'ādām*) and the word used for ground (אֲדָמָה/*'ădāmâ*). Thus, *'ādām* comes from *'ădāmâ*. Although there is no established etymological link[4] between *'ādām* and *'ădāmâ*, they are related by assonance.[5] A number of scholars have tried to reproduce the wordplay in English. Thus Hamilton translates 2:7: "God formed earthling from the earth"[6]; Blocher also refers to Adam as "the 'earthling'"[7]; Trible goes for "earth creature,"[8] and Alter suggests "humus" and "human."[9]

This places the human in a relationship with the ground, closer than that enjoyed by any other creature, with the corollary that Adam is uniquely suited to care for the ground and to reap its benefits (cf. 2:16). On the other hand, Adam's vulnerability is also clearly implied since, if the human is no more than dust brought to life by the breath of God, then if God withholds his breath Adam returns to *'ădāmâ*. The close relationship that humans have with the ground means that they are obliged to care for it and enabled to enjoy its produce, but it also means that anything adverse that affects the

---

3. Kidner, *Genesis*, 60.

4. Regarding the relationship between *'ādām* and *'ădāmâ*, Wenham comments that although *'ădāmâ* is grammatically the feminine form of *'ādām*, "it is doubtful whether there is any etymological connection between the two words"; *Genesis 1–15*, 59.

5. Words that sound the same are often used in Hebrew to emphasize an important truth (cf. Amos 8:2; Jer 1:11-12)

6. Hamilton, *Genesis 1–17*, 156.

7. Blocher, *In the Beginning*, 83.

8. Trible, *God and the Rhetoric of Sexuality*, 76.

9. Alter, *Genesis*, 8.

ground/land strikes deeply at the very basis of their existence. Nevertheless, the land would not be fruitful without humans to care for it.

When the Lord God breathes life into the creature he has formed from dust, Adam becomes a living creature (נֶפֶשׁ/*nepeš*). The KJV translates this as "living soul." This gives the impression that humans are distinguished from animals by *nepeš*. However, this is erroneous, since the same word *(nepeš)* is also used to describe the animals (1:20, 21, 24). The focus of the word *nepeš* in Genesis is on the physical rather than on the metaphysical, and it simply refers to "possession of life," whether human or animal. Modern versions avoid confusion by using alternative translations for *nepeš* such as "living being" (NIV, NJB) or "living creature" (RSV). Although the possession of *nepeš* does not make humans unique, the description of Adam receiving the divine breath is something that is never applied to the animals. Just as creation in the image of God marked the human beings as unique in the first creation account (1:26), the bestowal of the breath of God brought them into a much closer relationship with God and rendered them compatible with him at a level enjoyed by no other creature.

2:8-17 The Garden of Eden

The NIV introduces this section with a pluperfect, "the LORD God had planted a garden." Since there is no distinct form for the pluperfect in Hebrew, it is better to follow the vast majority of English translations and translate the first clause of 2:8 as "the LORD God planted a garden."

This special garden or parkland should be understood in the context of ancient appreciation of gardens. The kings of ancient Mesopotamia were proud of their gardens. Many Babylonian sanctuaries were surrounded by gardens. Other evidence of gardens in Mesopotomia include Nebuchadnezzar's legendary Hanging Gardens of Babylon. Ashurnasirpal II records building an aqueduct to conduct water from distant mountains to the gardens of Ashur. He lists 40 different species of exotic trees.

A Sumerian myth speaks of the wonderful land of Tilmun, where there were no beasts of prey and no illnesses. The sun-god brought forth water and made the land a fertile garden in which eight herbs sprang forth. Another myth mentions a garden in the middle of the sea whose trees bear precious stones instead of fruit. This myth also refers to a garden where a "plant of life" grows. In Egypt, garden parks with trees and flowers were popular and were associated with love poetry. A 15th-century B.C. wall relief depicts Queen Hatshepsut returning from Punt with trees for transplanting in her royal gardens.

The location "in the east" probably refers to east of Israel. The garden had all kinds of trees, but special mention is made of the two trees in the middle of the garden: the tree of life and the tree of the knowledge of good and evil. The idea of sacred trees was popular in the ancient Near East. In the British Museum a carved panel depicts the Assyrian king Ashurnasirpal in duplicate standing on either side of a sacred tree.

The tree of life suggests that the human beings were mortal but that eternal life was within their grasp while they lived in Eden. The meaning of the second tree, "the tree of the knowledge of good and evil," has given rise to numerous interpretations. Wenham gives a helpful summary of these.[1] Sarna makes the interesting suggestion that "the knowledge of good and evil" is a "merism" meaning the knowledge of "everything."[2] However, "knowledge" in this context does not denote omniscience but refers to knowledge ranging from good to bad.

Irrigation of the garden was by a river that rose in Eden and divided into four rivers: the Tigris, the Euphrates, the Gihon, and the Pishon.[3] The first two of these rivers are, of course, well known. The land of Mesopotamia (the land between two rivers) owes its name and probably its civilization to the Tigris and the Euphrates. The other two rivers are more puzzling. The identity of the Pishon is not certain, and the reference to the country it flowed through is of no help since this land rich in gold — Havilah — is also unknown. Gihon is the name of the spring that is located outside the earliest site of the Jebusite city of Jerusalem. However, the river Gihon mentioned in connection with the garden of Eden flowed to Cush (Ethiopia). It seems that these rivers that flowed from Eden watered much or all of the land of the ancient Near East, but this does not really help in locating the garden. Most scholars suggest Mesopotamia itself.[4]

2:18-25 The Creation of Woman

God, who seven times has declared various aspects of creation "good," now declares that "it is not good" for Adam to be without a suitable partner (2:18).

1. Wenham, *Genesis 1–15*, 63.
2. Sarna, *Genesis*, 19.
3. Genesis does not give enough detail to enable the reader to identify the precise location of the garden of Eden, and there has been a great deal of debate on this issue. The reference to the Tigris River limits the possibilities.
4. Porter, on the other hand, suggests that the garden of Eden was situated in the land of Canaan; "Where Was the Garden of Eden?" 3-4.

The reference to something that is "not good" sets the scene for one of the most evocative and beautiful stories in the OT. God forms the animals and birds and brings them before Adam; he gives them names, but no appropriate partner for him is found among them (2:19-20). The parade of the animals before the human would highlight their dual sexuality — male and female — and thereby accentuate the loneliness of the human being.[1] As in the formation of Adam, God is intimately involved; he forms woman from Adam's side. A deep sleep ensures that Adam could not take credit for his partner's existence. Together they stand equal before God (2:23). Although the woman is referred to as "helper," this is not an indication of inferiority or lower status.[2]

Adam's acceptance of his new partner and his delight in her are conveyed in three ways in the text. First, Adam's reaction when he meets Eve is presented as a poetic couplet, the first formal poetry in Genesis. Second, the words he speaks convey his relief that finally his ideal partner has been produced.[3] Third, Adam declares that his partner shall be known as "Woman." This name acknowledges that she is part of himself and they need each other to be complete.

This is more than just a beautiful story, since it provides a powerful polemic against polygamy. Although polygamy is practiced throughout the OT and many prominent characters have several wives, the ideal of one man and one woman is presented unequivocally in this passage.

3:1-13 The Serpent's Seductive Strategy and the Human Rebellion

Throughout the ancient world, the serpent was considered as a divine or semi-divine symbol. In the Gilgamesh Epic the hero finds a plant that could give immortality, but while he is swimming in a pond a snake swallows the plant. In Genesis the identity of the serpent is not given. Its identification as Satan is not made explicit until the intertestamental period.[1] However, its devious arguments and malicious intention are enough to make it clear that this

---

1. Sarna argues that "by observing the otherwise universal complementary pairing of male and female, he becomes aware of his own exceptional status and of his solitariness"; *Genesis*, 22.

2. Commenting on the term "helper," Sarna observes, "This term cannot be demeaning because the Hebrew *'ēzer*, employed here to describe the intended role of the woman, is often used of God in His relation to man"; *Genesis*, 21.

3. Hirsch renders Adam's opening words as "At last this is it!"; *Commentary on the Torah*, 1:69.

1. See, e.g., Wis 2:24.

snake symbolizes evil — not the belligerent, aggressive kind of evil, but the subtle and seductive kind. We may surmise that this was a poignant message for early readers to warn them that the most dangerous attacks may not be from armies with spears and battering rams but from the quiet seductive enticement to disobey the clear instruction of God. The enticement offered by the serpent had clear reminiscences of the temptation for Israel to follow the fertility deities.[2]

The serpent is described as "crafty" — a morally ambiguous word that could also be translated "prudent." It is similar in pronunciation to the Hebrew word for "naked" (2:25); there is an obvious contrast between the shrewd, calculating, seductive serpent and the naked, innocent human beings. In seeking to be shrewd like the serpent, the human beings would sacrifice their naked innocence. Wenham attempts to reproduce the wordplay in English and suggests, "They will seek themselves to be shrewd but will discover that they are 'nude.'"[3]

"Did God really say . . . ?" The serpent sows the seed of doubt in the woman's mind. He questions God's motives and suggests that God has placed unfair limits on the first couple. In her response to the serpent the woman displays her openness to temptation; she misquotes God by exaggerating the prohibition while weakening the penalty.

The serpent increases the pressure on the woman by assuring her that she would not suffer a severe penalty. It proceeds to undermine her confidence in God and to question her contentment with her present situation. "You will not surely die. . . ." "You will be like God knowing good and evil." These are subtle and seductive half-truths. Disobedience would not lead to immediate physical death and, as the serpent predicts, their eyes would be opened to good and evil. The serpent appears to be telling the truth, but in reality his words are dangerous half-truths that make disobedience seem innocuous.

After eating the fruit, the first human pair lose their innocence and two new emotions grip them; fear and shame. They attempt to deal with their shame by using fig leaves, and their fear drives them to hide among the trees of the garden. These strategies fail; fig leaves do not remove shame and it is not possible to hide from God. Since all else has failed, they resort to passing the blame.

2. However, we do meet the serpent elsewhere in the OT as Leviathan, the symbol of chaos and of opposition to God's created order (Isa 27:1).

3. Wenham, *Genesis 1–15*, 72.

3:14-24 The Divine Court in Session

In this passage God changes roles from Creator to Judge. This represents a watershed in Genesis and moves the narrative from the ideal world of Eden into the world familiar to the readers both ancient and modern who recognize that the post-judgment world is their world; its guilt, suffering, and pain are all too familiar to them. They know that the curse imposed on the ground is the curse that afflicts everyone who seeks to eke out an existence from the soil.

The serpent, the ground, and the human couple are all criticized and punished, but only the serpent and the ground are cursed. Found guilty of leading the woman astray, the serpent is condemned to crawl in the dust (3:14). Furthermore, Yahweh will cause enmity to exist between woman and serpent that will be perpetuated through their respective descendants, or seed (3:15).

Following the cursing of the snake, the text introduces the punishment of the woman (3:16). Unlike the serpent she is not pronounced "cursed," but she clearly loses some of the benefits of the blessing that God had pronounced earlier. Her punishment relates primarily to her role in procreation. Procreation is the foundation of all other blessings; it is the gift of life itself (1:22, 28). The punishment does not cancel the blessing of procreation, but it introduces pain (עִצָּבוֹן/'iṣṣābôn) into the process (3:16). Disobedience brings sorrow and distress to the woman in the very function that makes her distinctive from the man.[1] Just as the blessing is associated with the idea of "multiplication of seed," God now says "I will multiply your pains."

The final aspect of the woman's punishment is in relation to her husband (3:16). While the woman's longing will be for her husband, he will rule over her. This probably means that the harmonious relations that existed between the man and the woman would now be disrupted, leaving the woman vulnerable to exploitation.

Having punished the snake and the woman, the Creator, now turned Judge, addresses the man (3:17-19). Although not directly cursed by God, the man is deeply affected by the curse on the ground, which takes the pleasure out of his work and hinders his ability to obtain food. As McConville points out, there is "no longer responsibility as a dimension of blessedness, but hard labour."[2]

Two perspectives on work are highlighted in this passage. On the one

---

1. Wenham comments that she was "sentenced to pain and frustration at the center of her existence, in her distinctive role as wife and mother"; *Genesis 1–15*, 89.
2. McConville, "The Shadow of the Curse," 2.

hand, work can bring a great deal of fulfillment and blessing to a person, but on the other, work is not always fully satisfying and sometimes does not yield adequate returns for the amount of effort expended. The narrator explains that the unhealthy, stressful, and unfulfilling aspects of labor originate from the curse on the ground. From the perspective of Genesis, the ideal or Edenic conception of work is productive and fulfilling; it is a partnership between all who are involved. Unemployment is as far removed from this ideal and is just as much a curse as the sort of hard labor to which Adam was sentenced.

Blessing, as we have seen, was a powerful, beneficial directive made for the benefit of the created order. Cursing, on the other hand, was a powerful detrimental pronouncement aimed at punishing the disobedient creatures. The areas of human life affected by the pronouncement of divine judgment are reminiscent of those targeted earlier for blessing. In terms of procreation and authority, the pronouncement of blessing provided for well-structured, clearly defined relationships between the human couple themselves and between them and the animal kingdom (1:22–1:30; cf. 2:18-25). Furthermore, blessing was pronounced in the context of harmonious relations between humankind and their divine Creator (1:26-28). Cursing, however, introduced alienation instead of harmony, exploitation instead of structured authority. The comprehensive way in which the new situation affected the relationships of those involved may be seen from the following:

> Relations between the couple and the serpent are affected; "I will put enmity between you and the woman." (3:15)
> Relations between human beings suffer; "Your desire will be for your husband, and he shall rule over you." (3:16)
> The damaged relationship between humanity and deity is exemplified by the expulsion of the human beings from the garden.

While human beings still enjoy some of the benefits of blessing such as the ability to procreate, they must contend with the new situation where the world and its inhabitants are out of harmony with their Creator. The human beings are still distinguished from the animals because they have been made in the "image of God," but the harmonious relations that characterized their early existence are now history.[3] The punishment of the man and woman culminates in their expulsion from Eden (3:22-24). God, "like a landlord dissatis-

---

3. The fact that human beings are made in the image of God is used as an argument against murder in 9:6. The concept, therefore, has a bearing on interhuman as well as human/divine relations (cf. Jas 3:9).

fied with his tenants, evicts them."[4] The human beings are not expelled from the earth completely but only from the particular parcel of land on which they rebelled. This, however, does not cancel human responsibility in relation to the ground (3:23). Adam must still work the soil, but the benefits he receives are greatly reduced and thorns and thistles hamper his efforts (3:19, 23). Human beings will eat "the plants of the field"[5] until they return to the dust (3:18-19). The ground from which Adam was formed will eventually claim him again, but until then his life will be hard labor as he struggles to cultivate the soil.

This expulsion from the garden of Eden is the first record of exile in the Bible, and it happens as a result of disobedience. Many of the earliest readers of Genesis may have been exiles, and this record of the exile of Adam and Eve would have been very pertinent for them. The prophets clearly taught that Israel's exile from Canaan, like the exile of Adam and Eve, was decreed by God because of disobedience (e.g., Amos 7:11; Jer 7:14-15).

Interpretation of 3:15

Interpretations of 3:15 vary dramatically, and this variation has usually more to do with the reader's theological preconceptions than with the content of the text itself. God's prediction of enmity between woman and serpent and their respective offspring has been interpreted by some as little more than an attempt to explain why snakes crawl on their bellies (etiological interpretation), while others see it as a prophecy of Christ as the messiah who destroys the power of the serpent (Satan).[6] This latter interpretation approaches the passage as a protevangelium. Westermann argues that an aetiological interpretation is the best way to understand both the restrictions placed on the serpent and the forecast of enmity between woman and serpent and their respective offspring.[7] On the other hand, Wenham argues that while the primary meaning of the passage cannot be taken as a messianic reference, it "may be justified in the light of subsequent revelation."[8] According to this view, the messianic interpretation is a valid Christian way of reading the text, providing that we do not allow this *sensus plenior* to obscure the meaning of the text in the book of Genesis itself.

4. McKeown, "Unifying Themes," 256.
5. Wenham suggests that this term "probably covers both wild and cultivated plants in contrast to the fruit-bearing trees of the garden"; *Genesis 1–15*, 82.
6. This interpretation goes back at least as far as Irenaeus (ca. A.D. 180).
7. Westermann, *Genesis 1–11*, 259.
8. Wenham, *Genesis 1–15*, 81.

While these views of 3:15 are important and valid responses to the text for those who hold them, they fail, as Wenham points out, to do justice to the programmatic role fulfilled by this text in its present setting in the book of Genesis. The first readers of Genesis, unacquainted with the centuries of Christian theology, would expect the book of Genesis itself to explicate this promise of "seed." Since Genesis highlights the special status of one line of descent, a reference to the seed of the serpent and the seed of the woman suggests that the remainder of the book will shed further light on this mysterious pronouncement.[9] The identity of the "seed" of the woman is clearly delineated in Genesis as the line of chosen people whom God will bless. This line of descent is traced through Seth to Jacob and his sons. Ultimately, of course, this line does lead to Christ, as Matthew makes clear in the first chapter of his Gospel.

4:1-7 Two Brothers; Two Attitudes; Two Offerings

Since hope for the future is linked with the woman's offspring (3:15), the narrative now focuses on her first two children, Cain and Abel (4:1). The reader would expect the main focus to be on the firstborn son since he usually was honored with a higher status than his siblings. However, an important recurring theme in Genesis is that God often overturns accepted practice and chooses, not the firstborn, but one of his brothers. This trend begins with Cain, who, although the first son of Adam and Eve, is a huge disappointment.[1] One indication that the usual order will be reversed is that Abel's profession is given before that of Cain.

The name Cain is followed by a brief explanation of the name, "I have produced a man with the help of the LORD" (4:1 NRSV).[2] The clause "I have produced" translates the Hebrew קָנִיתִי/qānîtî, which sounds similar to Cain, קַיִן/qayin. Apart from assonance, any other link between the words is unlikely; Hebrew names and subjects are often associated with words that sound similar, regardless of meaning. However, the naming of Cain is significant because Eve involves God in the process, and even though she is outside Eden

9. Wifall suggests that this verse should be interpreted against a Davidic background; "Gen. 3:15 — A Protevangelium?" 361-65.

1. In Genesis, Ishmael, Esau, and Reuben were firstborn sons who were surpassed by younger siblings. In the Historical Books a similar pattern emerges with the accession to the throne by David and Solomon, even though both had older brothers.

2. The Hebrew of this verse is difficult to translate since it reads lit., "I have produced a man, with the LORD."

she recognizes that God has helped her. The name Abel is not explained, probably because the meaning was transparent to the earliest readers. Abel, הֶבֶל/*hebel*, is the Hebrew word which means "breath" or "vanity"; this is the word used in the refrain of the preacher in Ecclesiastes, "vanity of vanities."[3] Abel's life would be like a breath or vapor because of his premature death.

Farming and pasturing were two main sources of employment in the ancient world, and Cain and Abel represent these two traditions. Stories from Sumer, for example, reflect ancient tensions between farmers and shepherds. An example is the dispute between the shepherd-god Dumuzi and the farmer-god Enkimdu.[4] These farmer/shepherd tensions are very much in the background in the biblical story, which is about gaining acceptance with God, and the dispute between the siblings has no direct bearing on their respective professions.

The focus is on the two brothers and the offerings that they bring. Cain's offering of produce from the ground fails to gain him favor with God (4:5). Abel brings fat portions from the firstborn of his flock (4:4). The quality of the offering is emphasized because the fat portions were considered the best meat and the firstborn animals were the most prized. Abel carefully chooses his offering and brings the very best that he possesses to God regardless of expense. In contrast, Cain's offering is nondescript; he brings some of the produce of the ground. Abel brings God the firstborn of his flocks, but we are not told that Cain brings the firstfruits of the ground.

Because God does not accept his offering, Cain's face is downcast and he is "very angry." Why this strong reaction? Since the outcome is the murder of his brother, the crux of the matter for Cain is not just that his offering is rejected, but he is extremely jealous that Abel's has been accepted. Cain's position is not hopeless, since God gives him an opportunity to do better and to gain acceptance (4:7). God warns him that sin is crouching like a wild animal, ready to take advantage of his vulnerability.

We are not told why Cain and his offering are unacceptable. One possibility is that the produce that Cain brings is inappropriate because it came from the ground that had been cursed. However, only thorns and thistles are the result of the curse — not the fruit. Another popular suggestion is that Abel's offering is superior because it is a blood offering. Although the Hebrew word used for "offering" in this passage usually refers to a "gift" for God such

3. The link between names in Genesis and the explanations given is usually assonance. While the etymology of the name Abel is debated, it is probably not as significant as the more obvious link to the word with the same spelling.

4. "Dumuzi and Enkimdu: The Dispute between the Shepherd-God and the Farmer-God"; *ANET*, 41-42.

as grain or fruit (Lev 2:14), the offering of a living animal was a much greater sacrifice. The emphasis in the text is that Cain's attitude in bringing a nondescript offering of whatever came to his hand is not acceptable and his status as the elder son could not outweigh his failure. A recurring theme in Genesis is the rejection of the elder brother in favor of his younger sibling. The Cain-Abel story is the first episode that highlights this theme.

4:8-16 The First Murder and the Consequences

Cold-blooded murder is Cain's response; he reacts violently against his brother and kills him (4:8).[1] This represents an intensification of sin from disobedience to fratricide. Cain was the first person who was willing to hate and kill for religious reasons, and, sadly, many have followed his example. God's interrogation of Cain, "Where is your brother?" reminds us of the similar question to Adam, "Where are you?" Cain's attempt to avoid the searching question is no more effective than Adam's fig leaves had been; but whereas Adam had sought to avoid the question, Cain lies to God that he does not know his brother's whereabouts. Cain's own question, "Am I my brother's keeper?" goes unanswered because it is not a genuine inquiry but an arrogant retort that shows utter contempt for God and complete indifference to the crime that has taken place. Because of the fratricide, the blood of Abel cries out to God for vengeance and Cain cannot escape the consequences.

Although we would not normally link the crime of murder with the ground, this connection is made in the Cain-Abel narrative; the ground opens its mouth to receive the victim's blood (4:10). Furthermore, the ground also features in the punishment of Cain (4:11-12). Because of his crime, Cain is cursed "from the land/ground" (4:11). There are two possible meanings of this Hebrew construction: either he was cursed more than the ground or the curse would separate him from the ground, which in the past had been his source of food. The latter explanation seems more likely and is supported by most modern commentators. Cain is separated from the agent through which the blessing of Yahweh was channeled to him. Adam's punishment had rendered the ground difficult to cultivate, but through labor and toil he could still grow crops for food (3:18-19). In contrast, Cain's expulsion from the cultivated ground is a more serious chastisement because the ground will no longer

---

1. In v. 8 some ancient versions, including the Samaritan Pentateuch, include an invitation by Cain to Abel, "Let us go out to the field." This invitation is absent from the Masoretic Text.

yield its crops for him (4:11-14). God and the ground unite against the recalcitrant human to deprive him of his main source of food.

The punishment also involves the alienation of Cain from other members of the human race and from God. His exclamation, "My punishment is more than I can bear!" is a double entendre in Hebrew and also means, "My iniquity is too great to be forgiven." Cain's complaint is that his punishment is too great, but the second meaning, that he deserved no forgiveness, is obvious to Hebrew readers.

Cain's concern that whoever finds him will kill him raises the frequently asked question, "Where did all these new people come from?" The reader may expect that the total population of the earth was four people at this stage. Various explanations have been suggested, none of them fully satisfactory. This is further evidence that the narrator was not answering the sort of questions that people ask in the 21st century but was addressing the issues of his own generation. Since the text gives no clue to the answer, any attempt to provide one will be speculative and debatable.

Cain's complaint is not dismissed, and he is reassured that whoever kills him will suffer sevenfold vengeance. Yahweh places a mysterious sign or mark on Cain to protect his life. Cain goes to the land of Nod, which means "wandering," or as von Rad names it, "land of restlessness."[2] Whereas blessing had fostered harmony, cursing breeds separation and alienation.

The Adam-Eve and Cain-Abel stories feature an emphasis on the relationship between human beings and the ground. Concomitant with the deterioration in human behavior is a loss of productivity from the ground (3:17-19; cf. 4:10-12). Apparently, the narrator is establishing a principle that has important implications for the theme of land throughout the book of Genesis; the earth and all its land belong to the Creator, who has given humans authority and responsibility over the created order (1:1–2:9). Failure to treat the land properly (either eating forbidden fruit [3:6-19] or forcing the land to drink the blood of a brother [4:8-12]) is ultimately a sin against the Creator and will result in judgment. The role of God is consistent with the role of "supreme landlord." God supervises those who occupy the earth he has made. Those who do not behave in a worthy manner find the benefits that they receive from the land greatly restricted or removed completely.

Cain's story ends, like many stories in the OT, with exile. Once again disobedience leads to expulsion. However, by murdering his brother, Cain commits a much greater crime than his parents. The increased seriousness of the crime leads to a deeper sense of alienation from God and an intensified

2. Von Rad, *Genesis,* 107.

sense of exile. This was an important message to the earliest readers, since many of them were also facing or had faced exile. Genesis clearly attributes exile to alienation from God.

4:17-24 Genealogical Information

Few literary forms can compete with genealogical lists in terms of their soporific qualities and potential to bore the modern reader! However, societies that do not have our technology for keeping records often memorize, treasure, and perpetuate details about their family history. For example, Lacey and Danzinger, writing concerning the year 1000 in England, observe:

> The Anglo-Saxons learned most of their folklore by heart. They could tell long complicated tales of their family histories — who begat whom, back to when their ancestors had first arrived in England from the forests beyond the sea.[1]

For the first readers of Genesis family histories were highly significant, not just as historical records, but as part of their theological heritage explaining how God had chosen them for special blessing. Genealogical data is, therefore, a key element in the contents and message of the book of Genesis. Significantly, this first genealogical list (4:17-22) has been positioned between two accounts of murder (4:3-15 and 4:23-26). By sandwiching the list of Cain's descendants between "an impulsive act of murder" and "a deliberate reign of terror,"[2] the narrator gives a negative message about this particular line of descent. Chapter 4 conforms to a pattern found throughout Genesis, where the genealogy of a person whose career has been followed by the narrator but who is now about to disappear from the narrative, is given first.[3]

This genealogical information concerning Cain's family line concludes the narrative about him and his offspring. The information on Cain's descendants highlights their contribution to technological and sociological progress. Although out of harmony with God, Cain and his descendents are progressive and innovative. Enoch, Cain's first son, was born while his father was building

---

1. Lacey and Danziger, *The Year 1000*, 27.
2. Clines, "Theme in Genesis 1–11," 493.
3. As Wenham points out, "Genesis always records the descendants of the unfavored sons before the elect line. The genealogies of Japheth and Ham precede that of Shem (chap. 10); Ishmael's genealogy precedes Isaac's (25:12-34); and Esau's, Jacob's (chaps. 36-37). So here the genealogy of Cain precedes Seth's"; *Genesis 1–15*, 97.

a city and consequently the city was named Enoch.[4] It is somewhat surprising that Cain, who was doomed to be a wanderer, builds the first city. This is probably an indication that Cain refuses to accept God's verdict on his life and suggests his continued rebellion.[5] Other descendants of Cain are also mentioned: Mehujael, Methusael, and Lamech. Significant details are given about Lamech and his descendants. Lamech is the first person in Genesis who is on record as having married more than one wife. His two wives bear three children noted for their inventiveness. Jabal is described as "the ancestor of those who live in tents and have livestock" (4:20 NRSV) and his brother Jubal as "the ancestor of all those who play the lyre and pipe" (4:21 NRSV). Their half-brother, Tubal-cain, is credited with making "all kinds of bronze and iron tools" (4:22 NRSV). But on a more negative note, the passage includes the defiant claim of Lamech that he, like Cain, has committed murder. It is not clear why he can assert that, whereas the death of Cain would be avenged seven times, his own death would be avenged 77 times. Significantly, unlike Cain, Lamech has no direct encounter with God, which is part of the underlying message of these early chapters: the human race that had such a promising start in Eden was now hopelessly alienated from God and at odds with each other.

4:25-26 Genealogical Information about Adam and Eve

Genealogical information is given about Adam and his wife. She bears Seth and refers to him as "another child [lit., 'seed'] instead of Abel." For Adam and Eve, who have lost both Cain and Abel, Seth represents a new start. Seth's birth is significant for the story line of Genesis since it is his family line who survive the flood. Furthermore, Eve's reference to Seth as "another seed," זֶרַע אַחֵר/ *zera' 'aḥēr*, refers the reader back to 3:15 and to the "seed" of the woman who would bruise the head of the serpent's seed.

This passage fulfils a transitional role, redirecting the reader's attention from Cain and Abel to the family line of Seth. The chapter ends with a short statement about worship of Yahweh. According to Exodus 6, the name Yahweh was not revealed until the time of Moses, and therefore this verse seems anachronistic: how could people call on Yahweh if the name had not yet been revealed? However, in a polytheistic world it was important to identify early in Genesis who the Creator was. Perhaps for pragmatic reasons the

---

4. Cain's son Enoch should not be confused with a person of the same name in Seth's family line who "walked with God."

5. This point is made clearly by R. P. Gordon, *Holy Land, Holy City*, 24.

narrator of Genesis uses names that would not have been known until much later. For example, the city to which Abram pursues his enemies is named Dan (14:14), but the name of the city in the days of Abram was Laish. If the narrator was willing to replace an ancient city name with a name that the readers would be familiar with to avoid confusion, then it is likely that the same principle applied to the name of God.

5:1-32 The Family Tree from Adam to Noah

While the genealogy in ch. 4 concludes the detail of Cain and his family, ch. 5 opens with a genealogy that focuses on the future. The omission of any reference to Cain prepares the reader to look for future hope and blessing through the family line of Seth. Cain, the firstborn, had forfeited any right to a prominent role in God's agenda, and Seth takes his place (cf. 22:2).[1] Chapter 5 is much more positive than ch. 4 and traces its genealogy back, not only to Adam, but to God himself who created humankind in his image.

If 5:1-3 is read without considering its context, the reader will almost certainly conclude that human beings are no longer in the image of God. Thus whereas the Creator makes Adam in his own image — the image of God — Adam has a son in *his* own image. *The NIV Study Bible* jumps to the logical conclusion that "As God created man in his own perfect image, so now sinful Adam has a son in his own imperfect image."[2] However, given that the main message of this passage is that the line of Adam's firstborn son Cain has been rejected in favor of his younger brother Seth, the most likely interpretation is that Adam, who is made in the image of God, passes this image on to Seth. This argument is supported by the later affirmation that, even after the flood, human beings are superior to animals because they are made in the image of God (9:6). No reference is made in this passage to the image having become imperfect. Furthermore, the emphasis on death throughout the genealogy ("and he died") is put in perspective by this implication that the image of God has not been withdrawn.[3] In ch. 4 the increasing effect of sin is followed through one particular line. Now, in contrast, the effect of God's image in people and of his continued blessing on the human race is in focus through

---

1. A similar approach is taken in the Abraham narrative where, after Ishmael's genealogy is concluded, Isaac is described as Abraham's "only son."

2. *The NIV Study Bible* (Grand Rapids: Zondervan, 1985), 13.

3. Ross comments on 5:1-5, "The expositor should not miss the emphasis on the blessing of the image at creation or the intended contrast with the theme of death that suddenly takes over the passage"; *Creation and Blessing,* 173.

the progeny of Seth. The Sethite genealogy of ch. 5 is a uniform literary structure following the same pattern throughout. This takes the form:

> When Person^A had lived X years, he became the father of Person^B; and after he became the father of Person^B, Person^A lived X years and had other sons and daughters. Altogether, Person^A lived X years and then he died.

Obviously, any deviations from this order must be regarded as significant. These are:

1. In v. 3 Seth is said to be in his father's image and likeness.
2. V. 22 describes Enoch's walk with God and the consequent translation to be with God.
3. In v. 29 Lamech expresses hope that his son Noah will bring comfort from the hard labor experienced because of the curse on the ground.

These significant statements provide useful starting points to compare the genealogy of Cain with that of Seth. Cain's family line catalogues the movement of recalcitrant human beings away from God, whereas for Seth and his family line the movement is towards restoring the relationship with God. This can be seen by comparing the characters with the same names. Both genealogies (Cain and Seth) contain the name Enoch, and both include a short explanatory digression (4:17; 5:24). The Cainite Enoch is linked with the building of a city, a clear contrast with the much more spiritual Sethite Enoch who "walked with God." To emphasize the importance of Enoch's walk with God the narrator repeats the statement. Furthermore, the form used of the verb "to walk" (hitpaʿel) is the same as that used of God when he walked in the garden of Eden (3:8).

The name Lamech also appears in both genealogies (4:18-19; 5:25-31). The Cainite Lamech shows the direction in which his particular line is heading. As von Rad comments, it shows "the spirit of a growing irreconcilableness and fierce self-assertiveness, by which human community is more and more profoundly ruptured."[4] On the other hand, the Sethite Lamech is anticipating the birth of Noah and longing for a solution to the problems brought about by sin, a reference back to 3:15-17. Comparison of the two genealogies reveals a clear contrast between the line of Cain, with its murder and its steady movement away from God, and the line of Seth, with its spiritual emphasis and its hope of comfort from the effects of the curse.

4. Von Rad, *Genesis*, 111.

The verse in which Lamech names Noah (5:29) is pivotal; it looks back to the pronouncement of divine judgment in ch. 3 while at the same time it looks forward to Noah and his relationship with God. The reference to "the land/ground that Yahweh has cursed" is an obvious allusion to 3:17. This is further emphasized by the noun עִצָּבוֹן/*'iṣṣābôn* ("pain"), which occurs only three times in the OT: 3:16, 3:17, and 5:29. This word both defines and describes the power of cursing, just as the verbs "to fill" and "to multiply" described the nature of the blessing being pronounced. Lamech's use of this term highlights the seriousness of the situation that the human beings now face. Adam's disobedience has sentenced the humans to hard labor and pain from which there seems to be no relief. Lamech longs that his son may bring some comfort, and he calls him Noah with this in mind.[5]

Longevity in Genesis

Since we live in a scientific era when time can be measured accurately to thousandths of a second, it is difficult, if not impossible, to understand fully how the ancients recorded and understood time. Even people who live in tribal areas today have a different attitude; some of my African students have freely admitted that they do not know their own ages since in their societies this is not important. In Genesis we have people living up to 969 years. Some scholars think that these are literal years, while others suggest that they had a symbolic significance. If a symbolic significance is intended, we do not know what this was. However, convincing symbolic interpretations have been suggested for a few of the names. Thus, in ancient Egypt the ideal life span was 110, and, significantly, Joseph died at 110. Symbolism may also explain the age attributed to Lamech. As already mentioned, two men were called Lamech, one descended from Cain and the other from Seth. The Cainite Lamech refers to the number seven when speaking about revenge, but the length of his life is not given. For the Sethite Lamech, seven is also significant since he lives for 777 years. Also, Enoch, who "walked with God," lived for 365 years, which may have symbolized a full life.[6]

Large numbers in the Bible are puzzling, but many will feel that we shall not be taking the Bible seriously unless we take the numbers literally. Our

5. The name Noah, נֹחַ/*Nōaḥ*, means "rest," but Lamech links the name with a verb which sounds similar but means "to bring comfort" (נָחַם/*niḥēm*) As we observed in the context of Eve naming Cain, assonance was sometimes more important than etymology.

6. A Sumerian list, which like Genesis 5 contains 10 names, has exceptionally long ages (72,000 years) which also seem symbolic.

knowledge of the symbolic use of numbers is still very limited and does not provide, with present knowledge, a satisfactory alternative to the literal interpretation. Because of this uncertainty, a cautious approach to biblical numerology is highly advisable.

6:1-4 The Sons of God

It is impossible to disguise or ignore the intractable problems that face the interpreters of this short passage about the sons of God. Sarna suggests that the overwhelming difficulties of the passage have arisen because this is a "highly condensed version" of an original story which was told "to combat polytheistic mythology."[1] His theory cannot be proved since the only extant version of the story is the Genesis account, but certainly it is possible that the intended readers had additional information that would have made this passage much more easily interpreted. Sarna may be correct that we have only part of a longer original story.[2]

In the preceding genealogies the focus was on the male line of descent, but now the birth of daughters is introduced. A clear contrast is made between the "daughters of men" (NIV) and those who marry them — "sons of God." Assuming that the daughters were human girls, who were the sons of God?

a. Were they angels? Ancient Mesopotamian, Greek, and Egyptian stories describe divine and human interrelationships that result in semi-divine progeny. Moreover, the phrase "sons of God" in the book of Job refers to heavenly beings (Job 1:6; 2:1). If this interpretation is correct, its inclusion by the narrator develops the idea that God created everything within set boundaries, but now as wickedness increases even the boundary between human and divine is breached. An argument against this interpretation is that when God punishes the behavior of these sons of God, the judgment falls, not upon angels, but upon humankind. However, as Lucas observes, presumably the girls and their fathers consented to the illicit unions.[3] Others strongly oppose the theory that angels and women had sexual intercourse; Calvin describes the idea as "absurd."[4]

b. Were they members of the nobility? Rulers and judges were some-

1. Sarna, *Genesis*, 45.
2. This has occurred elsewhere in the Bible (e.g., Qumran texts contain a longer version of the Ammonite attack on Jabesh-gilead; 1 Sam 11:1-15).
3. Lucas, *Can We Believe Genesis Today?* 151.
4. Calvin, *Genesis*, 67.

times called gods, though this is not obvious to the English reader.[5] It is possible that these ancient rulers are condemned for creating large harems for themselves.

c. Were they the Sethites? If so, then 6:1-2 would mean that the descendants of Seth were married to those from the line of Cain. This does not seem particularly sinful, but Calvin argues that originally there was a clear distinction between Seth's descendants and everyone else; Seth's family was distinguished by their faithful worship while everyone else neglected God. If this scenario is correct, then the intermarriage of Seth's descendants "with the children of Cain and with other ungodly races" would represent the spread of Cain's culture of rebellion to the entire human race.[6]

d. Were they the "dramatis personae" who featured in the mythical stories of Israel's neighbors? While this may seem most unlikely to modern readers, mythical figures feature in the Psalms and in the Prophets. For example, Yahweh defeats the multiheaded monster and feeds his carcass to creatures in the desert (Ps 74:13-14). The book of Isaiah graphically describes the Exodus as Yahweh's victory over a monster (Isa 51:9). Furthermore, the readers of Genesis may have been familiar with legendary heroes, such as Gilgamesh, who were described as semi-divine. The text may be a polemic against these polytheistic myths, reminding Israel that those who worship Yahweh should regard as evil the religions and myths that glorified the concept of divine creatures marrying human beings.

e. Is the story linked to the fertility cults that were prevalent in the ancient Near East and which posed a serious threat to Israelite religion and worship? These cults linked the fertility of the field and the fertility of the womb, and their worship may have involved the practice of ritual prostitution. The priests of these religions represented the deity during ritual sexual acts, and it is possible that the title "sons of God" refers to them, while the female prostitutes may represent "the daughters of men."[7] The purpose of the passage, if this is the case, was to condemn pagan promiscuous worship.

Without further information, it is difficult to choose between the above options. However, if the crime is enigmatic (6:1-2), so also is the punishment (6:3):

---

5. In the property laws of the Torah (Exod 22:8-9), the parties involved are instructed to bring their case to God (cf. NRSV, ESV), but some translations translate the word for God in these verses as "judges" since this seems the most appropriate translation in the context of a property dispute (cf. KJV, NIV).

6. Calvin, *Genesis*, 67.

7. Lucas discusses this view and describes it as "plausible"; *Can We Believe Genesis Today*, 152.

> Then the LORD said, "My spirit shall not abide in mortals forever, for they are flesh; their days shall be one hundred twenty years." (NRSV)

To add to the confusion, the ages of people immediately after the flood are several hundred years. Some suggest that the 120 years is not the life span of human beings but the length of time before the flood.

It is interesting that the only NT passage that might be expected to shed light on this section of Genesis is equally enigmatic and controversial (1 Pet 3:18-22). However, these difficulties in interpreting the details of the passage should not prevent us from considering whether it has a useful theological message that is not affected by the hermeneutical problems. The passage upholds the sovereignty of God and demonstrates that rebellions against his authority will not succeed. God's decree that the human life span will be 120 years is an assertion that all life is a gift from God and even rebellious creatures must depend on him for their continued existence. "Only by his gift do they live. No attempted usurpation changes that."[8]

Verse 4 mentions the mysterious Nephilim and reiterates the statement that the sons of God had children with the daughters of men. The literal meaning of the Hebrew word נְפִלִים/*nĕphilîm* is "fallen ones," but this does not explain who they were and what was their relationship to the sons of God. The narrator regards these Nephilim as mighty men of renown (lit., "men of a name"). Commentators often refer to them as giants by comparing 6:4 with Num 13:31-33. However, the link between the preflood and postflood Nephilim is inconsistent with the Genesis narrative's insistence that all flesh were destroyed by the flood.

While a fully satisfactory explanation of this obscure passage is elusive, its purpose in the overall context is clear: the created order once declared "good" is now on a collision course with the Creator and sinister anti-God forces are on the increase.

6:5-8 God Observes Increasing Wickedness on Earth

A recurring theme in Genesis is that God observes the behavior of human beings and judges them accordingly. This theme is prominent, for example, in the tower of Babel story and in the account of the destruction of Sodom and Gomorrah (11:5; 18:20-21).

However, this passage not only highlights the idea that God is judge, but

---

8. Brueggemann, *Genesis*, 73.

it also emphasizes the idea that God suffers disappointment and grief. The cause of God's concern is the increasing wickedness of humanity. His initial blessing had promoted human multiplication on earth, but now a direct correlation is established between the number of humans and their increasing sinfulness.

The narrative describes the behavior of these early humans in negative terms. Without qualification, their every inclination and thought displease their Creator. Jewish theology postulates two inclinations in the human heart — a good inclination and an evil one — but this passage suggests that every action of these humans was guided and motivated by evil intentions.

God's observation of the evil multiplying among human beings on earth has a dramatic effect: God is grieved, and his heart is filled with pain (6:6 NIV). By attributing human emotions to God, the narrator shows that God's involvement with creation does not end with the seventh day. God is concerned with the continued progress of his created order, and using daring anthropopathy, the passage shows that God is deeply disturbed by human behavior. However, it is grief and not anger that is prominent in God's reaction to the situation. This shows that "he is not an angry tyrant, but a troubled parent."[1]

The translations of 6:6 vary because of the difficulty of translating the verb נחם/niham: "the LORD was sorry" (ESV, NLT, NRSV), "it repented the LORD" (KJV), "Yahweh regretted" (NJB), "The LORD was grieved" (NIV). The narrator is using language that with a human subject would express regret at having made a mistake. With the LORD as the subject the emphasis is on the change that has occurred; God who observed his creation and declared it "good" now observes it again, and his attitude towards creation is completely changed because it is no longer "good." Therefore, a human analogy is used to convey the utter revulsion of God towards the sin that has become rampant in his once perfect creation. The situation affects God deeply, and his heart is vexed or "filled with pain" (NIV); to quote the NLT, "it broke his heart." Although, unlike the putative fertility gods, Yahweh is not part of the created order, nevertheless he is not the distant, detached God of deistic philosophy. Rather, he is deeply involved and personally affected by the actions of humanity.

The emphasis on God's deeply felt pain prepares the reader for the extreme measures announced in 6:7 that will involve the removal of human beings and animals from the earth. The language of this verse is uncompromising; God will "wipe" (NIV) humankind and animals from the face of the

1. Brueggemann, *Genesis*, 77.

ground. A similar judgment is pronounced on Jerusalem in 2 Kings, where God declares, "I will wipe out Jerusalem as one wipes a dish" (2 Kgs 21:13 NIV).

Readers of Genesis in the exilic or postexilic period may have identified with the sentiments of this passage. They too had suffered, not the destruction of a flood, but the brutality of an expansionist regime. They did not fully understand why this had been permitted or why the exile lasted such a long time, and they felt that God did not care and was hidden from them (Isa 40:27). For all such situations when God seems indifferent or far away, Genesis offers the consolation that God is not unfeeling or uncaring but actually shares the suffering of his recalcitrant creation.

This tragic announcement of impending doom is countered immediately by the mention of Noah, who had "found favor in the eyes of the LORD" (6:8 ESV). Modern Hebrew has retained this idiom in expressions such as "Jerusalem finds favor in my eyes," meaning that I like the city of Jerusalem. Finding favor in God's eyes obviously means that God was pleased with Noah and would treat him favorably.

6:9-10 Introduction to Noah and His Sons

Verse 9 introduces the account of Noah and provides three new pieces of information about him. First, he is "a righteous man." This adjective refers to a person's behavior and affirms that s/he does what is right. In legal contexts, the righteous person is the one whom a judge declares innocent.

The account also describes Noah as "perfect" (KJV), "blameless" (NIV, ESV). When describing animals, this word connotes those that are physically perfect and fit for sacrifice (Lev 5:18). It is also used of a day to show that a "complete" or "whole" day is involved (Josh 10:13). Applied to people, it describes those that God wants to worship and serve him: people who do not practice sorcery and divination and who do not listen to fortune-tellers (Deut 18:13). In the context of Noah's life, it means that he was not implicated in the evil that was practiced all around him.

Earlier Genesis introduced Enoch as having such a close relationship with God that "God took him from the earth" (5:24). Now the narrator describes Noah in the same terms as Enoch; a man who "walked with God," which means that he had a close harmonious relationship with deity. It contrasts with the earlier story of God walking alone in the garden of Eden while his rebellious creatures hide themselves because their sense of harmony has been replaced by guilt and fear. This is probably an intentional comparison between Adam and Noah. Sarna observes that "Noah is the first man to be born after the death of Adam, according to the chronology of 5:28-29, and he becomes a second Adam, the second father of humanity." Sarna also points out that both Adam and Noah are in harmony with the animals, and both have three sons, one of whom is degenerate.[1]

Noah's behavior and his close relationship with God single him out from the other human beings on earth at that time and suggest that he was an example to others around him. The introduction to Noah and his character concludes with a reference to his three sons, Shem, Ham, and Japheth, but nothing is said about their behavior or about their relationship with God. The scene is now set to show how God involves this family in his plans. Even before God destroys the world he has chosen a family line through which his blessing pronounced at the dawn of creation will survive the coming judgment.

6:11-13 God Sees That the Earth Is Corrupt and Decides to Destroy it

In the creation narratives, everything that God sees is pronounced "good." Now it is corrupt and full of violence. Human beings have become corrupt themselves and have brought about the corruption of the earth, the consequences of which will be their own destruction. The emphasis that sin is the cause of the flood distinguishes the biblical Flood Narrative from the other extant flood accounts of the ancient Near East. The Gilgamesh Epic does not discuss the reason for the flood, and the Atrahasis Epic highlights human noise as the reason, rather than sin:

> And the country became too wide, the people too numerous.
> The country was as noisy as a bellowing bull.
> The God grew restless at their clamor,
> Ellil had to listen to their noise,
> He addressed the great gods,
> "The noise of mankind has become too much.
> I am losing sleep over their racket."[1]

The Atrahasis Epic gives no indication that the human beings have done anything morally wrong; they are simply creating too much noise. Genesis,

1. Sarna, *Genesis*, 49.
1. Dalley, *Myths from Mesopotamia*, 20.

however, emphasizes the moral dimension and claims that human beings through their wickedness and violence are destroying the earth. This clear connection between the transgression of the human race and the earth on which they live is emphasized by the repetition of various forms of the verb שחת/*šḥt*, which occurs four times in these three verses. The first two occurrences emphasize that the earth has become corrupt (nip'al). This state of corruption has been caused by humankind (hip'il), who, although placed on the earth to care for it, failed to fulfill their responsibilities (cf. 2:15; 3:23). Therefore, God devises a punishment that fits the crime; he will destroy (hip'il) humankind from the earth (6:13). Thus the root *šḥt* is repeated four times and used in three different ways in vv. 11-13; it describes the action of humankind, the state of the earth as a result of sin, and the action that God takes. Human beings have brought God's earth into a state of ruin, and now God brings ruin upon humankind.[2] The corollary is that human rebellion leads not only to their own destruction but to the destruction of the earth, since God's decision to destroy humankind (6:17) results in the earth losing its value as a life-supporting medium. Therefore, the behavior of human beings has repercussions, not only for their own welfare, but also for the welfare of the land.

Although the sinfulness of humankind is given as a reason for the flood, the violence that fills the earth is not limited to humans but "all flesh" is implicated, which of course includes the animals (6:12). Thus the passage suggests that the animals' behavior has become violent as a result of or, perhaps, in response to human violence. Animals are not to blame, but they are caught up and have adopted the dysfunctional behavior of their human cohabitants of earth. Sarna argues that the animals are included because they have become carnivorous "contrary to the implications of God's decree in 1:20."[3] In support of this view he cites the "utopian visions of Isaiah 11:6-7 and 65:25, which see the animal kingdom as ideally herbivorous."[4]

In an interesting article, Frymer-Kensky discusses the way in which the ground has been polluted. She argues that the contamination of the ground has been occasioned by the shedding of innocent blood.[5] This interpretation links the flood story very closely with the Cain-Abel story, suggesting that in both accounts the main crime is the shedding of blood with the consequent contamination of the ground. After the flood God issues laws aimed at preventing further contamination of the ground (9:1-7). These laws prohibit the

2. Wenham uses the English verb "to ruin" to translate שחת/*šḥt*, since "ruin" covers both senses of the Hebrew in this passage: "to spoil" and "to destroy"; *Genesis 1–15*, 171.

3. Sarna, *Genesis*, 51.

4. Sarna, *Genesis*, 51.

5. Frymer-Kensky, "Atrahasis," 154.

murder of humans and the eating of live animals. As is also demonstrated in the garden of Eden story, God reserves the right to act against people who mistreat the earth/land that he has provided for them (4:10).

6:14-22 The Ark

Noah's ark has caught the imagination of people both ancient and modern. Many attempts have been made to find evidence of it. Josephus quotes the Babylonian priest Berossus (3rd cent. B.C.), who claimed, "A portion of the vessel still survives in Armenia on the mountain of Cordyaeans and people carry off pieces of the bitumen as talismans" (*Ant.* 1.3.6).

The Hebrew word for "ark" is used in relation to only two objects in the Bible: the ark of Noah and the vessel used to conceal baby Moses. A different word is used when the ark of the covenant is the subject. This is only the first of a number of similarities and parallels in the text between Noah and Moses. For example, both receive detailed instructions from God for their most significant projects; Noah receives instructions to build the ark in similar detail to the instructions Moses receives to build the tabernacle. Both rescue others through their personal relationship with God. Both men became proverbial in later Israel as those whose intercession was particularly effective. However, the prophet Ezekiel points out that if Noah, Daniel, or Job had been alive in his day, they could have rescued only themselves since the entire population was beyond redemption (Ezek 14:14, 20).

Gopher wood, the main material for the ark, has not been identified with certainty. Suggestions include cypress, oak, and cedar. The ark was to be coated with pitch both inside and out (6:14). The word used for pitch is not the word normally used in the Bible but is closely related to the word used in the Babylonian flood stories. The dimensions of the ark were possibly 135m × 22.5m × 13.5m or 450ft × 75ft × 45ft (6:15). God warns Noah that everything which remains outside the ark will perish (6:17). Whether this implies a global deluge or a flood affecting the entire Near East has been, and continues to be, hotly debated. According to rabbinic lore, "the land of Israel was exempt from the flood."[1] In support of the global option, many argue that the text is unequivocal that the flood destroyed "all flesh in which is the breath of life under heaven" (6:17 ESV), which, it is argued, can only mean that every person and animal outside the ark perishes all over the world. On the other hand, in

---

1. Sarna points out that there is no evidence of a catastrophic flood at Jericho,"a town that dates back 9,000 years"; *Genesis*, 48.

support of a more localized flood, others argue that the Bible uses global language to describe the effects of the famine in the story of Joseph, which describes the extent of the famine as "over all the face of the earth" (41:56 KJV). However, it is quite clear from the Joseph story that this meant over that entire area. When the text declares that "all the world came to Joseph in Egypt to buy grain, because the famine became severe throughout the world" (41:57 NRSV), this does not mean that people came from India or Australia but that they came from all over the region of the world that was familiar to the narrator and the intended readers. This debate will not be settled easily, and it is greatly hampered by the problem that the Hebrew word for land, אֶרֶץ/*'ereṣ*, also means "earth" or "world" or "country." The range of meanings of this Hebrew term suggests that the distinction between the entire earth and the known world of the readers was not an issue for the narrator.

God will make a contract with Noah (6:18-22). This is the first occurrence of the word "covenant" in Genesis. According to Jewish tradition, God will make a total of 10 covenants before the end of the world. The covenant with Noah is considered to be number two. The concept of covenant was well known in the ancient world and referred to a wide range of contractual agreements. The concept of covenant included not only agreements between equals but also those between a superior such as a king and his subjects. God, the superior party in this covenant, binds himself to protect Noah and his family in the ark from the catastrophe of the flood. Noah, for his part, must obey the instructions that God has given him. Noah is not just escaping with his life. He is not entering a new relationship with God but is continuing an existing relationship and accepting the new responsibilities that the forthcoming events would involve. Noah's commitment to obedience requires him to bring two of every kind of animal and bird into the ark. God also instructs him to gather a supply of every kind of food, but water is not mentioned, presumably because it is not in short supply! Noah's diligence in fulfilling the divine instructions is emphasized in the text by repetition: "Noah did this; he did all that God commanded him" (6:22 ESV).

7:1-5 Instructions to Enter the Ark

Noah receives instructions regarding the necessary details. He is instructed to enter the ark with his family because God has found (lit., "has seen") him righteous. Noah's righteousness is not only the basis on which he personally is admitted into the ark but also includes his household. Further instructions include taking seven of each clean animal and two of the unclean into the ark.

This is in addition to the previous stipulation which mentioned only two of each animal. The purpose of the larger number is to provide animals for sacrifice or food without wiping out the species.

God gives Noah seven days to accomplish these tasks before he sends the rain that will fall for 40 days and 40 nights. This latter phrase probably refers to any lengthy period and provides a contrast with the first account of creation, in which the entire cosmos is completed in six days. The reiteration of Noah's obedience (7:5) confirms that he has fulfilled his part of the covenant stipulations and now he can do no more than wait for God to provide the protection that he has promised. Noah's behavior contrasts with that of Adam, who lost the protective environment of Eden through disobedience. Noah through obedience receives protection.

7:6-16 God's Instructions Obeyed

To this point, the emphasis has been on what Noah must do: he must take his household and specified numbers of certain animals into the ark. Although some of the details already given are repeated here, there is a significant change of emphasis from the responsibility of Noah to the initiative of those involved; Noah's family and the animals must enter the ark to escape the flood. Thus two aspects of the same truth are held in tension: God gives the instructions and does the work that is beyond human capability, but in return the human beings and even the animals must obey. This is an important theme for Israel, and it is repeated in the accounts of the settlement in Canaan. Moses brings the Israelites out of Egypt to the gateway of Canaan, but they are required to exercise faith and enter the land. Later in Israel's history, God will provide an opportunity for those exiled to Babylon to return to Jerusalem, but they must avail themselves of that opportunity. Noah has exercised faith in obedience to God, but the act of entering the ark is also an expression of obedience on the part of Noah's family and even of the animals. Every living creature in the ark is to some extent responsive to instruction conveyed through Noah.

When all are safely aboard, God shuts them in, suggesting that he supervises the entire operation. Since God takes personal control of closing the door, only those he chooses are permitted inside, and when they are within the ark only God can give permission to leave. Thus, the divine and human responsibilities are clearly delineated.

The description of the cataclysm itself suggests that the floodwaters come from below as well as from above. This is creation in reverse, with the chaotic waters breaking through the bounds that have held them in subjection. For ancient readers the miracle of creation was that the powers of chaos were subdued, but now God withdraws the restraints and the chaotic waters overwhelm the created order.

7:17-24 Every Living Thing outside the Ark Dies

The account of Noah and his ark is often romanticized as a children's story with the emphasis on the animals that are rescued. However, it is also a horror story in which human beings — men women, and children — and innocent animals are swept away by merciless floodwaters.

To ancient readers who had suffered calamities such as the exile, it is this horror dimension that would have been analogous to their situation. These verses emphasize the depth of this horror and the totality of the destruction. Outside the ark, nothing survives. The Hebrew is dramatic and dynamic as it describes the power of the chaotic waters prevailing over the land (lit., "the waters prevailed, very, very," 7:19). The depth of water covering the highest mountains is 15 cubits (7:20). Since a cubit was probably 18 inches (46 cm), the depth of water covering the mountains is 22.5 feet (6.9 m). This inundation continues for 150 days (7:24). If taken literally that this was a universal flood and that every mountain including Everest was covered, impossible amounts of water would have been involved. To obviate this difficulty while being fully literal, the creationist approach assumes that the high mountains were not formed until after the flood. However, this is not explicitly stated in Genesis or anywhere else in the OT and must be seen as pure speculation.

The shocking effect of this detailed emphasis on the totality and ruthlessness of the destruction caused by the flood is to show that the God who lovingly breathed into Adam the breath of life is now the executioner who pronounces the death sentence. Such a God must be feared and obeyed, since the failure to do so will be catastrophic. This chilling message harmonizes with the prophetic warnings to Israel to repent and avert disaster (e.g., Amos 1:2; Zeph 1:2-4).

While the fate of those outside the ark is inevitable and terrible, the fate of those inside is not enviable. Since the ark has no rudder, they have no control over their destination and all they can do is wait and hope. Exiled Israelites probably saw themselves in a similar situation to those in the ark. Both shared that most debilitating sense of uncertainty combined with an inability to control their own destiny. This is reflected in Isaiah, where the writer exhorts the people to wait expectantly on God, and he assures them that they will "soar on wings like eagles" (Isa 40:31). This would have been a wonderful prospect for those in exile and for anyone who feels that their situation is out of control and that circumstances have hemmed them in like the walls of a rudderless ark.

8:1-14 The Waters Recede

The turning point in the flood story is heralded by the words "God remembered Noah and all the wild animals and all the livestock that were with him in the ark" (8:1). The Hebrew verb "remember" does not always mean simply "to recall" an event or person. It includes the idea of acting on behalf of the person or thing that has been remembered. When the Psalmist prays, "remember David" (Ps 132:1 KJV, NIV), he is not asking God to recall who David is but is pleading for divine intervention on behalf of David's descendants.

This act of remembrance puts the flood process into reverse, completing the pattern creation–uncreation–re-creation. A wind commissioned by God blows over the earth and the waters begin to subside (8:1; cf. 1:2). Mountains reappear, their tops becoming visible at the end of the ninth month (8:5). Noah waits 40 days and then opens the window and releases the raven (8:6). We may assume that he waited seven days for the raven to return before sending the dove (8:8). He sends the dove out two more times (8:10-12). After a further 29 days Noah removes the covering (8:13). At the end of 57 more days the land is completely dry (8:14).

This part of the story is told in such detail that it contrasts sharply with the speed of the initial creation in just seven days. In the creation account the emphasis is on order, efficiency, and divine power. The flood narrative, on the other hand, emphasizes the slow, gradual restoration of the earth as the waters recede over a period of many days. Since these details of the slowly receding water are prominent in the text, we should think carefully about their significance. If we read the story through the eyes of the early readers, those in exile for example, the message becomes clear. After the immediate danger of the cataclysm has passed and after the intended victims of the judgment are long-since dead, the reader expects the flood to end quickly, especially if God can create a world in six days; why the delay? Israel as a nation had similar experiences and frustrations. Sometimes the promises of God seemed slow in materializing. Those in exile must have felt like the people and animals penned up in the ark. The immediate danger was over; they had been judged for their wrongdoing, and yet the agony dragged on with no indication of when it would end. The aftermath of the flood, like the aftermath of the exile, must have placed considerable demands on the patience and faith of those involved.

Comparing Genesis with the Mesopotamian flood story, the Gilgamesh

Epic reveals striking similarities as well as important differences in the way that the end of the inundation is described. The flood ends much more quickly in Gilgamesh, suggesting that the purpose of Genesis is to focus on the need for patient faith and hope in God for restoration after a time of judgment. The main point of contact between the accounts is the dispatching of the birds.

> When the seventh day arrived,
> I released a dove to go free,
> The dove went and returned,
> No landing place came to view, it turned back.
> I released a swallow to go free,
> The swallow went and returned,
> No landing place came to view, it turned back.
> I sent a raven to go free,
> The raven went forth, saw the ebbing of the waters,
> It ate, circled, left droppings, did not turn back.[1]

After this incident, the Gilgamesh Epic brings the flood story to a conclusion and introduces the details of the sacrifices offered. Although the story of sending out birds is a point of contact between the stories, this should not obscure from us the different emphases and different worldviews that separate the stories. This is evident even in the description of how the ark is evacuated. The Genesis account describes a very orderly evacuation under the supervision of Yahweh himself. The main point of the Genesis story is that God, who had earlier shut the door of the ark, now opens it, giving its inhabitants, animals and humans, permission to enter and populate the newly cleansed earth. This theological emphasis on Yahweh controlling the gift of the earth is also prominent in the story of settlement in Joshua, since Yahweh opens up the Jordan River to allow the Israelites to enter the land promised to them. For those reading Genesis in the postexilic period, the timely accession of Cyrus was judged as another example of Yahweh's controlling hand in history.

8:15-22 After the Flood

The human and animal inhabitants of the ark now leave, and the task of repopulating the earth begins. This process resembles the original creation of the earth (1:1-13). Noah offers sacrifices to God and receives a response of mercy and grace (8:20-22). Yahweh accepts the burnt offerings as "a pleasing

1. Foster, "Gilgamesh"; *COS* 1:460.

aroma." A brief divine pronouncement responds to Noah's sacrifices. Again, the focus of attention is the earth. God promises that he will never again curse the ground as he had done in bringing the flood (8:21). God assures the human beings that there will be no further destruction of all living creatures by a flood and that the normal seasons will continue while earth remains (8:22). The future of humankind is clearly linked with the future of the earth itself; the earth as a whole is portrayed as a gracious gift from the Creator to people who are not worthy of it (8:21). God reminds human beings that the earth they live on is still supporting life, not because humankind does not deserve another flood, but because God knows that periodic destruction of creation would not solve the problem. This dignified acceptance of Noah's sacrifice contrasts with the corresponding scene in the Gilgamesh Epic.

> I set up an offering stand on the top of the mountain.
> Seven and seven cult vessels I set out,
> I heaped reeds, cedar, and myrtle in their bowls.
> The gods smelled the savor,
> The gods smelled the sweet savor,
> The gods crowded around the sacrificer like flies.[1]

The Gilgamesh Epic portrays the gods in considerable disarray and disagreement because of the flood. In contrast, the Genesis account describes the evacuation of the ark and the occupation of the new earth as a dignified process controlled and supervised by God. Those on board disembark only after they receive a direct command from God (8:15-19). We have already observed a similar emphasis in the creation stories; the earth is provided by God; man is master of the earth, but it is delegated responsibility. It is this same emphasis that is now repeated after the flood.

Interestingly, the subject of land/ground that was prominent in the story of creation is also highlighted in the story of the flood. Throughout the flood narrative, a close connection is maintained between the land/ground and sin. The words for land/ground occur about 40 times in chs. 6–8.[2] It is true, of course, that a story dealing with a flood will necessitate some mention of the earth/land. However, comparisons between the Genesis narrative and

---

1. Foster, "Gilgamesh"; *COS* 1:460.

2. The term אֶרֶץ/*'ereṣ* occurs precisely 40 times in the passage, commencing with the announcement of the family history of Noah and ending with the declaration that the earth would not be destroyed again by a flood (6:9–9:11). It would be precarious to postulate that this is deliberate without a clear indication of what the number 40 is intended to symbolize. However, this large number of occurrences of "land" is, undoubtedly, significant.

the Atrahasis story show that the earth/land motif is much more prominent in Genesis than the story of a flood normally warrants.[3] Atrahasis 3:1:1–3:6:50 mentions earth/land only three times against 40 times in Genesis (6:9–9:11). Although land is never fully personified in Genesis, it has a prominent role in the drama. The Edenic ideal of a harmonious tripartite relationship is completely disrupted in the flood narrative. The humans who have already lost their close relationship with the Creator now lose their relationship with the land/earth when the flood covers it.

A story like the flood is ideally suited to a chiastic structure.[4] Such a structure is particularly evident between the reference to the animals and human beings entering the ark (7:13) and the subsequent reference to them leaving (8:19). Even if this structure was not in the author's mind, it does provide a useful way to show how the story is developed and helps to show the prominence given to the theme of land/earth as the water first covers it and then recedes again.[5]

Man, animals, birds and all that creeps on the earth enter the ark. (7:13-16)
　The length of time that the flood continues to cover the earth (7:17)
　　The waters prevail and increase greatly on the earth. (7:18)
　　　Waters cover the mountains, and everything on earth dies. (7:20-22)
　　　　Waters increase; all living creatures are blotted out from the earth.
　　　　　(7:23)
　　　　The waters cover the earth. (7:24)
　　　　God remembers Noah. (8:1)
　　　　A wind blows over the earth, and the waters begin to subside.
　　　　　(8:1)
　　　The waters recede from the earth continually. (8:3)
　　　The ark comes to rest, and the tops of the mountains become visible.
　　　　(8:4-6)
　　The water on the earth dries up. (8:13)
　The length of time from the start of the flood until the earth is completely
　　dry (8:14)
Man, animals, birds, and all that creeps on the earth leave the ark. (8:16-19)

3. Van Wolde discusses the frequent occurrences of the words for land and earth in the flood story, concluding that "the earth is central in God's concern"; *Stories of the Beginning,* 120.

4. This is because so many things happen in the flood story which must be reversed. People who enter the ark must leave; the waters which rise must fall, and mountains which are covered with water must appear again. Attempts to show the chiastic structure of the flood narrative include, e.g., Anderson, "From Analysis to Synthesis," 38; and Wenham, "The Coherence of the Flood Narrative," 338.

5. See the discussion in Wenham, *Genesis 1–15,* 156-58.

As the human beings and animals populate their new world, God promises that there will be no repeat of this disastrous, cataclysmic flood. This was not a promise that there would never be another flood but that God would not again use this method to punish sin. This was the worst flood that humankind had experienced. In the ark, winter and summer were the same and there was no seedtime or harvest. God promised that there would never be another flood like it. Both humans and animals could look forward to a future in which God guaranteed not to react to sin by destroying the world. People often ask whether the Genesis flood story gives us the mandate to say that nations that suffer great tragedies such as destructive floods are being punished for their sins. Genesis teaches the opposite truth; although natural disasters are a great problem and are difficult to reconcile with the existence of a loving God, the corollary of the postflood promises in Genesis is that God used a natural disaster to punish sin on that one occasion but would not do so again. This does not explain natural disasters, but it prevents us from adding insult to injury by asserting that those who have suffered so tragically are being punished. Genesis rules such judgments out of court, and so did Jesus (Luke 13:4).

This passage would have been particularly relevant to early Israelite readers who were longing to return to their homeland after a period of enforced exile with hopes of a new beginning. Evidence that this passage would be an encouragement to the exiles is found in the book of Isaiah:

> "In overflowing anger for a moment I hid my face from you, but with everlasting love I will have compassion on you," says the Lord, your Redeemer.
> "This is like the days of Noah to me: as I swore that the waters of Noah should no more go over the earth, so I have sworn that I will not be angry with you, and will not rebuke you." (Isa 54:8-9 ESV)

This passage shows that in spite of the long delay God did permit a new beginning. Some of the exiles were not entirely sure whether or not God had lost patience with the nation forever and had cast them off (Lam 5:20, 22). The message of the flood story is that after even the most severe judgment comes mercy, and a new beginning would bring encouragement and hope to the exiles and be an antidote to despair.

9:1-17 The Covenant

An important feature of the creation account in 1–2:4 was the bestowal of blessing on the birds and fish (1:22), on human beings (1:28), and on the seventh day (2:3). After the flood God pronounces blessing on Noah and his sons as the representatives of the human race (9:1-2). As in the previous blessing, this pronouncement focuses on fertility and authority, but with significant differences. While the exercise of dominion is prominent in both pronouncements, the rhetoric of the blessing on Noah and his sons creates a more sinister atmosphere. Humankind originally exercised authority in the harmonious context of the garden of Eden. Now, however, postflood humanity will exercise dominion that will lead to "fear and dread" rather than to harmony. The language of 9:2 in contrast to 1:28 holds the tension between the benevolent Creator with his willingness to bless all his creatures, on the one hand, and the effect of human rebellion with its power to sour relationships, on the other.

In the postflood era the animals will be part of the food chain, whereas before the flood humankind were vegetarians (9:3; cf. 1:28-29). Although postflood people were permitted to eat meat, the consumption of blood was prohibited (9:4; cf. Lev 17:11). Blood symbolized "life," and since only God could give life, the blood was his special domain and must be treated with respect by both humans and animals. Anyone who sheds human blood is accountable to God, whether animal or person (9:5). Murder of humans is in an entirely different category than killing animals for food since humans were made in the image of God (9:6). It is sometimes argued that human beings are no longer in the image of God because of their sinfulness, but even after the flood Genesis places a greater value on humankind than on any other creature because of this image. Even rebellious humans are different from animals because they are made in God's image. Thus it is the image of God that makes us human and makes it possible for us to have a closer and more profound relationship with him.

To confirm the promises of renewed blessing, God establishes a covenant with Noah and his sons (9:8-17). The impact and significance of the covenant are not limited to the humans, since God refers to it as "a covenant between me and the earth" (9:13) and "between me and all flesh that is on the earth" (9:16). Thus, while the covenant is communicated to Noah, it is made with every living creature and gives assurances about their continued existence (9:15-17).

Noah and Moses

The covenant with Noah recalls the covenant made with Moses, and it is one of a series of similarities between the two men. These similarities are emphasized so clearly that there is little doubt that Genesis intends the readers to see Noah as the forerunner of Moses. Both "found favor in God's sight" (6:8; Exod 33:12, 17); both are saved by an ark (the same rare word is used); both have a prophetic ministry, a priestly role, and both had key roles in an important building project constructed in accordance with a divine blueprint.[1] Furthermore, laws within the context of covenant are conveyed to both men. Jewish teaching regards Noah as the lawgiver for the Gentiles. Asked whether Gentiles may enjoy eternal life, the Jewish answer usually relates their standing before God in terms of the laws of Noah.

9:18-29 Noah's Family after the Flood

This enigmatic section comprises various motifs from the danger of drunkenness to family responsibility. Scholars, including Westermann, von Rad, and Vawter, argue that Lamech's hopes that Noah would bring rest (5:29) were fulfilled in his invention of wine-making. However, the text itself does not make this connection, and in this particular passage it is the danger of drinking too much wine that is highlighted rather than its benefits. Furthermore, there is no hint that the production of wine did anything to bring comfort from the ground. The aim of the passage is not to condone or condemn wine but to emphasize that Shem, the ancestor of the Israelites, was blessed while Canaan, the ancestor of the Canaanites, was cursed.

A comparison between the drunkenness of Noah and that of Lot raises the possibility that in both cases the narrator is implying a connection between wine and illicit sexuality. However, the specific sin of Ham is not disclosed. The outcome of Ham's impropriety is that for the first time in Genesis a curse is uttered by a human being. Since origins are of vital importance in Genesis, it is in this area that we must look for the key to the interpretation of the account of the cursing of Ham. As Ross explains, "Because these sons were primogenitors of the families of the earth, the narrator is more interested in the greater meaning of the oracle with respect to tribes and nations in his day than with the children of Shem, Ham, and Japheth."[1] If this is the case, it is significant that the Canaanites descended from Ham and the Ammonites and Moabites descended from Lot are all branded with sexual immorality in Genesis. Kidner has pointed out that since the curse is not pronounced on all

1. Noah built the ark and Moses built the tabernacle, but both projects were constructed according to divine plans.
1. Ross, "The Curse of Canaan," 224.

the Hamites but only on one branch (the Canaanites), "those who reckon the Hamitic peoples in general to be doomed to inferiority have therefore misread the Old Testament."[2]

If the motif of origins is one pointer to the meaning of this difficult passage, another important consideration is that of patterns. Certain aspects of the account of the postflood characters fall into the same pattern as the narratives about Adam and Eve. Noteworthy elements in this pattern are: blessing, nakedness, and cursing. God blesses Noah and his three sons just as he has blessed Adam. The first man and woman were naked; this caused no problems at first, but after their sin the nakedness became an embarrassment. In a similar way, Noah is found naked, but it is not implied that his nakedness itself is sin. It is the attitude and actions of Ham that are sinful and not nakedness itself. However, although nakedness is not described as sinful, it renders Noah vulnerable and provides the potential danger to which Ham succumbs. In both stories the naked person is covered by a third party — God provides skins for Adam and Eve (3:21) and Noah's sons cover him with a garment (9:23). The role that is encouraged and exonerated in Genesis is that of supporting the weak and vulnerable rather than exposing them. This idea that clothing the naked and helping the vulnerable is pleasing to God is exemplified in Israel's history:

> And the men who have been mentioned by name rose and took the captives, and with the spoil they clothed all who were naked among them. They clothed them, gave them sandals, provided them with food and drink, and anointed them, and carrying all the feeble among them on donkeys, they brought them to their kinsfolk at Jericho, the city of palm trees. Then they returned to Samaria. (2 Chr 28:15 ESV)

This idea is expanded in the teaching of Jesus (Matt 25:35-36).

Genesis 10

The location of ch. 10 is puzzling. If chronology had been the main consideration, ch. 11 would have preceded ch. 10 since the Table of Nations assumes the division of languages and the scattering that occurred at Babel. However, thematic considerations take precedence over chronology. If the tower of Babel incident had been located before the Table of Nations, it would empha-

2. Kidner, *Genesis*, 104. Kidner argues that this oracle was fulfilled by the subjugation of the Canaanites to Israel (cf. Josh 9:23; 1 Kgs 9:21).

size only the negative aspect of their origin and highlight the fact that nations developed as a result of the confusion of languages. However, while this negative aspect is still implied, the location of the Table of Nations following the covenant and blessing of ch. 9 emphasizes the positive aspect of their origin as the outworking of God's blessing and covenant. The growth of the vine provides anecdotal evidence of the adequate resources of the earth to provide for the needs of humankind. The Table of Nations is introduced to testify to the efficacy of the postflood blessing, which called upon humankind to "be fruitful and multiply" (9:1). The significance of the Table of Nations is that it shows the abundant measure in which this blessing is fulfilled. As von Rad says, "There is hidden pathos behind this barren enumeration, astonishment and reverence at the riches of God's majestic creativity."[1] This means that God has restored people to the earth/land to care for it and to supervise it; and in spite of their alienation from their Creator, he continues to bless them with fecundity.

Introduced as the "account of Shem, Ham and Japheth" (NIV), the Table of Nations fulfills the same purpose as the genealogies in chs. 4 and 5. Just as Cain's offspring were catalogued first and then forgotten while the offspring of Seth were dealt with in detail, the offspring of Japheth and Ham are given first and then, finally, the offspring of Shem. Thus the usual order of Shem, Ham, and Japheth is reversed to dispose of the less important lines of descent and concentrate on the line of Shem, which leads eventually to Abram. Furthermore, as Sarna points out, "while the genealogies of Japheth and Ham continue for only three generations each, that of Shem extends to the sixth generation."[2] The structure of the chapter, then, is clearly designed to highlight the line of Shem. Israel is not mentioned but is clearly implicit in the line of Shem, showing that "Israel belongs to and is derived from the nations but comes late in the history of humankind. . . . Israel, like Isaac, comes late as a child of God's surprise."[3]

10:2-5 The Descendants of Japheth

Seven of Japheth's sons are listed, including Magog. This interesting name occurs in Ezekiel as one of two powerful nations, "Gog and Magog." Identification of these nations is fraught with difficulty, and it is by no means clear

1. Von Rad, *Genesis*, 144.
2. Sarna, *Genesis*, 69.
3. Brueggemann, *Genesis*, 93.

whether there is a connection between Japheth's son and the nation of the same name.[1] Through two of Japheth's sons, Gomer and Javan, his descendants are traced to the third generation. Gomer refers to the Cimmerians, who, as Sarna points out, "came from beyond the Caucasus Mountains in the region of the Black Sea to invade and terrorize Asia Minor in the eighth and seventh centuries B.C.E."[2] Javan refers to the Ionians (Greeks), who established themselves on the west coast of Asia Minor. One of the sons of Gomer, Ashkenaz, will be familiar to many as the name given to the Jews (Ashkenazi) who came from Germany and Poland in contrast to the Sephardic Jews from Spain and Portugal. According to Sarna, in the OT the term refers to the Scythians, nomads from Armenia, "expert in cavalry and archery" (cf. Jer 51:27).[3] One of the descendants of Javan, Tarshish, is well known from the story of Jonah, but it is not certain where Tarshish is located; Sarna describes it as "one of the most enigmatic place-names in the Bible."[4] The Kittim, also descended from Javan, are the inhabitants of Kition, modern Larnaca, in Cyprus.

10:6-20 The Descendants of Ham

Four sons of Ham are listed: Cush, Mizraim, Put, and Canaan. Cush represents the region south of Egypt; Mizraim refers to Egypt, and Put is usually identified with Libya. With the exception of Put, the text provides information on each group.

A digression in the text transports the reader briefly from the territory of Ham to Mesopotamia and to the mysterious character Nimrod, who is described as "a mighty hunter" before Yahweh, or as Sarna translates, "by the grace of the Lord."[1] His kingdom is identified with ancient Babylon and Assyria, and he is credited with building major cities, including Nineveh and Calah (10:12). Nineveh is the well-known city where Jonah preached, while Calah is the site in Iraq known today as Nimrud. While attempts have been made to identify Nimrod with ancient heroes known to us, there is still no definitive solution. The name is also mentioned in Micah, where the land of Assyria is described as "the land of Nimrod" (Mic 5:6).

1. Sarna comments, "From the passages in Ezekiel, it is clear that the land of Magog was thought to be in the furthermost reaches of the north, which may possibly mean southern Russia or Asia"; *Genesis,* 70.

2. Sarna, *Genesis,* 70.

3. Sarna, *Genesis,* 70.

4. Sarna, *Genesis,* 71

1. Sarna, *Genesis,* 73.

Verse 19 provides the first delimitation of the borders of Canaan. The familiar boundary notices are mentioned "in all directions, from the cities of the plain to Gerar to the northern extremities."[2] This information obviously anticipates the future references to the land of Canaan in the patriarchal narratives and puts on the agenda for the first time the question of ownership of that small piece of land in the Near East that is, even now some three millennia later, still hotly disputed. However, the boundaries delineated are different from those specified elsewhere in the Bible. Sarna argues that the description of Canaan in the Table of Nations "corresponds to that of the Egyptian province of Canaan as it emerged following the peace treaty between the Egyptian king Ramses II and the Hittite king Hattusilis III (ca. 1280 B.C.E.), which defined the spheres of interest of the respective empires."[3]

10:21-31 The Descendants of Shem

Before the list of his sons is given, Shem is introduced as the ancestor of "all the sons of Eber." This immediately highlights Eber as the line that will later be delineated in more detail through Peleg to Terah and Abram.[1]

The first of Shem's five sons, Elam, represents modern Khuzistan, "the most easterly country" on the table.[2] Its capital was Susa, referred to in the book of Esther (Esth 1:2, 5). The second son, Asshur, represents the city of that name situated on the Tigris, from which the name of the surrounding area, Assyria, originated. Some confusion exists about the areas designated by the third and fourth sons, Arphaxad and Lud. The fifth son, Aram, may represent the confederation of Aramean tribes or it may be a reference to a specific tribe.

The fourth generation descendant from Shem through Eber includes two sons, Joktan and Peleg. While Joktan's descendants are listed, there is only a brief statement that during Peleg's lifetime the earth was divided (10:25). This is probably a reference to the confusion of languages at Babel. The list of Peleg's descendants is reserved for a more prominent position after the story of Babel. This is the familiar pattern found in Genesis; the genealogy of the most significant line of seed is given prominence by being kept to the last of those listed.

2. Ross, "The Table of Nations," 28.
3. Sarna, *Genesis*, 77.
1. Rashi, however, argues that the first mention of Eber in 10:21 means "the region beyond"; see Sarna, *Genesis*, 78.
2. Sarna, *Genesis*, 78.

11:1-9 An Ambitious Building Program

It is interesting to read this story with some of the earliest readers in mind, especially those who had been exiled to Babylon. Babylon is obviously the location of the tower building, and the first readers would be familiar not only with the kind of building implied in this story but also with the building materials and with the purpose of such buildings. The story would hold a poignant meaning for the exiles. It is a story about how to reach God and, whereas previously the Jerusalem temple played an important role, it had now been destroyed and the exiles had no resources or permission to build another one. We can only imagine how confused the exiles were, since the tragedy that had overtaken them suggested that the Babylonian gods were more powerful than Israel's God and that the Jerusalem temple which had been destroyed was less significant than the ziggurats and temples of Babylon.

This story illustrates that buildings are not a prerequisite for worship, since in the following narratives the patriarchs encounter and worship God without a building while the ambitious tower project does nothing to enhance worship or bring its builders closer to God. One of the lessons of Israel's exile was that God could be encountered and worshipped in a foreign country and even in the wilderness without a temple or shrine. This story is a warning that because a building has a religious purpose does not mean that it has God's approval.

The story of Babel begins with the phrase "all the earth," כָּל-הָאָרֶץ/*kol-hā'āreṣ*. This phrase is repeated five times in the story (11:1, 4, 8, 9 [twice]). Furthermore, the word "language," שָׂפָה/*śāpâ*, is mentioned five times (11:1, 6, 7 [twice], 9), as is the word "there," שָׁם/*šām*, referring to the location of Babel (11:2, 7, 8, 9 [twice]). Such repetition is usually not by accident in ancient Hebrew narrative, and here it fulfills important roles; it indicates that the extent of the problem of human rebellion is worldwide and also that the judgment represented by Babel is also worldwide. No one on earth was unaffected by human rebellion or by the divine response to it, and no place on earth was exempt. The repetition also links words in the passage through assonance. The repetition of "there," *šām*, is particularly effective because its sound is similar to two key words in the passage: "heavens," שָׁמַיִם/*šāmayim*, and "name," שֵׁם/*šēm*. These words "heavens" and "name" represent the main aspirations of the tower-builders, and the damning indictment was that they sought these things "there," at Babel! Postexilic prophets usually mentioned Babylon in derogatory terms. In the book of Zechariah, a woman called "Wickedness" is carried in a basket to Babylon between two women with wings (Zech 5:5-11). The meaning of the vision and the theological message of the tower of Babel story are similar: Babel is not the gateway to heaven but a place of sinfulness and confusion.

Most scholars agree that the building was a ziggurat, a term derived from the Akkadian verb *zaqaru,* meaning "to build high."[1] These stepped structures were built in Babylonian cities to replicate the concept of a sacred mountain where humanity and divinity could commune. Rooted on earth but with their heads in the clouds, sacred mountains were thought of as bringing heaven and earth together, since it was believed that the gods lived at the top. As Sarna comments,

> The most famous ziggurat of all, the one at Babylon, is the focus of the present narrative. It was known as the *e-temen-an-ki,* "The House of the Foundation of Heaven and Earth." In the flat, alluvial plain of Lower Mesopotamia, the ziggurat constituted a man-made sacred mountain in miniature, the physical means by which man and god might enter into direct contact with one another.[2]

Thus their aim — to reach heaven — is reflected in the name of this Babylonian ziggurat. The futility of their endeavor to reach heaven is emphasized in the narrative, which stresses that God is not at the top of the tower and its top is incapable of reaching heaven, since God must leave heaven in order to see what the builders are doing. Obviously this describes God's actions anthropomorphically and, no doubt with a touch of humor, suggesting that this building that is supposed to reach heaven is not even visible from God's abode and he has to come to earth to view it (11:5). The main point emphasized in the narrative is not that they are worshipping false gods, though this may be implied, but the truth being highlighted is that they are trying to reach God in the wrong way and with the wrong motives. Great buildings in themselves do not bring people closer to God. In the modern world we do not build towers to reach God, but extremely lavish and expensive buildings in deprived areas seem just as much a misappropriation of time, effort, and money as the tower of Babel.

Significantly, the purpose of the builders includes making a name for themselves. Building projects are often associated with human pride, and Nebuchadnezzar is reputed to have had his name stamped on every 50th brick to commemorate his building program in Babylon. The pride that he showed is reflected in the book of Daniel (Dan 4:30).

The divine decision to scatter the people prevents them from complet-

---

1. Sarna, *Genesis,* 82.
2. Sarna, *Genesis,* 82.

ing the city at this time. The significance of the confusion of their language is highlighted by a wordplay on the similar sounds of the word for Babel and the verb "to confuse": בָּבֶל/*bābel* and בָּלַל/*bālal*.

There are parallels between the Babel story and that of Cain. Like Cain the builders are driven from their home and become wanderers looking for a new place to live. But there is a difference; Cain was punished and had to wander aimlessly but the builders of Babel are scattered so that they can fulfill God's purposes and fill the earth. Even in the scattering there is grace and in the punishment there is mercy.

Both human audacity and the severity of God's punishment have reached a climax in the Babel narrative. The audacity is seen in the attitude of the human beings to God, and the severity of the punishment is evident in the permanence of the judgment. The scene is set for an unprecedented turning point in the book of Genesis with the introduction of Abram.

11:10-32 Introduction to the Family of Abram

This section, introduced as the "Toledot (Generations) of Shem," provides the link between the primeval history and the patriarchal narratives. Shem's family history has already been outlined and the names of his five sons given (10:22-31), so now only the son whose descendants lead to Abram is mentioned in a detailed genealogy that follows the pattern,

> When Person[A] had lived X years, he became the father of Person[B]; and after he became the father of Person[B], Person[A] lived X years and had other sons and daughters.

This pattern is unbroken as the line from Shem through Arphaxad is traced via Shela, Eber, Peleg, Reu, Serug, and Nahor to Terah (11:10-25). However, with Terah the pattern changes and his three sons, Abram, Nahor, and Haran, are named.

We have already observed that Abram is the final goal of the *Toledot* of Shem. This becomes obvious in 11:26, where the genealogy gives details of the family of Terah. This verse serves as a conclusion to the *Toledot* of Shem and as an introduction to the *Toledot* of Terah (11:27–25:11). Although three sons are mentioned, the only details given about Haran and Nahor are those that affect Abram and his line of descendants. We learn nothing about Haran except the birth of his son Lot and his death, details that explain how the circumstances arose in which Lot accompanied Abram to Canaan. Likewise, little is written about Nahor apart from the fact of his marriage. His story is resumed in 22:20-24, where his significance as the ancestor of the bride of Abram's son Isaac is revealed. However, these family details are covered fairly quickly since the main purpose of the author is to introduce Abram himself, his wife Sarai, and nephew Lot. To begin with, however, the main focus of attention is on Sarai. The most significant biographical detail in this section is the statement that Sarai, Abram's wife, is barren (11:30). This barrenness is the backdrop against which all the promises of a multitude of seed are made to Abram. After this introductory section, the call of Abram is recorded (12:1-3), and this is followed by a record of his obedience (12:4-9).

GENESIS 12–24 THE LIFE OF ABRAM/ABRAHAM

12:1-3 Blessing Promised to Abram and His Descendants

The call of Abram marks a turning point in the book of Genesis, since the focus now narrows down from the whole world to one man and his family history. The international dimension, however, is still important since the objective of the blessing promised to Abram is to bring blessing to all nations. A dramatic change also occurs in the direction of the narrative: chs. 1–11 depict a movement away from the perfect relationships of the garden of Eden, while ch. 12 introduces a relationship that will culminate in a covenant between God and Abram.

In chs. 1–11 the downward spiral of divine-human relations is marked by a series of curses and punishments in which God is mainly reactive as he punishes and curtails the activity of his recalcitrant subjects. In contrast, ch. 12 opens with a new divine initiative introduced by God in a speech. Creation had come into being through divine speech, and now at this strategic turning point in the history of the created order God speaks again. While the content of this speech is a call to Abram to leave his country,[1] its main thrust is indicated by the fivefold repetition of the Hebrew root signifying blessing, ברכ/ *brk*. God will bless Abram and his descendants, and through them the rest of the world. This is God's agenda for reclaiming the initiative and stopping the destructive cycle of rebellion and cursing followed by further rebellion and

---

1. Yahweh calls Abram away from his land, his relatives, and his father's house. The progression is from the general category of land to the personal category of family. This threefold gradation emphasizes the cost of this decision to Abram: he must relinquish his land, but it would be replaced by another; however, his birthplace and father's house were irreplaceable.

consequential punishment. A new ray of light has begun to shine through the darkness of human rebellion and disobedience, as reflected in von Rad's perceptive comment that 12:1 marks "the new point of departure in the divine revelation of salvation."[2]

This promised blessing in 12:1-3 is clearly intended as a contrast to the cursing that is mentioned in the primeval history (3:14, 17; 4:11; 5:29; 9:25). It is probably not coincidental that cursing occurs five times in chs. 1–11 and the Hebrew root conveying the idea of blessing appears five times in the "call of Abram" (12:1-3). Numerical patterns were very significant in ancient literature, and some numbers, particularly "three," "five," and "seven," carried symbolic value that modern readers often miss. The underlying message in this passage is that God now counters the power of cursing with blessing. Cursing began because of the disobedience of human beings (Adam), and it led to alienation and disaster. Now attention focuses on Abram to show that blessing and the success it brings are possible through obedience and faith.

Strategically, this short pericope acts as a bridge passage between the Babel narrative and the Abram story, contrasting the account of rebellion at Babel with that of Abram's call and response. Both implicit and explicit contrasts between Abram and the builders highlight Abram's significance and show that what the builders wanted most was available to Abram through a close relationship with God. A corollary of the nationhood promised to Abram was the sense of cohesion and security that the tower-builders sought without success. Furthermore, while the aim of the builders is to make a name for themselves (11:4), Abram is promised a great name through blessing (12:2).[3] Babel brings the primeval period to a close on a very pessimistic note with its emphasis on the scattering of the nations, but Abram's call offers a long-term hope for all these scattered nations through divinely promised blessing (12:3). Babel represents human beings making their own plans, while the Abram narrative features a person who discovers that God has a plan for the world into which his personal life plan would fit. Acting in obedience to that plan, he lives in a harmonious relationship with God. In the primeval narrative, all creation had been in harmony with God and had received his blessing; now Abram also receives the promise of blessing within the context of peaceful relations and divine approval (cf. 1:22, 28; 2:3).

The divine directive to Abram could not have been clearer: he must

---

2. Von Rad, *Genesis*, 159.

3. There is possibly also an intentional contrast between Abram and the "heroes" of 6:4, who were, lit., "men of a name." While the reference to these men is obscure, it is clear that the name they acquire for themselves is illegitimate in God's sight. Abram does not seek a great name but receives this unsolicited honor from God.

leave the place and the people he knows and follow God's leading. The command "Go" (לֶךְ-לְךָ/*lek-lĕkā*) is an unusual construction, and Wenham translates it, "Go by yourself."[4] It occurs again in ch. 22, when God calls Abraham to "Go" to the land of Moriah and offer Isaac as a burnt offering. Thus by this unusual construction two of the most difficult decisions in Abram's life are linked: the decision to leave his homeland and the decision to offer up his son Isaac.

Abram's divinely appointed destination is described in the vaguest possible terms as simply "the land I will show you." This is not a question of comparing one place with another and deciding which is best. He must head for this new land without knowing anything about it. Adam had not consciously chosen to live in the garden of Eden, but this destination had been chosen for him, and now analogically Abram must acquiesce in God's choice for him. Adam had forfeited his privileged tenancy through disobedience (2:8; 3:24), but Abram has the opportunity through obedience to receive the land that has been divinely chosen for him. Abram does not choose the land he wants and then seek God's approval; he is not even told the name of the land that God has chosen for him. He must trust that the divine choice is right for him, and he must have confidence that God could be trusted to make wise and beneficent choices for his worshippers.

God promises Abram five main benefits on condition that he obey the divine commands. First, he will become a great nation, in territory as well as numerous progeny. Second, he will be blessed with the power necessary to succeed in his divinely chosen role. Third, God will make his "name" great so that he will be a blessing to others (12:2).[5]

Fourth, God promises to bless those who bless Abram and curse those who curse him, providing vindication and protection against any who might despise him. Two verbs are used for cursing here: קלל/*qll,* which means "to despise or treat lightly," and ארר/*'rr,* which means "to curse." In most translations, both verbs are translated "to curse," but this is misleading since the second verb is much stronger than the first and this affects the meaning of the verse: anyone who disdains or despises *(qll)* Abram will be dealt with most severely and cursed *('rr).* As Wenham comments, "Those who merely 'disdain' Abram will be 'cursed' by God himself."[6] Sarna suggests that the reason for

4. Wenham, *Genesis 1–15,* 265.
5. Commenting on the phrase "make your name great," Wenham argues that it "has its closest parallel in the promise to David in 2 Sam 7:9: 'I will make for you a great name'. Otherwise, only the name of God is described as 'great' (Josh 7:9; 1 Sam 12:22; Ps 76:2 [1]; Mal 1:11)"; *Genesis 1–15,* 275.
6. Wenham, *Genesis 1–15,* 277.

this promise to Abram is that as "an unprotected stranger in an alien land, he will have particular need of God's providential care, and whoever maltreats him will be punished with exceptional severity."[7] Many of the early readers of Genesis would be able to identify with this promise, since Israel was often despised by her neighbors. Those who were despised and who could call themselves children of Abram had good reason to be encouraged, since God had promised that he would judge their deprecators.

Finally, God assures that through Abram all nations would be blessed. Exactly how this is to come about is not explicit. Most likely, his descendants are to provide an example for other nations so that they might also receive God's blessing.[8]

Members of the early church identified themselves as heirs of the promises to Abraham (Acts 3:25). Paul regarded the promise of blessing to the nations as an early statement of the gospel message and claimed the promises to Abraham for all who shared the faith:

> Know then that it is those of faith who are the sons of Abraham. And the Scripture, foreseeing that God would justify the Gentiles by faith, preached the Gospel beforehand to Abraham, saying, "In you shall all the nations be blessed." So then, those who are of faith are blessed along with Abraham, the man of faith. (Gal 3:7-9 ESV)

Excursus: Technical Problems Involved in Translating and Interpreting 12:1-3

A number of technical problems associated with translating these verses can only be dealt with very briefly in this commentary. First, the final clause of 12:2 is in the imperative voice. A literal translation would render it, "Be a blessing." Hamilton argues that the imperative sense should be retained, since it is related to the first imperative, "go" (12:1); he suggests that the second half of v. 2 should be translated,

> I will make your name famous, and be a blessing.[9]

However, this translation is awkward, and the imperative "be a blessing" does not follow logically from the promise, "I will make your name famous." Furthermore, it would create a disjunction between vv. 2 and 3. Moreover, as

---

7. Sarna, *Genesis*, 89.
8. Brueggemann, *Genesis*, 120.
9. Hamilton, *Genesis 1-17*, 369.

Gesenius' Hebrew Grammar points out, an imperative may be translated as imperfect or jussive:

> The imperative, when depending (with *wāw copulative*) upon a jussive (cohortative), or an interrogative sentence, frequently expresses also a consequence which is to be expected with certainty, and often a consequence which is intended, or in fact an intention.[10]

In the light of this, it is best to follow the NRSV and ESV: "I will bless you and make your name great, so that you will be a blessing."[11]

A further problem arising in 12:1-3 is related to the translation of נִבְרְכוּ/ *nibrĕkû* in v. 3.[12] This is the nip῾al third person plural perfect and may be translated either as a passive[13] ("they may be blessed") or as a reflexive("they may bless themselves"). In the parallel passages in 22:18 and 26:4, the corresponding word is in the hitpa῾el and would normally be translated as a reflexive and not as a passive. Accordingly, some prefer to use the reflexive translation in 12:1-3. The difference between the reflexive and the passive in this context is significant. The passive translation would imply that Abram would be a source of blessing on an international scale.[14] The reflexive would indicate that Abram would become proverbial as an example of blessing and that the nations would invoke his name in the hope that they might enjoy similar blessing.[15]

Dumbrell makes the interesting suggestion that the use of the nip῾al in ch. 12 and of the hitpa῾el in ch. 22 is deliberate because neither theme of the verb quite conveys the precise sense intended. Thus according to Dumbrell, the best translation is found in "a middle sense" such as "win for themselves a blessing."[16] A middle meaning would seem a strong possibility, since, as

10. GKC, §110i.

11. Cf. 20:7: "He will pray for you and you shall live." The verb "to live" is imperative, but it is translated as imperfect in the main versions.

12. The RSV text reads, "By you all families of the earth shall bless themselves," but a footnote provides the alternative reading: "in you all the families of the earth shall be blessed." The NRSV gives priority to the passive voice, and the reflexive alternative, "bless themselves," is mentioned in a footnote. The NEB has, "All the families on earth will pray to be blessed as you are blessed."

13. The LXX translates it as a passive (cf. Acts 3:25).

14. This is the view taken by Cassuto, who argues that "it appears preferable to take the meaning to be that the father of the Israelite nation will be privileged to become a source of benison to all peoples of the world, and his merit and prayer will protect them before the Heavenly Court of Justice"; *A Commentary on the Book of Genesis*, 2:315.

15. Vawter suggests that the meaning here is "simply that Abraham will be for all mankind the exemplar of divine blessing: 'May God bless us as he blessed Abraham'" (*On Genesis*, 177).

16. Dumbrell, "The Covenant with Abraham," 49.

Wenham points out, "a middle sense here complements and completes the earlier remarks."[17] There is an obvious progression of thought beginning with God blessing Abram and making his descendants a great nation, followed by the assurance that blessing will flow to others through his great name. The blessing of others is also emphasized in the idea that those who bless Abram will receive blessing.

We can now summarize this study of 12:1-3. The promises made in this pericope include an implicit promise of land, nationhood, a great name, a protective relationship, and the mediation of blessing to others. Blessing is the bestowal of God's favor and power in the realization of all these promises. When all the promises have been fulfilled, it will be evidence that Abram has been blessed. Blessing is the power to succeed in his God-given commission.

12:4-9 Abram's Journey of Faith

Unquestioning obedience is Abram's response to the divine commission, even though this meant exchanging the security of familiar surroundings for the uncertainty of wilderness travel. None of the promises was provable, and the crucial promise of "land" was vague. However, sustained by faith in God's promises, Abram commences his journey, committing not just himself but also his wife and his nephew Lot and their entourage to an uncertain future. They journey in the direction of Canaan without any indication that this is their final destination. Details of the long journey from Haran to Canaan, the expectation of the travelers, and the events that occurred on the way are not included in the narrative, so that nothing can detract from the central focus of the passage — the arrival in Canaan. Repetition of the words "land of Canaan" emphasize the arrival of Abram for the first time in the land that would have far-reaching consequences for him and for his descendants, not to mention those who were already living in that land.

Abram's first significant stopping place is Shechem and the oak of Moreh.[1] The poignant remark that "the Canaanites were then in the land" (12:6) highlights that, although the land is a gift from God, it is a land that is already possessed by others. However, if Abram questions whether this land that is already occupied could be the "promised land," then his doubts are

---

17. Wenham, *Genesis 1–15*, 277.

1. The word translated "oak" in the NRSV and ESV is disputed. Some think that it should be "terebinth." The word Moreh means "teacher" and suggests that the tree was a place where the community gathered for instruction or to receive an oracle. Deborah fulfilled her role under a palm tree (Judg 4:5).

quickly allayed by an appearance of God to him. No detail is given regarding this appearance because the emphasis is on the content of the divine utterance rather than on its form. This first divine speech in the land of the Canaanites promises Abram (12:7 NRSV), "To your offspring I will give this land." Yahweh's initial instruction to Abram was simply to go "to the land I will show you" (12:1 ESV). Now the identity of the land is revealed as Canaan, which, as Clines comments, was "good news for Israelites and bad news for Canaanites."[2] However, there is still considerable uncertainty, since it is not clear that this is the land where Abram himself should settle; it is the land that will belong to his offspring, but is it the place where he should stay?

Abram acknowledges this gift of land for his descendants by building two altars, one at Shechem (12:7) and one between Bethel and Ai (12:8). These serve as monuments in honor of God, who has claimed the right over this land and promises to give it to Abram's posterity.[3] As well as building an altar, Abram also pitches a tent, but this is a strange detail to include here. Abram has traveled hundreds of miles from Haran, and on that long journey he would have pitched his tent many times, but it is never mentioned. Significantly, in Genesis most references to pitching tents are closely associated with building an altar. However, it is not altogether clear what significance should be attached to this. Wenham suggests that the mention of pitching a tent means that Abram spent a long time in that place:

> Since presumably Abram pitched his tent wherever he went, the mention of the fact here probably suggests that he settled near Bethel for some time; cf. 26:25; 33:19; 35:21; Judg 4:11.[4]

While this is feasible, this first reference to pitching a tent seems to be quite significant since it is referred to again (13:3). Kidner sees this significance in the "contrast" between the building of the altar and the pitching of the tent.

> There is force in the contrast between *pitched* and *builded* (8), the one for himself, the other for God. The only structures he left behind were altars: no relics of his own wealth.[5]

---

2. Clines, *What Does Eve Do to Help?* 56-57.

3. Strangely, however, the type of sacrifice and the method of offering are not related. The main subject of the narrator is not sacrifice but the establishment of a shrine for the worship of Yahweh.

4. Wenham, *Genesis 1–15*, 280.

5. Kidner, *Genesis*, 115.

If this is correct, the contrast between building and pitching emphasizes the idea that this land belongs to God but it does not belong to Abram yet and he must wander around from place to place, pitching his tent, having no permanent house. According to this approach this contrast illustrates that building personal wealth and prestige is transitory compared to the more enduring effect of influencing the world for God.

D. J. Wiseman, on the other hand, suggests that there is a religious significance for both the tent and the altar since they are often closely associated (12:8; 13:18; 26:25). He argues that the erection of a tent by Abram "refers not so much to his mode of living as the setting up of a tent-shrine to mark his acceptance of the divine land-grant, a form of token take-over of the promised land."[6]

Wiseman's suggestion (if correct) explains why the reference to patriarchs pitching their tents only occurs in Canaan, and it shows why the exact location where a tent had once been pitched should be significant.

12:10-20 A Famine in the Promised Land

Ironically, the land that God shows Abram and promises to his offspring is in the grips of a severe famine. Just as possession of land is incompatible with the land that others already inhabit, so famine is incompatible with the promise that Abram would be blessed in the land that Yahweh would show him. This is just one of a number of obstacles that seem to make the land either impossible to possess or undesirable; the life of faith is full of disappointments for Abram. The repeated mention of the famine both at the beginning and end of the verse in which it is introduced (12:10) and the description of the famine as severe increase the tension in the narrative and suggest that Abram, having discovered the land that God promised to show him, now must either leave it or face starvation. The severity of the famine effectively clears Abram of any blame in his decision to leave the "promised land." Wenham comments,

> The reader is disconcerted to learn that Abram is deserting the land of promise: to underline the fact that he had no other option, the famine is again mentioned, and this time is said to be "severe."[1]

Indeed, the question is not whether Abram will leave Canaan but whether he will return, since doubts are cast on both its availability and its

6. Wiseman, "Abraham Reassessed," 141.
1. Wenham, *Genesis 1–15*, 287.

dependability. The text is silent about whether Abram is disappointed. If he is disappointed, which would not be at all surprising, we are not told whether he is disappointed merely with the land or whether he is also disillusioned with God and with the promises that have led him to leave a fertile country to come to one in the grips of a severe famine.

It is easy to imagine how early readers of Genesis, such as Israelites returning to Jerusalem after the exile, would have been able to identify with Abram's predicament. They returned to Jerusalem with hopes of blessing and divine approval but found, as Abram did, that the promised land was inhabited by others hostile to their cause and that famine was often a reality (cf. Hag 1:6). If the promised land fell short of Abram's expectations, it undoubtedly disappointed those who returned from Babylon expecting blessing and a renewed Davidic kingdom. As Haggai observes, they "looked for much, and behold, it came to little" (Hag 1:9 ESV). They were bitterly disappointed, and it required the preaching of Haggai and Zechariah to rekindle their faith and hope. We do not know if the book of Genesis was read by them or whether it encouraged them to know that their disappointment had been foreshadowed in the experience of Abram. However, the experiences of Abram are certainly helpful to us in making it clear that disappointments do come to those who are convinced that they are doing God's will and such disappointments do not always have an easy explanation. Genesis encourages worshippers in such circumstances to remain strong in their faith and to maintain confidence in God's ultimate goodness but not to expect easy answers. Genesis never explains why there is a famine, just as we cannot explain why there are hurricanes and earthquakes. Abram discovered that sometimes bad things happen to good people and even those who believe they are fulfilling God's will can face unexpected difficulties that defy any logical explanation. We, like Abram, are part of a bigger plan with divinely promised blessing as its goal but plenty of troubles along the way.

Abram is forced because of the severity of the famine to travel to Egypt in order "to sojourn there." Cassuto argues that the verb "to sojourn" refers to a short-term visit. He believes that Abram's intention is "not to settle permanently, but to dwell there temporarily for a little while."[2] Wenham, on the other hand, argues that Abram went to Egypt as an immigrant, suggesting "the intention of long-term settlement."[3] This view is supported by other occurrences of the same verb "to sojourn" in the OT which, with the possible exception of Jer 14:8, refer to lengthy periods of settlement rather than short-

---

2. Cassuto, *A Commentary on the Book of Genesis*, 2:346.
3. Wenham, *Genesis 1–15*, 287.

term visits. We do not know the patriarch's intentions as he travels to Egypt, but it seems that he is prepared to settle there indefinitely. His eventual return to Canaan is not a further expression of faith in God's promises but is due to the eviction order issued by Pharaoh (12:19-20). Even though Abram's journey to Egypt is understandable, his return to Canaan is not as honorable as his first encounter with that country; his return is precipitated by circumstances brought about by his deceit.

Abram is portrayed as jeopardizing Sarai and sacrificing the possibility of descendants through her (12:11-15). Abram expects the worst from the Egyptians, but contrary to Abram's expectations, the Egyptians act honorably and it is Abram's behavior that is questionable. Abram's fears that the Egyptians will seize Sarai and kill him are irrational since he contemplates a strong moral revulsion to adultery among them but thinks that they will not shrink from murder in order to take his wife. Abram sees his own well-being as the priority and expects Sarai to sacrifice her life to save his. As Coats suggests, Abram submits Sarah to "intentional adultery."[4] Ironically, Abram seems to value his own survival but fails to recognize that without Sarai the promises will not be fulfilled. Abram the father of the nation puts its existence in grave peril, and the recipient of the promises acts as if they have never existed![5] Through Abram's duplicity, his wife is taken into Pharaoh's harem and he receives sheep, cattle, servants, donkeys, and camels as a result. These are a poor substitute, however, for the one through whom God's promises are to be fulfilled. Apparently, Abram has lost interest in the promises that encouraged him to leave Haran; he trades Sarai for material wealth, but with her he has traded his future blessing and the promises of God. By treating his wife as a disposable commodity, Abram jeopardizes his own future and the future of his family.

However, a theme running through Genesis is that the plans of God will be carried out in spite of human failure and disobedience. He has a clear plan for Abram and Sarai that he will not allow to be thwarted (12:17-20). Plagues fall on Pharaoh and his household (not for the last time) until Sarai is released. Pharaoh acts honorably; he is not a tyrant, and he is not portrayed as a pseudo-god. Egypt suffers because of Abram's lapse and not because of any failure on their part. As Brueggemann comments,

> When Abraham acts faithlessly, as he has obviously done, curse is released in the world. The faith and/or faithlessness of Israel matters not only to

---

4. Coats, *Genesis*, 111.

5. Von Rad makes a similar point concerning the seriousness of Abram's visit to Egypt: "One must remember that the jeopardizing of the ancestress called into question everything that Yahweh had promised to do for Abraham"; *Genesis*, 169.

Israel. It is decisive for the nations. In this strange way, Israel has the capacity to impact the affairs of nations.[6]

The story of Abram in Egypt emphasizes that custodians of God's promises have responsibilities as well as blessings and must live in a way compatible with God's plan for their lives. Abram is appropriately rebuked and expelled from the country but is otherwise unharmed. Having fared rather badly in this first opportunity to bring blessing to the nations, he heads towards southern Canaan once more.

13:1-4 The Return from Egypt

Abram retraces his steps northward, passing through a region known as the Negev, a semi-desert area in the south of Canaan. Its name is probably related to a verb that means "to be dry." This was the most direct route back to Canaan from the south. In the Exodus story this route was rejected in favor of the circuitous route via the river Jordan.

Encumbered by an expanded entourage and increased wealth, Abram's journey back would have been very slow, but the details are not given. Like the journey from Haran to Canaan, it is not recorded since the focus is on what happens in the land of Canaan itself where the Israelites would be living. The details in Egypt were significant because this is where Abram's descendants would later be enslaved, and the wealth he acquired is important because the large herds and flocks have a bearing in the later story. No incidental details appear; the entire narrative focuses on material that has a bearing on Abram's life and on the significance of that life for future Israel and her relationship with the surrounding nations.

Significantly, Abram returns to the place of his first altar and tent and there calls on the Lord's name. The return to this area is not just a geographical detail. Rather, it signifies a renewed commitment to the promises associated with Canaan. Later in the story of Jacob the narrative emphasizes his failure to return to Bethel. In the context of Abram's journey to Egypt, his return to the place of his first encounter with God represents a new start and a renewed faith in God's promises.

Lot returns from Egypt with Abram. He too has acquired substantial wealth, but fewer details are given since the focus is primarily on Abram.

6. Brueggemann, *Genesis*, 129.

13:5-13 Abram and Lot Separate

In the previous section, the question arose about whether the land is fertile enough to be the land God has promised since it was in the grips of a famine. A similar theme pervades this narrative, raising the question of whether the land is big enough.

The success of Abram and Lot in acquiring large flocks and herds has negative consequences since quarrels arise among the herdsmen as they seek to pasture their livestock in inadequate territory. Abram and Lot themselves do not quarrel but recognize that the problem must be resolved. Since they are living in a land where they are both strangers, they would put themselves in danger if people such as the Canaanites and Perizzites[1] should see them quarreling (13:7). Thus in these circumstances, to separate amicably seems better than to stay together and allow their relationship to deteriorate.

Abram, the senior partner in the relationship, acts to defuse the crisis by generously offering Lot the opportunity to choose whichever part of the land he wants. He invites Lot to turn either right or left. In antiquity, people faced the east to give directions (the rising sun); therefore, since Canaan was a narrow stretch of land, Abram invites his nephew to go either north or south. However, Lot looks east. Perhaps with memories of the famine still vivid in his mind, he is attracted by the well-watered plains of the Jordan. This area was probably not part of the land that Abram believed he had been promised, and it was not included in the area that he had walked through, since he had kept mainly to the central ridge routes, avoiding the main centers of population (13:12). However, Lot is not party to those promises, and he feels free to choose for himself.

This portrayal of Lot looking out to the east and making his own choices dramatically emphasizes that, in contrast to Lot, Abram did not choose his own land; his land was chosen for him by God. Furthermore, in Genesis east often symbolizes movement away from God. The gate out of Eden was to the east, and when Cain was driven away he went towards the east; this was also the direction that the tower-builders traveled to attempt their doomed building project.

Since Lot is the ancestor of the Moabites, his choice is significant for the narrator since it denies the Moabites any claim to the land of Canaan. Lot's separation from Abram is a further stage in the fulfillment of God's promises.

---

1. The Perizzites cannot be identified with certainty, but it has been suggested that they were people who dwelt in rural villages in contrast to the inhabitants of the fortified Canaanite cities.

Lot leaves the land inhabited by Canaanites and makes an ominous move towards Sodom and Gomorrah. There is a tinge of sadness and regret in the text that excessive wealth should separate two kinsmen (13:6, 8). Wealth has divided them so that the brothers can no longer live together.

The narrative makes a contrast between the choices of Lot and Abram. The latter chooses to live among the Canaanites, who are not yet sinful enough to merit divine judgment, but Lot pitches his tent towards Sodom, where the inhabitants are wicked and are sinning greatly before the Lord. Moreover, Lot's decision, governed by what he sees, is reminiscent of how Eve decided to follow the serpent's advice. Decision-making based on physical appearances only leads Lot to make a serious mistake.

Ironically, the reader knows that the physical features of the well-watered plains and fertile land that Lot chooses are transitory and will change dramatically. Lot cannot see the storm clouds of judgment on the horizon that will change the features of the idyllic landscape beyond recognition. Had Lot been privy to the future, his choices would have been different.

13:14-18 God Renews the Promise of Land to Abram

Following the departure of his nephew, God renews the promise of land to Abram. God not only restates the promise but develops the detail to clarify that the land of Canaan is promised not just to Abram's offspring but also to him personally. Lot has "lifted up his eyes" and chosen the land that he wants; but now, using the same idiom, God commands Abram to lift up his eyes and look around, north, south, east, and west, with the assurance that all the land that he can see will be given to him and to his offspring forever (13:15). The promise is more explicit than in ch. 12. Both Abram and his offspring are beneficiaries of the promise and the land is promised to them, not for a period of time, but "forever." An analogy with the dust of the earth reinforces the idea that Abram's seed will be numerous (13:16). God invites Abram to walk throughout the land. He pitches his tent at Hebron, near the great trees of Mamre, and he builds an altar there (13:17-18). This symbolic pitching of a tent probably has some religious significance and represents Abram accepting the land as a gift from God.

No reference is made to Lot building an altar, and the only mention of his pitching a tent is the negative reference that he "moves" (NRSV) his tent in the direction of Sodom and towards trouble (13:12). Lot has greedily grasped the best land for himself, and he suffers the consequences because the benefits are short-lived. But Abram has patiently accepted what God gives him, and although the benefits are slow in materializing, they have long-term significance.

14:1-12 War and the Abduction of Lot

Having dealt with the effect and aftermath of famine, the narrator introduces the other common occurrence in the Middle East — war. Nine kings are involved in conflict. Some of their kingdoms, such as Shinar and Elam, are easily identified, while others are obscure.[1] Efforts to harmonize the names of the kings with those mentioned in extrabiblical sources have been disappointing and unconvincing. A strong alliance of kings led by the king of Elam exercises control over a number of city-states around the Dead Sea area. Having been subject to this alliance for 12 years, five kings rebel in the 13th year (14:1-4). Their freedom is short-lived, since one year later the alliance moves into the area, successfully attacking a number of minor ethnic groups. Finally, the forces meet and the allies defeat their former vassals in a pitched battle in the valley of Siddim. This story explains why the hapless Lot ends up, with his family and substance, as part of the spoils of war (14:8-12).

14:13-24 Abram Rescues Lot

As Sarna points out, the "city of Hebron, where Abram resided, lay outside the path of hostilities, and the patriarch had no reason to intervene."[1] Lot's capture, however, brings Abram into the conflict. Although the reader already knows who Abram is, he is introduced as "Abram the Hebrew." While this title may refer to Abram as the father of the future Hebrew people, it is more likely that it is associated with people known as Habiru/Apiru, found throughout the ancient Near East at that time. Without affiliation to any particular land or country, some of them were pressed into slavery, especially in Egypt, while others became mercenaries. As Wenham observes,

> The Apiru are usually on the periphery of society — foreign slaves, mercenaries, or even marauders. Here Abram fits this description well: he is an outsider vis à vis Canaanite society, and he is about to set out on a military campaign on behalf of the king of Sodom as well as Lot.[2]

1. Shinar is Babylonia, and to its east was the kingdom of Elam.
1. Sarna, *Genesis*, 107.
2. Wenham, *Genesis 1–15*, 313.

No suggestion is made that Abram hired out his military muscle for payment but, "as Abram the Hebrew," he is credited with his own private army of 318 trained men. Amorite allies of Abram — Aner, Eshcol, and Mamre — accompany him. Remarkably, with his small army and his three Amorite allies, Abram routs the coalition of five nations (including Babylon and Elam). He pursues the enemies from Dan[3] to Hobah, north of Damascus (14:15). Effectively this means that he drives the invaders out of the land of promise.[4] Whereas in the previous chapter Abram has sacrificed the land to avoid strife, here he is willing to drive out aggressors and robbers. All this makes Abram, even as a sojourner in the land, a good ally and a formidable foe. He has begun to bring blessing to the nations (cf. 12:3).

After his victory, Abram is welcomed and given hospitality by Melchizedek, king of Salem, who is not one of the aforementioned combatants (14:18-20). The name of this mysterious person means "My king is righteous." If Salem is an abbreviation for Jerusalem, it is remarkable that an earlier king of this city had a similar name — Adonizedek, which means "My lord is righteous" (Josh 10:1). Melchizedek is also described as "priest of God most High" (אֵל עֶלְיוֹן/'ēl 'elyôn). Melchizedek is the first person in the book of Genesis to bless Abram personally.

> And he blessed him and said, "Blessed be Abram by God Most High, Possessor of heaven and earth; and blessed be God Most High, who has delivered your enemies into your hand!" And Abram gave him a tenth of everything. (14:19-20 ESV)

Abram's payment of a tenth to Melchizedek is a recognition of his authority and jurisdiction. As Brueggemann argues, this payment or "tithe" is not a "freewill offering" but "acknowledgement of a relation to a superior by a subordinate."[5]

The details given about Melchizedek are important for understanding the references to him in the Psalms (Ps 110:4) and in the NT (Heb 5:6, 10; 6:20; 7:1-17). His significance must be understood in the light of David's capture of ancient Jerusalem.[6] Unlike the Aaronic priesthood, the authenticity of

---

3. The name Dan is anachronistic, but that is the name with which the early readers of Genesis would be familiar. The name of the town in the time of Abram was "Laish."

4. So Wenham, *Genesis 1–15*, 315.

5. Brueggemann, *Genesis*, 135.

6. Although the traditional identification of Salem as Jerusalem has been widely accepted (cf. Ps 76:2), there have also been serious objections, such as the long distance between Jerusalem and the Dead Sea and also references to Jerusalem in ancient texts such as the execration texts indicate that Salem was not the ancient name for Jerusalem.

Melchizedek does not depend on who his parents were. David was probably able to carry out limited priestly functions as a priest of the order of Melchizedek. Later this title gained messianic significance, and this is developed in the NT book of Hebrews.

A tragic foil is provided for Melchizedek in the person of the king of Sodom, who meets Abram empty-handed. As Sarna points out, his first word to Abram is "Give!"[7] Melchizedek's provision of bread and wine makes the king of Sodom seem inhospitable and ungrateful in contrast. Compared to the warm reciprocal relationship between Abram and Melchizedek, there is unmistakable frostiness and animosity between Abram and the king of Sodom. Abram will accept nothing from the king of Sodom, giving him no excuse to claim that he has contributed to his wealth.

In the context of Genesis, the importance of the narrative is to establish that Abram is under Yahweh's protection and blessing. At this stage Abram does not own any land, but the reader is reminded here that he has received promises from God, under whose control is the entire earth (14:22). Yahweh has given Abram victory, and this victory is a sign of God's ability to deliver the promises that he has made.

15:1-6 A Dialogue with God

Brueggemann argues that this chapter is "pivotal for the Abraham tradition," and he claims that "Theologically, it is probably the most important chapter of this entire collection."[1] The passage highlights the tension between the doubts and fears of the servant of God and faith in the ultimate purposes of God, and it establishes that the covenantal relationship with Abram and his descendants is based on an oath sworn by God.

The chapter commences with a dialogue between God and Abram. Since Cain, no one in the Genesis account has had such an interchange with God. Cain's dialogue represented the end of his close relationship with God, but Abram's leads to a deepening relationship.

Abram enters this exchange in a vision. This particular noun, translated "vision," מַחֲזֶה/*maḥăzeh*, is found four times in the OT (Gen 15:1; Num 24:4, 16; Ezek 13:7). While the recipients of these revelations see something, the content is not primarily a visual experience of God but the revelation of his word. In spite of the visual vocabulary, the significance is in the words that God speaks rather than on a visual representation of his appearance.

7. Sarna, *Genesis*, 109.
1. Brueggemann, *Genesis*, 140.

Dialogues often occur at important junctures in narratives and serve to slow down the pace of the narrative and focus the reader's attention on something significant. As Alter points out,

> In any given narrative event, and especially at the beginning of any new story, the point at which dialogue first emerges will be worthy of special attention, and in most instances, the initial words spoken by a personage will be revelatory, perhaps more in manner than in matter, constituting an important moment in the exposition of character.[2]

In the light of the importance of dialogue, it is not surprising that the subject chosen for this first dialogue between Yahweh and Abram is one of considerable importance for the development of the narrative. The subject in question is that of covenant and seed or lines of descent, a theme that clearly links this vision with the preceding Abram stories.

Another link with what precedes is the injunction not to fear. In Egypt Abram had made unwise decisions motivated by fear, but now there are very justifiable reasons to be afraid. Worries about possible reprisals from Kedorlaomer could have tempted Abram to leave Canaan, but he receives this timely promise of divine protection. Furthermore, God promises Abram a very great reward. The Hebrew is ambiguous and could mean, "I am your shield; your reward shall be very great" (NRSV) or "I am your shield, your very great reward" (NIV). Shields are mentioned frequently in the Bible; they were an essential part of a soldier's equipment. The term is also used metaphorically to connote protection (Deut 33:29). God is not only a shield against physical weaponry but also against the verbal abuse and hostility of Israel's enemies. The word for "reward" can refer to wages (Gen 30:28; Prov 11:18) or the fare for a journey (Jonah 1:3).

Abram's response to God's opening words of assurance (15:1) is to ignore any fears that he may have had and to plead with God for a child ("seed"). In Egypt, fear had dictated Abram's behavior, but now even fear cannot distract from the disappointment that, in spite of all the wonderful promises that he had received about becoming a great nation, he has not even one child to whom he can pass on his inheritance. Not only is Abram disappointed about the failure of the promise to materialize, he is even looking at what his alternatives are if the promised offspring does not appear. Since Lot has now left him, Abram's heir will be his chief steward Eliezer. Abram's impassioned complaint is an admission that the provision of descendants is the

---

2. Alter, *The Art of Biblical Narrative*, 74.

prerogative of Yahweh; he gives (4:1) or he withholds (cf. 20:18). This is true in a general sense, since Genesis recognizes that children are a gift from the Lord (1:28; 4:1; 9:1; 29:31). But in Abram's situation, we have gone beyond that general gift of children to a special expectation of a gift of "seed" who will be the key to the fulfillment of Yahweh's promises (cf. 3:15; 4:25).

The earlier promises of descendants and nationhood (12:1-3) would be meaningless if Abram's heir is Eliezer of Damascus. Abram's concern, however, is not the long-term issues of whether or not he will become a great nation but the immediate need for someone to inherit the wealth he has acquired. Abram does not indicate any concern about the future greatness of his offspring, but he relates passionately to the problems facing him as a wealthy person with no heir. The possibility of Eliezer being the promised heir is ruled out (15:4). Now for the first time it is made unmistakably clear that Abram's heir will be not be an adoptee but rather a natural son. However, the mother's identity is still not revealed, and this maintains tension in the narrative by keeping the reader's curiosity alive.

There follows a promise similar to that already given in 13:16, with the difference that here (15:5) Abram's seed will be as numerous as the stars,[3] rather than the dust as previously promised. This is a repetition of the same promise as before but underlined this time by a different metaphor; Abram's seed will be so numerous as to make counting impossible. Once again, this promise is made against the backdrop of Sarai's barrenness, making the point that Abram is unable to contribute anything to the future greatness of his progeny. The change of metaphor from the dust to the stars is probably an indication that this vision occurred at night.

Verse 6 concludes the initial dialogue with an affirmation of Abram's faith and a brief assurance of God's acceptance of him.[4] Abram's faith that the promise of descendants will be fulfilled is credited to him as righteousness. Abram had left Ur to find a country that God promised him without knowing its name and now he believes the promise about descendants even though, from a human standpoint, it seems highly improbable or even impossible.

---

3. The creation of the stars is virtually an afterthought in ch. 1, but now they are described as numerous. God speaks about the stars with the authority of their creator.

4. The fact that the dialogue is taken up again in v. 8 has led many to reject the unity of the chapter. Westermann is typical. He argues that in ch. 15 "two central promise narratives have been juxtaposed"; *Genesis 12–36*, 216. Wenham, on the other hand, following Lohfink, argues for the essential unity of the chapter. He shows that vv. 7-21 develop the theme of land running in close parallel to the theme of seed in vv. 1-6; *Genesis 1–15*, 325. The two themes are closely connected, since the theme of land cannot stand isolated from the promise of descendants; the land is essentially a provision for the offspring of Abram.

Abram's righteousness is not linked to particular acts that he performs but to his faith in God. His faith, of course, leads to actions and provides a paradigm that is used and developed by NT writers leading to the idea of Abraham, the father, not just of the Jews but of all who share his faith in God (Rom 4:16; 9:7-8; Gal 3:6-9).

Abram is declared righteous because of what he believes rather than what he does. His actions in offering the choice of land to Lot or his attack on the enemy kings would have qualified as righteous acts but his faith in God's promises is seen as more significant. This does not imply that his actions are unimportant, but since Abram's actions are the outcome of his faith, it is faith that is of primary importance.

Genesis makes a clear distinction between those who take what God says seriously and those who disobey him. Eve and Adam believed the serpent rather than God. Their unbelief resulted in their expulsion from the privileged land of Eden and, ultimately, led to the death of their son Abel. Now Abram shows that he can believe God, even in difficult circumstances, and this leads to further assurances that, although Adam lost the benefits of living in communion with God through unbelief, Abram will receive these benefits through faith.

15:7-21 God Confirms His Promise to Abram by an Oath

Verses 1-6 deal mainly with the promise of a son and heir, but this section (vv. 7-21) concentrates on the promise of land, which is confirmed by an oath. Two separate occasions are involved since the first vision occurs during the nighttime (15:5) and the second commences in daylight but extends into the hours of darkness (15:12). However, in the final form of the text, the two visions are unified by the theme of faith (15:6).

The promise of land commences with a restatement of God's dealings with Abram in relation to land (15:7). The statement "I am the LORD who brought you out of Ur" is reminiscent of Israel's famous creedal statement, "I am the LORD who brought you out of the land of Egypt." This assertion reiterates the reason why Abram is landless. Unlike Adam or Cain, he has not been driven out; rather, God brought him out of his homeland with the specific aim of giving him a new land (cf. 12:1-3, 7).

Abram's response to this promise, "How can I know that I will gain possession of it?" (15:8 NIV), reflects his growing frustration. He has access to much of the land and he benefits from its resources, but the land does not belong to him and others have prior claims to it and jurisdiction over it (cf.12:6;

13:7). In substance, Abram's question is "How can land that is occupied and owned by others become mine?" This is not lack of faith but a search for a deeper understanding of the promise of land rising out of Abram's desire to believe. In this context, a failure to inquire for more detail or a neglect to ask for a sign would be evidence of lack of faith (cf. Isa 7:10-14).[1] God recognizes the question as legitimate and answers it in the vision that follows (15:13-16). First, however, Abram must comply with the divine request to bring a heifer, a goat, and a ram, each three years old. Abram is instructed to cut the animals in half and then to lay them out, together with a dove and a young pigeon.

Abram is not told why he must carry out this procedure. He is not asked to sacrifice the animals and birds but simply to lay them out. Having done this, he is faced with a problem, since the carcasses attract birds of prey and Abram must ward them off. This was probably an exhausting task, especially for an elderly man, since these were certainly not timid garden birds but vicious and determined scavengers such as buzzards and vultures. Carcasses lying out in the open would attract these birds in large numbers. According to an ancient proverb, quoted in the Talmud, a vulture in Babylon could spot a carcass in Palestine! Allowing for some rhetorical exaggeration, the proverb makes the point that where carcasses are available the vultures will find them. We should not allow our lack of familiarity with birds of prey to diminish the impact of the passage. Without Abram's presence, these carcasses would have disappeared rapidly. This story emphasizes the danger that lies ahead for Abram's offspring. Tasty pieces of meat under attack from birds of prey illustrate how vulnerable Israel would be to attack from the surrounding nations.

When evening comes, an exhausted Abram falls into a deep sleep that leaves him powerless to protect the carcasses. The same word for "deep sleep" is used in the story about God making the first woman when Adam was in a deep sleep. Adam and Abram have comparable experiences. Like Adam (2:21), Abram is removed from his duties and rendered helpless.[2] Adam has no part to play in the making of Eve, and Abram can do nothing to protect his offspring from the dark times ahead of them. As the sun sets, deep dread and darkness fall upon Abram. God warns him that the occupation of Canaan by his descendants will be preceded by a period of enslavement in a foreign land (15:13). Eventually, the nation that enslaves them will be punished (15:14) and Abram's descendants will be released from the foreign land with great possessions (15:14). On a more personal level, Abram is assured that he will die in peace

---

1. Cf. Wenham, *Genesis 1–15*, 331.
2. The rare word תַּרְדֵּמָה/*tardēmâ*, which occurs just seven times in the Bible, is used in both stories to describe the deep sleep.

(15:15). His descendants will return to the land of promise, which will be given to them when the sins of the Amorites have reached a certain level (15:16).

When it is dark, fire moves among the carcasses; this probably represents the presence of Yahweh and is reminiscent of the "burning bush." This is the setting for the covenant between God and Abram. The verb translated "to make" is, lit., "to cut." The origin of the idiomatic expression "to cut a covenant" is unknown, but it is particularly appropriate in this context. The covenant focuses specifically on the promise of land: the borders of the land are delineated[3] and the list of the present inhabitants is given (15:18-21).

The significance of this passage lies first in the fact that the promise of land is now made by God under oath and second, in the clear display of divine authority reminiscent of the creation event. The same God who brought a deep sleep on Adam is now at work in relation to Abram, the land of Canaan, and the present and future inhabitants of that land. While still awake Abram is able to drive away the predators, but he is relieved of this role when he falls into a deep sleep. A person in a deep sleep has no control over the situation. Abram cannot control future events and must leave this to Yahweh. As in chs. 1–11, God allocates land to people (cf. Adam in the garden of Eden, 2:15). He can terminate the tenancy of any person or nation when their sin reaches a certain level (cf. Adam, 3:24; Cain, 4:12; humankind, 6:7).

Yahweh's sovereignty over land was an important subject for many of the early readers of Genesis. The twofold promise of descendants and land highlighted in this chapter would provide assurance and encouragement especially during the period of the exile. As Westermann writes,

> It was supremely important for the later period that the promises to the patriarchs were unconditional. Later generations, under imminent threat, could reawaken the promises adapted to their situation and dealing with the preservation of the people and the retention of the land, so as to cling to God's assurance when both were in jeopardy.[4]

It may seem elementary to us, but in a community where the dominant view was that when you are living according to God's will, all will go well with you, any disaster or hard times could lead to the mistaken assumption and

---

3. Commenting on 15:18, Martens makes this useful observation: "The territorial extent [of the promised land] is designated as including an area from the river of Egypt to the river Euphrates. . . . The river of Egypt is not the Nile but 'Brook of Egypt', which enters the Mediterranean 87 km south-west of Gaza. The north-south boundaries are not spelled out here but are listed elsewhere (*e.g.* Nu 34:3-12); *God's Design*, 40.

4. Westermann, *Genesis 12–36*, 230.

debilitating conclusion that troubles indicated that God had forsaken them. This was the view of Job's three friends, who assumed that his problems resulted from his sinfulness and, consequently, God's judgment. Genesis shows that there are periods of darkness even for the most faithful of God's servants and times when they feel inadequate to change the situation.

Ten names are given of peoples who will be driven out by Abram's descendants: the Kenites, the Kenizzites, the Kadmonites, the Hittites, the Perizzites, the Rephaim, Amorites, the Canaanites, the Girgashites, and the Jebusites. This is the "longest list of the pre-Israelite inhabitants of Canaan found in the OT."[5]

16:1-16 Hagar and Ishmael

Chapter 15 has left the reader in no doubt that God has promised Abram personal progeny to inherit his wealth and that this must be a natural son of Abram (15:4). However, in sharp contrast to the unequivocal promises and the clear assurances of ch. 15, this episode deals with the human uncertainty and panic that arise because the fulfillment of the promises is slow in arriving. Furthermore, the period of waiting had fostered new doubts about the parentage of the promised offspring. It has been established unequivocally that Abram will be the father, but what about the mother? Must Sarai be the mother of the promised seed, or is it necessary only for Abram to be the father to meet Yahweh's requirements? The story of Abram's relations with Hagar the Egyptian explores this question. The Hagar incident also emphasizes that the promised seed will be a gift from Yahweh. The story is prefaced with a clear repetition of Sarai's continuing problem (16:1). As von Rad aptly comments,

> The narrator mentions only the prominent fact of childlessness, but the reader who has read chs. 12; 13; 15 perceives the real problem at once: the delay — indeed, the failure — of the promise proclaimed with such display. Sarah formulates this fact in all its paradoxical harshness: Yahweh himself has spoken and acted in this affair.[1]

Abram and Sarai, while acknowledging the overall control of Yahweh in the situation, paradoxically, out of desperation, invite a third person into their relationship. As Trible points out, the opening sentence of this scene (16:1) reverses the usual order in Hebrew of placing the verb first and then the subject. This means that the opening verse, one sentence in Hebrew, begins

---

5. Wenham, *Genesis 1–15*, 333.
1. Von Rad, *Genesis*, 191.

with the word Sarai and ends with the word Hagar. Since the name Abram oc-curs between the names of the two women, Trible comments that "two fe-males encircle Abram."[2] He is indeed caught between the two women, and throughout the story he merely obeys. In this incident the person with patri-archal authority obeys and meekly follows his wife's proposal without objec-tion. Ultimately, it is Abram who is to blame in this situation.

However, before we condemn the patriarch completely, we should note that in the OT, reflecting the customs of the ancient world, the ideal of mo-nogamy was not always practiced. Evidence from Nuzi has been cited to sup-port the actions of Abram and Sarai in seeking to provide an heir through a maidservant. If Abram and Sarai were resorting to "a proper legal practice," then as Brueggemann suggests, "No moral judgment need be rendered against the alternative device for securing a son."[3] The problem with their ac-tion is not that it was immoral in that society but that it showed lack of faith. This story illustrates that even those who desperately want to believe God may find it almost impossible to keep faith alive when all the evidence argues against it. Brueggemann aptly comments, "Faith is not easy. It calls for a per-sistence which is against common sense. It calls for believing in a gift from God which none of the present data can substantiate."[4]

Sarai believes that Yahweh has prevented her from having children (16:2). In desperation to give Abram an heir, she seeks to fulfill her perceived obligation to her husband by proxy through her handmaiden (16:1-3). Hagar is treated deplorably; her opinion is not asked for; she is a possession rather than a person.

Wenham argues that this passage is evocative of Genesis 3. He points out that the phrase "listen to the voice of" occurs only twice in the Bible (3:17; 16:2). Just as Adam accepted the temptation from the hand of Eve, Abram now succumbs to Sarai's tempting proposal. The verbs used and the sequence in which they occur are the same in both stories. Both women take and give something to their husbands, and in both cases the decision to accept the of-fer brings serious consequences and alienation.

But the focus is not just on what Sarai does, since Hagar is probably one result of the debacle in Egypt when Abram passed off Sarai as his sister.[5] Fur-

---

2. Trible, *Texts of Terror*, 11.

3. Brueggemann, *Genesis*, 151. Wenham makes a similar point: "This practice of surrogate motherhood is attested throughout the ancient Orient from the third to the first millennium B.C., from Babylon to Egypt"; *Genesis 16–50*, 7.

4. Brueggemann, *Genesis*, 152.

5. While Abram was in Egypt, he "acquired sheep and cattle, male and female donkeys, menservants and *maidservants,* and camels" (12:16 NIV).

thermore, subtle irony pervades the narrative since the readers have information not available to the characters in the narrative. Abram does not know that the nation that will enslave his seed will be the Egyptians, so he seeks to provide seed for himself through an Egyptian maid.

The anticipated birth of Ishmael actually leads to a worsening of Sarai's position. She still lacks offspring, but the situation is exacerbated by Hagar's change of attitude; Sarai is now despised in her eyes (16:4). We are not told how Hagar despises Sarai, but it may mean that the Egyptian refuses to acknowledge Sarai's claim to the baby in her womb. The point of Sarai giving her handmaid to Abram is that, according to custom, Sarai could have a baby by proxy, and Sarai's proposal to Abram that he should marry Hagar is so that "I can build a family through her" (16:2 NIV).[6] However, in Genesis, the baby is always referred to as Hagar's and not Sarai's. It is unlikely that Hagar in her deprived social status could have refused to recognize the child as Sarai's had her mistress insisted. It is more likely that Sarai is so offended by what she perceives as Hagar's bad attitude that she refuses to accept the child as hers.

Sarai's mistreatment of Hagar, apparently with the connivance of Abram, is not excused or minimized in the text (16:5-6). Abram's attitude is that Sarai owns the slave and can treat her accordingly, but he ignores the fact that Hagar is also his wife and that he should have protected her (16:3). Both Sarai and Abram treat the slave deplorably.

Having fled from her mistress, Hagar receives reassurance from the angel of Yahweh that she will be the mother of a multitude of descendants, and more specifically that she will bear a son called Ishmael (16:10-11). Significantly, the angel of Yahweh addresses Hagar by name and speaks to her personally. Abram and Sarai do not use her name, and they treat her as a possession and a convenience. To Yahweh, however, she is a person with a personal name, and he communicates with her. Hagar is one of only a few characters who have a dialogue with Yahweh; even her mistress Sarai is not afforded this privilege. Furthermore, the promised blessing of multiple descendants that Hagar receives is clearly parallel to the promise made to Abram (cf. 15:5). Abram fails to protect Hagar and Sarai treats her badly, but she is acknowledged and blessed by God. Later the Egyptians will act unjustly and enslave the Israelites, but Abram and Sarai show that they, representing Israel, are also capable of unjust behavior.

Hagar is told by the angel to return to Sarai and submit to her. This is wise advice. When the angel meets Hagar she is on her way to Shur, which was on the caravan route to Egypt. Apparently, she is attempting to return to her

---

6. Sarai probably uses the verb "to build" in the context of having children because it has a similar sound to the word for sons.

native land, but it was an impossible journey for a pregnant woman on her own. Therefore the angel sends her back to the family of Abram and Sarai, where she may be mistreated but nevertheless will receive protection until the baby is born. The angel's instruction to return to Sarai does not condone the harsh treatment meted out to the Egyptian but is in Hagar's best interests.

The annunciation of Ishmael's birth gives Hagar hope for the future. His name means "God will hear" and suggests that the God who later "heard" the cry of the Israelites because of their oppression also heard the cry of an Egyptian slave girl who was maltreated by Abram and Sarai (16:11; cf. Exod 3:7). The prediction that Hagar's son will be like a "wild ass" does not seem encouraging or complimentary to us, but for the slave Hagar it speaks of freedom (16:12). Ishmael would never be a slave like his mother but a free man who roams the desert and who is answerable to no one.

Submissively, Hagar returns to Sarai and Abram. The situation has not changed, and no indication is given that Sarai treats Hagar better. But something has changed: Hagar now has the assurance that God is with her and sees her problems. The name by which she refers to God — "the God who sees me" — reflects Hagar's new hope and confidence. The exact meaning of Hagar's words is unclear, and this is reflected in the different renderings of modern versions (16:13):

> So she called the name of the LORD who spoke to her, "You are a God of seeing," for she said, "Truly here I have seen him who looks after me." (ESV)
>
> And she called the name of the LORD that spake unto her, Thou God seest me: for she said, Have I also here looked after him that seeth me? (KJV)
>
> She gave this name to the LORD who spoke to her: "You are the God who sees me," for she said, "I have now seen [or 'seen the back of'] the One who sees me." (NIV)
>
> Thereafter, Hagar referred to the LORD, who had spoken to her, as "the God who sees me," for she said, "I have seen the One who sees me!" (NLT)
>
> So she named the LORD who spoke to her, "You are El-roi"; for she said, "Have I really seen God and remained alive after seeing him?" (NRSV)

In spite of the difficulties in understanding Hagar's words, the general sense is clear, that she is greatly encouraged to know that God is watching over her and that he is aware of her maltreatment at the hands of her mistress. Her master had received great promises from God but now so has she; she was treated badly by her mistress and even worse by Abram, who should have protected her. She can now accept the harsh treatment because now, quite wonderfully, she is a person with a purpose because God has acknowledged her cruel situation and has promised to protect her and her offspring.

Abram is 86 when Ishmael is born. The birth of a son means that in one sense Sarai's plan has succeeded — a child has been born. However, the text makes it clear that the plan has been a disastrous one for her since this is Abram's child and not hers.

Many early Israelite readers of Genesis were probably able to identify with Hagar more easily than with Sarai. Hagar was oppressed, and when she had no hope of a better future, this oppression drove her to despair. Israelites in exile who abandoned their historic faith left themselves vulnerable to a similar sense of despondency and hopelessness. However, if they believed in God and had confidence in his plans for them, they would be better able to endure the alienation as exiles. The story demonstrates that a realization that God is in control of a given situation is the antidote to despair.

17:1-6 Abraham, the Father of Nations

Thirteen years lapse between the end of ch. 16 and the beginning of ch. 17, reminding us that Genesis is not presenting the history of Abram's life but only the incidents that have theological importance. Abram at the age of 99 is addressed by Yahweh, who introduces himself as El Shaddai. This is the first occurrence of this title in the OT. In the Exodus story, this name is closely associated with the patriarchs. When God appears to Moses in Egypt before the Exodus he says,

> "I am Yahweh. I appeared to Abraham, to Isaac and to Jacob as El Shaddai but by my name Yahweh, I did not make myself known to them." (Exod 6:2-3; my translation)

In Genesis, however, El Shaddai is only one of a number of names used to address God, and the name Yahweh appears frequently. The name El Shaddai is usually translated "God Almighty," but its etymology is uncertain. An early rabbinic tradition suggests the meaning, "He who is Sufficient."[1]

Abram is exhorted to walk before God (17:1). Sarna suggests that the ex-

1. See the discussions in Sarna, *Genesis*, 384-85, and Wenham, *Genesis 16-50*, 20.

pression "walk before me" "seems originally to have been a technical term for absolute loyalty to a king." He observes that

> In the Bible, "to walk before God" takes on an added dimension. Allegiance to Him means to condition the entire range of human experience by the awareness of His presence and in response to His demands.[2]

God exhorts Abram to "be blameless." When describing animals, this word connotes those that are physically perfect and fit for sacrifice (Lev 5:18). It is also used of a day to show that a "complete" or "whole" day is involved (Josh 10:13). Applied to people it describes the type of people that God wants to worship and serve him (Deut 18:13): they do not practice sorcery and divination, and they do not listen to fortune-tellers. Noah is described as "blameless" to show that he was not implicated in the evil that was practiced all around him. Unlike Noah, however, Abram is not described as "blameless" but called to "*be* blameless."

Since Abram is called upon to attain this blameless life, we may assume that he has not yet reached this standard. His faith was acclaimed when God initiated the covenant earlier, and on that occasion God declared him "righteous" (15:6). The exhortation to be blameless may be a hint that God does not condone the actions of Abram in relation to Hagar the Egyptian, but it is more likely that this is a stipulation of the covenant that is being made with him and highlights the requirement of not just Abram but all those who claim a covenant relationship with God.

El Shaddai declares that he will "give" his covenant between Abram and himself. This is an unusual verb to use in relation to covenant and may mean "to confirm"(NIV) the covenant previously made in ch. 15. The promise of the covenant is followed by the promise that El Shaddai will multiply the descendants of Abram (17:2). Abram responds by "falling on his face," a symbolic act of prostration signifying complete submission. Ezekiel adopts the same position when he sees a vision of God in Babylon (Ezek 1:28). Prostrate before God, Abram hears a restatement of the divine intention both to make a covenant and to give him numerous posterity (17:4). Abram's faith is at breaking point. He believed God's promise of a multiplicity of descendants when he was younger, but he is now called upon to believe the same promises when he is almost 100 years old. The delay in the promises being fulfilled not only emphasizes that this is a test of faith but also shows that fulfillment is delayed until no one could deny that only divine intervention could have achieved

2. Sarna, *Genesis,* 123.

this result. Many of the readers of Genesis would have been able to identify with Abram, since the nation of Israel went through a similar trial of waiting for the fulfillment of God's promises on a number of occasions, but particularly in relation to the return from exile and the rebuilding of the temple.

The promise of numerous posterity permeates these six verses, making this the most explicit statement so far. Repetition of key words in the passage and the gift of a new name for the patriarch heighten the rhetorical impact and deliver the unmistakable message that, in spite of the unexplained delay, God intends to fulfill his promises. Repetition is an important device for producing emphasis in Hebrew, and this device is applied twice in this passage. The words that are repeated are:

> vv. 2 and 6 — מְאֹד בִּמְאֹד/*biměʾōd měʾōd*, lit., "very, very" but usually translated "exceedingly."
>
> vv. 4 and 5 — אַב-הֲמוֹן גּוֹיִם/*ʾab-hămôn gôyīm*, "father of a multitude of nations"

The new name for Abram, now called Abraham, symbolizes God's personal interest and concern for the patriarch (17:5). As Coats observes, "The name change is rooted in the divine promise: 'Your name shall be Abraham, for I have made you father of a multitude.'"[3]

The entire pericope is summed up in 17:6. The only new element in v. 6 that is not in the preceding verses relates to the promise that the patriarch's posterity will include kings. This additional element emphasizes that the promised posterity will not only be distinguished by numerical greatness but also by the high social standing of some of its number.

These promises of 17:2-6 are very general and do not point to the nation of Israel in particular. There is no mention of a specific land, and the promise is about a plurality of nations rather than about one single nation or one specific line of "seed." The contents relate clearly to the concept of blessing on an international scale.

17:7-14 The Covenant of Circumcision

Verse 7 begins a new section in which the implications of the covenant are unfolded in more specific terms. In 17:2-6 the personal dimension is to the fore, and the special personal relationship that Yahweh established with Abra-

---

3. Coats, *Genesis*, 134.

ham is emphasized with the change of name. Now the extension of that covenant to his descendants is explicit (vv. 7-9). The words "covenant," "seed," and "everlasting" give a long-term dimension to the covenant relationship, and the use of the verb קוּם/*qûm* ("to establish") underlines the idea that something is being established that will endure. Furthermore, now a specific land is mentioned, the land of Canaan, which will be the everlasting possession of the heirs of the Abrahamic covenant.[1]

The promise of the land is both introduced and concluded by the important statement that God's relationship with Abraham will be perpetuated among his descendants. Abraham's special links with Israel are the main focus of Genesis, but this is not an exclusive relationship and Abraham's descendants are found in other nations too.

Abraham's covenant responsibility is to observe the rite of circumcision. This stipulation also applies to his descendants, whether they are his by descent or purchase. Failure to be circumcised would have serious consequences resulting in an uncircumcised person being "cut off" from the covenant community (17:10-14).

17:15-27 Sarai's Name Changed and the Birth of Isaac Predicted

As the theophany develops, the promises focus specifically on, not just the descendants of Abraham, but also on the offspring of his wife Sarai. Her inclusion in the promises made to her husband is emphasized by a new name, Sarah, and by the twofold repetition of the verb "to bless" with her as its object. There is no difference in meaning between the name "Sarai" and "Sarah," but the name change is significant because Yahweh gives her this new name and, by doing so, acknowledges her as a member of the family line through which blessing will be mediated to the world. She will be the mother of nations, and kings will be among her descendants.[1] Abraham's incredulity at the idea that his wife Sarah will bear him a child leads him to fall facedown and laugh. This is the second time that Abraham falls facedown: he adopts this posture reverently in response to the theophany, but now he adopts the same posture to avoid showing that he is laughing. Although his posture suggests compliance

---

1. Von Rad notes this new emphasis from v. 7: "In v. 7, a new paragraph begins with another covenant declaration. What is new is the express statement that the covenant is made not only with Abraham but also with all his descendants. It is therefore a reference to its timeless validity" (*Genesis,* 200).

1. The fulfilment of this promise is realized in Esau being among Sarah's descendants, since through him she becomes the ancestress of the Edomites.

and submission, his innermost thoughts, and particularly his laughter, suggest a sense of incredulity and hopelessness.

The laughter is highlighted by the verb used, which is spelled the same as Isaac's name. As Abraham laughs, he expresses doubts about God's promises, and, ignoring the possibility of Sarah having a son, he petitions God on behalf of Ishmael (17:17-18). It is not entirely clear what Abraham asks God for on behalf of Ishmael. Literally, he requests that his son might live "before God's face," which means that he might live in the presence of God. This could be a request that Ishmael will experience, as Abraham did, an awareness of the presence of God. Hagar, Ishmael's mother, had experienced the blessing of knowing that God was watching over her, and perhaps Abraham is asking a similar blessing for Ishmael. However, it is more likely that Abraham is praying that Ishmael will become heir to all the blessings promised to Abraham.

The divine reply draws a clear distinction between the blessing Ishmael will share because he belongs to Abraham's posterity (17:20) and the covenant relationship that will be the special prerogative of Abraham's line of descendants through Sarah and her son Isaac (17:19, 21). Coats summarizes the promises concerning Ishmael as follows:

> God promises for Ishmael (1) blessing, (2) numerous descendants, (3) twelve princes, and (4) nationhood. But for Ishmael no covenant appears. The promise for posterity is thus of a different order from the one for Abraham-Isaac. V. 21 then returns to the promise of a covenant for Isaac and the announcement of the coming birth.[2]

Two facets to God's promises appear in ch. 17. On the one hand, God promises to bless all Abraham's posterity with fruitfulness and nationhood, but no specific land is mentioned. The heir to this promised blessing is Ishmael. On the other hand, God promises to enter into a covenant with a special line of Abraham's descendants, and they will inherit the land of Canaan. This special line is represented by the promise of Isaac. Following the theophany, Abraham circumcises every male in his household in obedience to the covenant requirements.

18:1-15 Abraham's Three Visitors

This passage describes a visit of three strangers to Abraham's tent at Mamre (18:1-2). At least one of these is Yahweh himself (cf. 18:13). This very daring

---

2. Coats, *Genesis*, 135.

presentation of deity in human form, speaking face to face with Abraham and accepting hospitality, is the high point of divine revelation in the patriarchal narratives allowing divinity to show a human face.[1] An important concept in Genesis is that the human form is fully compatible with deity, since human beings are made in God's image. By the same reasoning, and contrary to Egyptian belief, God could not appear as an animal or bird, since they are not made in his image.

Von Rad observes that Abraham does not see these strangers approaching and, following Gunkel, comments aptly that "Divine events are always so surprising."[2] This account of God appearing in human form will not surprise or trouble Christian readers, since the NT's main focus is on God's appearance as a human being. However, in the context of Genesis this is a very special event. Since there has been no mention of God walking on earth since his appearance in the "garden of Eden," the narrator must have an important purpose for this particular passage. Gibson considers what this purpose could have been and concludes,

> It can only have been to emphasize the crucial significance of the drama that was being played out in this portion of Genesis. Or to phrase it differently, the author wanted God to be seen to be present in these events in a very special way. Abraham's life was fast approaching its climax, and in the truest of senses the world's future hung on what was now happening.[3]

Abraham's offer of hospitality could not have been more generous or have been provided with more enthusiasm. Twice in the story Abraham runs; he runs to meet the men and he runs to the herd to obtain a calf. Running emphasizes Abraham's determination to be hospitable, because, not only was it undignified for an old man to run, but it was also very difficult in the heat. Abraham's offer to the men — some water and a morsel of bread — is a gross understatement of what he actually provides, which is a feast fit for royalty with ingredients that include about 20 liters of fine flour and a choice animal from the flock. Abraham provides this high quality food before the identity of his guests is revealed to him. The narrative portrays him as the ideal host who enthusiastically welcomes strangers with the best hospitality he can provide.

Through their dialogue with Abraham, the visitors reveal the purpose of their mission. This is to announce that Sarah will have a son, even though,

---

1. From this point on there will be a gradual distancing of Yahweh from people until in the Joseph stories he appears only in dreams.

2. Von Rad, *Genesis*, 206.

3. Gibson, *Genesis*, 2:77.

from a human standpoint, this is impossible because of her age (18:9-15). There has been a previous announcement with similar content (17:16), but this time Sarah is present and her reaction is important; she laughs at the idea of bearing a child at her age (18:12). It is a cynical laugh in the face of what seems a cruel joke reminding her of what had once been her fondest dream but is now out of the question. Now with tremendous skill the writer juxtaposes against this account of human disappointment the almighty power of Yahweh, making the point very clear that the birth of Isaac will be as a result of special divine intervention (18:14).[4] In these words ("Is anything too hard for the LORD?") we find the key to understanding the entire incident. They focus on the importance of Yahweh's intervention to give Abraham descendants. As Willis comments,

> The question **Is anything too hard for the Lord?** is actually the central issue throughout the story of the divine announcements that Abraham would have a son in his old age (Gen. 15:1–18:15). It is also one of the most vital questions facing contemporary man as he agonizes with the difficult problems of life.[5]

The promise of a special line of descendants is clearly taken out of the human realm and presented as a sovereign act of God. Furthermore, this incident highlights the truth that sometimes the fulfillment of God's promises may be delayed until even the faith of an Abraham and Sarah cannot prevent them both from indulging in cynical laughter. We can surmise that many of the early readers may have been in a situation where their faith was severely tested and where many were beginning to doubt if the great promises made to the nation could still be relevant for them. The exile is one obvious context when these stories of faith severely tested would be pertinent and relevant.

18:16-33 Abraham Intercedes on Behalf of Sodom and Gomorrah

As the three visitors leave, Abraham walks part of the way with them and God reveals to him his future plans for the destruction of Sodom and Gomorrah. God, reasoning with himself, explains why he should reveal his intentions to a human being. The reason given is that Abraham is special in God's sight and

---

4. This key question is referred to by von Rad as "a precious stone in a priceless setting"; *Genesis*, 207.

5. Willis, *Genesis*, 256.

will become a great and powerful nation that will be the source of blessing to all nations. Thus, the reason for informing Abraham about the destruction before it happens links directly with his role of bringing blessing to the nations. Moreover, Abraham is the counterpart of all that is wrong with the doomed cities. He is an example of righteousness and justice for his household, and he has a close relationship with God that will benefit not just himself and his family but the entire world.

At least two of the visitors go on their way, but the third person, identified as "the LORD," remains with Abraham and allows him to bargain with him about the cities.[1] Abraham has influence with the highest authority and is on speaking terms with the one who can change history. Face to face with deity, Abraham negotiates about how the cities might be spared the threatened judgment. This description of the patriarch bargaining with God is one of the most daring portrayals of human-divine relations in the entire OT. Even the intercession of Moses on behalf of Israel is portrayed in less intimate terms (Exod 32:11-14). The lack of success of Abraham does not detract from the clear message that he has special influence with God. While Abraham's attempt to strike a bargain with God may seem strange and out of place to readers in the West, it fits well with the context of the East, where striking a bargain is an everyday occurrence at the marketplace. The amazing aspect of the story is not that Abraham bargains but that he does so with God.

This passage is also important because of what it teaches us about God. He is the Judge of all the earth, and its inhabitants are responsible to him for their behavior. Those who emulate Abraham in his key qualities of righteousness and justice may have a close relationship with him, but those who are wicked may expect unrelenting judgment. There has been an outcry to God because of the sins committed in the cities of the Jordan Valley (18:20). God investigates these complaints by coming down to judge them, as he had previously come down to judge the builders of the tower of Babel (11:7). The word "outcry," according to von Rad, "is a technical legal term and designates the cry for help which one who suffers a great injustice screams."[2] Sarna observes that it connotes "the anguished cry of the oppressed, the agonized plea of the victim for help in the face of some great injustice."[3] From whom does this outcry come? We are not told, but in an earlier story the blood of the innocent cried out to God from the ground (4:10). Violence and unrequited mur-

---

1. Originally 18:22 probably read, "The Lord stood on before Abraham," but the Scribes, presumably, felt that this was inappropriate and changed it to read, "Abraham stood on before the Lord."

2. Von Rad, *Genesis*, 211.

3. Sarna, *Genesis*, 132.

der defiled the ground on which they were committed. However, in this context no specific crimes are mentioned, and lawlessness in a general sense is probably envisaged (cf. Lev 18:25).

The questions raised by Abraham's bargaining with God are significant, not just for the theology of Genesis, but also for the theological interpretation of events in Israel's history. Events such as the destruction of the northern kingdom of Israel by the Assyrians or the destruction of Jerusalem by Nebuchadnezzar raised similar objections and questions to that asked by Abraham, "Shall not the Judge of all the earth do what is just?" (18:25 NRSV). In particular, one of the most pertinent questions raised by the judgment of a nation is the issue of the innocent individual caught up in the punishment of the masses. This is highlighted by Abraham's negotiations with God about how many righteous would be necessary to avoid the destruction of the city. Genesis does not provide all the answers, but it does reassure people that God is aware of their questions and conscious of their pain and confusion.

19:1-11 Lot Entertains Strangers

Two visitors arrive at Sodom in the evening. Lot meets them at the entrance to the city. Gateways were meeting places in ancient cities.[1] Lot offers hospitality to the strangers, just as Abraham had done earlier, though the language is more subdued. Unlike Abraham, Lot does not run to greet or serve his guests, and the provision he makes is much more modest than that provided by Abraham. Strangely, the men are reluctant to accept Lot's hospitality and initially, at least, decide to lodge in the city square. Why were they reluctant? Perhaps they were waiting for some of the Sodomites other than Lot to offer them hospitality.[2] It is certainly a tremendous slur on the town that only a resident alien (Lot) offers the customary hospitality to strangers. However, several elements in the story contrast Lot unfavorably with Abraham, and this is probably the role of the reluctance motif. Abraham's visitors immediately accept his hospitality, but Lot must plead with them, suggesting that Abraham has a closer relationship to God and his messengers than Lot. God honors Abraham and shares privileged information with him but, although God rescues Lot and is merciful to him, he does it for Abraham's sake (19:29). However, although Lot compares unfavorably with Abraham, when compared to the people of Sodom, he is a righteous man (cf. 2 Pet 2:7-8).

1. At the archaeological site of Tel Dan there is an interesting reconstruction of a city gate that shows clearly where people could have congregated and sat.
2. Cf. Willis, *Genesis*, 262.

Chillingly, the description of the mob, surrounding Lot's house to demand that he hand over the strangers, leaves the readers in no doubt about the depravity and licentiousness of the inhabitants of Sodom (19:4-9). Their demand that the strangers should be brought out in order that "we may know them" (19:5 NRSV) is probably a reference to sexual knowledge.[3] The alternative interpretation that this is simply a request to become acquainted with the men is unsustainable in the light of Lot's willingness to give them his daughters to pacify their lust.

The rabble gathered around Lot's house were not a small contingent of troublemakers but "all the people to the last man" (19:4 NRSV). The insistence that everyone was involved in the wickedness of the city rules out the possibility of finding 10 righteous people in such a place. In spite of Abraham's intercession, the city will be destroyed. This continues one of the main themes of Genesis, that God will remove from their land those who fail to meet his demands for righteous conduct. It also suggests that the city was more wicked than Abraham realized.

The story shows how foolish Lot has been to associate with the inhabitants of Sodom. Earlier, Abram and Lot were described as "brothers" (13:8), but in this passage Lot refers to the men of Sodom as "brothers" (19:7). However, the city-dwellers despise Lot and threaten him with personal violence, even reducing him to offering his daughters to them as sexual playthings (19:8). Abram and Sarai had not treated their slave as a person with rights, but Lot's behavior is even more outrageous in treating his daughters as disposable assets who can be sacrificed to extricate him from a difficult situation. Ironically, while Lot is trying to save his visitors, they save him by inflicting blindness on his attackers (19:11). The word for blindness is סַנְוֵרִים/*sanwērîm*. According to Sarna, the reference is not to "the usual kind of sightlessness," "but a dazzling brightness."[4] This story was a solemn warning to the first readers to avoid the temptation of developing close relationships with the heathen and adopting their lifestyle (cf. Isa 3:9).

19:12-29 Lot's Departure and the Destruction of Sodom and Gomorrah

The incident provides the evidence that the angels require that the city is ripe for judgment, and they inform Lot that they will destroy the city; they urge

---

3. The verb "to know" is frequently used in the OT to refer to sexual relations.
4. Sarna, *Genesis*, 136.

him to leave and take all his kindred with him immediately (19:12-13). Lot's lack of influence is further illustrated by his futile attempt to persuade his two daughters' fiancés to leave the city; his appeal seems like a joke to them (19:14). Lot is less successful than Noah, who was able to save in the ark his sons and their wives. Again, the comparison with Abraham is pertinent, since he is able to negotiate with the Hittites and even with God himself; but Lot has no credibility, even in his own family.[1]

The reluctance of the sons-in-law to leave Sodom is shared by Lot and his family.[2] In his account of the family's departure, the narrator creates palpable tension by clearly juxtaposing the urgency of the angels with the apathy and complacency of Lot. Even though he has been told that the city is about to be destroyed, Lot needs further persuasion from the angels, and still he lingers until the angels virtually drag him and his family from the city (19:16-17).[3]

Lot disputes the advice given to flee to the hills and asks permission to flee to a city instead, albeit a small one. He seems to believe that a small city will be less sinful than a large city. The angels permit Lot and his family to flee to Zoar, which will be spared for their sake (19:22). Lot's intervention leads to Zoar being excluded from the destruction. His failure to settle there suggests that the city actually deserved the judgment from which he saved it. Thus, both Lot and Abraham bargain with God about a city. Lot does so to provide a home for his family, whereas Abraham's motives are altruistic, reflecting his concern for justice.

In spite of the angels' best efforts, Lot's wife fails to escape. This carefully narrated drama shows that Lot, having once forsaken city life to follow his uncle in obedience to God, has been drawn again into city life and finds it almost impossible to leave. City life is not presented as necessarily sinful, but in the context of the ancient world it is certainly presented as a place where rebellion against God can easily develop. We can speculate that this narrative may have provided a warning to the early readers of Genesis against becoming entangled in the lifestyle of polytheistic city life. This may have been a particularly relevant message to readers in the exilic period.

Significantly, the description of the destruction of the cities includes a reference to the animals and the plants of the ground suffering ruin.

Then the LORD rained on Sodom and Gomorrah sulphur and fire from the LORD out of heaven. And he overthrew those cities, and all the valley,

---

1. The Hittites refer to Abraham as "a mighty prince" (23:6).

2. Lot's daughters are betrothed but not yet married (cf. 19:8).

3. Wenham observes that there is a wordplay between the name Lot and the verb "to escape," and he reproduces this in English as "Lot was *let* out of Sodom"; *Genesis 16–50*, 58.

and all the inhabitants of the cities, and what grew on the ground. (19:24-25 ESV)

This continues the theme that began with the curse on the ground as a result of Adam's sin: the welfare of the ground and its vegetation are adversely affected by the rebellion of human beings against God. In the time of Noah the great flood destroyed innocent animals as well as plants. Although animals are not mentioned in the account of the destruction of Sodom and Gomorrah, the destruction of vegetation is specifically highlighted. This is probably an etiological reference to the utter barrenness of the region around the Dead Sea.

In 19:27 the focus of the passage returns to Abraham as he views the destruction from the place where he had pleaded with God to spare the cities. However, although he had not been successful in saving all the inhabitants, God has rescued Lot for Abraham's sake. The phrase "God remembered Abraham" is reminiscent of the turning point in the flood story when "God remembered Noah" (8:1). As Wenham observes,

> Similarities between the account of Sodom's destruction and the flood story have often been noted. Both stories are tales of universal destruction brought about by human wickedness, a destruction from which one righteous man and his family are saved by divine grace. Both stories are followed by the hero's intoxication with wine and the disgraceful actions of his children.[4]

This means that the narrator of Genesis is making both favorable and unfavorable comparisons: Abraham reflects the most positive aspects of Noah's life since they both found favor with God; but Abraham's integrity in passing on the blessing of God to his descendants is untainted, and there is nothing in his career to compare with Noah's intoxication. Lot, on the other hand, reflects the negative sequel to Noah's life through the sordid story of his daughters' relationship with him.

19:30-38 Lot and His Daughters

Lot's demise continues in this passage. His choice of Zoar as a place of refuge following the destruction of Sodom seems to have been unwise, and he was too afraid to remain there. Whereas his uncle Abraham had received assur-

---

4. Wenham, *Genesis 16–50*, 42.

ances from God that he need not fear, Lot does not have this benefit. In ch. 13, while he was with Abraham, Lot possessed flocks, herds, and tents; but as the narrator prepares to leave him and focus on Abraham and his direct descendants, Lot is homeless apart from a cave and friendless apart from his daughters. His choice to leave Abraham and join city life have cost him dearly.

Lot, in his state of abject misery, is not afforded a genealogical record, since he leaves nothing for his descendants to inherit. However, his descendants through an incestuous relationship with his daughters are traced to Israel's neighbors, the Moabites and the Ammonites.

20:1-18 Sarah and Abimelech

An overwhelming sense of déjà vu greets the reader of this passage as Abraham once again refuses to call Sarah his wife and claims that she is his sister. This story creates problems for the modern reader. Not only is it difficult to believe that Abraham could repeat the same deception that resulted in expulsion from Egypt earlier, but there is now the added problem that Sarah is an old woman and the deception would seem unnecessary since she is now over 70. Moreover, God has promised Abraham a son through Sarah. Is Abraham disregarding this promise because of some misguided fear about his own safety?

In spite of the difficulties associated with this story, its location here fulfills an important literary function by slowing down the pace of the narrative to direct the reader's attention to God's perseverance with Abraham. It shows that, but for the protection and intervention of God, the birth of Isaac would never have taken place. Through deception Abraham endangers the promises, but God does not allow this to happen. Abraham's characterization is not that of a superhuman who never makes mistakes. He is a vulnerable human who does not fully appreciate all that God is doing for him. God blesses Abraham in spite of himself.

A careful comparison between this story and the earlier story situated in Egypt (12:11-20) shows an important difference. In both accounts Abraham pretends that his wife is his sister. However, in the Egyptian story the possibility of relations between Pharaoh and Sarah is envisaged, whereas in this case it is made clear that Yahweh prevents Abimelech from having a relationship with Sarah. Yahweh intervenes in two ways: he warns Abimelech in a dream (20:3-7), and he renders all the women of his harem barren (20:18). Eventually, Sarah is restored to Abraham, together with a large gift to compensate (20:16). Abraham then prays for Abimelech, and the fertility of his household is restored (20:17). The barrenness of Abimelech's wives and the restoration of their fertility in answer to prayer show that the process of procreation is derived ultimately from God. This applies not only to the special line of seed through Abraham but even to the offspring of the "Philistine"[1] monarch. Subtle irony pervades this story since Abraham's prayers for other people's wives are immediately efficacious, but he has to wait a lot longer for his prayers for Sarah to be answered.

Other points of interest in the passage include the favorable portrayal of the Philistine chief, a somewhat surprising accolade from an Israelite text. Abimelech has high moral standards, and apparently these are shared by his servants, who are very afraid when they hear how they could have inadvertently sinned against God (20:8). Abraham is accused of having brought guilt upon Abimelech and his kingdom. As in the story of Jonah, God's servant seems oblivious to the trouble that he has brought upon others.

God communicates with the Philistine chief and acknowledges his innocence by intervening to prevent the Philistine from sinning unwittingly (20:6). Abraham's excuse to Abimelech for his irresponsible behavior is that he thought there was "no fear of God in this place." Thus, Abraham underestimates the spiritual and moral standing of the Philistines. He attempts to vindicate himself, arguing that he has not told a lie since Sarah and he have the same father, though different mothers. However, this does nothing to lessen the crime of sacrificing Sarah in order to save himself.

Abraham, who earlier refused to accept gifts from the king of Sodom, shows no reticence in accepting generous gifts from Abimelech. Whereas Pharaoh had driven Abraham from his land during a similar incident, Abimelech generously allows Abraham to sojourn anywhere on his land. However, in making this offer the Philistine refers to the land as "my land." This is not disputed in the text. All land belongs to Yahweh, but he gives it to others as their possession, including Philistines. God's provision of land for others as well as Israel is one of the themes of Amos' preaching (Amos 9:7). Abimelech describes his gift as "a covering of the eyes" (20:16). This interesting idiom has been translated in a number of ways:

> To Sarah he said, "Behold, I have given your brother a thousand pieces of silver. It is a sign of your innocence in the eyes of all who are with you, and before everyone you are vindicated." (ESV)
> And unto Sarah he said, Behold, I have given thy brother a thousand pieces of silver: behold, he is to thee a covering of the eyes, unto all that are with thee, and with all other: thus she was reproved. (KJV)

---

1. The word "Philistine" is used here in a locative rather than an ethnic sense since the Philistines did not settle in Canaan until the late 13th and early 12th century B.C.

> To Sarah he said, "I am giving your brother a thousand shekels [that is, about 25 pounds (about 11.5 kilograms)] of silver. This is to cover the offense against you before all who are with you; you are completely vindicated." (NIV)
>
> Then he turned to Sarah. "Look," he said, "I am giving your 'brother' a thousand pieces of silver to compensate for any embarrassment I may have caused you. This will settle any claim against me in this matter." (NLT)
>
> To Sarah he said, "Look, I have given your brother a thousand pieces of silver; it is your exoneration before all who are with you; you are completely vindicated." (NRSV)

God has promised that Abraham would be a source of blessing to the nations, and this is one way that this promise is fulfilled. However, the irony would not escape readers that Abraham has irresponsibly caused the problems in the first place. At the same time, his misdemeanor does not prevent Abraham from playing a prophetic role and bringing blessing through prayer.[1] As Brueggemann aptly comments, the "preeminence of Abraham here rests not on Abraham's virtue, but on God's promise."[2] Similar examples of God protecting those whom he has chosen are found in the Jacob stories, in which we read that God protects Jacob from Laban although Jacob is not entirely the innocent party.

21:1-7 The Birth, Naming, and Circumcision of Isaac

Sarah's barrenness, which is so prominent in the narratives, does not highlight any flaws in her character or any failure on Abraham's part. Rather, it accentuates the promissory aspects of the narrative and illustrates the helplessness of Abraham and Sarah to contribute in any way towards the fulfillment of the promises. The future greatness of Abraham's seed is placed entirely in the realm of special divine intervention. The verb used to emphasize God's role in the birth of Isaac is פקד/*pqd*. Although it is often translated "to visit," this is rather inadequate since the Hebrew verb implies intervention in a human situation. It is often employed in the text to describe God intervening in human affairs either to bless or to punish. In this case, it means that God is true to his word and enables Sarah and Abraham to have the child they have longed for, even though

---

1. Abraham is the first person to be described as "a prophet" in the Bible (20:7).
2. Brueggemann, *Genesis*, 178.

in spite of their faith they have laughed at the very idea. Indisputably an act of God, the birth fulfills the divine promises since God has been gracious to Sarah as he had said and has done for her what he had promised (21:1). Moreover, the event happens at the time God had predicted to Abraham (21:2).

Isaac's name, which means "he laughs," links the story of his birth with previous occasions when his parents both laughed incredulously at the idea of bearing a child in their old age. This link with laughter is emphasized again by Sarah's assertion that through the child God has brought her laughter that would be shared by all who hear her incredible news. A child born to a 100-year-old man is well worth a laugh (21:6-7). However, a double entendre is intended, since the idea of laughter also highlights the great joy and relief that herald Isaac's birth. Isaac is the missing piece in the jigsaw puzzle, since without him the promises made to Abraham make no sense. The joy and laughter associated with the birth of Isaac are clearly analogous with the theme of Psalm 126:

> When the LORD restored the fortunes of Zion,
> we were like those who dream.
> Then our mouth was filled with laughter,
> and our tongues with shouts of joy:
> then they said among the nations,
> "The LORD has done great things for them."
> The LORD has done great things for us: we are glad.
>
> (Ps 126:1-3 ESV)

The reference to "restoring fortunes" is, as Brueggemann observes, "the way Israel speaks about the end of exile." He applies this very effectively to the story of Isaac: "Isaac is the end of every exile in the kingdom of necessity."[1]

Laughter and joy are not the only themes of the birth narrative, since it also highlights the obedience of Abraham to the covenant stipulations. The child is born into the covenant relationship established by God with Abraham, and, as a sign of this privileged position, he is circumcised when eight days old.

21:8-21 Hagar and Ishmael Expelled

The tension in the text does not relax with the birth of Isaac, since immediately comparisons with Ishmael surface. Abraham's favoritism is the first indication

---

1. Brueggemann, *Genesis*, 182.

of future trouble. When Isaac is weaned his father provides a sumptuous feast (21:8), but no such feast was mentioned when his brother was weaned. Probably, like the brother of the Prodigal Son story, Ishmael could not show any enthusiasm for his younger brother for whom this lavish feast was prepared while no such honor had been paid to him (cf. Luke 15:25-27). We are not told anything about Ishmael's feelings. The story is told from Sarah's point of view, and she notices Ishmael "laughing." Some versions translate this "mocking" (KJV, NIV) or "scoffing" (NKJV), since they believe that Sarah has found some misdemeanor in Ishmael; however, the verb used to describe Ishmael's action is the verb from which the name Isaac is derived. It does not indicate that Ishmael was doing anything wrong and, therefore, is misleading to use the pejorative word "mocking" to describe Ishmael's action. Other versions make this clear, translating the verb as "playing" (NRSV, NJPS) or simply as "laughing" (ESV). So although tradition has been unkind to Ishmael, the text itself does not unequivocally blame the boy. Rather, it explains his expulsion as the natural outworking of Sarah's jealous protection of her own son Isaac. To Sarah, Ishmael is merely "the son of Hagar the Egyptian, whom she had borne to Abraham" (Gen 21:9 NRSV), and she ruthlessly demands his expulsion. It is very clear from Sarah's plea to Abraham that she feels strongly that Ishmael is inferior to Isaac. Her demand seems very wrong to Abraham, and most readers will feel alienated from her since it was originally her idea that Abraham should have a child by Hagar. Once again, the hapless Hagar is caught up in a drama that is not of her own making, and Sarah demands her expulsion along with Ishmael's, even though neither she nor her son was implicated in any crime. Throughout the entire narrative, Hagar is the innocent party, the expendable pawn in an important game. Through no fault of her own, she must play a subservient role and accept the lot of one who is not part of the central drama.

Yet Sarah's actions may have been, not the jealous reaction of a paranoid mother, but a necessary step to preserve Abraham's inheritance for Isaac. Ishmael was the firstborn of Abraham and was destined to receive the larger part of his father's wealth. An ancient law, which Sarna notes, stipulates that "the father may grant freedom to the slave woman and the children she has borne him, in which case they forfeit their share of the paternal property."[1] Sarah may have been persuading her husband to protect Isaac's birthright in the accepted way, a step that Abraham was reluctant to take.

God, however, has the last word in the story. Abraham, whose personal displeasure at Sarah's demands is made clear, receives instructions to do as she says. This does not amount to divine approval for Sarah's harsh and cruel

1. Sarna, *Genesis*, 147.

treatment of her slave girl, but it is God's reassurance to Abraham that he will take care of Ishmael and his mother and that she shall share in the blessings promised to the seed of Abraham. This reassurance enables Abraham to carry out Sarah's instructions, knowing that Ishmael and his mother will enjoy God's protection.

Although the story of this expulsion leaves the reader with mixed emotions, it fulfills an important role in the narrative by drawing attention to the distinction between Isaac and Ishmael. It follows the pattern repeated throughout Genesis where two people live or work together and then something happens to separate them. Following this separation, one of them fades from view while the other becomes the focus of attention. Cain moves to the East, leaving Seth; Lot moves towards Sodom, leaving Abraham in the land; Esau moves to Mount Seir, leaving Jacob in Canaan.

Abraham's provision for Hagar and Ishmael is hopelessly inadequate, especially when compared with his earlier hospitality. Isaac gets a great feast (21:8), but Hagar and Ishmael only as much bread and water as Hagar can carry on her shoulders (21:14).[2] This is inadequate for their survival, and divine intervention is required to prevent Ishmael's death. Abraham's failure to provide for his Egyptian wife and her son contrasts with God's care and future plans for the lad. He reveals a spring of water to Hagar, which is reminiscent of the provision of water in the wilderness for the Israelites. Furthermore, God's appearance to Hagar becomes the opportunity for a reiteration of the divine promise that Ishmael will become a great nation (21:18). The narrator finishes his account of Ishmael with a brief description of how his mother arranges his marriage to an Egyptian.

The Christian interpretation of the story of Hagar receives its classic expression in the NT book of Galatians (Gal 4:21-31). Paul strips the story of its sympathetic undertones towards Hagar and typifies Isaac as the son of the free woman while Ishmael is the son of the bond woman. In this allegorical approach, the characters lose their personal human significance and become types and visual aids in the presentation of timeless theological truths.

21:22-34 A Treaty with Abimelech

This is a strange location for a further story about Abimelech. However, it provides an interesting contrast between the provision of water for Hagar and

---

2. According to Jewish tradition, the original supplies were adequate, but Hagar got lost; Sarna, *Genesis*, 147.

Ishmael and the need for Abraham to bargain with Abimelech over the wells. Furthermore, it explains how Beer-sheba, mentioned in the previous story, receives its name.

Abraham's relationship to the other inhabitants of Canaan is the main subject of this short passage. Recognizing that Abraham has divine protection, Abimelech and his military leader acknowledge to Abraham, "God is with you in all that you do" (21:22 NRSV). This is evidence that the promises of blessing to Abraham are being fulfilled and that this is obvious to foreigners who have not been privy to the promises made to Abraham (12:1-3). Abraham agrees to take an oath of friendship, but doubt is immediately cast on the practical value of such accords by the complaint of Abraham that almost immediately Abimelech's servants break the agreement. Access to water is the main issue in the dispute. As the two men confirm their covenant relationship, Abraham declares his right to the well in question by giving Abimelech seven ewes, establishing the etiology for naming the well "Beer-sheba" (lit., "the well of seven") as the "well of the oath." The incident shows the struggle that Abraham has in establishing that even one well belongs to him and yet God had promised to give him the entire land. After the departure of Abimelech and his men, Abraham plants a tree and prays to El Olam (the "Everlasting God"). Abraham knows that any agreement with Abimelech may be short-lived, and so he calls on God as his witness that Beer-sheba is his property.

The importance of the number seven is not always apparent to English readers, but it often appears in the OT to highlight important events. In this story the number is prominent, not only because there are seven ewes, but also the names Abraham and Abimelech both occur seven times in the Hebrew text. Furthermore, as Sarna points out, the consonants of the Hebrew word for seven are found both in the verb "to swear" and in the name Beer-sheba.[1]

22:1-19 The Command to Sacrifice Isaac

This highly charged passage begins with the assertion that "God tested Abraham." The Hebrew verb "to test" is used, for example, in 1 Sam 17:39, where David refuses to wear Saul's armor or to use his fighting implements because he has not tested them, meaning that he has not had the opportunity to use them. The implication of God testing Abraham is that he gives the patriarch

---

1. Sarna, *Genesis,* 148.

an opportunity to demonstrate his faith. A purely theoretical faith is inferior to a faith that has been tested and tried through the experiences of life. No hint that Abraham might fail the test arises in this story.

Isaac belongs to God, and Abraham must acknowledge God's prior claim to his life. Abraham must now respond with obedience and faith to the command to sacrifice Isaac, just as he had responded earlier when he left Haran (12:4). The command "go" is given in an unusual way: לֶךְ-לְךָ/*lek-lĕkā*. This phrase was used previously in the command to Abraham to leave his country (12:1). Clearly, the repetition of this unusual phrase is not accidental and indicates that God's relationship with Abraham that commenced when he was called to leave his country has now reached a new and critical junction. The fulfillment of the promises depends on obedience in both cases. Following God is not just a matter of initial commitment: for Abraham it means life-long commitment with more than a few unexpected demands along the way.

The test in ch. 22 demands that Abraham renounce any personal rights over Isaac and express unquestioning faith. The seed given by God's intervention belongs to God, and the divine will concerning him must be given priority. Abraham must accept that the future is in safe hands, even though God's decisions and requests do not always make sense.

Sarah is not involved in this test, and her previous protectiveness suggests that she would have attempted to prevent anything that brought danger to Isaac. Jewish sources argue that her relationship with Abraham deteriorates considerably after this event, but the biblical text is silent on the matter.

Abraham's obedience is unqualified; he sets out "early in the morning," having saddled the donkey himself and prepared the wood for the sacrifice (22:3). Normally a servant would have performed these tasks, and Abraham's personal involvement is an indication that he keeps the details of the vision secret and makes low-key preparations to leave on his long journey. A three-day journey is involved, so Abraham has time to consider all the consequences of what he has been asked to do. This test should not be considered in isolation, since it is part of Abraham's journey of faith. It will teach him more about himself, but in particular, more about God.

As the narrative unfolds, the clear impression is given that Abraham's resolve does not weaken (22:4-5). As they draw near to the appointed place, the servants are left behind and Abraham and Isaac proceed alone, "together" (22:6). The servants do not understand what is happening, and they are not permitted to travel to the place of sacrifice. Abraham's assurance to them that he and Isaac will return indicates that he is convinced that the test will not necessarily lead to the death of his son. Abraham knows that God has a plan to bless and not to harm Isaac, and therefore he obediently follows God's instructions.

The unique recognition given to Isaac in this passage is emphasized in the description of him as "your only son" (22:2, 12, 16). This is very significant since the reader knows that Isaac is not Abraham's only son (16:16). The point is that Abraham has already lost Ishmael in a practical sense, and now he is threatened with losing Isaac as well. Isaac is Abraham's only son in another sense, since it is through Isaac that the promises will be fulfilled; he is the seed through whom the blessing must come (cf. 12:1-3; 13:16; 17:19).[1]

Isaac's question "where is the lamb?" increases the tension in the narrative, as does his father's reply, "God himself will provide the lamb" (22:7-8). The drama reaches its climax as Isaac is bound and Abraham raises his knife to kill his son (22:9-10). The importance of this is that Abraham is portrayed as willing to forgo every aspect of the promised blessing for the sake of his relationship with God; all other blessings are subordinate to this relationship. The tension is quickly released with the intervention of the angel and the substitution of the ram for Isaac (22:13). The episode concludes with a blessing pronounced by God on Abraham (22:16-18). Abraham is assured that his descendants will be as "numerous as the stars in the sky and as the sand on the seashore" (22:17 NIV).

Has the passage anything to say about child sacrifice? Child sacrifice was probably never a major problem in Israel, and it is not the main theme of this story. Nevertheless, there is a clear message that God valued the willingness of a parent to give his or her firstborn to him; but it was the life of the child that God wanted, not his death (cf. 1 Sam 1:24-28). The name of the place encapsulates the significance of the story as God's provision and is very significant for biblical theology: God makes demands but then provides his worshippers with what is needed to fulfill those demands.

The importance of the passage containing the angel's speech must not be overlooked (22:15-18). This speech reaffirms the promises of 12:1-3.[2] Chapter 12 called for Abraham's obedience (12:1). This has been demonstrated, not only in the patriarch's departure from Haran (12:4-6), but also in his willingness to sacrifice the land to Lot (13:8) and Isaac to God (22:10-12). Further-

---

1. As von Rad aptly observes, "Isaac is the child of the promise. In him every saving thing that God has promised to do is invested and guaranteed. The point here is not a natural gift, not even the highest, but rather the disappearance from Abraham's life of the whole promise"; *Genesis*, 244.

2. A similar point is made by Brueggemann: "In 22:18, the promise of 12:3 is reaffirmed. To be sure, there are other chapters yet to follow. But after this one, the dramatic intensity of the whole is noticeably relaxed"; *Genesis*: 185.

more, the promises made by Yahweh in ch. 12 are guaranteed by the provision
of Isaac and by the assurance that Yahweh intends that he shall live (22:12, 17).
This reaffirmation of ch. 12 completes the main purpose of the Abraham narrative; the passages which remain tie up the loose ends and prepare for the
transition to the Jacob stories.

One aspect of the story is disturbing: could God still make such an un-
reasonable request? On some television programs where contestants meet
challenges with risks involved, the viewers are warned not to try this at home.
The story of Abraham offering Isaac should carry a similar warning. This is a
one-off incident that is related in Genesis to fulfill a particular purpose. It was
not intended to suggest that God asks his subjects to carry out particular tasks
for which they must suspend their judgment and act against reason. I remember hearing about seminary students in Africa who decided to test God with
their strong faith, so they stepped out into a lake to walk on the water like St.
Peter. As far as I remember the incident, a number of them were drowned!
The story of the offering of Isaac suggests that God tested Abraham's faith,
but it does not give us permission to test God by putting our own or someone
else's life at risk to prove a point.

22:20-24 Genealogical Information about Abraham's Brother, Nahor

Part of this process of bringing the Abraham cycle to a conclusion while preparing for what still lies ahead is seen in 22:20-24. This pericope provides genealogical information relating to Abraham's brother, Nahor. Twelve sons of
Nahor are named, eight borne by his wife and four by a concubine. However,
the most important character in the genealogy for the continuation of the
Genesis story is Nahor's granddaughter, Rebekah. Normally a granddaughter
or even a daughter would not be mentioned in a genealogy, but in the context
of the death of Sarah the introduction of Rebekah gives hope for the continuation of the family line. Chapter 22 confirms Isaac as the one through whom
the promises to Abraham will be fulfilled. It is, therefore, an appropriate context in which to introduce the girl who will eventually be his wife.

While the chapter emphasizes the faith and obedience of Abraham, at
the same time it points beyond him to the future of the promised line of descent through Isaac and his offspring. The reaffirmation of the promises
(22:15-18) points back to the initial divine communication with Abraham
(12:1-3) and underscores Yahweh's commitment to the fulfillment of his
promises.

23:1-20 Abraham and the Purchase
of Land from the Hittites

A crisis regarding land arises after the death of Sarah, because Abraham does not own any land. He describes himself as "an alien and a stranger" (23:4 NIV). The Hittites reply, describing Abraham as "a mighty prince among us" (lit., "prince of God"). They insist that Abraham does not need to own property in order to bury his dead, since they will make their choicest sepulchres available to him (23:6). This seems a very generous offer, but it is probably an attempt to prevent Abraham from owning property.

Perhaps the Hittites are concerned that if Abraham becomes a landowner he will be a threat to them. Responding to their offer, Abraham proposes that he purchase land from a specified individual, Ephron son of Zohar. As Kidner suggests, Abraham makes "skilful use of the fact that while a group tends to resent an intruder the owner of an asset may welcome a customer."[1] Abraham's ploy is effective and he becomes the legal owner of the property. Those who have made purchases from a Near Eastern market will recognize that the initial offer, "I will give it to you," is not a serious suggestion but a way of opening the haggling. As von Rad comments, the negotiations are "a delightful miniature of adroit Oriental conversation!"[2]

Abraham, in a dignified manner, does not haggle but accepts the first price mentioned, even though it is very high (23:16).[3] The necessity of a burial site for his wife, his own wealth, and the significance of the legal possession of the land make the price irrelevant. As Westermann suggests, "it is so important for Abraham to gain unimpeachable possession of the burial place that he will pay any amount for it."[4]

The narrator undoubtedly intends us to regard this acquisition as part of the fulfillment of the promise of land; otherwise, that promise is never fulfilled personally to Abraham.

Von Rad is emphatic on this point:

---

1. Kidner, *Genesis*, 145.
2. Von Rad, *Genesis*, 247.
3. As Vawter comments, "We have no way of being sure, but we may doubtless surmise with the greatest probability that it was a noble sum indeed that Ephron exacted. . . . David bought the temple site and the materials for sacrifice for fifty silver shekels (2 Samuel 24:24). In any case, Abraham paid the stipulated price without protest. It undoubtedly pleased the biblical author to record that the patriarchal tombs at Machpelah had passed from Hittite ownership into that of the Hebrews by no deed of condescension from the inhabitants of Canaan but only through a munificent gesture of Israel's great ancestor"; *On Genesis*, 264-65.
4. Westermann, *Genesis 12–36*, 375.

Did the patriarchs who forsook everything for the sake of the promise go unrewarded? No, answers our narrative. In death they were heirs and no longer "strangers." A very small part of the Promised Land — the grave — belonged to them; therefore they did not have to rest in "Hittite earth" or in the grave of a Hittite (cf. v. 6), which Israel would have considered a hardship difficult to bear.[5]

The importance of the fact that Sarah is buried in the land of promise is underscored by repetition of the location of the tomb at Hebron "in the land of Canaan" (23:2, 19). The purchase of this land completes the development of the theme of "land" in the Abraham narratives. The theme began as "the land I will show you" (12:1). Then the land of Canaan is identified as the land which Abraham's seed will possess (12:7), and later it is promised to Abraham personally (13:15). One final development before Abraham actually possesses a token part of the land is the promise of the land under oath (15:18). In each case the development of the promise of land is preceded by an act of obedience or an indication of faith on the part of Abraham. Thus, the first explicit promise that Canaan will be the possession of Abraham's seed is given after he arrives there in obedience to the divine command (12:4-7). Second, the land is promised to Abraham personally, after he has refused to fight over it and after he has given Lot the opportunity to choose (13:9). Third, the promise of land on oath follows the statement that "Abram believed the LORD, and he credited it to him as righteousness" (15:6). Finally, the test of Abraham in relation to Isaac and his unfaltering obedience (22:1-10) are the background against which he acquires possession of the land at Machpelah (ch. 23). Thus Sarah is buried at the age of 127 years, but Abraham will live on for a further 48 years.[6]

24:1-67 The Selection of a Bride for Isaac

Chapter 24 records how a bride is obtained from Aram-naharaim for Isaac. The chapter divides into two main sections: the commission of the servant (vv. 1-9) and the servant's journey and return (vv. 10-67). This structure permits the narrator to emphasize the main points of the story by twofold repetition: first by Abraham to the servant and second by the servant to Rebekah's

5. Von Rad, *Genesis*, 250.
6. While Sarah's age at death (127) may be understood literally, Wenham mentions that "the midrash saw symbolism in it: 100 stands for great age, 20 beauty, and 7 blamelessness"; *Genesis 16–50*, 125.

family. Thus, v. 3, repeated in v. 37, describes how Abraham made his servant swear that he would ensure that Isaac did not marry a Canaanite. In v. 4, repeated in v. 38, Abraham commands the servant to take a wife for Isaac from Abraham's own relatives. This repetition highlights the insistence that the line of descent through Isaac must be through endogamous marriage.[1]

Another issue raised in ch. 24 relates to whether Isaac should return to the land of Abraham's kindred in the event of it being impossible to persuade a girl to travel to Canaan. For reasons of diplomacy this cannot be repeated by the servant to Rebekah's family, but the point is highlighted by its repetition in the question/answer format in which Abraham emphatically refuses to permit Isaac to return to Aram-naharaim (24:5-6). Furthermore, the refusal is repeated once more in v. 8, leaving an indelible impression in the reader's mind that Isaac must under no circumstances leave Canaan. The reason for this insistence that Isaac stay in Canaan is that the offspring of Abraham and the land of Canaan together symbolize the early stages of the fulfillment of God's promises. As Van Seters observes,

> It is precisely in v. 7a that we are given the reason why Isaac is not to return to Abraham's homeland. It is because God took him from there to give, under oath, this new land to his offspring, and, therefore, for Isaac to return to his father's homeland would be a rejection of that promise.[2]

At the same time, the insistence that Isaac should not return seems strange in the light of Jacob's later return to the same place. Isaac is also warned not to go to Egypt during a famine. Abraham went to Egypt and Jacob to both Haran and Egypt, but Isaac never leaves Canaan.

The name of the servant is not given, but perhaps it was the person named earlier as "Eliezer of Damascus" (15:2). The servant must swear by the Lord, "the God of heaven and the God of the earth" (24:3). Is there any particular significance in these titles? We saw that in his meeting with Melchizedek God is "God most high, Possessor of heaven and earth" (14:19-20), and after the oath with Abimelech he is described as "Everlasting God" (21:23). Probably the significance here is that no matter where the servant travels — even if he goes back to Damascus — he will not leave the jurisdiction of the God of heaven and earth.

The servant is obviously not alone on this journey. With 10 camels laden with valuables he probably has an armed escort. These are very different circumstances from Jacob's lonely journey to Aram-naharaim via Bethel.

1. See Ezra 9:12 for the postexilic view on marriage.
2. Van Seters, *Abraham in History and Tradition*, 241.

As in earlier stories, no details of the journey are given until the servant reaches the desired destination. He addresses God, not in the earlier impersonal terms of "God of heaven and the earth," but more personally as "the God of my master Abraham" (24:12). He does not question whether God has power to help him but simply pleads that God will show "steadfast love" to Abraham. The servant recognizes that he is merely Abraham's representative, but he believes that God can influence events and give him success. The servant has deep personal faith in his master's God, and he prayerfully proposes a way that God can help him.

The servant asks God to bring the chosen girl to him and then to confirm to him that she is the chosen one. His prayer indicates that he believes that God has made a decision already and that a particular girl has been chosen. All that is needed now is for her to be revealed to him. The servant's confident assumption is that God is totally in control and has already picked a wife for Isaac. The God of heaven and earth is also the God of Abraham.

The servant's proposal that the chosen girl not only offer him something to drink but also water his camels is a good test because the servant has 10 camels, each of which could drink considerable amounts of water, and it is not the sort of job that anyone would take on lightly. The servant relies on God to influence the chosen person to undertake voluntarily a task that is well beyond the usual obligation to a stranger.

We are not told whether Rebekah is the first girl with whom he tries his chosen formula, but when she comes there is no doubt that she surpasses all expectations. She lowers her jar quickly to give Abraham's servant a drink, and then she not only offers to water the camels but to draw water until they have had their fill — a very generous offer. Apparently this in itself does not fully convince the servant, but when he hears that she is from Abraham's kith and kin he praises the Lord and acknowledges that he has been led by the Lord to the right place (24:27).

Laban, who will play a major role later in the narrative, meets the servant, but the main emphasis is on the qualities of Rebekah, the prospective heiress of the promises made to Abraham and Sarah. First, Rebekah's diligence and haste in offering hospitality to the stranger are noteworthy (24:15-21) and are comparable with the practice of her great-uncle Abraham (18:1-5). Sternberg describes this as an "elevating analogy" which "stamps her as worthy of the patriarch himself."[3] At the same time, Rebekah's selfless action contrasts sharply with the reaction of her brother Laban, whose offer of hospitality seems directly related to his perception of the wealth and generosity of the

3. Sternberg, *The Poetics of Biblical Narrative*, 138.

visitor (24:28-32).[4] Second, the narrative highlights the willingness of Rebekah to leave home (24:58). By leaving Aram-naharaim to go to the land of Canaan, she follows in the footsteps of Abraham. Rebekah is, therefore, much more active in the story than Sarah has been.

The link between Rebekah and Sarah is made in 24:67; Isaac brings her (Rebekah) into the tent of his mother Sarah, he marries Rebekah and she becomes his wife, and he loves her; and Isaac is comforted after his mother's death. Von Rad comments on this verse:

> The series "he took Rebekah, she became his wife, and he loved her" is not the one familiar to us from novels. . . . With that the story has reached its goal: there is now another ancestress for Abraham's seed. Precisely because of this goal the mention of Sarah's tent is important.[5]

The marriage of Isaac and Rebekah is the result of the successful mission of Abraham's servant, but the reader is aware that the entire episode has been controlled and accomplished by God himself.

25:1-11 Isaac in Relation to the Other Descendants of Abraham

Chapter 25 introduces Abraham's third wife, Keturah. Their marriage produces six children, and the family line of two of them is given. An unknown number of concubines are also credited with bearing children to Abraham, but details are not given (25:6). The narrative implies no criticism of Abraham, and his large family is evidence of the fulfillment of the earlier promises that he would have numerous progeny (15:5). Nothing disparaging is said about Keturah, the concubines, or their offspring, but there is a clear demarcation between them and Isaac. Isaac is given a position of unmistakable prominence as the son of Abraham in a special and unique sense, and through him Abraham's most significant line of descent is traced — the line of promise and blessing. This special status of Isaac is reflected in the distinction made between the inheritance Abraham bequeathes to Isaac, to whom "he left everything he owned," and the gifts that he provides for the children of his concubines, who are exiled eastwards away from Isaac (25:5-6).

Abraham's death is recorded briefly; he died at "a good old age, an old man and full of years, and was gathered to his people" (25:8). This is the idi-

---

4. Roth speaks of "Laban's suspiciously quick reaction to precious metal"; "The Wooing of Rebekah," 182.

5. Von Rad, *Genesis*, 259.

omatic way of conveying that Abraham's life was successful and even his death was exemplary. His sons bury him in the cave of Machpelah. This is the last recorded occasion when Ishmael and Isaac are seen together as brothers. They are united as sons of Abraham but divided by the special status afforded to Isaac. Ishmael's reaction to his inferior status is not recorded since the story is told from the point of view of those who regarded themselves as descendants of Abraham through Isaac.

These 11 verses are not just an exercise in tying up loose ends; rather, they provide a smooth transition from the life of Abraham to the story of Isaac and his descendants. They show that the promises made have been fulfilled. They end Abraham's life on a satisfactory note. Even good men must die, but Abraham dies with all his hopes realized and his dreams fulfilled. He had a good life followed by a good death. As Brueggemann comments,

> Abraham had lived a long, blessed life. He had a good burial plot. The death of Abraham is peaceable because he dies midst the generations, confident that all things valuable have been transmitted to his son(s).[1]

The reader's attention is now focused on Isaac by the comment that "after Abraham's death, God blessed his son Isaac" (25:11). Isaac is related to Abraham, not just as his son, but as the one to whom the promises of blessing and descendants have been passed on.

25:12-18 Family History of Ishmael

A short section entitled the family history of Ishmael records his age at death as 137 and lists the names of his 12 sons who became tribal chiefs. The only detail given about Ishmael and his descendants is ambiguous in Hebrew, as the following sample of versions shows (25:18).

> They settled from Havilah to Shur, which is opposite Egypt in the direction of Assyria. He settled over against all his kinsmen. (ESV)
> And they dwelt from Havilah unto Shur, that is before Egypt, as thou goest toward Assyria: and he died in the presence of all his brethren. (KJV)
> His descendants settled in the area from Havilah to Shur, near the border of Egypt, as you go towards Asshur. And they lived in hostility toward all their brothers. (NIV)

1. Brueggemann, *Genesis*, 203.

(They dwelt from Havilah as far as Shur, which is east of Egypt as you go toward Assyria.) He died in the presence of all his brethren. (NKJV)

They settled from Havilah to Shur, which is opposite Egypt in the direction of Assyria; he settled down alongside of all his people. (NRSV)

The record of his death is shorter than that of Abraham: Ishmael "breathed his last and died, and he was gathered to his people" (25:17). Though Ishmael's age at death seems very impressive by modern standards, it is not described as a "good old age," nor is he described as "full of years." Even in these details of his death the narrator gives the minimum details because his focus is fixed on the line through Isaac. Thus when Isaac dies he is described as "old and full of days" (35:29).

Although he is overshadowed by Isaac, Ishmael is an important character in Genesis and his relationship to Abraham is carefully explicated. Ishmael is more closely related to Abraham than Lot, and it is clearly emphasized that Ishmael, in contrast to Lot, shares in the blessings promised to Abraham. On the other hand, a clear distinction is made between Isaac and Ishmael, and it is the former who is recognized as the heir to the divine promises.

25:19-28 The Birth of Esau and Jacob

Now that Ishmael's family history has been summarized briefly, the spotlight falls on the family of Isaac, and his history, of course, is much more detailed. A short genealogy featuring Isaac, the son of Abraham, and Rebekah, the daughter of Bethuel and sister of Laban, introduces the section (25:20) and acquaints the reader with the people who will feature in the following narratives.

The genealogical material is followed immediately, not with the account of the births of Jacob and Esau, but with a short passage informing the reader that, to begin with, Rebekah is unable to have children and Isaac must entreat Yahweh on her behalf (25:21). It is important to recall, at this stage, that fertility is a particularly significant aspect of blessing in Genesis (cf. 1:22, 28; 9:1; 12:2; 13:16; 15:5; 17:2, 16; 22:17). At the time the OT was written, the earth was not overpopulated, and the success of people seems to have been calculated in correlation to the size of their families. Men could multiply progeny by recourse to polygamy, but while this is not explicitly condemned in Genesis, the impression given is that it leads to serious interfamily feuds. Isaac was born into a home where explosive tensions were caused by the second wife and her son. It is not reading too much between the lines to see Isaac's monogamy as his reaction to his own experience when he saw the pain and sorrow that Abraham's relationship with Hagar had introduced into their home. Thus when Isaac discovers that his own wife is childless, rather than marry another, he prays for her.

One reason for the emphasis on Rebekah's childlessness is that it provides a link with the Abraham story (cf. 11:30); it also places the birth of Jacob and Esau in the category of special divine blessing.[1] Isaac's birth demonstrated that children are a gift from Yahweh, and even the timing of birth is firmly in God's control. Now in order to have children himself, Isaac acknowledges Yahweh's power and control over childbirth. Isaac's faith is not disappointed, and in answer to his prayer Rebekah becomes pregnant with twins.

During the pregnancy a struggle takes place between the twins. Now it is Rebekah's turn to pray; alarmed by what is happening in her womb, she appeals to Yahweh (25:22). She is informed that she will be the mother of two boys who will be the fathers of two nations. Contrary to normal expectation, the older will serve the younger (25:23). These comments predict that the disturbance in Rebekah's womb is just the beginning of the struggles between her offspring; they will also struggle for approval and blessing during their lifetimes, and when they die their descendants, the Israelites and the Edomites, will continue the struggle. The reference to the two nations invites the readers to view Jacob and Esau, not only as individuals, but also as ancestors of their respective nations. The lives and characteristics of these twins reflect in microcosm the nations that they foreshadow.

Isaac and Rebekah are caught up in a struggle that they do not fully understand, one that will eventually put strains on their own relationship; nevertheless, they acknowledge that Yahweh is in control and both prayerfully entreat him for help and guidance. Although their favoritism will divide them later, at this stage prayer unites them as supplicants of Yahweh's mercy and grace. This may represent an intentional contrast to the prayerful way that Isaac and Rebekah approach the question of childbirth and the later shenanigans of Jacob's wives.

The text makes an important statement about Yahweh: the power to give life is in his hands, and the mysteries of life, even including what happens inside the womb, are open to him. The passage highlights Yahweh's independence; his plans are not constrained by human traditions or what is the ex-

---

1. Hirsch observes, "We see here how, not only the first stone, but the further building up of the House of Israel had to come only as a direct gift from the Almightiness of God"; *Commentary on the Torah*, 1:422; cf. Brueggemann, *Genesis*, 212.

pected norm. Yahweh does the unexpected and makes no apology for ignoring the traditional rights of the firstborn in favor of his younger brother. A similar situation arises in the choice of David as king, where the explanation is that God makes the unlikely choice of the youngest son because he can see what is in his heart. No such comment is made to exonerate Jacob; he is not chosen because of his character but in spite of it. As Brueggemann aptly comments,

> Jacob is announced as a visible expression of God's remarkable graciousness in the face of conventional definitions of reality and prosperity. Jacob is a scandal from the beginning. The powerful grace of God is a scandal. It upsets the way we would organize life.[2]

Following Yahweh's disclosure to Rebekah, the two boys, Esau and Jacob, are born (25:24-26). Esau is the firstborn, but apparently only by a short time since Jacob is born holding his brother's heel. Jacob's name is linked to this incident and, in particular, to the word "heel," which makes powerful wordplays based on Jacob's name. It is unlikely that the parents intentionally give their son a name with a pejorative implication; their intended meaning is probably "may God protect."[3] According to Sarna, the origin of the name is "a plea for divine protection of the newly born."[4] However, because of the similarity between the name and the word for heel, the name also suggests the idea of tripping someone up. Jacob's grasping his brother's heel at birth followed by his act of deceiving his father and his dogged determination to get his own way means that his name becomes synonymous with deviousness (27:36; cf. Jer 9:4). Esau's name is linked to the comment that at birth his entire body is like a hairy garment.

Although twins, it is the differences between the boys that the account emphasizes. Esau, a man of wide open spaces, knows how to hunt, but Jacob, the quiet man, prefers to stay inside the tent. Parental preferences develop — Isaac loves Esau and Rebekah loves Jacob. Rebekah's preference for Jacob is not explained, leaving the reader to ponder whether her preferences are based on Jacob's lifestyle and his predisposition for the domestic scene or whether she has some deeper intuition based on Yahweh's revelation to her before the birth of the boys. Isaac's preference, however, is clearly explained; he likes Esau because of his hunting skills, since Isaac is "fond of game" (25:28).

2. Brueggemann, *Genesis*, 217.
3. Von Rad, *Genesis*, 265.
4. Sarna, *Genesis*, 180.

25:29-34 Jacob Strikes a Bargain with his Brother

The account of the birth is succeeded by an incident in the early adult life of the two sons. Esau the firstborn, who becomes a hunter, sells his birthright[1] to his brother Jacob (a quiet man, living in tents) for a plate of stew (25:27-33). Later, Esau claims that Jacob has deceived him over the birthright, but the nature of this deception is not clear in the text. Von Rad makes the interesting suggestion that when Esau saw the red food being prepared he thought that it was "blood soup" and was disappointed to find that it contained only lentils.[2] Whether the price agreed was "blood soup" or lentil stew, the narrator's verdict is that Esau "despised his birthright" (25:34). Perhaps Esau later regrets his rashness and tries to suggest that it was only a joke, but in making his birthright the subject of a joke he had indeed despised it.

26:1-11 Déjà Vu

This passage recalls an incident in the life of Abraham (12:10-20) and offers the reader an opportunity to compare and contrast the reactions of Isaac with those of Abraham in similar circumstances. The text refers back to Abram's arrival in the land when Canaan was in the grip of a severe famine, an affliction that recurs in Isaac's time (26:1). Although Abram left the land and went to Egypt during the famine, Yahweh commands Isaac not to leave (26:2). Yahweh declares that if Isaac remains in the land he will give it to him and to his descendants, who will be as numerous as the stars (26:2-4). Furthermore, all nations will be blessed through his offspring. This divine reassurance enables Isaac to endure the hardship, believing that the famine will end soon and that God will faithfully fulfil his promises. This decision to stay in Canaan should have avoided the necessity of repeating his father's deceptive wife/sister strategy, but in spite of the promises of God, Isaac repeats this folly. Like Abram, he declares that his wife is his sister. This deception leads to Abimelech's confronting Isaac in much the same way as he confronted Abram. Abimelech fears the guilt that even inadvertent adultery would bring on his people, while Isaac, like Abram, remains indifferent to the danger that he has imposed on the ancestress of Israel. The story demonstrates that the low opinion that Abram and Isaac had of the heathen kings was unjustified.

1. The birthright was the special status of the firstborn which included the right to extra inheritance (cf. Deut 21:17).
2. Von Rad, *Genesis* 266.

They believed that men like Pharaoh and Abimelech and their servants would have no scruples about taking another man's wife and that they would be afraid of being killed. However, both Abram and Isaac were wrong, and the behavior of the two kings was exemplary. Could this be a message intended for later Israelite readers, that although the heathen did not have the Torah, they still knew right from wrong and were to be respected when they acted on this knowledge? Canaan before the Israelites entered was not a lawless society, and it was well known to the early readers of Genesis that the act of killing a man and taking his wife was done by an Israelite king and not by the heathen (2 Sam 11:1-27).

26:12-33 Blessing and Trouble

As a result of Isaac's personal obedience demonstrated by his remaining in the land, he "reaped a hundredfold, because the LORD blessed him" (26:12 NIV). A hundredfold is an exceptionally high yield. In medieval Britain a yield of two or three times was normal. However, documents from ancient Mesopotamia record yields as high as 75 times, but Isaac's one hundredfold is a tremendous crop and clear evidence that Yahweh was blessing him. Verse 13, which describes the exponential growth of Isaac's wealth, is difficult to translate into English without losing something of the movement and energy of the original Hebrew, which suggests that Isaac was becoming richer all the time. English translations obscure the fact that the Hebrew root גדל/*gdl,* which means "to be great," is repeated three times in this verse. Brueggemann links the use of this terminology with God's promise to make Abram a "great nation" and to make his name great, and he describes this as "the prototype of Israelite blessedness."[1]

The recurring theme of famine in the Abraham, Jacob, and Joseph cycles is obviously an important element in the stories. But what is their purpose? Just as the patriarchs themselves experience periods of childlessness, the land also goes through times of barrenness, which would lead the reader to question whether Yahweh had a purpose in allowing this to happen.[2] In this context, the fertility of the land is causally related to the obedience of Isaac, providing evidence that he is the recipient of blessing. If this is so, may

1. Brueggemann, *Genesis,* 222.
2. Hirsch argues that the repeated references to famines are a reminder that "the blossoming of this land is not to be dependent merely on the work of man and the favour of nature, but, in the first place, on the morality and integrity of its inhabitants"; *Commentary on the Torah,* 1:429.

we then expect that the absence of blessing (during a famine, for example) should be linked with a particular failure on the part of the patriarchs? But this is not the case, since the role of the "barrenness" and "famine" motifs seems to be "testing" rather than punishment.[3] Thus when Abraham first arrives in Canaan, there is no record of any failure or misdemeanor on his part, and yet Canaan is in the grips of a famine severe enough to force him to leave the land and go to Egypt. It is possible that the famines are linked, not to misdemeanors of the patriarchs, but to the sins of the Canaanites. However, if this is the case, no explicit link is made.

Blessing and trouble are not necessarily experiences that we think of as closely associated, but in this passage they are inseparable. It is a mistake to think that blessing is the absence of problems. A person may experience many problems and still maintain a sense of being richly blessed and sustained through the difficulties. In Isaac's situation, the material blessing is the root cause of some of his troubles. His wealth and blessing attract unwelcome attention from the Philistines, who are envious of his success (26:14). Quarrelling continues because of disputed water rights (26:19-21). Throughout this dispute, Isaac is the innocent party whose wells are either seized or filled in by his enemies. Since the wells are deliberately sabotaged, this is not a question of one group depriving the other of essential supplies of water; it is an example of wanton vandalism motivated by jealousy.

Isaac is a peace-loving man who avoids conflict where possible. When Abimelech's men claim one of his wells, he does not protest and make a fuss but quietly moves on until he finds another well. Some would say he was foolish not to claim what was rightly his, and undoubtedly his son Jacob would have taken an entirely different approach. However, Isaac's patience pays off, and eventually a well is discovered that the Philistines do not dispute. Isaac gives it the significant name Rehoboth, which means "wide open spaces," commenting, "Now the LORD has made room for us, and we shall be fruitful in the land" (26:22). Isaac recognizes the benefit of possessing territory that no one else claims. This is a blessing indeed and a rare commodity in many parts of the world today where the majority of wars relate to conflicting terri-

---

3. On the other hand, Donaldson argues that the barrenness of the wives of the patriarchs is linked to incorrect marriage relationships: "Barrenness is used here [i.e., in Genesis] as the key indicator of an 'incorrect' relationship. In each case the barrenness of the matriarchs is overcome by an act of God (21:1-2; 25:21; 30:22)." Thus, according to Donaldson, "the narratives reflect the tension between types of kinship relationships and legitimate marriages"; "Kinship Theory," 83. The difficulty with this approach is that the barrenness of the matriarchs is presented as testing and not as punishment. Furthermore, not all exogamous marriages in Genesis result in barrenness (cf. 36:1-43).

torial claims. As Isaac recognizes, conflicts are counterproductive and hinder people and nations from realizing their full potential. Brueggemann highlights the importance of this concept of space and suggests that it is "a major motif of the blessing theme," reflecting the "awareness of people who have had no safe place" or who are "often facing exile."[4]

Isaac's satisfaction and fulfillment is the realization that Yahweh has made room for him related to physical space, but many who read Genesis today are suburbanites who expect water to flow from a tap or buy it bottled in a supermarket. Can this be applied to us? While the territorial claims about water rights will not apply to many readers, the underlying concept may be applied to our psychological and sociological needs to have our own space. We all need the satisfaction of having our own "breathing space" or "sphere of service" in which we can exercise our gifts and feel fulfilled. It is helpful, therefore, to think about the space God gives us — it may be our work that we feel particularly called to, or it may be the role we fulfill in our church — like Isaac, it is good to thank God for making room for us. Such gratitude for the "room" we have been given is an excellent antidote to the attitude that craves someone else's gifts and envies the work that they are doing.It can prevent us standing like cows with our heads over the fence trying to eat the grass on the other side and trying to occupy the space given to someone else. It is good to recognize and to value our own uniqueness and the special room that God has given each one of us.

Following the discovery of Rehoboth, Isaac travels to Beer-sheba, where Yahweh appears to him promising blessing and numerous progeny (26:24). In response, Isaac builds an altar and pitches his tent, much as Abraham had done. An unexpected visit from Abimelech and his top officials surprises Isaac, since he believes they hate him. However, their fear outweighs their hate and they want to make a treaty (26:26-30). The narrative emphasizes that Abimelech has been forced to make peace with Isaac because it is now obvious, even to Abimelech, that Yahweh has blessed Isaac (26:29). It was when Abimelech recognized that God was with Abram that he sued for peace, and this is repeated in relation to Isaac. Thus the presence of God with the patriarchs brought, not just fertility, but the prerequisite protection for living as a resident alien among the indigenous inhabitants of the land. Isaac prepares a feast for Abimelech, and his men and exchange oaths with them, thus ending the conflict (26:31). That day Isaac's servants find another well, leading to the naming of that place "Beer-sheba," the "well of the oath" (26:33).

The story of Isaac's life is short and comparatively uneventful, but as the

4. Brueggemann, *Genesis*, 225.

heir of the promises made to Abraham, he is highly significant. Closely linked with the land of Canaan, which he never leaves, Isaac's story epitomizes the life of faith in the promised land — a life with many trials and enemies, but lived in harmony with Yahweh and enjoying his protection and showing clear evidence of blessing. Promises and blessing provide the main linkage between Abraham and Isaac. The blessing that Isaac receives is clearly identified as the continuance of the blessing that God promised Abraham. The fertility of Isaac's land and his increase in wealth are highlighted as evidence that Yahweh is blessing him (26:12, 29). In a divine speech addressed to Isaac (26:2-5), God promises him fruitfulness — a multitude of descendants who will become a great nation through which all nations will receive blessing. This is clearly the same blessing promised to Abraham, now entering a new stage in its fulfillment through Isaac and his offspring (cf. 12:1-3).

26:34–27:40 A Divided Family

Blessing is an unmistakable theme in ch. 27. Since the ancients were fascinated by numbers, especially three and seven, it is particularly significant that the Hebrew noun בְּרָכָה/*berākâ* occurs seven times in this passage and its verbal form 21 times.[1] The patriarchal blessing is the main focus of a struggle between Esau and Jacob to receive Isaac's blessing. Although the blessing belongs by right to Esau, the firstborn, the reader's sympathy has been wooed on Jacob's behalf through the prenatal prophecy (25:23) and by the comment that Esau married two Hittite women who "made life bitter for Isaac and Rebekah" (26:35 NRSV). The prophecy leads the reader to see, even in the deceit of Jacob and Rebekah, the controlling hand of Yahweh, while the Canaanite marriages give the impression that Esau is not a worthy custodian of the blessing.

Isaac's love of wild game has already been indicated, and as he prepares to bless his firstborn he prefers to accompany it with enjoyment of his favorite food. The food also has a symbolic significance. Just as in covenants, food helps to bring the parties together, and it creates an atmosphere of harmony and communion. Rebekah overhears the instruction given to Esau; she conspires with Jacob to deceive her husband and claim his blessing for her favorite son. She and Jacob obviously feel that this blessing is something valuable and effective, a prize to be grasped, something that will make a real difference to the life of the recipient.

Blessings in Genesis are passed on within the context of a relationship.

1. Sarna, *Genesis*, 189.

In the creation accounts God blesses his creatures when his relationship with them is harmonious, but he curses them when the harmony breaks down. If blessing is something to be grasped, then cursing is a powerful malediction to be avoided at all costs. This explains Jacob's initial reluctance to deceive his father; if his father discovers the deception, their relationship will break down, resulting in cursing instead of blessing (27:12). Jacob's reluctance to deceive is not on the basis of any moral or ethical qualms; he is afraid of being caught and exposed.

It is interesting to note the seriousness attached to blessing by the main characters in this drama. Rebekah risks bringing a curse upon herself and her favorite son (27:13); Jacob is prepared to trick his father, knowing that as soon as his brother returns the deception will be uncovered and he will incur his brother's wrath and his father's displeasure (27:19-24); Isaac shows how seriously he takes the matter by trembling violently when he learns that he has been tricked (27:33); and finally, Esau's bitter regret speaks for itself (27:38).

When Rebekah reports to Jacob what she has overheard, she adds to Isaac's words the phrase, "before the LORD." As Sternberg comments, the additional words probably represent an attempt "to affect the addressee's attitude."[2] Sarna suggests that Rebekah added the words "in order to impress upon Jacob the importance and solemnity of the occasion."[3] Whatever the reason, Rebekah involves Yahweh in her deception, either to justify her deceit by giving it a spiritual dimension or to highlight why the blessing is important. Perhaps she is recalling the prenatal prophecy when Yahweh informed her that the older son would serve the younger.

Rebekah instructs her younger son to bring not just one kid but two from the flock, so this is a very big meal. No expense is spared in order to deceive Isaac. She is confident that she can prepare a meal using domestic animals in such a way that Isaac will not know the difference and will think that wild game has been used. As Kidner points out, she may have "smarted" over her husband's preference in the past and now has a chance to show decisively that her cooking is equal, if not superior, to Esau's.[4] Although flocks and herds are part of Isaac's wealth and evidence that he has been blessed, these products are used to take advantage of him. He is not only deceived about the identity of the person he is blessing but also about the nature of the food he is eating; it is not wild game as he has requested but his own animals, and he does not know the difference.

2. Sternberg, *The Poetics of Biblical Narrative*, 392-93.
3. Sarna, *Genesis*, 190.
4. Kidner, *Genesis*, 156.

Aware of the danger that Jacob has already highlighted, that if his father touches his smooth skin the deception will be discovered, Rebekah covers Jacob's exposed skin with the skin of the kids. She also dresses Jacob in Esau's best robes. Since catching kids in a domestic flock is a great deal easier than shooting wild animals with a bow and arrow, unsurprisingly Jacob is first to present a meal to his father. But he is almost too fast, because Isaac becomes suspicious; he is old and blind, not stupid. In reply, Jacob must compound his deception with a lie that implicates Yahweh as he falsely claims, "the LORD your God granted me success" (27:20). This does not allay Isaac's suspicions, since he realizes the voice is Jacob's; but when he feels the hairy skin of the goats covering Jacob's smooth skin, he becomes less suspicious (27:23). Nevertheless, he asks again, "Are you really my son Esau?" (27:24). Thus the narrator shows that Isaac is very cautious. But in spite of the precautions he takes, he is the victim of a carefully orchestrated plan to divert the blessing from Esau to Jacob.

The proceedings begin with the consumption of the meal, presumably by both parties, though the text mentions that only Isaac partakes. Isaac then kisses his son and comments on the fresh outdoor odor coming from his garment (27:26-27). It is a wonderfully evocative scene as Isaac, his other senses having been dulled by age, allows the smell of the open countryside to fire his imagination and awaken within him memories of his lifetime relationship with the land. From these memories and from the depths of his being, Isaac utters the words of blessing:

> "Ah, the smell of my son is like the smell of a field that the LORD has blessed. May God give you of heaven's dew and of earth's richness — an abundance of grain and new wine. May nations serve you and peoples bow down to you. Be lord over your brothers, and may the sons of your mother bow down to you. May those who curse you be cursed and those who bless you be blessed." (27:27-29 NIV)

The content of this blessing is agricultural success and dominance (27:27-29). Its provisions would be more appropriate for a farmer than a hunter and reflect Isaac's own interest as a cultivator of crops. Isaac's reference to "the dew of heaven" reflects the climate of the Near East, where most of the rainfall is concentrated in four months of the year. During the growing season much of the moisture for crops comes from the dew and, therefore, heavy dew is considered a blessing. Sarna explains:

> The significance of dew as a factor in the hydrology of the Land of Israel gives special meaning to this aspect of the blessing. It continued to be re-

flected in the Jewish liturgy throughout the ages. Rabbinic sources report that in the days of the Second Temple, when the High Priest emerged safely from performing the sacred service in the Holy of Holies on the Day of Atonement, he uttered a short prayer for the welfare of Israel during the coming year. Among other things, he asked for an abundance of dew. To the present time, the end of the rainy season and the commencement of the rainless summer is marked in the Jewish liturgy by a prayer for dew *(tefillat tal/tikkun tal)*, which forms part of the Musaf, or Additional Service, on the first day of Passover during the reader's repetition of the Amidah. Even during the winter season, the ninth benediction of the daily Amidah couples a petition for dew with that for rain.[5]

"The fatness of the earth" is a blessing referring to healthy crops, while "plenty of grain and wine" envisages prolific growth. A second aspect of Isaac's blessing relates to relationships, to bestowed dominance and victory over friend and foe alike, and in particular refers to his mother's sons bowing down to him (27:29). The blessing also calls for cursing on those who curse the recipient and promises blessing for those who bless him. This clause repeats an aspect of the blessing pronounced on Abraham (12:1-3), but there is no reference to any direct relationship to God or to many descendants, and no direct reference is made to the blessing mediated through Abraham. This was a traditional patriarchal blessing that, though greatly valued by those concerned, is not the same as the blessing promised to Abraham and later communicated to Jacob at Bethel. The blessing promised to Abraham has an international dimension in the blessing of the nations, whereas in Isaac's blessing the main benefits are dominance in the immediate family circle and success in farming.

As Jacob exits the scene, having executed the plan to deceive Isaac successfully, Esau now appears before Isaac with yet another meal (27:31). This is a comic, though tragic, scene; Esau appears with the sort of meal that his father has requested but finds that his food is no longer required because his brother has provided a carefully disguised substitute meal. Worse still, Isaac has already uttered the formula of blessing that he believed as head of the family he had the right to bestow on his eldest son. From the point of view of our Western culture, in which we are accustomed to the idea of "taking our words back," it seems strange that Isaac should tremble while Esau weeps bitterly when they discover what Jacob has done (27:33-34). Surely, the deceitfulness of Jacob is sufficient grounds for his blessing to be annulled and redi-

---

5. Sarna, *Genesis*, 192-93.

rected to Esau. However, the story reflects the belief that when the blessing has been bestowed, it cannot be recalled. The expedient of "taking one's words back" is not an option, since the blessing cannot be undone. An earlier story tells how Esau despises his birthright and treats it lightly. This is not the case with the blessing, which he takes very seriously indeed, pleading with his father twice to bless him also (27:36-38).[6] The blessing that Isaac does eventually bestow on Esau is not a blessing at all but an acknowledgment that Jacob will be superior until eventually Esau breaks off his yoke.

Surprisingly, Isaac's blessings do not reflect the relationships between Esau and Jacob that are described in Genesis but seem to relate more to the nations of Israel and Edom, the descendants of Jacob and Esau respectively. According to the historical narratives in Kings, Edom was a vassal nation of King David but later gained independence.

However, to the lives of Jacob and Esau, the blessing that they struggle over is, apparently, irrelevant; Esau never serves Jacob and seems to be more powerful in the following narratives. The blessing stipulates that Jacob's brothers will bow down to him, but he bows seven times to Esau (33:3). The blessing of Isaac seems to be a traditional patriarchal blessing made to a set formula without much relevance to the lifestyles of Jacob or Esau, both of whom seem more involved with livestock than with cultivation. The important themes of being the father of numerous seed, possession of Canaan, and being a source of blessing for the nations are absent from this blessing. Isaac's blessing is an impassioned expression of his innermost desires as a farmer, but it lacks the vision and depth of other blessings in Genesis, including that bestowed by Isaac on the eve of Jacob's departure for Paddan-aram (28:3-4). Thus the blessing that Jacob and his mother value so highly and obtain so deviously is irrelevant to Jacob's life, and yet it cost them dearly since they would never see each other again. Their best efforts and most daring schemes are aimed at achieving the blessing of Isaac that is only a pale shadow of the blessing that Yahweh has in store for him and will bestow at Bethel. Like Abraham's marriage to Hagar, the deceitful acquisition of blessing is an attempt to obtain by human efforts that which has been divinely promised. Yahweh is working to a plan and schedule for Jacob's life that are far superior to anything that he has envisaged, and Jacob's own devious schemes cannot hinder Yahweh's plan and purposes.

6. There is an interesting play on the words "blessing" and "birthright" in 27:36: בְּכֹרָתִי/ *bĕkōrātî* ("my birthright"); בִּרְכָתִי/*birkātî* ("my blessing").

27:41–28:9 Jacob's Departure from Home

Jacob's departure is directly linked to the blessing that he gained by deceit (27:1-40). Esau is so greatly outraged by what Jacob has done that the latter's life is in danger (27:41). News of this reaches Rebekah, who decides that Jacob should seek refuge with her brother Laban "for a few days" (27:43-45 NKJV). The deceit has backfired, and Rebekah must now bear the consequences and either send her son away or risk Esau killing Jacob, just as Cain killed Abel.

Before Jacob departs, Rebekah, now working with Isaac rather than against him, encourages him to send Jacob away to her brother Laban so that he can arrange an endogamous marriage. Isaac agrees and gives Jacob a blessing before his departure (27:46–28:5). Once again Isaac blesses Jacob, but this time he is fully aware who is the recipient of the blessing. This perhaps signals the reconciliation of Isaac to his son Jacob, but more importantly it represents the reconciliation of Isaac to the divine purposes. Isaac is now blessing the son whom God has chosen for blessing without having to be tricked into doing so.

The use of the verbs "be fruitful" and "multiply" in this blessing is reminiscent of the prominence of the same verbs in the creation blessings (1:22, 28) and also in the blessing on Noah and his sons after the flood (9:1, 7). Jacob and his descendants are chosen to be God's new creation upon whom his blessing rests.

Isaac invokes the blessing of El Shaddai upon Jacob (28:3). This significant name has been linked in 17:1 with the concept of the covenant between God and Abraham. It leads Isaac on naturally to express the desire that Jacob will experience the blessing of Abraham, not only for himself but for his descendants also. The blessing is, in this context of Jacob's departure from Canaan, specifically linked to the possession of the land by his descendants (28:4). The message is clear that Jacob, as the one who has been blessed, will be absent from Canaan for only a limited period. He must return to it, since the promised blessings are inextricably bound up with that land.

The clause "that you may become a company of peoples" (28:3 NRSV) emphasizes the multiplicity of Jacob's offspring. As we have seen, this relates to fertility, which is often closely associated with blessing.

Following this blessing on Jacob, a brief pericope indicates that Esau is still anxious to be blessed. When Esau hears that Jacob has gone to Paddan-aram to marry a relative with his father's blessing, it seems that, for the first time, he realizes that his father disapproves of Canaanite women (28:6). Esau reacts by marrying a daughter of Ishmael (28:7-9). It seems that by marrying a granddaughter of Abraham he hopes to please his father and attract his blessing. Esau is portrayed as someone who tries hard but who does not really understand the main issues. Esau is deluded if he thinks that marrying another woman will lessen the problems for Isaac and Rebekah posed by his present wives.

However, the main emphasis in the passage is that Jacob's departure from Canaan receives the blessing of his father and the support of his mother (28:1-5). His father's blessing is linked with the earlier blessings bestowed on Abraham, and the content is similar; prominence is given to the idea of fertility and to the return of Jacob to the land of Canaan where the promises made to Abraham will be fulfilled.

As Jacob goes into exile he foreshadows the experience of the nation of Israel. Jacob was not innocent and deserves the enforced exile, just as Adam deserved expulsion from Eden. However, in spite of all his faults, Jacob is the heir to the promises of Abraham, and ultimately with the help of God he will return. His experiences are reflected in the history of Israel and would provide a source of courage and reassurance for others who like him found themselves in exile.

28:10-22 Jacob's Encounter with God at Bethel

While Bethel is mentioned in the Abraham narrative (12:8; 13:3), it is during the Jacob Cycle that the place becomes prominent. It is the scene for the blessing of Jacob by Yahweh, and it is the place to which Jacob will return again when in need of guidance and encouragement (cf. 35:1). Like the Babel incident, this story deals with questions about communications between heaven and earth. It shows that the aim of the builders to reach heaven with their tower was not impossible, but such contact between heaven and earth must be initiated by God. Humans cannot build up to heaven, but God can reach down to them. The fear of the temple-builders about being scattered is reflected in Jacob's own experience as he is forced away from home. Jacob, like them, had tried to force his father, and ultimately God, to bless him. In doing this he sought to take control of his destiny and make a name for himself. Now he must learn that while he is struggling to snatch blessing from others God is freely offering it to him. God's encounter with Jacob occurs, "not in wakeful control but in a time of vulnerable yielding, while he is asleep."[1] Jacob, who from that moment of birth, when his tiny hand grasped his brother's heel, sought to take the initiative, must now yield control to God.

---

1. Brueggemann, *Genesis*, 241.

Jacob's encounter with God at Bethel is set in the context of a dream during which he sees "a ladder set up on the earth, and the top of it reached to heaven. And behold, the angels of God were ascending and descending on it!" (28:12 ESV). The Hebrew word for "angel" also means "messenger"; therefore, we may assume that they were actively involved in carrying communications between heaven and earth. We should not envisage these as creatures with wings, since winged creatures in the OT are referred to as "cherubim" or "seraphim." Jacob is aware, not only of the angelic beings, but, more significantly, of the presence of Yahweh, the God of his fathers. The text is not entirely clear about the exact location of Yahweh in the dream. He is described as standing עָלָיו/'ālāyw. This could mean that he stood "above (the ladder)," or it could also be translated that he stood "beside him (Jacob)." Most versions, including KJV, NIV, and NLT, opt for "above it," as referring to the ladder or stairway, but the NRSV translates "the LORD stood beside him," and a similar translation is adopted by NJPS. Either translation is possible, but the idea that God stood beside Jacob seems very appropriate in the light of his later comment, "Surely the LORD is in this place — and I did not know it!" (28:16 NRSV). Jacob experiences God's presence very close to him. God is not far away at the top of the stairs or ladder but right beside him as he sleeps. God is not inaccessible but has come down to renew the promises of Abraham to this fugitive.[2]

This is the first time that Yahweh addresses Jacob directly. As we have already observed, the introduction of direct speech in a narrative is particularly significant. However, when the speaker is Yahweh, it gives the passage special significance.

The blessing itself is prefaced by Yahweh's self-introduction as "the LORD, the God of your grandfather Abraham and the God of your father Isaac" (28:13). This makes a clear connection, therefore, between the revelation to Jacob and the earlier revelations and promises of blessing given to Abraham and Isaac. It is very significant to have these three names mentioned in the same verse: Abraham, Isaac, and Jacob are together the founding fathers of the Israelite nation, God's chosen people.

After the divine speaker has identified himself, he promises that Jacob and his descendants will inherit the land on which he is lying. We see here the close link between two main aspects of God's promises to the patriarchs: land and blessing. The reference to Jacob's descendants being as numerous as the dust of the earth reminds the reader that the same promise was made earlier

---

2. Jesus was probably alluding to this incident when he referred to "the angels of God ascending and descending on the Son of Man" (John 1:51).

to Abraham (13:16). Concomitant with this is the idea that his descendants will "spread out to the west and to the east, to the north and to the south." This not only underscores the idea of multiplicity but also suggests victory and dominance over other nations (28:14). However, the result of the dominance of Jacob's descendants is not tyranny but blessing to other nations (28:14). The link with the blessings bestowed on Abraham is unmistakable (cf. 12:3; 18:18). Furthermore, the idea that Jacob's descendants can spread in every direction is a further reflection on the Babel story, in which the people are scattered because of divine disapproval of their plans. Now Jacob's descendants will be dispersed throughout the earth with God's approval. Finally, the pronouncement of blessing on Jacob at Bethel includes the promise of divine protection:

> "I am with you and will watch over you wherever you go, and I will bring you back to this land. I will not leave you until I have done what I have promised you." (28:15 NIV)

We have already observed that divine protection can be an aspect of blessing. God protects Noah and his family from the flood when the rest of mankind suffer from the effects of cursing, which, of course, is the antithesis of blessing (7:21–8:1). Protection is also implicit in the promise to Abraham that whoever blesses him will be blessed, whereas any who despise him will incur divine malediction (12:3). After Abraham's victory over his enemies, Melchizedek acknowledges that he has been blessed by God (14:19-20). Furthermore, divine protection is included in the blessings that Rebekah's family bestow on her and that Isaac bestows on Jacob (24:60; 27). Now God, in this special divine speech, promises protection to Jacob. It is important to note that this protection is promised in terms of a close relationship between God and Jacob; Jacob is promised that the divine presence will accompany him wherever he goes.

Jacob's response also emphasizes a close relationship with God, since he builds an altar and makes a vow that, if God will protect him and make the return possible, he will worship God and give tithes to him (28:20-22). While Jacob's response is a grateful acknowledgment of the promises made to him, it is also a cautious response prefaced by the word "if"; as Brueggemann suggests, even in this solemn moment Jacob "sounds like a bargain-hunter"[3] (28:20). The specific expectations that Jacob mentions in his vow are a rather pale reflection of the benefits God promised; whereas God has spoken of Ja-

---

3. Brueggemann, *Genesis*, 248.

cob becoming a great nation and being a blessing to all nations, Jacob's vow is about much more immediate needs such as food and clothes. Perhaps Jacob is expressing indifference to how many descendants he has or to the promise that his descendants will be a great nation, or he may be underestimating the significance of the promises. More likely, Jacob is pragmatic in his response to God. Realizing that the fulfillment of many of the promises lies well in the future, he highlights a number of ways in which he will know that God is with him by contextualizing the promises to his situation, and particularly to his need for food and clothes and a safe journey home. Jacob will be confident in God's long-term promises when he sees evidence of God's presence in his daily life. There is an important principle in this story, since no experience of God that offers blessing only after we are dead can make a serious beneficial impact on our lives or on the lives of those among whom we live. Unless our relationship with God means something here and now, our religion will appear as nothing other than "jam yesterday, jam tomorrow, but no jam today." Too often eternal life is thought of as life after death; but religious experience should change our expectations of life on earth, and eternal life should have an effect on relationships and how we live long before we die. Like Jacob, we have to translate the longer-term promises into what it means to have God's presence with us today.

Jacob's vow is sealed by the symbolic act of setting up as a sacred pillar the stone on which he has slept. Stones were often used as memorials by later Israelites (Deut 27:2), but the use of sacred pillars in Israel's cult was prohibited because of their association with Canaanite worship, and particularly in the worship of Baal. Anointing with oil was also a frequent symbolic act in later Israelite practice used at the coronation of kings.

As we have seen, this is a particularly significant passage in which God directly addresses Jacob in a dream. Jacob is blessed in a way that is reminiscent of previous divine blessings. He is promised ownership of land, a multitude of descendants, the mediation of blessing to others, and, finally, divine protection. He will look for God's provision on a daily basis and will accept such provision as evidence that God is with him (cf. Matt 6:5-15).

29:1-13 Jacob's Arrival in Paddan-aram

As Jacob departs from Bethel, the Hebrew reads literally that "Jacob lifted his feet." This short clause is seldom translated literally and is usually rendered "Jacob continued on his journey." However, the reference to Jacob's feet in the Hebrew is probably deliberate, since his feet are mentioned again when at the end of his life "he drew his feet up into the bed" (49:33). Thus the pilgrimage of Jacob is bracketed by these two statements about lifting his feet. Sarna outlines three possible meanings of the clause: (1) the going was now easier; (2) he directed his feet, that is, he went with resolve and confidence; (3) he had to force himself to leave the site of the theophany.[1] It is not necessary to choose between these suggestions, since the significance of the clause probably lies not so much in its meaning as in the new beginning that it represents. Later, Jacob looks back on his departure from home as a time of great distress and uncertainty; but his experience of God at Bethel is a turning point, one that represents the beginning of a pilgrimage that will only end when he eventually lifts his feet into the bed. God's appearance to Jacob at Bethel and the reassurances that he received mean that he now goes on his journey with a new "spring in his step."

Jacob's arrival and his introduction are told in detail. Most aspects of the account are clear, but the reference to the stone over the mouth of the well is ambiguous. Why do the shepherds not remove it? Is it too heavy? Can Jacob, the quiet man, remove a stone that usually needs several shepherds to move? Is there a link between this stone and the one that Jacob anointed at Bethel? The text does not answer these questions, but it seems that Jacob breaks local protocol in order to impress Rachel, with whom he falls in love "at first sight." Rachel immediately informs her father about the visitor, and Jacob is warmly welcomed (29:13-14).

29:14-30 One Love Story but Two Weddings

After Jacob has stayed one month, Laban bargains with him about his wages since it is now apparent that Jacob's sojourn will be a long one. Laban has two daughters, Leah and Rachel. The text refers to Leah's eyes, but modern versions disagree about what is implied (29:17).

> Leah was tender eyed; but Rachel was beautiful and well favoured. (KJV)
> Leah's eyes were delicate, but Rachel was beautiful of form and appearance. (NKJV)
> Leah's eyes were weak, but Rachel was beautiful in form and appearance (ESV)
> Leah had weak eyes, but Rachel was lovely in form, and beautiful. (NIV)

1. Sarna, *Genesis*, 201.

143

Leah had pretty eyes, but Rachel was beautiful in every way, with a
lovely face and shapely figure. (NLT)

Leah's eyes were lovely, and Rachel was graceful and beautiful. (NRSV)

Jacob fell in love with Rachel at their first meeting, and he agrees to work for
seven years for Laban with no other payment than the hand of Rachel in
marriage.

The seven years pass quickly for Jacob because he is deeply in love with
her. However, this is the same Jacob who cheated his father, and he now receives his comeuppance because his uncle Laban is also deceptive. These two
deception stories, the deception of Isaac by Jacob and the deception of Jacob
by Laban, are linked by the repetition of the same vocabulary and motifs.
Isaac eats a meal, but because of the darkness brought about by failing eye-
sight he thinks he is blessing his elder son, while in reality he is blessing the
younger. Now Jacob partakes of the feast provided by Laban, and because of
the darkness produced by his bride's veil and by the unlit tent he thinks he is
embracing as his wife the younger girl, while in reality he marries the elder.
The deceiver is now deceived.

Jacob has struggled with his elder brother, and now he enters a home
where a similar struggle is taking place. Ignoring the firstborn, Jacob prefers
her younger sister, but Laban manipulates the situation to his own advantage
and ensures that his less attractive elder daughter is married first. Laban ex-
cuses his deception by citing local custom. Jacob could justifiably have argued
that this information might have been given seven years earlier, but such objections could not alter the facts. Powerful irony permeates the passage because Jacob had duped his father into breaking his local custom of giving the
blessing and birthright to the firstborn son; now Jacob himself is duped, and
his attempt to ignore the rights of the firstborn is thwarted. Jacob's indigna-
tion is subdued because Laban agrees that, after Leah's wedding week is past,
Jacob may marry Rachel and then work for the next seven years to pay the
debt.

By his deception, Laban secures Jacob's services for an additional seven
years in exchange for his marriage to both Leah and Rachel, but it is clear that
he loves Rachel more (29:30). Already the seeds of discord have been sown,
and Jacob's favoritism will lead to some of his most painful experiences. For
obvious reasons, later Levitical law prohibits the marriage of two sisters to the
same husband while both sisters are alive. However, this law did not exist in
Jacob's time, and initially he only intended to marry Rachel (Lev 18:18).

The concept of service is prominent in this passage. In the blessing that
Jacob purloined, he was assured that nations would serve him, and Isaac, ex-

plaining to Esau, declares, "I have made all his relatives his servants" (27:37 NIV). But now in reality, Jacob is the servant of his relative Laban, rendering the narrative rich with irony.[1] The man who wanted to be master of all and deceived his father is now a servant, having been deceived by his uncle.

29:31–30:24 The Struggle for Jacob's Love and Respect

Earlier struggles for blessing between Jacob and Esau (25:22-34; 27:1-41) are mirrored in this section by a new struggle between Leah and Rachel (30:1-24). It is Leah, the one Jacob loves less, who bears more children. The narrator points out that this is because Yahweh saw her predicament and opened her womb. This close involvement of Yahweh in human affairs is consistent with the portrayal of God in the creation narratives, where he is shown as separate from creation but personally involved in it with deep concern for its welfare. However, more significantly, Yahweh's involvement on behalf of Leah indicates that God is caring and loving to the unloved or despised. Leah's deep sense of rejection is reflected in the names she gives to her first three children, Reuben, Simeon, and Levi — names that sadly reflect her desire to be loved. When she names Reuben, she wistfully says, "now my husband will love me" (29:32 NRSV). The naming of Simeon is accompanied by the comment "the LORD has heard that I am hated" (29:33 NRSV). When Levi is born, she says hopefully, "Now this time my husband will be attached to me because I have borne him three sons" (29:34 ESV). However, with the birth of her fourth child, Leah acknowledges that Yahweh has blessed her, and the name Judah is linked to gratitude and praise. The explanations given for the names should not be confused with etymologies. For example, the name Reuben probably was a common name that literally means "see, a son." But the explanations given refer, not to the literal meaning, but to the thoughts and emotions of the person pronouncing it. Sometimes the sound of the name is more important than the meaning because of the ideas that it triggers by association.

Rachel's frustration at seeing her sister produce four children while she has none leads to an outburst against Jacob (30:1). His reply is interesting because he clearly thinks that it is Yahweh who is preventing Rachel from having children, but he does not acknowledge that at least part of the problem between his wives is his favoritism. He had to leave his mother and father because of problems created by their favoritism; but far from learning from this,

---

1. Sarna points out that the verb stem relating to "serving" occurs seven times in the narrative (29:15-30) and argues that "serve" is therefore a key word; *Genesis*, 203.

Jacob creates divisions in his own family, and when things go wrong he gets angry with Rachel and blames God for her problems (30:2). However, the readers can perceive that Jacob's favoritism is a key factor (29:31).

Rachel seeks to solve the problem of descendants in much the same way as Sarah did when she gave Hagar to Abraham. Her maidservant Bilhah bears Dan and Naphtali, both names explained in terms of the struggle between Jacob's wives. Following her sister's example, Leah gives her maidservant Zilpah to Jacob. Zilpah gives birth to Gad and Asher, names reflecting Leah's happiness.

The curious passage about the mandrakes (30:14-21) shows the bitterness of the struggle between Leah and Rachel. Leah must bargain with the favorite wife in order to sleep with her husband. Jacob acquiesces in this arrangement. The mandrake is a plant that grows in the wild and produces a bell-shaped violet flower and edible yellow fruits. Its root looks like two bodies intertwined in a loving embrace, which is probably why folklore gave the plant the reputation for assisting women to become pregnant and as an aphrodisiac (cf. Song 7:13). Chemical analysis has shown that the plant does have medicinal qualities, but these have nothing to do with sexuality or pregnancy.[1] Not surprisingly, the fruit does nothing to help Rachel in her desperation to have children; but ironically her sister Leah does benefit from the situation and bears Jacob two more sons and a daughter, Dinah (30:17-21). While the birth of daughters is usually not mentioned, an exception is made with the reference to Leah's daughter Dinah, since she has an important role to play in one of the later stories.

Finally, Rachel has a son, her first but Jacob's 11th. She gives him the name "Joseph," which means "may he add" and is explained by Rachel's longing that, now she has one son, God will add another. The turning point for Rachel is highlighted by the phrase "then God remembered Rachel" (30:22). God's effective action on Rachel's behalf is in contrast to her own futile endeavor with the mandrakes and reflects the similar phrase, "God remembered Noah" (8:1). Both Noah and Rachel were hemmed in by circumstances, and only God's action on their behalf could resolve the situation. The passage emphasizes the need of dependence on God and the need to wait for his time to act on our behalf. It highlights the ineffectiveness of ill-conceived strategies designed to force God's hand. Those who have faith will not be forgotten or forsaken by God, and he will remember them and answer their prayers. In the nation of Israel, the people endured times of hardship and oppression when any thought of success or fruitfulness seemed wishful thinking. But the nar-

1. See Sarna, *Genesis,* 209.

ratives of Genesis remind God's people that they should have courage in even the most "barren" circumstances and should believe that eventually God will remember them (cf. Isa 40:27-31).

30:25-43 Jacob Acquires Wealth in Laban's Employ

After the birth of 11 sons to Jacob, the narrative concentrates on his acquisition of wealth. Jacob decides to return to his parental home following the birth of Joseph, but first he requires permission from Laban, who is effectively his master. Jacob is not a slave whom Laban purchased, but he is a hired servant and is not free to leave until Laban releases him. Thus Jacob's request, "Send me on my way" (30:25 NIV). Furthermore, Laban must also release his daughters and their offspring into Jacob's care, and so Jacob's request includes "Give me my wives and children" (30:26 NIV). In a later encounter Laban makes it clear that he believes that all that Jacob acquires is legally his (31:43). Like early Israel in Egypt or later Israel in Babylon, Jacob is not free and must wait until he is released by Laban or else take an opportunity to escape.

Laban clearly wants Jacob to stay, and he speaks in a very conciliatory way. He informs Jacob that by divination, probably using his household gods, he has discovered that his recent increase in wealth has come from Jacob's God because of Jacob's presence with him. In other words, Laban's gods have informed him that Jacob's God is blessing him. Although the implications are not discussed in the text, the inferiority of Laban's gods is clearly implied and, in particular, their inability to bless. As Lot was blessed while he lived alongside Abraham (cf. 13:5), Laban has become prosperous because of the presence of Jacob. Jacob confirms this: "you had little before I came, and it has increased abundantly; and the LORD has blessed you wherever I turned" (30:30 NRSV).[1] Therefore, Laban starts the negotiations by asking Jacob what he wants. Laban seems to assume that Jacob's proposal to leave is just an attempt to agree wages. Jacob rejects this and declares, "Don't give me anything" (30:31 NIV). In these tense negotiations where the men do not trust each other, this surprising declaration gives Jacob the advantage and allays Laban's fears that he will have to give too much. Jacob then outlines his proposal. He realizes that any agreement with such a slippery person as Laban needs to be clear,

---

1. At the same time, when Jacob first met Laban he himself had nothing; he accumulated all his wealth in Aram. Ross comments, "The Jacob stories in effect describe a patriarch who came to the land of the Arameans to receive God's blessing. In that account there is a similarity with the history of Israel, for the abundant blessing that turned the family of Jacob into a great nation occurred in the land of Egypt"; *Creation and Blessing,* 517-18.

unambiguous, and verifiable. He agrees to stay providing he can have all the speckled or dark animals from Laban's flock as his wages (30:32). This strange request is made so that it would be obvious which animals belonged to whom (30:33). Since the name Laban is also the word for "white," there is a wordplay in the Hebrew that does not translate easily into English. Sheep in the Near East are usually white and goats generally brown or black, but a few animals are spotted or striped. Laban agrees that all the spotted or striped animals born from that time will belong to Jacob, but he alters one important aspect of the agreement. Jacob has proposed that he remove all the spotted and striped animals that already exist, but on that very day Laban performs that task himself. Furthermore, he takes the precaution of moving all the animals that are spotted or striped three days journey away from the flocks that Jacob is attending. Laban does not trust Jacob, and he takes these precautions to make it impossible for Jacob to steal any of his flock that are already speckled or spotted. He acts swiftly to limit Jacob's gains and to ensure that Jacob cannot deceive him. It is interesting that a person as devious as Laban is very concerned about being deceived. However, by moving his own flocks three days journey away from Jacob he provides Jacob with an opportunity to escape that he will avail of later.

Jacob, intent on increasing the number of speckled or dark animals, believes that he can induce his animals to have speckled or spotted offspring by displaying spotted and striped objects in front of them at their drinking troughs and during mating. The subtle introduction of the color white provides a further subtle wordplay on the name Laban (30:37). Jacob deviously selects the strongest animals for this treatment in order to increase the number of animals that will belong to him while ensuring that fewer and weaker ones will belong to Laban. This seems to work, and Jacob becomes very wealthy. However, in spite of his attempts to influence the outcome of the deal, Jacob later admits that it was not his own schemes that gave him success but the blessing and protection of the God of Bethel (31:9).

31:1-21 Jacob's Secret Departure from Paddan-aram

Two reasons are given for Jacob's departure from Laban. First, he is guided by circumstances: Laban's sons become envious of Jacob's wealth and accuse him of enriching himself at the expense of their father, while Laban's attitude towards Jacob is changed. Second, Jacob receives a command from Yahweh to return to his native land. The language used is similar to that of the call to Abraham (12:1-3). Yahweh has already blessed Jacob and has made him prosperous in Paddan-aram in spite of Laban's attempts to claim all the blessings for himself (31:18; cf. 31:42).

Jacob in his speech to his wives reveals that Laban has changed his wages 10 times. Laban has attempted to exploit Jacob, but the God of his father has come to Jacob's aid and has blessed him (cf. 31:42). Even though Laban, like Lot, tries to choose the best for himself, attempting to outwit Jacob, God works to Jacob's advantage. Laban's shrewdness and craftiness do not bring blessing. God alone is its source, and Jacob is the one whom he chooses to bless. Jacob explains to his wives that the God of Bethel, where he had made a vow and anointed a stone, has commanded him to return to his native home. Jacob's communication with his wives and his attempt to explain the situation to them is significant in literature where the men seem to make all the decisions. It reveals a caring and tender side to Jacob's character that helps to balance the less attractive traits that have been made known in his relationships with others.

Rachel and Leah express solidarity with Jacob in his decision to depart, and they show considerable resentment towards their father, whom they accuse of selling them, regarding them as foreigners, and using up what he was paid for them (31:16). This resentment must have been very strong for them to want to leave home without saying their farewell. The extent of the alienation between Laban and his daughters is also reflected in the theft of Laban's household gods by Rachel (31:19). Since Laban has already admitted the use of divination, he may have used these gods for that purpose. We are not told why Rachel takes them, but she may have wanted to prevent her father from using divination, as Sarna suggests, "to detect Jacob's escape" or to discover his whereabouts.[1]

This story showing the approval of Jacob's wives to his departure from Laban fulfills two functions. First, it shows that the wives are not being taken as prisoners, as Laban later implies; and second, it assures the readers that, although Jacob does not refrain from devious dealings when necessary, the main cause of the breakdown of the relationship is Laban's greed and duplicity. Jacob's departure from Canaan was his own fault, but his departure from Paddan-aram is more honorable; his departure has not only divine sanction but the full support of his wives, who agree with the decision to leave their father, who they feel has treated them badly.

---

1. Sarna, *Genesis,* 216.

31:22-55 Laban Confronts Jacob

Three days pass before Laban discovers Jacob's departure (31:22). Not surprisingly, Laban is infuriated by Jacob's furtive departure; they have been together for 20 years. It takes Laban seven days to overtake the fugitives, but by that time they have reached Gilead and are not far from Canaan. Since this is a journey of about 400 miles, either Jacob travelled with his flocks and family at the incredible speed of 40 miles per day and Laban at almost 60 miles per day or, as Sarna suggests, the figures three and ten may be figurative rather than literal.[1]

During the journey God warns Laban in a dream to "say not a word to Jacob, either good or bad" (31:24). This is an example of a merism, an expression that uses two opposites to include everything in between. Thus, to say nothing either good or bad means to say nothing at all. This seems to be an idiomatic expression warning Laban not to harm Jacob. On Laban's own admission he has power to harm Jacob, but he takes the nocturnal warning seriously. God protects Jacob and his family from Laban's hostile intentions. We observed earlier that the promise of divine protection is an aspect of the blessing bestowed on Jacob at Bethel. This incident in which God actually warns Laban in a dream not to harm Jacob is clear evidence that God is with Jacob and is protecting him. Nevertheless, Laban has a great deal to say as he expresses his grievances. He probably believes that Jacob has carried his daughters away by force, and it does not occur to him that because of his treatment of them they willingly departed (31:26-27). Jacob defends his decision to leave and explains that he was afraid that Laban would take his daughters from him by force. This seems unlikely to us, but in the ancient world was the practice (cf. Exod 21:4).

The tension in the narrative, already intense because of the animosity between Laban and Jacob, is heightened by the incident about Laban's household gods (31:30). The reader knows that Rachel has stolen them (31:19); but Jacob, ignorant of this, puts her in danger by declaring that whoever has stolen the gods will be put to death (31:32). Like Jephthah (Judg 11:30-31), he makes a rash statement that endangers the one he loves. Laban commences a search, but he is deceived by Rachel and fails to find the gods (31:34-35). Fishbane compares this incident to Jacob's deception of his father in ch. 27, when Jacob seeks to acquire his father's blessing. He argues,

> [In v. 11] Jacob is described as smooth-skinned; he consequently fears that his father will "feel" him (stem: *mashash*) when he approaches, and so

1. Sarna, *Genesis*, 217.

discover his duplicity. Although Isaac did "feel" him (vv. 21-22), he was nonetheless duped. Years later, in an ironic reversal, Jacob's wife Rachel (the younger sibling) stole the household gods . . . from her own father Laban, who "felt" (stem: *mashash*) her baggage in search of them (31:34, 37). The search was inconclusive, and a patriarchal blessing was again abducted deceitfully.[2]

Another underlying motif of the narrative is a comparison between the gods of Laban and the God of Jacob. The narrative pours scorn on Laban's gods because they have been kidnapped and have no power to defend themselves. They suffer the ultimate indignity of being sat upon. In comparison, Jacob's God has called him on this journey and has protected him by appearing to his antagonist in a dream. It is doubtful if Rachel wants these gods in order to worship them; it is also unlikely that she has any faith in their power, otherwise she would not have treated them so ignominiously. In the period of the Judges, when the ark of the covenant is captured, Yahweh afflicts the Philistines until he returns the ark to Israel. Yahweh has power, but Laban's gods are helpless and indeed are mere fabrications.

When Laban fails to find the gods, Jacob, having gained the high moral ground, upbraids Laban for his behavior. He repeats the accusation that Laban changed his wages 10 times, and Laban does not dispute this. Jacob argues that Laban would have sent him home empty-handed if it had not been for the protection of his God. Jacob refers to God, significantly, as "the God of my father, the God of Abraham and the Fear of Isaac" (31:42). The appellation the Fear of Isaac probably refers to the reverent fear that Isaac showed to his God and also to the danger involved in harming the person protected by this deity.

Laban, now duped not only by Jacob but also by his own daughter, permits Jacob and his entourage to continue on their journey. Their mutual distrust is reflected not only in their respective speeches but also in the terms of the covenant that they make. This involves creating a pile of stones that becomes witness to their oaths. Laban's concerns include the fear that Jacob will mistreat his daughters or take other wives besides them. Laban and Jacob both feel aggrieved with each other and consider that they have been treated badly; but the text makes clear that they have both been devious and Jacob's superiority was not in his moral rectitude but in the decision of Yahweh to choose him for special blessing. Yahweh chooses Jacob not because of what he is like but in spite of it.

2. Fishbane, *Text and Texture*, 51.

Jacob and Laban swear that they will not pass the pile of stones with the intention of harming each other. Three names are given to the pile of stones that they create. The best known of these in Christian circles is Mizpah, which is linked to the statement "May the Lord keep watch between you and me when we are away from each other" (31:49 NIV). The literal meaning of *Mizpah* is "watchtower." After making a covenant with Jacob and blessing his daughters and grandchildren, Laban returns to Paddan-aram (31:53-55).

32:1-21 Preparations to Meet Esau

As he proceeds towards Canaan, Jacob must prepare to meet his brother Esau. His tense departure from Laban and the grudges that Laban now carries against him mean there is no possibility of returning to Paddan-aram. However, Jacob has no guarantee of a welcome from his brother Esau, who has even more reasons for bearing a grudge. Jacob has deprived Esau of his father's blessing, which meant a great deal to him as firstborn son, and this had led to Jacob's enforced departure from Canaan since he feared that Esau would seek revenge. Now, however, Jacob has not only his own safety to consider but the welfare of his large family. Therefore, an apprehensive Jacob leads his extended family with their flocks and herds towards Canaan and the inevitable reunion with Esau.

Jacob's preparations to meet Esau are interrupted by a vision of angels (32:1-2). Jacob names the place where he sees them Mahanaim (lit., "two camps," 32:2).[1] Presumably, the reference is to Jacob's camp and God's camp. There may be a connection between these angels and the messengers that Jacob sends to Esau (32:3). This connection is more obvious in Hebrew, since the word for "messenger" and that for "angel" are the same (מַלְאָךְ/*mal'āk*). As Brueggemann suggests, this "double use of messengers" is important because it highlights the "two dimensions" of this account and shows that Jacob has not only to establish his relationship with Esau but also to consider his relationship with God.[2] Not only is the narrative preparing for a meeting with Esau; it is also preparing for a meeting with God.

These angels are also a reminder that Yahweh has the resources to protect his people. The stories about Elisha include an incident in which the servant is alarmed because an Aramean army surrounds the city where Elisha is

---

1. Mahanaim is later designated as one of the Levitical cities of refuge.
2. Brueggemann, *Genesis*, 262.

staying. The prophet is not perturbed because he can see an even larger army of Yahweh in the hills surrounding the city, and he assures his servant, "those who are with us are more than those who are with them" (2 Kgs 6:16 ESV). In a similar way, this vision seems to be reassurance for Jacob that God is protecting him. In both stories the angels take no active role because their presence is enough to remind the people concerned that Yahweh is protecting them.

The reader gets an insight into Jacob's strategy by studying carefully the conciliatory message that he sends to Esau. Jacob describes Esau as his master and himself as Esau's servant. By using subservient language, Jacob reverses the terms of his father's blessing and clearly renounces the superiority that Isaac had bestowed on him. The purpose of the message is to be accepted by his brother.[3] When the messengers return, they bring news that heightens the tension in the narrative: Esau is coming to meet Jacob with 400 men. Since 400 men are not necessary for a welcoming party, Jacob is terrified, assuming that his brother intends to attack him. Jacob fears the worst and plans for the possibility that Esau will not just want to kill him but also his wives and family. Unlike Abraham, Jacob does not have his own private army, so armed combat with Esau is not an option. Jacob's strategy is to provide as many as possible of his entourage with an escape route should an attack occur, and so he divides them into two groups (32:6-8).

In desperation, described as "great fear and distress" (32:7 NIV), Jacob turns to the God of his fathers and pleads for help and protection. Jacob recalls that the decision to return from Paddan-aram was a response to God's command (32:9). He acknowledges that God has blessed him and confesses his own unworthiness. Thinking back to the time when he left Canaan, Jacob recalls that his only possession as he left home was his staff, but now God has greatly enriched him. Jacob freely admits his fear of Esau, and, in particular, his anxiety is not just for himself but for his wives and children (32:11). The prayer finishes with a reminder that God has promised to make his descendants "like the sand of the sea, which cannot be counted" (32:12 NIV). This short, urgent prayer gives us an excellent insight into the patriarch's personal faith in a God who responds to prayer. This prayer is the outpouring of a heart that is being torn apart by fear and doubts. Jacob, on the verge of the land he has been promised, is also on the brink of disaster. He cannot turn back to Laban, but to go forward he must face his past and the mistakes that he once made; he must face Esau, who stands between him and Bethel. He

---

3. The idiomatic phrase "to find favor in your eyes" is still used in Modern Hebrew. If you like Jerusalem, then this can be expressed idiomatically as "Jerusalem finds favor in my eyes."

knows that his only hope is that God will answer his prayer and somehow resolve the situation.

Jacob combines prayer with activity. He selects a gift from his flocks and
herds and cleverly arranges these in a way that would help to appease Esau.
The verb translated "to appease" is כפר/*kpr*, which belongs to the vocabulary
related to penitence and forgiveness. The outcome that Jacob sees is, literally,
that Esau "will lift up my face." This is an idiomatic way of expressing hope of
forgiveness and acceptance; a similar hope is expressed in the priestly blessing
(Num 6:24-26). However, in spite of these allusions to the possibility of forgiveness, Jacob's main motivation is not penitence but fear.

32:22-32 A Strange Encounter at the Jabbok

Jacob faces another important crisis as he fearfully looks forward to his meeting with Esau. Having sent his entourage across the river, he wrestles alone
with an unknown combatant. Eventually, Jacob becomes aware that his opponent is the angel of Yahweh. On his outward journey to Paddan-aram, Jacob
had seen God in his dreams, but now a face-to-face encounter takes place. Jacob has been wrestling with Esau, Isaac, and Laban, always trying to win the
blessing. This passage shows him wrestling with Yahweh as the one who truly
holds the key to that blessing. Commenting on 32:26, Fokkelman writes,

> Although lame below the belt Jacob keeps clasping the man in his arms.
> He does not let him go until he, the adversary, has blessed him. Blessed
> him! That is Jacob all over! From the most miserable situation he wants to
> emerge an enriched man. The key-word of the first phase of his life, also
> found in the Haran-period, here appears in the third period. At Bethel he
> had, among other things, received the blessing of Abraham, at his depar-
> ture; now, at his return, he wants to receive a blessing from the mysterious
> adversary, on the eve of his most difficult moment.[1]

Jacob's wrestling opponent is a formidable foe. Jacob, as at birth, cannot
win, and therefore he just holds his opponent with a tenacious grip. Jacob's
request for his opponent's name is refused. This not only adds to the mystery
of the account, it also invites comparison with the story of Moses, to whom
the divine name was revealed. God explained to Moses that he had not revealed this name to the patriarchs:

---

1. Fokkelman, *Narrative Art in Genesis*, 215.

I appeared to Abraham, to Isaac, and to Jacob, as God Almighty, but by my name the LORD I did not make myself known to them. (Exod 6:3 ESV)

Thus the divine name is not something to be squeezed from a reluctant deity but a gift of God's grace that would be given to Moses in the context of the deliverance of Jacob's descendants from slavery in Egypt.

It is significant that as Jacob left the land, because he feared Esau, God blessed him at Bethel (28:11-22). Now on his return, as he stands on the outskirts of the land with apprehension about meeting Esau, God blesses him once again (32:29). This incident shows that true blessing and possession of the promised land come, not by deception or strife, but from Yahweh himself. So far Jacob's whole life had been a continual struggle, and even his wives turn the natural act of giving birth into a struggle for supremacy. Now he must learn that true blessing is a gift of God.

The change of name from Jacob to Israel plays an important role in this narrative. The name Jacob is a reminder that even his birth had been a struggle (cf. 25:22). The name Israel is given by God as a reminder that his greatest struggle is with God. The fact that Jacob limps away from the place where he has been blessed helps to put Jacob's struggles in perspective. He limps back across the brook "blessed"; but the result implicit in the story and highlighted by gentle irony, you "have prevailed," is that at last Yahweh has prevailed and Jacob is conquered. Kidner's apt comments give a fitting conclusion to the Jabbok story:

> After the maiming, combativeness had turned to a dogged dependence, and Jacob emerged broken, named and blessed. His limping would be a lasting proof of the reality of the struggle: it had been no dream, and there was sharp judgment in it. The new name would attest his new standing: it was both a mark of grace, wiping out an old reproach (27:36), and an accolade to live up to. The blessing, this time, was untarnished, both in the taking and in the giving: it was his own, uncontrived and unmediated.[2]

The impact of Jacob's new name on the readers who called themselves Israelites must not be underestimated. This passage would have been particularly poignant for those returning to the promised land after the exile in Mesopotamia. It is no longer just Jacob who is entering the land from which he was exiled. Now with his new name he represents the nation, just as Esau represents Edom. Therefore, to get the most from this passage we must read it

2. Kidner, *Genesis,* 169.

through Israelite eyes. The nation in exile had many struggles with the surrounding nations represented by the very people with whom Jacob struggled. However, the most important struggle for Israel was with God; and in spite of the temptation to give up the struggle and release their grip of God, they must retain the kind of tenacity exemplified in their forefather Jacob.

Jacob calls the name of the place Peniel ("the face of God") because he saw God face to face. When Moses saw God face to face, his face shone reflecting the glory of God and the harmony between the deity and his prophet. When Jacob meets God, he comes away with a limp as a reminder of the most daring and significant struggle of his life. Those who have an encounter with God are never the same again.

The meeting with Esau is portrayed as a turning point in Jacob's life. He and his wives have been involved in a struggle for fertility. For Leah and Rachel, this was related to the desire to have children (30:1-24). Jacob, while not remote from the struggles of his wives, was engaged in a battle of wits with Laban in relation to the fertility of the herds and flocks (30:25-43). Now at the Jabbok River, both of these situations are resolved and Jacob has made peace with Laban in a covenant treaty. He will no longer be the deceiver and the fighter. He begins his new role by making peace with his brother Esau.

33:1-17 Jacob and Esau Meet

Jacob's humiliation is complete in his meeting with the brother he has wronged. Mercilessly, the narrator emphasizes that he bows before Esau, not once but seven times, and his wives and children follow suit. Jacob's favoritism is still apparent, since the handmaidens and their children are the first to meet Esau and hence the most vulnerable should there be an attack. Leah and her children follow the handmaidens, with Rachel and Joseph coming last (33:2). Jacob describes himself as Esau's servant and compares seeing Esau to seeing the face of God. This is an interesting allusion to Jacob's encounter with God at Peniel on the previous evening. Jacob's face-to-face struggle with God was not easy, but he prevailed, and now he refers to his meeting with Esau in the same terms. Seeing God when he wrestled with him was both a terrifying encounter and an opportunity; now meeting Esau is terrifying, but it also provides an opportunity for reconciliation and a new beginning. Like God, Esau has power to harm and power to forgive. God allowed Jacob to meet face to face, and this opened up the possibility of blessing; now Esau meets face to face, and Jacob sees acceptance rather than vengeance in his brother's facial expression. In this way, meeting Esau is like meeting God.

Jacob appears before Esau as humble and unassuming, and three times he mentions that his aim is to "find favor" with Esau (33:8, 10, 15). This is certainly not the language of brotherly love or the vocabulary of affection but the diplomatic terminology of one seeking mercy and reconciliation.

This meeting of the two brothers reverses the roles anticipated in Isaac's blessing of Jacob. That blessing promised Jacob dominance over his brothers, but he now relinquishes these ambitions and accepts that he must bow before Esau. The narrator clearly presents two types of blessing: the patriarchal blessing, with its emphasis on short-term dominance, and the divine blessing, with long-term promises. In the long term the Israelites will dominate the Edomites, but in the short term Jacob's struggle with his brother is over; God is the one who will deliver the definitive blessing.

Esau, in spite of his capacity to harm Jacob, runs to meet him, embraces him, falls on his neck, and kisses him. At first Esau shows reluctance to accept a gift from Jacob, but eventually he relents under pressure (33:9-11). Jacob refers to his gift to Esau as "my blessing" (33:11 ESV). As Westermann points out, this is Jacob's way of saying that "he wants to give back the 'blessing' to his brother."[1] Jacob is paying a debt and making an apology to the one he has wronged.

Although Esau wants Jacob to go to Seir and Jacob agrees to join him there (33:12-14), this agreement is never kept. The text shows clearly that Esau is associated with the land of Edom and Mount Seir but Jacob settles in Canaan. Jacob still has obvious reservations about living side by side with Esau. Such an arrangement had not worked for Abraham and Lot or for Jacob himself with his uncle Laban.

33:18–34:31 Jacob Dwells among the Shechemites

At first Jacob settles at Succoth (33:17), which is on the borders of Canaan. According to Jewish tradition, he stays at Succoth 18 months. This is a strange decision, since the reader is expecting a return to Bethel. If Jacob has been called to return to his homeland, why does he settle outside it? At last Jacob moves in the direction of Bethel but stops short at Shechem, which was a crossroads of trade; and, buying a piece of land, he settles among the Hivites[1] (33:19; cf. 34:2). This is a new departure for a patriarch. Abraham had bought

---

1. Westermann, *Genesis 12–36*, 526.

1. The Hivites were one of a number of ethnic groups living in Canaan at that time. They are probably to be identified with the Hurrians, who are mentioned in extrabiblical sources.

land for a burial place but not to live on. Kidner argues that, by settling at Shechem just one day's journey short of Bethel, Jacob is making a compromise and is acting in disobedience to the call back to Bethel.[2] Following the example of Abraham, Jacob pitches his tent and builds an altar, claiming the land for both God and his posterity by naming the altar "El-Elohe-Israel" (lit., "God the God of Israel"). This name conveniently applies to the patriarch himself and also to the future nation of Israel.

After Jacob's return to Canaan, Shechem, a young Hivite, becomes infatuated with Dinah the daughter of Jacob and rapes her. Unlike other occasions when rape leads to repulsion (2 Sam 13:10-15), here Shechem's love increases and he persuades his father to make a proposal of friendship to Jacob (34:9-10). Hamor's enthusiasm for establishing a covenant with Jacob is not just related to his son's desire for Dinah. Hamor can see evidence that Jacob has been blessed, and he knows that, if such a person should dwell among them, they could share the blessing (34:23).

Obvious questions are being raised here in relation to the future of the blessing. Is this how Jacob is to fulfill his role of bringing blessing to the nations? If Jacob accepts the proposal of the Hivites, surely he will jeopardize the future of the blessing by compromising the purity of the descent from Abraham. Undoubtedly Jacob's inaction shows him in a bad light. As Sternberg comments,

> His inaction amounts to an acquiescence in what a patriarch, whatever his paternal instincts, must fight tooth and nail: exogamous marriage. Dinah must be extricated even at risk. But Jacob proves blind to tradition and destiny as well as to morality.[3]

Jacob, who had been subservient to Laban and then Esau, is now subject to his sons' desires: Jacob has lost his authority. His sons cite their traditions in order to deceive the Hivites, just as Laban had used a similar strategy against Jacob. They claim that Dinah cannot marry someone who is uncircumcised, but if the Hivites submit to this rite, then they can be one people (34:15-16). Shechem is described as the most honorable in his family. This removes any thought that he has ulterior motives: he is genuinely in love. Yet despite this, the appeal to the men of that city to accept circumcision is made on the basis that the livestock and property of Jacob and his sons will become available to them. Tempted by this prospect, the Hivites agree to submit to circumcision. However, this ritual is a special sign of inclusion in the

2. Kidner, *Genesis*, 172.
3. Sternberg, *The Poetics of Biblical Narrative*, 474.

covenant community, and it seems that the brothers are using it to their own devious ends.

The danger of Jacob's descendants losing their identity is avoided when Jacob's sons massacre the Hivites in retaliation for Shechem having raped Dinah. The way in which they deceive the Hivites is a reminder of the earlier deceptions perpetrated by their father Jacob (34:13-17; cf. 27:18-20). However, Jacob had never resorted to violence, even though threatened by both Esau and Laban. His sons continue his deviousness but add a dangerous dimension by their violent and merciless attack. Not all Jacob's sons are implicated in the murders that take place. Simeon and Levi seem to have been the main perpetrators of the atrocity, but Jacob and all his sons are involved in taking the wives of those who were killed together with livestock and other property. This means that Jacob's entire household could be held responsible for what happened and could be considered a legitimate target for anyone seeking to avenge the violent deaths. Jacob, aware of these dangers, accuses Simeon and Levi of having made him odious to the inhabitants of the land (34:30). His accusation that his sons have brought "trouble" (עָכַר/*ʿākar*) uses the same word as the story of Achan (Josh 7:24-25). Achan brought trouble by breaking the rules laid down by Moses. Jacob's sons brought trouble by taking the law into their own hands and breaking the rules of normal civilized behavior.

Abraham, Isaac, and Jacob lived as resident aliens in Canaan, and their continuance there depended on good relations with the other inhabitants of the land. Up until the massacre the relations, while sometimes strained, had always been resolved without bloodshed. Jacob's sons crossed a boundary and entered uncharted territory. In the past difficulties had been resolved through negotiations, but Jacob's sons showed that they could not be trusted since they broke a mutually binding covenant. This is serious for Jacob, who needs the goodwill of those surrounding him; he cannot keep running to stay out of trouble. He has fled from Esau and from Laban, but now when he intends to settle peaceably he must move again. His rebuke of his sons is uncompromising and direct, but they do not concede that they are wrong. They try to excuse themselves by referring to the terrible thing that was done to Dinah by Shechem, but seem oblivious to the greater wrongs that they themselves have committed on the pretext of vengeance. Brueggemann makes the following apt comment:

> Sadly, at the end of the narrative Jacob's sons have learned nothing and conceded nothing (v. 31). They are fixed on the narrow sexual issue. The sons remain blind to the larger economic issues, blind to the dangers they have created, blind to the possibilities of cooperation, and blind even to

the ways they have compromised their own religion in their thirst for vengeance and gain.[4]

This thirst for vengeance is still a motivating factor in the world today. It is so easy for violence to rage out of control as one side seeks retribution against the other. In the dark days of the "troubles" in Northern Ireland, the most frightening episodes were the sectarian killings when people were killed because of their religion in response to earlier killings by "the other side." Reason and common sense gave way to blind sectarian vindictiveness and thirst for revenge. This is what Jacob feared.

35:1-15 Jacob Returns to Bethel

Jacob is horrified by the incident, but his objections are based on fear of reprisals rather than on moral or ethical grounds. These circumstances are reminiscent of the events earlier in Jacob's life when he was afraid of Esau. On that occasion he was encouraged and reassured at Bethel, where he had received Yahweh's blessing (28:10-22). The reader is not told why Jacob did not return and renew his vows at Bethel earlier, especially since Bethel is only about one day's journey from Shechem. It seems that Jacob's prayers and pilgrimages are made only when he is in danger. Fear is the controlling emotion in his most significant encounters with God. Now once again God calls him to return to Bethel.

The only hint about why Jacob did not go to Bethel earlier is provided by the preparations that he must make. Before leaving Shechem, he collects the symbols of idol worship from his company and buries them under a tree. Was an unwillingness to get rid of these objects earlier the reason why Jacob lived so close to Bethel without actually going there? He also stipulates that his people should change their clothes; Bethel represents a new start. As he describes his purpose in going to Bethel, Jacob explains its significance. However, he avoids the impression that God dwells at Bethel and cannot be contacted anywhere else; the God he had met at Bethel in that time of distress has been with him ever since, wherever he has gone (35:3). Nevertheless, Bethel evokes special memories for him, and it is a place where he feels particularly close to God.

Throughout the journey Jacob's fears of vengeful attacks do not materialize because the inhabitants of the cities he passes are terrified. The descrip-

---

4. Brueggemann, *Genesis*, 279.

tion "terror of God" (35:5 NIV) is similar to our idiomatic expression "to put the fear of God into someone." It is an indication that Jacob is now a threat to others and his earlier reputation of being peaceful is now lost. He is a symbol of danger rather than of blessing. Harmonious relations have suffered because of his sons' bloodthirsty actions, and Jacob desperately needs reassurance and protection.

Following the announcement that Jacob has arrived at Bethel is a brief etiological note on how the place received its change of name from Luz to El-bethel (35:7). Then follows an interesting interruption to the main story while the death of Rebekah's nurse is recorded. She is buried under an oak, giving the place its name Allon-bacuth, which means "the oak of weeping" (35:8). This is an unusual detail, because Rebekah's nurse has not been part of the narrative and yet the note occurs in a location where it clearly disrupts the narrative. No reference to Rebekah joining Jacob has been made and her death is not recorded in Genesis, which makes it all the more unusual that her nurse is with Jacob and that the nurse's death is recorded. According to Jewish tradition, Rebekah had sent her nurse to Paddan-aram to encourage Jacob to return home, but there is no record of this in the text.

At Bethel, God appears to Jacob as El Shaddai and renews the promises of descendants and land (35:11-13). The change of name from Jacob to Israel is confirmed. Once again there are reminiscences of Genesis 17, where Abraham is promised that he will be the ancestor of kings. After the events of the preceding chapter, this is a reminder that the covenant still stands in spite of the misuse of the rite of circumcision. Here also is the renewal of the promise given only to Jacob that he will become a company or an assembly of nations (35:11).

35:16-29 Family Matters

The narrative has now reached a turning point when the focus begins to shift from Jacob to his sons. The birth of Benjamin and the death of Rachel in childbirth signal the end of the struggle of Jacob's wives to produce offspring. This struggle dominates the story of Rachel's life and also accounts for her death. Because of serious complications, Rachel dies while giving birth, but the child survives (35:16-18). Reflecting her experience, on her deathbed she names the child "Ben-Oni" ("son of my sorrow"), but Jacob changes his name to "Benjamin" ("son of the right"; 35:18). Jacob's sorrow at losing his favorite wife is not mentioned except for the brief note that he set up a pillar on her grave, which the narrator observes "is there to this day" (35:20 NRSV).

161

Rachel's death occurs near Bethlehem, and just outside the modern town the traditional site of her tomb is still honored. The birth of Jacob's youngest son is followed by a record of a lewd act by the eldest, Reuben, who sleeps with his father's concubine, Bilhah, an incident that is reported to Jacob (35:22). Like David, Jacob does not approve but takes no action. However, because of this act of immorality, Reuben loses the traditional advantages of the firstborn (49:4).

Now that the patriarch's family is complete, a short genealogy lists the names of his 12 sons. Finally, the death of Isaac and his burial by Esau and Jacob are recorded here. The father who divided them during his lifetime unites them in his death. He dies at the age of 180 and is described as "old and full of days," an idiomatic expression denoting that he lived a full life (35:29). Brueggemann comments that the order in which Isaac's sons are mentioned in this narrative is important:

> Most important, the burial is conducted by both sons, Esau and Jacob, even named in that order. When the brothers had separated (33:16-17), it was not clear whether this was a reconciliation or a truce. But this text makes clear that there was a reconciliation. Even in this Jacob-oriented tradition, the older brother is remarkably valued. The venom has been removed from the oracle of 25:23.[1]

Jacob's previous meeting with Esau had been preceded by fear and foreboding. The meeting itself was held in an atmosphere of distrust and uncertainty. Now Esau and Jacob appear together in harmony.

36:1-43 Genealogical Information about Esau's Family

Edom's relationship with Israel is a recurring theme in biblical literature, and it is obviously an important theme for the narrator of Genesis, who takes time and space to reproduce a lengthy genealogy of Esau's descendants. The section is introduced by a brief explanation that Esau did not live in Canaan because there was not enough room for him and Jacob. This is similar to the emphasis in ch. 13 that Lot and Abram could not dwell together because their herds and flocks had become too numerous. It is a clear statement that the Edomites do not have a claim to the land of Canaan in spite of their ancestry. Territory is a prominent subject throughout this section. Esau is described as the "ancestor of the Edomites, in the hill country of Seir" (36:9 NRSV; cf. vv.

1. Brueggemann, *Genesis*, 285.

21, 30). Following the list of Esau's descendants with the references to their territory, there is a note that "Jacob settled in the land where his father had lived as an alien, the land of Canaan" (37:1 NRSV). The location of this verse at the end of the genealogical references to Esau and before the introduction to the "*tôlĕdôt* of Jacob" sets it apart from either section as a significant editorial note. This emphasis on where people lived is evidence of the struggle for territory between Israel and Edom.

The genealogy lists a number of Edomite kings, with the explanatory note that the Edomites had kings before the Israelites (36:31). One of these, Hadad, is credited with defeating Midian in the land of Moab (36:35). These Edomite kings recall the promises to Abraham and Sarah that kings would be among their offspring. Esau and his offspring are not afforded the same role of bringing blessing to the world as Jacob and his descendants, but Esau is not rejected and through him some of the promises are fulfilled.

37:1-11 Introduction to Joseph

The *tôlĕdôt* of Jacob begins a new section which deals mainly with the story of Joseph. As a young man of 17, he alienates his brothers by reporting their misdeeds to his father. His unpopularity increases when Jacob provides him with a coat that reflects the special relationship he has with the boy.[1] Favoritism figures in Jacob's story from his own childhood and was a source of tension in his marriage.[2] Now in old age he continues the practice, with the result that the other brothers, with the possible exception of Benjamin, hate Joseph (37:4). As Westermann explains, this concept of hatred should not be confused with the modern use of the term.

---

1. Joseph's coat is often described as a "coat of many colors." This comes from the Greek translation (LXX). The meaning of the Hebrew word for this special coat is uncertain, but the same expression is found in 2 Sam 13:18, where it refers to the garment worn by a princess. This would indicate that the garment was not just very ornate but was an indication of status. As Westermann suggests, "it is safe to assume that Jacob was doing more than simply giving Joseph a nice gift; he was raising the boy to a level above that of his brothers"; *Joseph*, 6.

2. A recurring theme in Genesis is that people do not learn from the mistakes of earlier generations. Isaac passed his wife off as his sister just as his father had done, and Jacob and Joseph both have favorites in their families in spite of the problems that this unwise practice had brought into the relationship of Isaac and Rebekah. However, Westermann takes a different approach to Jacob's favoritism, arguing that "The storyteller's perspective of Jacob's favouritism is utterly free of criticism; his intention is to present it merely as one special — and fateful — . . . phenomenon of human nature. So, too, should we understand it"; *Joseph*, 5.

When we use the word "hate," we usually mean something that is a personal position or attitude. However, in the Hebrew, the verb "to hate" has a different meaning: it is a deed or the inception of a deed. To practice this kind of hate is like pulling a bowstring taut — it has no purpose unless an arrow is then unleashed. By the same token, hate makes no sense unless one follows through with a corresponding deed. . . . Thus, when our storyteller says that the brothers hated Joseph, we should expect that a hate-fulfilling deed will follow.[3]

Joseph stokes the fires of jealousy by describing dreams that clearly indicate his superiority. The dreams vary in detail, but the result is the same. One of the dreams envisages the family binding sheaves of corn, when suddenly Joseph's sheaf stands straight and all the other sheaves bow down to it. The second dream carries the same message, but this time the sun and moon and 11 stars bow to Joseph. Even his biased father has reservations about this dream, which needs little interpretation, because it obviously suggests that father, mother, and 11 brothers bow to Joseph. The reference to Joseph's mother must refer to a stepmother, since Rachel is dead. This emphasis on being the person to whom others bow down recalls the blessing that Isaac bestowed on Jacob; Joseph is now following the same aspirations. Is this why Jacob is so concerned and rebukes him?

Yet, there is no suggestion that Joseph concocts these dreams. Later in the story it becomes apparent that these dreams are from God and that they reveal the future. Joseph cannot be faulted for having the dreams, but perhaps the insensitive way that he relates them shows that he is unaware of the hatred growing against him in his brothers' hearts and minds. While Jacob rebukes Joseph, he does not dismiss the dreams out of hand but "kept the matter in mind" (37:11). Why should Jacob keep the matter in mind if he does not privately hope that there may be some truth in these dreams, unless he is reliving his own dreams through his favorite son?

37:12-36 Brotherly Love!

Jacob, oblivious to the danger, sends Joseph to his brothers, who are grazing their livestock near Shechem. Note the similarity with the David story. David also is sent by his father to his brothers, and he also experiences sibling jealousy. Arriving at Shechem, Joseph discovers that his brothers have moved

---

3. Westermann, *Joseph*, 7.

from there towards Dothan. As Joseph approaches them, he is visible from a distance so that when he reaches them they have already conspired to kill him.[1] Their purpose is to ensure that his dreams do not come true. Ironically, they actually ensure by their actions that the dreams are fulfilled. Reuben plays his role as the eldest son and proposes a plan that will give him an opportunity to rescue Joseph. At Reuben's suggestion the brothers do not kill him but strip off the special robe, the hated symbol of Jacob's favoritism, and throw him into a pit. Before Reuben can carry out his rescue plan, at the suggestion of Judah Joseph is sold to a group of merchants traveling towards Egypt. Thus Joseph becomes the first of Abraham's descendants to be enslaved in Egypt, but eventually many more will follow.

A great deal of discussion has centered on the two names of the people to whom Joseph is sold. They are referred to as both Ishmaelites and Midianites. In source-critical studies, occurrences of two names in stories like this are used as evidence of a conflation of sources. While this is possible, another equally plausible suggestion is that the traders were Ishmaelites who came from a Midianite tribe.[2]

Among the brothers, only Reuben expresses regret about what has happened, showing how deeply rooted their hatred of Joseph has become. Together they invent a story to deceive their father, and it works perfectly; the man who had so successfully deceived others is completely duped. However, the brothers underestimate the effect this would have on Jacob, and having convinced him that Joseph is dead, they are unable to console him. This is reminiscent of the story of the death of Absalom and David's refusal to be consoled (2 Sam 18:19-33). So while Jacob mourns for Joseph, his son commences work in the employ of Potiphar, one of Pharaoh's senior officials.

38:1-30 The Judah/Tamar Incident

A strange report about Judah interrupts the Joseph story. Why is this account allowed to disrupt the Joseph narrative with material that seems irrelevant and out of place? Furthermore, the Judah story also seems out of harmony with the rest of the Joseph story. Judah is not living with his father and broth-

---

1. Joseph does not get the opportunity in the text to express how he feels about this conspiracy (cf. Ps 105:17-22), but the prophet Jeremiah gives vent to the most extreme emotions when he discovers that members of his own family are plotting against him (Jer 11:20; 12:3).

2. Longacre draws attention to Judg 8:24, where "Midianite" invaders are described as "Ishmaelites." He argues, therefore, that these two names "refer to the same group of people"; *Joseph*, 31.

ers, and he has his own home and flocks. At first it does not seem to have any thematic unity with what precedes it or with what follows.

However, Redford's claim that "chapter 38 has nothing whatever to do with the plot of the Joseph Story" fails to recognize that in the final chapters of Genesis Judah and Joseph are compared since they are both contenders for the special privileges due to the firstborn.[1] Chapter 38 should not be considered as irrelevant to the Joseph story since it highlights the importance of the comparison that is taking place between Judah and Joseph.[2] Judah's three older brothers have all forfeited any claim to special blessing, and Judah is next in line. Eventually it is Joseph who receives the firstborn blessing through the adoption of his two sons. Therefore, a comparison between the two provides reasons why this should happen.

38:1-11 Judah's Marriage to a Canaanite

In this chapter, Judah is living separately from his other family members. Unlike Lot who leaves Canaan when he separates from Abram, Judah remains in Canaan and lives in a town called Adullam. This town is on the western border of the territory allotted to the tribe of Judah in the conquest narratives. The man whom Judah chooses to live with in Adullam is called Hirah and is otherwise unknown. Judah's wife is also one of the virtually unknown characters in the Bible. We know nothing about her, except that she was a daughter of a Canaanite man named Shua and that she bore three children to Judah: Er, Onan, and Shelah. The story focuses on Tamar, Judah's daughter-in-law. She is married to Judah's firstborn Er, who dies, or as the narrator bluntly records, Yahweh "put him to death" because of his wickedness. Since Er has no family, the custom under what was known as levirate law was that the nearest kinsman must marry the widow and raise children who would be regarded as the offspring of the deceased relative.

Er's brother Onan marries Tamar, but since he knows that any children would be regarded as his brother's descendants and not his, he refuses to fulfill his duty. In this way he too displeases Yahweh, who we are told also puts him to death (38:10). When both sons die, Judah blames Tamar; but she is innocent, as the text makes clear that her husbands both die as judgment from God. Judah refuses to allow Shelah, his youngest, to marry Tamar; but since

1. Redford, *A Study of the Biblical Story of Joseph*, 16.
2. Longacre supports the view that "the story of Judah and Tamar is not, of course, without significance to the broader story"; *Joseph*, 26 n. 1.

this would be against custom, he deceives her and tells her to wait in her father's home and when the time is right he will allow Shelah to marry her.

38:12-23 Tamar Deceives Judah

Realizing that she has been deceived, Tamar, in a quest for offspring and an identity, deceives Judah. Dressed as a prostitute, she seduces him and cleverly secures personal belongings from him to guarantee the agreed payment of one of the kids from his flock. The pledge comprises very personal items that could belong only to Judah; perhaps they would be the modern equivalent of his credit cards. Judah falls into her trap and apparently is easily seduced. However, when he seeks to provide the agreed payment, Tamar cannot be found and Judah is not able to retrieve the pledge that he gave her.

38:24-30 Tamar Gives Birth to Twins

Judah's ruthlessness and hypocrisy in these verses are counterbalanced by his admission of guilt. At first when he hears that Tamar is pregnant, he demands that she should be burned to death; but when she produces the articles that he has given her as a pledge, he admits that she is more righteous than he. Tamar gives birth to twins, Perez and Zerah. Like the daughters of Lot, Tamar has struggled to have offspring and succeeded.

Obvious similarities exist between the story of Tamar and the story of Potiphar's wife that immediately follows it. Both women attempt to seduce a man, and both take some of his personal belongings as evidence of their encounter. However, the differences between the two characters are more significant than the similarities. The motives of the Egyptian are selfish and sensual, whereas Tamar is motivated by the need to raise children who will continue the family line of her dead husband. Thus, Tamar honors her husband though he is dead, but the Egyptian dishonors her husband while he is still alive. Furthermore, Potiphar's wife withholds Joseph's garment to incriminate an innocent man, but Tamar retains Judah's personal effects to reveal the truth. This comparison between the two narratives suggests that, although Tamar's actions are unusual and certainly not to be condoned, she pragmatically makes the best of the situation in which she is placed through no fault of her own.

39:1-5 Joseph Sold to Potiphar

No details are given of Joseph's journey to Egypt or about the circumstances regarding his sale except that he is bought by Pharaoh's captain of the guard, Potiphar. Joseph's success as a slave is emphasized; Potiphar is pleased with him and puts him in charge of his entire household and of all that he owns. This success results from Yahweh's presence with Joseph (39:2); even Potiphar recognizes that Yahweh gives him success (39:3). Yahweh had promised Abraham that through him and his offspring all the nations would be blessed, and now in this passage Yahweh blesses the Egyptian because of Joseph. The importance of this rather unusual statement that Yahweh blesses the Egyptian is underlined by repetition. The richness and abundance of blessing channeled through Joseph is also emphasized by the repetition of the word "all," which occurs five times in this pericope (39:1-6). According to Alter, this repetition shows that "the scope of blessing or success this man realizes is virtually unlimited; everything prospers, everything is entrusted to him."[1]

39:6-19 A Woman Spurned

Ancient narrators do not usually describe the appearance of their characters unless this impinges on the story. Joseph is described as well built and handsome as a prelude to the account of how Potiphar's wife tries over a period of time to seduce him. Like Eve, she sees something that she desires and reaches out for it. The pace of the story is slowed down by a dialogue between Joseph and Potiphar's wife in which Joseph explains clearly why he refuses her request. Joseph bases his refusal on the trust that his master has placed in him; he cannot possibly betray such trust. He also explains that what she asks him to do is a "wicked thing" and to agree would be to "sin against God" (39:9). Unimpressed by Joseph's moral quibbles, Potiphar's wife keeps up the pressure and tries to force Joseph into bed by grasping his clothing. In alarm, Joseph runs away from her, leaving his cloak in her hands. The emphasis on the importunity of the woman effectively highlights the morality and trustworthiness of Joseph. Even under pressure he will not betray his master or his God.

Potiphar's wife now seeks revenge and screams for help to the members of the household, claiming that Joseph attacked her. She ultimately accuses not just Joseph but also her husband, blaming him for bringing a Hebrew

1. Alter, *The Art of Biblical Narrative*, 107-8.

into the house to "insult us." Contrary to the NRSV, she does not refer to Potiphar as her husband but uses the impersonal "he," probably an expression of her alienation from him (39:14). In her hypocritical speech to Potiphar, she repeats her accusation that Joseph attacked her. She describes him in derogatory terms as "the Hebrew servant" (39:17) and produces his garment as evidence. Once again in Genesis a woman deceives a man. Lot's daughters deceive their father, Rachel deceives her father, but this woman deceives her husband.

39:20-23 Joseph in Prison

This short section explains that Yahweh's blessing is evident in Joseph's life, even in prison. His treatment is much better than one would expect for a slave suspected of sexual assault, suggesting that Potiphar is not totally convinced of Joseph's guilt. More importantly for the story line, Joseph is placed in the prison that Pharaoh uses for his servants. The continuing providential care of Joseph results in his gaining favor with the warden, who gives him a position of responsibility over the other prisoners. Like Potiphar the warden discovers that his new assistant is completely trustworthy (39:23). This is further evidence of Yahweh's presence with Joseph granting him success.

40:1-23 Prisoners' Dreams

Two prisoners are highlighted, the chief cupbearer and the chief baker. Since both men have responsibilities over culinary matters, we may assume that Pharaoh was unhappy with the food prepared for him or perhaps he even had food poisoning. Such details are of little interest to the narrator, whose main concern is to bring the subject of dreams back into the story. The reader already knows that Joseph has dreams himself, but there is still no evidence that he can interpret them accurately. Indeed, the problem with Joseph's dreams is that anyone could interpret them and their message is clear, even if unwanted.

Since in biblical times dreams were regarded as highly significant, it was important to have them interpreted, and there were people who specialized in this task. However, when Pharaoh's cupbearer and baker have mysterious dreams, they know that it is unlikely that they will get them interpreted in prison. Their dejection is so obvious that Joseph asks them for the reason, and this leads to the dreams being repeated to him.

169

An important statement in this account is Joseph's declaration that the interpretation of dreams belongs to God. He listens to the butler's dream and offers the interpretation that in three days he will be restored to his previous employment. Joseph explains his own misfortunate to the butler, describing how he had been "stolen out of the land of the Hebrews" and wrongfully imprisoned in Egypt. He pleads with the butler to speak to Pharaoh on his behalf (40:14-15).

Joseph also interprets the baker's dream faithfully, even though the meaning is less welcome since Joseph explains that he will be hanged in three days. Joseph can be trusted to give a faithful interpretation, even when it is not favorable. The third day is Pharaoh's birthday, and his actions towards the prisoners confirm Joseph's predictions. However, Joseph's position is unchanged; the baker cannot help because he is hanged, and the butler, relieved to be back in favor, forgets about prison and Joseph (40:23).

41:1-8 Pharaoh's Dreams Baffle Egypt's Wise Men

The time between Joseph's interpretation of the prisoners' dreams and his opportunity to appear before Pharaoh is given as two years. God's purposes are being fulfilled, but very slowly. Abraham had to wait for God's timing, and now Joseph must do likewise. By drawing attention to the length of time involved, the narrator highlights the extent of Joseph's suffering. Waiting and uncertainty were trials that many of the readers of Genesis had to endure as they longed to return home from exile.

Pharaoh's first dream is located by the river Nile, the longest river in the world. Egypt owed its existence to the Nile, and it would be among the reeds of its banks that the baby Moses would be hidden; it would be by those same banks that Moses would challenge Pharaoh and his wise men. These wise men would be baffled by the wonders that God would perform through Moses, and their magic would be shown to be inferior and impotent when opposed by the power of God.

In his dream Pharaoh witnesses seven "attractive and plump cows" coming out of the Nile, followed by seven "ugly and thin cows" that eat the "attractive and plump ones" (41:1-4 ESV). Pharaoh awakes and then falls asleep again when he has a second dream. The second dream has the same story line as the first, but the location is a harvest field and, instead of cows, the subject matter is stocks of grain.

Troubled by his dreams, Pharaoh summons "all the magicians and wise men of Egypt." Wisdom and magic were synonymous in Egyptian society, but even though the entire company is involved they are unable to interpret the dream. Later Moses will also show the inadequacy and limitations of Egypt's magicians and wise men, and later still the same will happen in Babylon as Daniel shows the superiority of Yahweh over Babylon's wise men and enchanters.

41:9-38 Joseph Appears before Pharaoh

Confessing his lapse in memory, the chief cupbearer relates how a young Hebrew lad has successfully and accurately interpreted dreams in prison. But even his lapse in memory is providential, because now is the opportune time to introduce Joseph to Pharaoh.

The narrator's fondness of detail is reflected in the observation that Joseph is shaved prior to appearing before Pharaoh. Although shaving was not the norm in the ancient world, it was practiced by the Egyptians. Thus Joseph must shave before he can serve Pharaoh (41:14).

Joseph's first words to Pharaoh highlight the important point that Joseph himself does not claim to be a professional interpreter of dreams. He claims that the interpretation comes from God (41:16). Pharaoh relates his dreams to Joseph, including all the detail given earlier and adding that when the lean cows swallowed the fat ones they were not improved or fattened themselves. He reiterates his dilemma that no one is able to explain these dreams (41:17-24).

Joseph does what no one else can do and gives Pharaoh a detailed interpretation. He explains that the two dreams have the same meaning but the repetition in two forms underlines that the matter is fixed by God and will occur quickly (41:25-32). Modern interpreters of OT literature place great significance on the repetition of stories, and it is interesting that Joseph does likewise.

Joseph follows his interpretation with advice about how Pharaoh and his officials should react to the warning of the dreams that there will be seven years of plenty followed by seven years of famine (41:33-36). In advising Pharaoh to choose someone to oversee the preparation for the famine, Joseph essentially composes his own personnel specification. He advises Pharaoh to choose a discerning and wise man to be in charge; and Pharaoh recognizes that, not only is Joseph discerning and wise, but also the spirit of the gods is in him.

41:39-57 Joseph Takes Charge

Pharaoh makes Joseph his second in command, so presumably even Potiphar is now subject to Joseph. Questions that we might ask about whether he takes revenge on Potiphar's wife, or even meets her again, are not on the narrator's agenda. The narrative reports Joseph's exaltation in detail. Complete authority in the land of Egypt is his, with only Pharaoh on his throne able to overrule him. Pharaoh takes his signet ring and places it on Joseph's finger, and he also renames Joseph. These are symbolic acts by which Pharaoh claims Joseph as his protégé. The meaning of the new name that Pharaoh gives Joseph is not known. Pharaoh also chooses a wife for him. Exchanging his prison clothes for fine linen and a gold neck chain, Joseph rides in a chariot with servants calling before him, "Bow the knee." Joseph the Hebrew slave has become Joseph the Egyptian prince at the age of 30 (41:46).

Joseph's position would have been untenable if his predictions had proved untrue; therefore it is not just Joseph's natural ability that sustains him in office but the continued blessing of God on his life. Pharaoh exalts Joseph, but the narrative exalts Joseph's God, since without God's help Joseph would still have been languishing in prison.

Joseph's prediction of seven years of abundant harvests is fulfilled, and he wisely stores the surplus grain. In superlative terms the surplus is described as immeasurable, like the sand on the seashore, making it impossible to keep records. Thus, agricultural fertility is described in terms that mirror the fertility that God promised Abraham would characterize his descendants. Joseph is also blessed with two sons through his wife Asenath, daughter of Potiphera, priest of On. Joseph chooses the names Manasseh and Ephraim for his boys, linking these names to his experiences. Significantly, in explaining the name Manasseh Joseph claims that God has enabled him to forget his father's household (כָּל-בֵּית אָבִי/kol-bêt 'ābî, "all the house of my father"; 41:51). This would indicate that Joseph does not intend to travel to Canaan to seek out his family; he has a new family now in Egypt. It is the first indication that he intends to seek neither reconciliation nor revenge. Some scholars are very critical of Joseph in this regard. Pirson comments,

> This remark on forgetting his father's house sheds a not entirely favourable light upon Joseph. All the more so, since Joseph has been the man in charge for at least a year now (and perhaps even more) — and he has not made any attempt yet to contact his family in the land of Canaan. Nor will he for the years to come![1]

1. Pirson, *The Lord of the Dreams*, 92.

As far as possible he has put his past life behind him, unaware that his task of providing food for the famine years will bring him into touch with them again and at that point he will be faced with the decision whether to forgive or to punish.[2]

Joseph links the name of his second son, Ephraim, with the positive aspect of his experience and, in particular, that God has made him fruitful. Blessing is manifest in fruitfulness, and Joseph has experienced the blessing promised to Abraham and his descendants, in spite of the hardship that he has suffered. Indeed, Joseph's hardship was the gateway to his exaltation in Egypt.

In his task of providing for the famine years, Joseph shows that God not only has blessed him personally but also has given him the ability to appropriate the blessing and to make it available to others (41:49, 56-57). This clearly recalls the promise to Abraham in 12:3, that through his offspring all nations would receive blessing. Nowhere else in Genesis is this promise fulfilled on such a grand scale as that seen in this portrayal of Joseph providing essential food for Egypt and the surrounding nations. He acquired the grain when it was surplus and worthless, but now he sells it as an essential commodity that cannot be obtained anywhere else.

42:1-24 Joseph's Brothers in Egypt

Back in Canaan, the other members of Joseph's family are starving, but the brothers are helpless and are described by Jacob as doing nothing more productive than "looking at one another" (42:1 NRSV). Presumably these exchanged glances from one to another are reminders of their guilt and reflect their conviction that they are being punished. The debilitating effect of guilt is clearly illustrated in these stories. Every time the brothers face a crisis, it is not faith that comes into play but guilt. Guilt destroys their ability to face life's crises positively, and they helplessly wallow in feelings of self-pity and regret. Jacob learns that food is available for sale in Egypt; but if the brothers are burdened by guilt, Jacob is weighed down by grief and fear. He sends 10 brothers to Egypt but keeps Benjamin at home, "for he feared that harm might come to him" (42:4 NRSV).

Joseph sees his brothers when they arrive in Egypt since he personally supervises the sale of grain. However, they fail to recognize him, which is un-

---

2. Fung asks, "Why does Joseph want to forget it all? Is it because it matters no more? Or is it because it hurts?"; *Victim and Victimizer*, 105.

derstandable because he was only 17 when they sold him. More importantly, they expect him to be working as someone's slave and not acting as second in command to Pharaoh. Joseph reacts with hostility when he first recognizes his brothers, and he refuses to reveal his identity to them. It is not clear whether Joseph is motivated by revenge or suspicion, but we may suspect that he has taken years to get over the way in which his brothers had treated him; seeing them now brings back many unwelcome memories and confuses him with conflicting emotions. The text informs us that seeing Joseph's brothers reminds him of his dreams (42:9). Since these dreams had been the cause of the brothers' animosity, their recall would be in the context of his acrimonious relations with them. These are not loving brothers whom Joseph yearns to see again but people who had been jealous of him, who had planned to murder him, and who had sold him into slavery. While his present position is not one he could complain about, Joseph also has 13 years of hard labor to thank them for.

By questioning the brothers through interpreters, Joseph discovers what they are saying about his own disappearance, and he ascertains that his father and Benjamin are both well, though still in Canaan. In a tension-filled narrative, the brothers explain to Joseph who they are, unaware that their identity is already known. His false accusation that they are spies terrifies them, since this serious accusation can only mean slavery or death.[1] The fate to which they had condemned Joseph is now staring them in the face. Their claim to be honest or upright men is ironic, since Joseph and the readers know their guilty secret (42:11). To prove that they are not spies, they are instructed to send one of their number for Benjamin and bring him to Egypt (42:15). Joseph is emotionally disturbed in the presence of his brothers, and he desperately wants to see the one brother that he can trust.

Joseph has had to exercise patience as he languished for years in prison, and now he makes his brothers wait while he decides what to do, imprisoning them for three days. When Joseph meets them again he allows them to return to Canaan, not out of any feelings of sympathy but because "I fear God" (42:18). However, he insists on keeping Simeon in prison as guarantor of their return with Benjamin. The brothers know that they are in deep trouble because Jacob will not want Benjamin to leave him; they discuss the matter among themselves, unaware that Joseph understands their language. In his hearing they reveal their belief that they are being punished for their treat-

---

1. The irony of this accusation is that in his youth Joseph had spied on his brothers and brought back reports to his father (37:2). As Pirson suggests, the one accusing the brothers of spying "used to be a spy himself"; *The Lord of the Dreams*, 95.

ment of him earlier; this is nearer to the truth than they realize. Joseph learns from their conversation that Reuben was not involved in the plot and was opposed to it. This sign of his brothers' regret softens Joseph's attitude towards them, causing him to weep; but he still keeps Simeon in prison and persists with his plan, even though it is not just the brothers that he is punishing but also his father. The choice of which brother should remain in prison is made by Joseph himself, but we are not told why he chooses Simeon and why he not only imprisons him but binds him (42:24).

We are not told why Joseph refuses to reveal himself to his brothers during this first visit. However, he had resolved not to contact his family during the seven years of plenty, and while this resolve may have been softened by his brothers' appearance and by the things he heard them say, Joseph is not ready yet to forgive.[2]

42:25-38 The Brothers Return to Canaan

Mysteriously, Joseph arranges for the brothers' money to be returned to them. If this is intended as an act of generosity, it only adds to the brothers' misery and fear, since their guilty consciences lead them to suspect that this is further evidence of God working against them (42:28). Their report to their father keeps the issue of whether or not they are honest men to the forefront.

When the brothers return to Jacob and describe what happened, their speech creates a sense of drama and tension because they and their father are not aware of the identity of this person they describe as "the lord of the land"; but the narrator and the readers know. Significantly, the brothers do not tell Jacob the whole story. For example, they do not mention that they have all been in prison three days. Redford argues that they tell Jacob only the essential part of the story because they "are anxious not to upset him."[1] The tension deepens with the discovery of the money in all of the sacks. Up to this point they think that the money has inadvertently been returned in one sack only, but now they are "dismayed" to discover that it has all been returned (42:35).

Their misery is reflected in the apprehension and grief of Jacob. The promised blessing seems irrelevant in their family at that stage of uncertainty and utter desperation. Jacob's dilemma seems to have no solution, since if he

2. Pirson suggests that Joseph was torn between his emotions and his reason; *The Lord of the Dreams*, 99.

1. Redford, *A Study of the Biblical Story of Joseph*, 82.

does nothing they will die in the famine; yet what is required, the sending of Benjamin to Egypt, is unbearable. In this plight there is no revelation from God, no reassurance, and no clear guidance. Jacob must make the inevitable decision that he dreads, while the narrator and the readers know that this painful decision will in fact lead to the denouement of his predicament.

Jacob's favoritism is evident in this passage. He is prepared to sacrifice Simeon rather than risk sending Benjamin to Egypt. Reuben, fulfilling his role as firstborn, tries to reassure his father with the proposal that Reuben's own two sons can be put to death if he refuses to bring Benjamin back (42:37). This is reminiscent of the equally preposterous proposal made by Lot to sacrifice his daughters to the whim of a crowd (19:8). Such an offer did nothing to satisfy the mob's lust, and Reuben's suggestion is equally ridiculous and futile.

43:1-34 Judah Persuades His Father

Following the failure of Reuben to persuade his father to allow Benjamin to go to Egypt, Judah takes the lead. This is the beginning of Judah's increasing prominence in the narrative. Against the background of continued famine, Judah explains that he will be responsible for Benjamin's safety (43:8-10). In the Tamar story, Judah deceptively protected his youngest son, but now he must protect his youngest brother. The gift that Jacob sends to Egypt includes balm, spices, honey, almonds, and pistachio nuts plus double the amount of silver. They are sent with Jacob's best wishes expressed in the name of El Shaddai.

Joseph's behavior is enigmatic. He organizes a banquet for his brothers but does not inform them, serving to increase their anxiety (43:17). They must wait without knowing what will happen, just as Joseph had to wait in the wilderness pit while they decided what to do with him. Still worried about the silver that had been returned, they raise the matter with the steward, who assures them that he received their silver; he tells them that "the God of your father has put treasure in your sacks" (43:23 ESV). The tension in the narrative reaches breaking point as Joseph's intentions are withheld from the reader, and the action is slowed down to a crawl by the dialogue.

Joseph's special relationship with Benjamin is highlighted in two ways: Joseph is overcome emotionally when he sees Benjamin, and he turns aside to weep; he shows his favoritism by ensuring that Benjamin receives a larger portion of meat than the other brothers (43:34). Seating at the feast is prearranged, and the brothers are amazed that they have been seated according to age (43:33). They are seated separately from the Egyptians, since the latter did not eat with Hebrews. Obviously, this reference to "Hebrews" cannot refer to Israelites, and the rule about food may be a general one, indicating that the Egyptians would not eat with Semitic herdsmen. Some have also suggested a link with the term Habiru, which refers to an ethnically diverse group scattered through the ancient Near East who were not linked to any specific land or territory.

44:1-34 The Silver Cup

Joseph does not reveal his identity to his brothers during the meal, increasing the tension in the narrative and suggesting that self-revelation is not his intention. Joseph orders his servant to place his silver cup in Benjamin's bag. Joseph's plan is that when the cup is discovered Benjamin may be separated from the others and returned to Egypt. Benjamin is Joseph's only full brother, but he is also the only brother who was not involved in the plot against Joseph. Therefore, it seems that Joseph intends to keep Benjamin with him in Egypt and to reveal himself to him alone. Accordingly, Joseph's steward pursues the brothers. When the cup is discovered in Benjamin's bag, the steward makes it clear that only Benjamin is required to return to Egypt; but realizing the grief that this would cause their father, the others tear their garments in despair and insist on returning too. Joseph's scheme to separate Benjamin from his brothers and to keep him in Egypt fails.

When the brothers return to Joseph's house, the group is described as "Judah and his brothers" (44:14). This time the brothers do not simply bow before Joseph but fall to the ground before him; their humiliation is complete before the one whom they had wronged. Joseph is unrelenting and accuses them not only of theft but also of stupidity, since they should have known that someone in his position had special powers of divination. Incidentally, the word used for divination has the same consonants as the word for serpent, probably suggesting a link between the serpent cult and divination.[1]

Judah makes no defense at this stage, accepting that "God has found out the guilt of your servants" (44:16 NRSV). Judah, on behalf of the others, is not speaking about their guilt in stealing the cup because he knows that they are innocent; but he accepts that their earlier sin of selling their brother into slav-

---

1. Sarna seeks to defend Joseph from actually practicing divination by suggesting, "It is not stated that Joseph actually believes in divination. He wants his brothers to think he does"; *Genesis*, 304. Pirson, however, suggests that Joseph's use of the divining cup "may be another indication that he has forgotten his father's house during the years spent in Egypt [cf. 41:51]"; *The Lord of the Dreams*, 117.

ery is now being uncovered by God. He therefore offers himself and the others as Joseph's slaves. The story has come full circle, with the chief instigator of Joseph's slavery suggesting that they all become his slaves.

Joseph repeats his decision that only Benjamin must stay and the others are free to return to their father. This is the cue for Judah to step forward and make a moving speech, the longest and most detailed discourse in Genesis. Judah's defense begins in the humblest possible terms, admitting that Joseph is "like Pharaoh himself" (44:18). He accurately summarizes the story so far, with the addition that Jacob believes that Joseph has been torn to pieces. Judah, in this impassioned speech, reminds Joseph of Jacob's great love for the two sons of his favorite wife, and he offers himself as a slave instead of Benjamin. This is poetic justice, since the reader knows that Joseph was sold into slavery at the suggestion of Judah.

45:1-28 Joseph Reveals His Identity

Moved by Judah's speech, Joseph orders the Egyptians from the room as he reveals his true identity, not just to Benjamin, as he originally planned, but to all the brothers. Joseph's emotional state is important to the narrator, who emphasizes that Joseph weeps so loudly during his self-revelation that the Egyptians hear it. More than 20 years of pent-up emotions are being released. Joseph's earlier decision to "forget his past life" has failed, and his loud weeping is a sign that he is now ready for reconciliation. His immediate concern is about his father, and his first full sentence inquires about Jacob's well-being (45:3). The brothers do not answer immediately. The emotion of the occasion is conveyed skillfully by the narrator as he conveys the idea that the brothers are speechless with shock. Their reaction is translated variously by English versions as "troubled" (KJV), "stunned" (NLT), "terrified" (NIV), "dismayed" (ESV, NRSV), "dumfounded" (NJPS).

Joseph not only reveals himself to the surprised brothers, he also explains his understanding of what had happened. He declares that his brothers should not blame themselves, since God had planned it all to provide a means of survival from the famine. He points out that "it was not you who sent me here, but God" (45:8 NRSV). God's providential care is clearly the main theme in the Joseph narratives (cf. 50:20). Life with all its hurdles and troubles is not without purpose, and while God's presence is not always obvious, he nevertheless is still working out his plans. Joseph's rise to power shows that he has been the recipient of blessing. His dreams have now come true, and there is obvious evidence of blessing in his life: he has children (41:50; cf. 1:28), he is very successful (41:39-43; cf. 24:35; 26:12-14), and his brothers bow before him (42:6; cf. 27:29). In contrast, his brothers lack such blessing: they need to plead with an Egyptian to get food (42:6), and they are aware that they are riddled with guilt because of the way in which they mistreated their brother (42:21-22).

Joseph sends his brothers back to their father with carts laden with provisions. Joseph, still not completely convinced about their integrity, warns them not to quarrel on the way back to Canaan (45:24).

46:1-34 Jacob and His Household Depart Canaan for Egypt

Eventually Jacob himself comes to Egypt from Beer-sheba. Beer-sheba is also linked with Jacob's first departure from Canaan (28:10). Previously, Jacob left Beer-sheba because Esau was threatening to take his life (27:42-45). Before departure, Jacob offers sacrifices to the God of his father Isaac (46:1).[1] He does not leave without careful consideration and an assurance from God, who appears to him "in visions of the night." The injunction to "fear not" suggests that he is afraid to leave Canaan.

Compared with Jacob's earlier dream at Bethel, this divine communication is more personal and involves a two-way conversation, during which God assures him that he will go with him and his offspring would become a "great nation there" (46:3-4). God also affirms that Jacob is going to Egypt with a "return ticket," since he promises "I will surely bring you back again" (46:4 NIV). This promise will be partially fulfilled with the return of Jacob's body to Canaan for burial, but ultimately the promise relates to the return of Jacob's offspring to dwell in Canaan.

The narrative lists Jacob's children and grandchildren. The total comes to around 70, including Joseph's sons. Only two daughters are included. These details appear in other accounts to explain that, although comparatively few went down to Egypt, a large company left there after just a few years. One important characteristic of the list is that Judah is treated differently than the others. A note explains that Judah's first two sons died in the land of Canaan. Whereas all the other sons are listed with their immediate progeny, two of Judah's grandchildren (Jacob's great grandchildren) are also listed.

Judah's prominence in the genealogy is continued in the narrative. It is Judah whom Jacob sends ahead to receive direction to Goshen from Joseph. Judah is now clearly in a leadership role.

---

1. Beer-sheba is also closely associated with Isaac, the one patriarch who never left Canaan — not even to find a wife.

The account of Joseph's meeting with his father at Goshen reflects an emotionally charged reunion of a father and son who had despaired of seeing each other again (46:29). The biblical expression "fell on his neck and wept on his neck" is an idiomatic usage equivalent to an deeply emotional embrace. Joseph arranges for his father and brothers to settle in Goshen. This is the most appropriate place because of the aversion of Egyptians to shepherds (46:34).

47:1-12 Jacob Arrives in Egypt

When Jacob and his sons arrive in Egypt, Joseph must obtain permission for them to settle in the land. He takes a delegation of five of his brothers to meet Pharaoh, but we are not told which five. Presumably he chooses those who would make the best impression, or who would be least likely to make a faux pas in the presence of Pharaoh. Asked by Pharaoh about their occupation, the brothers say that they are shepherds and that they have suffered greatly because of the severe famine. They ask Pharaoh for permission to settle in Goshen. Joseph has chosen the five delegates well, since apparently they acquit themselves appropriately; Pharaoh not only grants them permission to stay in the best of the land but also instructs Joseph to employ any of the brothers with special skill to oversee the care of the royal livestock (47:6).

After the brothers leave, Pharaoh has a brief meeting with Jacob, during which he inquires about the herdsman's age. Jacob speaks in a self-deprecatory way and informs Pharaoh that he has lived 130 years. He describes these years as "few and hard" and points out that his life span does not compare with that of his ancestors. Isaac had lived to 180 and Abraham to 175.

When Jacob meets Pharaoh he blesses him, and as he leaves his presence he blesses him again. Jacob's blessing of Pharaoh was a traditional herdsman's greeting appropriate for a powerful foreign dignity. It is not inappropriate for a mere herdsman to bless a king, because the patriarch's superior age would have given him this credibility.

47:13-26 Joseph's Management of the Famine

Joseph had collected the surplus food during the years of good harvests so that it could be distributed during the years of famine. However, it was not given free of charge, not even to the Egyptians themselves. When money was exhausted, Joseph accepted land, and when that was all given over he mortgaged the people themselves as slaves to Pharaoh. Eventually the Egyptians would enslave the Hebrews, but Joseph, a Hebrew, had thought of it first! Joseph makes an agreement with the people that, since they and their land now belong to Pharaoh, they must give one fifth of their produce to the royal coffers. The narrator notes that this rule is still in force at the time of writing (47:26).

47:27-31 Joseph's Oath

Although the story of Jacob's life is not yet complete, at this juncture the narrator summarizes his time in Egypt. Jacob lived there 17 years, and his life span was 147. Jacob makes Joseph swear that he will be buried, not in Egypt but in Canaan. Having gained his wish, Jacob worships God, leaning on the top of his staff (47:31).[1]

48:1-22 Jacob Blesses Ephraim and Manasseh

The aged Jacob recounts to Joseph how Yahweh blessed him in the land of Canaan (48:3-4). Jacob emphasizes especially the facets of blessing relating to land and descendants. The promise that through his descendants all nations would be blessed (28:14) is omitted. Presumably, this is not important here in the family context, especially since it has been dealt with in the preceding story (41:57; cf. 50:20).

The chapter goes on to describe the blessing of Joseph's sons Ephraim and Manasseh (48:5-22). This makes it clear that, although their mother is an Egyptian, they are still to be reckoned in the line of blessing. They are adopted by Jacob. The adoption is linked with a mention of the death and burial of Rachel (48:7). Presumably the purpose of this is to indicate that Ephraim and Manasseh will take the place of other sons whom Rachel might have borne had she not died, or it may be that Joseph and his children remind Jacob of the sad time when he lost his beloved Rachel.

Before the actual blessing of the two lads, Jacob draws them near to him and kisses and embraces them (48:10). There is a wordplay between the noun "knee" and the verb "to bless," since the same consonants are used for both words (ברך/*brk*). This emphasis on those who are to be blessed coming near

---

1. The Hebrew text reads, "Jacob bowed himself upon the head of his bed," a reading followed by several versions including ESV, KJV, and NRSV. The LXX has the alternative reading, "Jacob leaned on the top of his staff," and this is followed by the NIV.

to the one who will bestow the blessing emphasizes the harmony required between the donor of the blessing and the recipient. This is reminiscent of the blessing bestowed on Jacob, who was told to draw near to Isaac, who kissed him before bestowing the blessing (27:26-27). There could be no blessing until there was communion between the giver and the recipient; the kissing and embracing establish this communion.

Joseph expects his father to pronounce the blessing with his right hand on the head of the firstborn Manasseh but, significantly, his right hand is placed on the younger son Ephraim (48:14). Once again we have the younger being given preeminence over the older (48:17-20).[1] The incident recalls the blessing of Jacob by Isaac, when the usual conventions were broken in favor of the younger son (27:1-40). In this case, however, the recipients are passive and there is no repetition of the deception perpetrated by Jacob. Furthermore, although Jacob is now old and blind, as Isaac had been in ch. 27, Jacob has a clear prophetic insight about which of the boys before him should receive the blessing reserved for the firstborn (48:19).

The blessing commences with Jacob's ascription of three titles to God (48:15-16).

(1) "The God before whom my fathers Abraham and Isaac walked" (48:15 NIV), identifying his God as the God who promised blessing through Abraham and his seed (12:1-3).

(2) "The God who has been my Shepherd all my life to this day" (48:15 NIV). The picture of God as shepherd occurs in the Psalms (23:1; 80:1) and prophets (Isa 40:11; Ezek 34:11-31), but in Genesis it is used only here and in the blessing of Joseph (49:24).

(3) "The Angel who has delivered me from all harm" (48:16 NIV).

These three statements reflect Jacob's close relationship with God and highlight his dependence on God's presence. As von Rad points out, the third

---

1. Vawter gives a useful outline of how this pattern develops throughout Genesis and discusses its significance in this context: "Abel (then Seth) is chosen over Cain (chapter 4), Japheth supersedes Ham in the order of precedence after Shem (9:18-27), Isaac is preferred to Ishmael, Jacob to Esau, Perez to Zerah (38:27-30), Judah over his elder brothers (cf. 49:8). In this story Joseph brings his sons before his father in the proper order, so that his firstborn will be in the place of honor, at Jacob's right hand. When Jacob crosses his hands in bestowing his blessing, thus reversing Joseph's protocol, the latter naturally thinks that blindness or senility has befuddled the mind of the aged patriarch and seeks to rectify the mistake. But Jacob has in his final breaths been gifted with prophetic insight, which counts for more than the wisdom of Joseph"; *On Genesis*, 455.

of these statements is "the most important theologically."[2] The "Angel" referred to is not a third party but God himself.[3] The word translated "delivered" in the NIV is the verb "to redeem" or "to ransom" (cf. NRSV, ESV). In the OT the concept of redemption is primarily related to family relationships and responsibilities, and it shows that God "is the closest relative, prepared to redeem man."[4] Jacob does not indicate how or in what circumstances God "redeemed" him, but he is probably referring in a general sense to God's intervention on his behalf to protect him from his enemies.

Jacob's threefold identification of God introduces and emphasizes the prayer of blessing that the boys may be blessed and perpetuate the names of Jacob himself and also of his ancestors Isaac and Abraham (48:16). By giving Joseph's sons his name, Jacob makes them his heirs, and this in turn makes them heirs of the promise of a great name given by Yahweh to Abraham (12:2). The blessing concludes with the idea that they should "grow into a multitude," a major emphasis in almost every blessing pronounced in Genesis, not just in the patriarchal narratives but also in the primeval history (cf. 1:22, 28; 9:1; 12:2; 22:17; 28:3; 35:11).

The wording of the blessing makes no distinction between Ephraim and Manasseh (48:16). The difference lies in the formalities and symbolism involved (cf. 48:17). The symbolism and the etiquette of blessing are probably as important as the words used.

After blessing the two boys, Jacob gives a piece of land to Joseph (48:22). Two things are said about this gift. First, it is an extra portion beyond what the other brothers receive; and second, it is land that Jacob took by force from the Amorites. Jacob explains that he took the land "with my sword and with my bow." This altercation with the inhabitants of the land is not mentioned elsewhere in Genesis.

49:1-28 Jacob Blesses His Sons

Chapter 49 is devoted, apart from a short account of Jacob's death, to the blessing Jacob bestows upon his sons. These blessings are without parallel in Genesis, and indeed some of them actually are curses rather than blessings (49:7). In the light of this, Willis comments:

2. Von Rad, *Genesis*, 417.

3. Westermann observes that the term "Angel" is used in this context "as an alternative for God"; *Genesis 37–50*, 190.

4. Von Rad, *Genesis*, 418.

Perhaps "bless" (Heb. *barakh*) is to be interpreted as a polar word here, meaning both "bless" and "curse" as the individual case demands, or at least is to be taken as a relative term depending on the character of the father of the tribe and/or that of the tribe itself.[1]

Clearly, Jacob is not speaking simply as a wise old patriarch, but he is endowed with prophetic insight and is outlining the future history of the tribes with divine enabling. While the prophecies are addressed to individuals and may even be corollaries of their merits or faults, ultimately these predictions are about intertribal relationships and the future of the nation of Israel.

Reuben, the firstborn, is addressed first (49:3-4). At one time Jacob had been proud of Reuben. However, Reuben loses the preeminence that he should have enjoyed as Jacob's firstborn because of sexual impropriety (35:22). By this act Reuben destroyed the communion existing between his father and him, and as a result he forfeits the blessing. Not only Reuben suffers a loss of preeminence, but the tribe named after him endures the same fate. When the tribes are called to battle in the period of the judges, the warriors in Reuben's clan are apparently indecisive (Judg 5:15-16). The Chronicler preserves the tradition of Reuben's failure and states that the rights of Reuben as firstborn were transferred to the sons of Joseph:

> The sons of Reuben the firstborn of Israel (for he was the firstborn, but because he defiled his father's couch, his birthright was given to the sons of Joseph the son of Israel, so that he could not be enrolled as the oldest son; though Judah became strong among his brothers and a chief came from him, yet the birthright belonged to Joseph). (1 Chr 5:1-2 ESV)

This deprecation of Reuben is reflected in the tribe's nondescript history. As Wenham observes, "the Reubenites seem to fade out of national history: no prophet, judge, or king came from this tribe."[2]

The comment that introduces the next blessing, "Simeon and Levi are brothers" (49:5), seems superfluous. The reader already knows that they are brothers, and furthermore the people addressed are all brothers. However, the statement is not made to confirm their physical kinship but to establish that they are partners in crime. Jacob condemns their anger in which they killed men and hamstrung oxen, and he distances himself from their crime, which

---

1. Willis, *Genesis*, 446.

2. Wenham, *Genesis 16–50*, 473. A similar point is made by von Rad: "The tribe produced no significant man, no judge, no king, no prophet"; *Genesis*, 423.

probably refers to their massacre of the Hittites (34:25-31). Jacob pronounces a curse on Simeon and Levi that emphasizes that they will be scattered and dispersed. This is reminiscent of the fate that befell the builders of Babel (11:8). These brothers have brought alienation and not harmony; therefore, the blessing becomes a curse. This is the very thing that Jacob feared himself when his mother prompted him to deceive his father (27:12).

The blessing pronounced on Judah, the fourth son of Leah, is positive and lavish, apparently giving this tribe a leadership role.[3] Supremacy and fertility are the two main elements of the pronouncements. Judah is pronounced preeminent over both allies and enemies. Judah's subjection of his enemies is described in uncompromising terms as having his hand on their neck, indicating complete subjection. His allies (brothers) are also in subjection to Judah and bow down to him, but the relationship is introduced on a laudatory note with a wordplay emphasizing that Judah will be praised by his brothers (49:8).[4] The wordplay is based on the similar sounds of the name Judah and the verb "they will praise you": יְהוּדָה/*yĕhûdâ* ("Judah"); יוֹדוּךָ/*yôdûkā* ("they will praise you"). We are not given any details about why the brothers should praise Judah, but there seems to be a reference to a heroic deed performed by Judah for which his brothers praise him. The emphasis on Judah's supremacy is intensified by an animal metaphor in which Judah is characterized as both a ferocious young lion devouring prey and an older lion or lioness lying down, defying anyone to disturb it.

Judah's "curriculum vitae" is further enhanced in 49:10 by the role of ruler represented by a scepter and a ruler's staff, the symbols of authority. It is not entirely clear how the second half of the verse should be translated. Three main approaches have developed.

> The sceptre shall not depart from Judah, nor a lawgiver from between his feet, until Shiloh come; and unto him shall the gathering of the people be. (KJV)

> The scepter will not depart from Judah, nor the ruler's staff from between his feet, until he comes to whom it belongs and the obedience of the nations is his. (NIV)

3. But according to the Chronicler, the tribe of Joseph received the blessing due to the firstborn and forfeited by Reuben (1 Chr 5:1-2).

4. As Westermann points out, the wordplay is on the basis of assonance rather than etymology: "This is not an etymology, i.e., the purpose of the saying is not to explain the name Judah (as in Gen. 29:35); it is a pure wordplay"; *Genesis 37–50*, 227.

The sceptre shall not depart from Judah, nor the ruler's staff from be-tween his feet, until tribute comes to him; and to him shall be the obedi-ence of the peoples. (ESV)

In spite of a great deal of scholarly debate, there has been no definitive interpretation of Shiloh.[5] The KJV simply reproduces in English the Hebrew word "Shiloh" (שׁיל֑ה/*šîlōh*). However, it is difficult to make sense of this, since elsewhere in the OT Shiloh is a place and not a person (Josh 18:1; 1 Sam 1:3).[6] Moreover, it is a place associated with judgment rather than hope (Ps 78:60; Jer 7:12). Therefore, scholars have explored possible meanings of Shiloh, which has sometimes involved changing the vowels of the word.[7] One suggestion is that the reference is not to Shiloh but to Shelah, Judah's son.[8] Another suggestion reflected in the NIV is to understand *šîlōh* as the relative pronoun *še*, meaning "which" plus a preposition with the third person pro-nominal suffix meaning "to him," to give the reading, "to whom it belongs." A slightly different change in vocalization is used in the ESV to give "until trib-ute comes to him."

In spite of these difficulties, it is clear that the passage indicates that the dominance of the tribe of Judah will not be lost until the coming of a person or event that will firmly establish it. While the details are debatable, the general import of the blessing is clear: Judah is promised a period of prominence over the other tribes until this culminates in the authority of the monarchy and the domination of the surrounding nations. Since the dominance of Judah results in "the obedience of the nations," Westermann observes that this "corresponds exactly to the historical reality under David and Solomon."[9]

The remainder of the pronouncements on Judah focus on wealth and fertility (49:11-12). Idyllic imagery is now introduced as a man is portrayed tying his foal or donkey to the choicest of vines while he washes his clothes in wine. The image of the animal tied to a vine represents a carefree atti-tude, since it implies that the owner has so many vines that he does not care if the donkey eats one of them. Likewise, washing clothes in wine is evoca-tive of fertility and abundance. Minor details such as the inadvisability of

5. Cf. Westermann, *Genesis 37–50*, 231.

6. Nevertheless, in Jewish tradition *Shiloh* was sometimes understood as a reference to the Messiah (cf. *Targum Onkelos to Genesis*, 284).

7. Biblical Hebrew was a consonantal language, and the vowel system used today was not finalized until the 9th century A.D.

8. This view is discussed by Carmichael, "Some Sayings in Genesis 49," 438-44.

9. Westermann, *Genesis 37–50*, 230.

washing clothes in wine are not an issue since the passage is deliberately metaphorical.

The pronouncements on Judah conclude with images of health and well-being. Eyes darker than wine and teeth whiter that milk are not modern ways of describing a healthy person, but in the context of the ancient farming community they evoke an image of someone whose appearance reflects a good diet and healthy lifestyle.

In summary, the main advantages bestowed on Judah are: victory over his enemies (49:8), supremacy over his brothers (49:8), sovereignty over other nations (49:10), abundant provision (49:11-12).[10] Judah is given a very prominent position among the brothers and is identified as the one through whom the future leadership of the tribes will come. The prominence given to Judah and the most generous blessing he receives mark him and his descendants as having a special role to play in the future fulfillment of the promises initially made to Abraham (12:1-3). In spite of the uncertainty involved in translating some of the details of these pronouncements, they unmistakably point to the kingdom of David and underline not just the authority of David himself but also of his descendants.

In sharp contrast to the detailed and complex blessing on Judah, the pronouncements on Zebulun are brief and low key. Animal metaphors give way to nautical images, identifying the tribe's future as being "by the seashore" and as becoming "a haven for ships" with its border extending towards Sidon (49:13). Nothing pejorative is said about Zebulun, yet nothing positive is promised either. References to the sea in this blessing are at variance with the land-locked territory allotted to the tribe in Josh 19:10-16. However, there was a clear tradition linking Zebulun with the sea, since the blessing of Moses uses the same imagery (Deut 33:19). In the book of Judges, Deborah praises the role of Zebulun in defeating the Canaanites and describes Zebulun as "a people who risked their lives to the death" (Judg 5:18 ESV).

The indictment on Issachar relates to a willingness to accept servitude (49:14-15). The precise imagery used is debated because of the uncertainty about the translation of the word הַמִּשְׁפְּתָיִם/*hammišppĕtāyim*. The word occurs only twice in the Bible, here and in Judg 5:16. It is a dual Hebrew form and refers to two of something. One possibility is that it should be translated as "two saddlebags." If this is correct, Issachar is portrayed as a donkey that is

10. The poetic imagery here of tying the donkey to the vine is not just one of abundance but of extravagance, according to von Rad: "No Judean would tie his ass to a vine, for it would be eaten up, of course. Anyone who can be so careless and who can wash his garment in wine, lives in paradisiacal abundance. Probably these statements intend to say just this in antiquated poetry . . . he who will come will live in an aeon of paradisiacal fertility" (*Genesis*, 425).

unwilling to bear the burden placed upon it, and so, resting the two saddle-bags on the ground, it lies down between them.[11] Others translate the disputed word as "two campfires" or as "sheepfolds" (cf. NRSV). Whichever translation is used, the meaning is clear; the passage accuses Issachar of being like a lazy donkey that remains inactive when there is work to be done. The work that Issachar refuses to do is to secure their territory, and apparently this passage suggests that they accepted servitude without resistance. If this reflects a particular tradition about the history of the tribe, it has been lost.

The pronouncement on Dan makes two main points. The tribe would provide "justice for his people," and it would be "a serpent by the roadside" (49:16-18). Jacob's characterization of Dan as a serpent that bites a horse, resulting in its rider being thrown to the ground, may reflect the history of the tribe. Dan settled by the coast, but under pressure from their enemies, the tribe was eventually forced to move further inland to the north at the end of the Judges period. The exploits of Samson, one of Dan's most colorful and enigmatic descendants, suggests that Dan responded to the Philistines and other enemies, not with all-out war but with guerrilla attacks. In this case, the imagery of the serpent that buried itself in the sand and attacked anything that passed by is an apt metaphor for Dan.

A short prayer follows the blessing of Dan: "I wait for your salvation, O LORD" (49:18 NRSV). The use of the first person suggests that this is Jacob's personal prayer. Perhaps this is his response to the bad news that he is predicting for his sons and their descendants.

The brief mention of Gad relates to its retaliation against an enemy (49:19).

> Gad shall be raided by raiders, but he shall raid at their heels. (NRSV)
> גָּד גְּדוּד יְגוּדֶנּוּ וְהוּא יָגֻד עָקֵב
> *Gād Gĕdûd yĕgûdennû wĕhûʾ yāgūd ʿāqēb*

This short statement resembles one of those tongue twisters that are difficult to say quickly. This reflects the unmistakable play on the name Gad, the consonants of which occur in four of these six words. The last word, "heel," reminds us of Jacob himself, who grasped his brother's heel at birth (25:26). The passage refers to a situation where Gad, or more likely the tribe descended from him, will be vulnerable to raiders but will fight back. This is appropriate, since the tribe settled in Transjordan, where they were continually forced to

---

11. This view is reflected in KJV and NIV.

defend their territory.[12] The name Gad occurs in the Moabite inscription, which records the military exploits of Mesha, king of Moab.

> And the men of Gad lived in the land of Ataroth from ancient times, and the king of Israel built Ataroth for himself, and I fought against the city, and I captured it.

This inscription suggests that Mesha thought that Israel was allied to Gad; but he apparently did not know the tradition that Gad was a tribe of Israel. However, Mesha's reference to war with Gad suggests that the blessing was appropriate.

For Asher an abundance of food is envisaged (49:20). Asher's name means "happy one," reflecting the jubilation of his mother when he was born (30:13). Asher's descendants settled in a fertile area of western Galilee and were in an ideal position to trade with the neighboring Phoenicians. The reference to "royal delicacies" (NRSV) suggests that, because of their fertile land and strategic location, the people of Asher may have supplied food for foreign royal courts.[13] It is also possible that they supplied the courts in Samaria and Jerusalem.[14]

Naphtali's blessing is obscure and various interpretations are possible. If we follow the MT pointing,[15] the blessing compares Naphtali to a wild doe that has been released from captivity (49:21). This doe, according to most versions, produces beautiful fawns, but the KJV translation, "he giveth goodly words," is a more literal translation. To add to the confusion, the LXX supplies different vowels to the word that is usually translated "doe" and renders it as the stem or branch of a plant:

> Naphtali is a spreading stem, bestowing beauty on its fruit. (LXX)

---

12. Sarna observes that "for most of its history, Gad was engaged in a series of wars with its neighbors, Ammonites (Judg. 11), Moabites (Mesha Inscription, lines 10-13), and Arameans (1 Kings 22:3; 2 Kings 10:33). Its members acquired a reputation as fighting warriors (Deut 33:20; 1 Chr 5:18 and 12:8) and, doubtless, the Testament of Jacob reflects this"; *Genesis*, 341.

13. The view that Asher supplied foreign royal courts is supported by Wenham. He observes that it is unclear "whether this remark is a compliment or a rebuke, or simply a comment on Asher's affluence"; *Genesis 16–50*, 482.

14. This is von Rad's view, *Genesis*, 427.

15. Hebrew is a consonantal language originally written without vowels. The vowel system used in our Hebrew Bibles is referred to as "pointing"; it was developed by Jewish scholars known as Masoretes, leading to the designation of the text they produced as the Masoretic Text. Although the earliest extant copies of the MT are from the 10th century A.D., the Masoretes were following established traditions for vocalization and orthography.

Nothing that we are told about the history of Naphtali sheds light on the problem, and all the suggested translations are very tentative. Von Rad suggests that "the saying about Naphtali can scarcely be interpreted by us any more."[16]

Jacob then goes on to pronounce a lavish blessing on Joseph (49:22-26). The considerable differences in the translations of this passage in modern versions reflect textual difficulties. Von Rad comments that the text of the blessing on Joseph "is in bad condition and filled with questions that concern first of all the meaning of the words and their syntactic relation to one another."[17] Wenham describes the passage as "an exegete's nightmare."[18] This problem did not begin with modern versions, since the Samaritan Pentateuch and the LXX differ considerably from the MT.

The blessing on Joseph reflects his experience of being ostracized and hated by his brothers and other enemies. His deliverance occurred because God was with him. Several names are used for God in this passage. He is the Mighty One of Jacob. This title, Wenham suggests, "seems to be an ancient epithet for God that is echoed in Ps 132:2, 5; Isa 49:26; 60:16; cf. 1:24."[19] Joseph's success both as a person and as a tribe reflects not so much the personal qualities of Jacob's son but the mighty power of Jacob's God, who could protect his chosen one, even in Egypt.

God is also described as "Shepherd," a title that came from Jacob's own experience as a successful herdsman and shepherd who knew how to care for his flock and had a deep interest in their health and fertility (30:31-43).

Although the RSV introduces the title "Rock of Israel," the Hebrew word is אֶבֶן/'eben, lit., "the Stone of Israel" (so KJV). This may be a reference to the stone that Jacob anointed at Bethel, where his first encounter with God took place. Two other titles of God that appear in the passage express continuity and protective presence: "the God of your father" and "the Almighty" (49:25; cf. 17:1).

In 49:25-26 the key word "blessing" occurs five times and the verb "to bless" occurs once, emphasizing that God had turned the efforts to destroy Joseph into blessing. The benediction on Joseph is mainly related to fertility in the field and in the home. The efficacy of these blessings is lauded and claimed to be stronger than the blessings of the mountains or the bounties of the everlasting hills. These blessings, Jacob prays, will rest on the brow of Joseph, who was separated from his brothers.

16. Von Rad, *Genesis*, 427. See the detailed discussions in Wenham and Sarna.

17. Von Rad, *Genesis*, 427.

18. Wenham, *Genesis 16–50*, 484.

19. Wenham, *Genesis 16–50*, 486.

Benjamin receives the final blessing, which describes him as a "ravenous wolf" (49:27). Very little information is given about Benjamin's personal character, but nothing suggests that he was like a ravenous wolf. Sarna describes Benjamin as Jacob's "lamblike youngest son."[20] Therefore, Jacob's statement relates to later activities of the tribe of Benjamin rather than to any particular incident in the book of Genesis (cf. Judg 19:1–21:25).

The blessing of Jacob's sons concludes with a note that he has blessed each one with an appropriate blessing (49:28).

49:29–50:14 The Death and Burial of Jacob

Jacob announces that his death is imminent and instructs his sons to bury him in the cave that Abraham bought from the Hittites, the place where Abraham, Sarah, Rebekah, and Leah are already interred. Having given these instructions, Jacob draws his feet up into the bed and dies (49:33). After Jacob's dream at Bethel, the Hebrew text mentions that "he lifted his feet" (29:1), and now the same phrase occurs again. His pilgrimage is framed between these references about lifting his feet. The pilgrimage that began at Bethel, took him to Aram, and back to Canaan finally concludes in Egypt.

Jacob's body is embalmed, an expensive practice indicating high status and wealth. This process takes 40 days, but the ceremonial period of mourning continues for a further 30 days. At the end of this period, Joseph requests Pharaoh's permission to take his father's body to Canaan for burial. Joseph makes his request to Pharaoh's household and not directly to Pharaoh himself as previously (47:1). This suggests that Joseph's status in Egypt is on the wane and prepares the reader for the time when a pharaoh will not know Joseph (Exod 1:8). It is also significant that Joseph must ask permission to leave Egypt. His request is made on the basis that he has found favor in Pharaoh's sight; furthermore, he supports his request with the claim that his father made him swear on oath that he would bury him in Canaan. While the permission is granted readily, the stage is set for a later pharaoh's refusal to a similar request.

A large Egyptian entourage accompanies the funeral procession to Canaan, and a seven-day period of mourning is observed. Significantly, the Canaanites who see these proceedings believe that it is an Egyptian who is being buried. This is another subtle warning about the dangers of Jacob's descendants losing their identity if they become too closely related to other nations.

20. Sarna, *Genesis*, 345.

50:15-21 Joseph's Relationship with His Brothers after Their Father's Death

This passage demonstrates that Joseph's brothers are still haunted by guilt and fear because of their crimes against Joseph. They do not believe that he has forgiven them, and they fear that following their father's death Joseph will take revenge.

Driven by guilt and fear, the brothers develop a plan to preempt Joseph's vengeance. Their scheme involves a concocted story that Jacob had requested before his death that Joseph should forgive them. It is very unlikely that their report of Jacob's request is genuine, since if Jacob had such worries he would have spoken to Joseph personally. Joseph weeps when he receives their message, probably because he realizes that they still do not trust him, or perhaps because he is disappointed that they resort to a deceptive scheme to win his favor. It is significant that a book which has a story of deception by the serpent near its beginning draws near its conclusion with a further act of deception. Joseph's reply to his brothers is very significant, because it highlights the theme of God's providence. His brothers had acted with evil intent, but God was in control and turned their evil into something good (50:20; cf. 45:8).

Joseph's brothers have one final way of averting his anticipated reprisals, and this is to offer themselves as slaves. The reader knows that slavery will befall the Israelites in Egypt, but this is still in the future. Joseph refuses their offer and repeats his earlier declaration that God had overruled by turning their evil into good. Once again, prominence is given to the important theme that, even when things are going wrong, God is still in control and will fulfill his purposes.

50:22-26 Joseph's Death

The final five verses of Genesis are about Joseph. Following a brief pericope with information about Joseph's offspring, the passage records his death, burial, and last requests. Two pieces of information are given twice in these verses, emphasizing their importance. First, we are told twice that Joseph died when he was 110. While most of the ages given in Genesis are mysterious and we do not know whether to take them literally, this is the exception. The age of 110 was an ideal age in Egypt, and the successful pharaohs also died at 110. This ideal Egyptian age establishes Joseph as a success in his work as a senior Egyptian official. However, the second piece of information that is repeated reminds us that Joseph was not an Egyptian but a Hebrew from the land of

Canaan. Thus, we are told twice that Joseph affirmed that God would surely come to his people's aid and take them from Egypt to the land sworn by divine oath to Abraham. Joseph makes his listeners swear that they will take his bones from Egypt to the land that God has promised.

The final detail given in Genesis is that Joseph died and, like his father, his body was embalmed. In a subtle way the embalmed body of Joseph waiting its transfer to Canaan is a fitting end to the book of Genesis.

Theological Horizons of Genesis

THEOLOGICAL MESSAGE OF THE BOOK

Main Unifying Themes

The book of Genesis, as indeed the Pentateuch, is a collection of fairly diverse materials including narratives and genealogies that may have circulated independently of each other at one time. A great deal of work has been done to analyze the Pentateuch with a view to discovering the sources underlying the finished work. The results of this approach may be seen, for example, in Westermann's detailed three-volume commentary on Genesis. This approach allowed scholars analytically to examine and critically to evaluate passages in microscopic detail in order to understand their provenance, interrelationship, and respective theological perspectives.[1] One of the main drawbacks was that it was not an appropriate method for understanding the overall message of a book. It was more suited to discovering the "Kerygma of the Yahwist" or the theology of the Priestly writer than the theological message of an entire book such as Genesis.

One of the legacies of the analytical approach to the study of the Pentateuch is the consensus that books such as Genesis were not written in the way that a modern author would write a book from cover to cover. Genealogical data, stories, and poetic passages have been brought together with an overall purpose and particular readership in mind to produce a finished work. This does not imply, however, that Genesis, is just a collection of ancient documents or a scrapbook of religious memorabilia. The book has an overall purpose and a logical sequence of events that lead towards a conclusion and de-

---

1. A brief history of this approach is given in the introduction to this book.

nouement. The present chapter seeks to answer the questions "What was this overall purpose?" and "How do we discover it?" More specifically, how do the books of the Pentateuch and Genesis in particular hang together as we now have them; what unifies them and makes them readable as a whole?

In this chapter I argue that there are unifying themes in Genesis that can be identified in every major narrative. These themes provide an explanation for the structure, content, and main emphasis of the work, and they also provide continuity between Genesis and the other books of the Pentateuch. Unifying themes are not just important topics such as "covenant," for example. No one can deny that "covenant" is important, but it is an event related to a theme rather than a theme in its own right. Unifying themes will not simply be recurring motifs but will easily be identified as the continual emphasis of the book woven into the woof and fabric of every passage. If we can identify themes that affect the structure and content of Genesis to the extent that they are essential for the cohesion and coherence of the work, then we will have identified the interpretative key to the message and significance of the text. If we fail to identify these themes, then we risk misunderstanding the book. We can never know even what a modern author's intention is for writing a particular book because we cannot access the writer's inner mind to discover his or her motivation; and in this sense it seems futile to attempt to understand the overall purpose of an author of an ancient book such as Genesis. Nevertheless, at a functional level, the themes that unite diverse material and give a book its final form will be invaluable in shedding light on the raison d'être and theological purpose that gave the book its final form. These themes will also have a bearing on the overall message of the Pentateuch and will show the significance of the message of Genesis in its canonical setting of the Torah and of the Hebrew Bible.

Genesis does not stand on its own but is a component of the Pentateuch. The book ends with the placing of Joseph's embalmed body in a coffin in Egypt. This ending anticipates the book of Exodus and the story of the return of Joseph's body to the land of Canaan. In order to identify the unifying themes of Genesis we should, therefore, study the book in its wider context of the Pentateuch and inquire about the themes that provide cohesion for all five books and not just Genesis.

One of the best known attempts to identify the unifying themes of the Pentateuch is provided by Clines in *The Theme of the Pentateuch*.[2] According to Clines, the single theme that enables the Pentateuch to be read as a unity is the partial fulfillment of God's promises to the ancestors. Clines divides these promises into three groups: land, a relationship with God, and descendants.

---

2. First published in 1977, the work was revised and updated in 1997.

These three groups of promises are clearly significant for the book of Genesis as well, and I suggest that they should be identified as the unifying themes of the book. The second theme, a relationship with God, is best approached through the concept of blessing. As we shall see, blessing is God's way of showing his favor to those who are in a harmonious relationship with him. I intend to deal with these themes in the following order:

1. Descendants
2. Blessing
3. Land

These are not to be understood as independent or parallel concepts running through Genesis but as interrelated and interdependent themes that are part of the rhetorical, theological, and structural distinctiveness of the work. Nor are these themes equal in status and significance. The theme of descendants is the foundational or key theme, since the others, blessing and land, can only be recognized by their relational function to those who benefit from them — the descendants. Therefore, the order in which these themes are studied should be first descendants and then blessing and land.

Descendants

The identification of descendants as, not just a theme, but the key unifying theme of Genesis relies on a number of factors. One obvious indication is the frequent occurrence of the Hebrew word "seed." It is not just the number of occurrences that is important, but the fact that they occur in all the main narratives. Another unique feature of Genesis is the occurrence of the *toledot* formula. This will be discussed in more detail below, but it is a formula that is linked to the theme of bearing children and is integral to the structure of Genesis, dividing the book into 10 sections. Another obvious indication of the importance of the theme of descendants is the genealogical material in Genesis. We shall see that these lists are not cosmetic in the book of Genesis, but that they contribute to its theological message and purpose. Moreover, the significance of the theme of descendants is clearly indicated by the way in which the theme is integrated into the story line and plot of every main story in the book. Finally, the theme of descendants provides continuity between Genesis and the other books of the Pentateuch in order to show that the Israelites in Exodus are heirs to the promises made to the patriarchs. The accumulative weight of this evidence is very strong and points unequivocally to the importance and significance of the theme of descendants in Genesis.

We shall now study this theme in more detail.

The frequent occurrences of the word "seed" in Genesis reveal its thematic importance.

Throughout Genesis descendants are referred to using the Hebrew word "seed," זֶרַע/*zera'*. This word is used, first of all, in relation to the plants that are created by God with their seed to produce further plants after their kind. The idea that plants produce more plants of the same kind is repeated frequently in ch. 1. The seed of a specific fruit can be traced back to a parent tree of the same type. This emphasis on the generation of plants prepares the reader to recognize the importance of human genealogical data. Just as the seed of a particular fruit can be traced back to the parent tree, the seed of Abraham[1] can be traced back to him and they are heirs of the promises he received.

Modern versions of the Bible often translate the word "seed" with alternatives such as "offspring" or "descendants." As a result, the English reader may be unaware of the frequency with which the subject of seed occurs. Therefore, a brief survey of the occurrences of "seed" will be helpful to show how this concept is woven into the fabric of the entire book.

After the disobedience in Eden, God pronounces that there will be enmity between the woman's seed and the serpent's seed (3:15). Eve refers to Seth as "another seed instead of Abel" (4:25). Noah builds the ark "to keep seed alive on the earth" (7:3). When the flood has abated, God establishes a covenant with Noah and his seed (9:9). In the patriarchal narratives, God promises that Abraham's seed will inherit the land (12:7; 13:15) and that his seed will be as difficult to number as particles of dust (13:16). However, because Sarah cannot have children, Abraham complains to God that he has no seed (15:3). Again, God confirms that Abraham's seed will be as numerous and as difficult to number as the stars (15:5). In a vision, Abraham is warned that his seed will be enslaved (15:13). God establishes a covenant with Abraham; his seed will inherit the land (15:18). After Abraham's relationship with Hagar, an angel tells her that her seed will be too numerous to count (16:10). In ch. 17 God establishes a covenant with Abraham and his seed (17:7), and as part of the proceedings he promises land to Abraham and to his seed (17:8).

---

1. For consistency, in the theological discussion the patriarch and his wife will be called Abraham and Sarah, even though these names were not given until ch. 17.

The text emphasizes that it is not only Abraham who is bound by God's covenant but also his seed (17:9), and like Abraham his seed must observe circumcision (17:10). Moreover, males in Abraham's household who are not his seed
also must be circumcised (17:12). God promises that Isaac will be born and
that he will establish his covenant with him and his seed (17:19). The subject
of seed is important for others as well as Abraham, and we are informed that
Lot's daughters are anxious to have seed (19:32, 34). Although Ishmael will become a great nation (21:13), it is emphasized that Abraham's seed will be reckoned through Isaac (21:12) and will be as difficult to number as the stars
(22:17). All nations will be blessed through Abraham's seed (22:18). The importance that Abraham places on the line of descent through Isaac is emphasized by his insistence on an endogamous marriage for his son; he reminds
his servant that God has promised the land of Canaan to his seed (24:7). Seed
is also an important issue for Rebekah's relatives, who wish that her seed will
dominate their enemies (24:60).

After the death of Abraham, God confirms the promise of land to Isaac
and to his seed (26:3-4). God also promises that Isaac's seed will be as numerous as the stars and that all nations will be blessed through his seed; to emphasize its importance, the word seed occurs three times in 26:4. God also promises Isaac that the number of his "seed" will be increased for Abraham's sake
(26:24). The concept of seed is also emphasized in connection with Jacob. Isaac
wishes for Jacob and his seed the blessing of Abraham (28:4). Furthermore, Jacob receives promises at Bethel; the land will be for him and for his seed
(28:13). Indeed, God promises that Jacob's seed will be like the dust of the earth
and that all peoples will be blessed through him and his seed (28:14). Later,
when he is afraid, Jacob recalls that God promised that his seed would be as
numerous as grains of sand (32:12). When Jacob returns to Canaan and eventually to Bethel, God renews the promise of land to him and to his seed (35:12).

Three interesting occurrences of the word "seed" that English readers
may easily miss relate to Onan, who was responsible for raising seed for his
dead brother. The Hebrew contains an evocative wordplay, since the word for
both offspring and semen is "seed." So Onan, unwilling to raise seed for his
brother, spills his seed on the ground (38:8-9).

In the Joseph narrative, Jacob and all his seed go to Egypt (46:6-7). There
are also several references to seed in relation to the crops in Egypt related to the
famine (47:19-24). When Jacob is dying, he recounts the promise of land to
him and to his seed (48:4). When Joseph brings his sons to Jacob, the old man
rejoices that, not only has he seen Joseph alive, but also his seed (48:11). Jacob
prophesies that Ephraim's seed will become a group of nations (48:19).

This survey of the use of the word "seed" in Genesis shows how the term is found in every major narrative, highlighting the importance of the subject of family and, in particular, of lines of descent throughout the book. These occurrences are one of the distinguishing aspects of Genesis and contribute to its overall message.

The toledot *formula underlines the structural significance of seed.*

Modern readers have the benefit of reading Genesis in a well-structured format with the work clearly divided into chapters and verses, so that with the aid of modern lexical tools we can find any given word or phrase in seconds. Ancient readers did not have the advantage of chapters and verses, but there is evidence that the text was originally divided into 10 sections by a phrase, often called the "*toledot* formula." This is usually translated in English as "these are the generations of . . ." or "this is the family history of. . . ." The most significant Hebrew word in this phrase, which occurs only in the construct form in the Bible, is תּוֹלְדוֹת/*tôlĕdôt*, "generations of," and hence the name. Ten times the phrase *'ēlleh tôlĕdôt* occurs (2:4; 6:9; 10:1; 11:10; 11:27; 25:12; 25:19; 36:1; 36:9;[2] 37:2), and on one occasion there is a similar expression: *zeh sēper tôlĕdôt*, "this is the book of the generations of" (5:1 ESV). These occurrences seem to be a deliberate attempt to divide Genesis into 10 main sections and to provide a unifying framework. The noun *tôlĕdôt* is linked to the verb יָלַד/*yālad*, which means "to bear children." The use of the word *tôlĕdôt* in this way draws the reader's attention to the importance of birth and genealogical lines in Genesis. Genesis is a complex family tree augmented with material from family histories. It traces the eponymous ancestors of Israel back to the first man and woman and their son Seth. The *tôlĕdôt* are often closely linked with genealogical data about the main characters. This is further evidence on the significance of lines of descent.

The genealogical data is presented as essential to the narrative.

Any attempt to understand the theme of seed or descendants in Genesis must take account of the genealogical lists in the book. The genealogies are a practical outworking of the theme of "seed" and give the book a sense of movement and future hope.

---

2. 36:9 repeats 36:1. Verse 9 is not considered to be the beginning of a new section, since the information in vv. 9-43 merely expands the brief introduction to the *tôlĕdôt* of Esau in vv. 1-8.

In the material relating to the preflood period there are two collections of genealogical data. The first of these collections is in 4:17-26.[3] In this list Cain's descendants are followed through Enoch, Irad, Mehujael, Methusael, and Lamech. Lamech's two wives are named, and his children are also named with a short description of the contribution that each made to the spread of civilization (4:18-22). Lamech confesses that he has murdered a young man, and he makes a cryptic remark about Cain being avenged sevenfold and Lamech seventyfold (4:23-24). The genealogical information in ch. 4 finishes with a brief note that refers back to Adam again. Resulting from the union of Adam and Eve, Seth is born and is described as "another child (seed) instead of Abel" (4:25-26). Seth himself has a son whom he calls Enosh. The chapter ends with a short statement that people began to worship Yahweh.

The location of Cain's genealogy is probably significant, since it is sandwiched between the story of the murder of Abel and the reference to the murder that Lamech committed. This suggests that Cain's family history begins and ends with murder, and it gives a negative message about this particular line of descent.[4] In contrast to this, the reference to the birth of Seth is not linked with murder but is linked with the worship of Yahweh; Seth's line is linked with a relationship with God, while Cain's line is linked with ever increasing rebellion and murder.

Another genealogy occurs in ch. 5 that features both close similarities to and major differences from ch. 4.[5] Immediately one is struck by the omission of any reference to Cain in ch. 5. Taking ch. 5 on its own, one would conclude that Seth was the firstborn of Adam. However, in the context of the final form of Genesis, in which the writer has juxtaposed these two genealogical lists, we must ask what reason the narrator has for making the link between Seth and Adam uninterrupted. It seems that the narrator wants to focus on the importance of one line of seed, allowing all other lines of descent to fade into insignificance or become nonexistent.

Chapter 5 traces its genealogy not only back to Adam but also to God himself, who created the human being in his image. The idea of the image of God is closely linked with the blessing that God bestowed on the first humans (1:27-28). The emphasis on death throughout this genealogy is put in perspective by this reference, with its implication that the image of God has not been withdrawn. In ch. 4 the increasing effect of sin is followed through one partic-

---

3. In the parlance of the Documentary Hypothesis, this genealogy is referred to as Yahwistic (J).

4. Cf. Clines, "Theme in Genesis 1–11," 493.

5. The genealogy in ch. 5 is often referred to as the Priestly genealogy (P).

ular line, but now, in contrast, the effect of God's image in human beings and of his continued blessing on the human race are in focus through the progeny of Seth.

When the genealogical data in these early chapters is compared, the references to Cain and his line of descent are mainly negative, related to murder and rebellion, while by contrast the references to Seth and his descendants relate to the worship of God, the image of God, walking with God, and future hope of comfort from God. In this way the theme of a special line of seed is introduced who will have a close relationship with God and enjoy his favor and blessing.

After the flood, the story of the tower of Babel is preceded by a genealogical list usually referred to as the Table of Nations (10:1-32). Noah's descendants are linked with the main nations known to Israel. The list begins with Japheth as the one least pertinent to Israel's history, followed by Ham and then finally Shem. An interesting feature of the list is that the sum of the nations is seventy. As Wenham points out, "Seventy was a traditional round number for a large group of descendants." Since Jacob's family that went to Egypt numbered seventy, "Israel is thus a microcosm of the wider family of humanity described in this chapter."[6] Thus, the purpose of the Table of Nations is not to give a comprehensive history of the world's population but to set the political context for the choice of Abraham as the one through whom God's promised blessing would come to the world.

The genealogical lines of Japheth and Ham conclude in the Table of Nations, but the family line of Shem continues after the tower of Babel story. There is probably an intentional wordplay, since the tower-builders wanted to make a "name" for themselves and in Hebrew "Shem" means "name." The genealogy of Shem is traced to the family of Terah and his three sons Haran, Nahor, and Abram/Abraham. The main purpose is to introduce Abraham, to whom God will promise "a great name" as the descendant of Shem ("the name"). Shem's genealogy is the bridge from world history to family history and from the story of the nations to the story of the patriarchs.

Abraham has two brothers, Haran and Nahor, but we are given only a few details about them. We learn nothing about Haran except the birth of his son Lot and his death, details that explain how the circumstances arose in which Lot accompanied Abraham to Canaan. Likewise, little is written about Nahor except for the fact of his marriage. This story is resumed in 22:20-24, where Nahor's significance as the ancestor of the bride of Isaac is revealed. However, these family details are covered fairly quickly, since the main pur-

---

6. Wenham, *Genesis 1–15*, 214.

pose of the author is to introduce Abraham, his wife Sarah, and nephew Lot. The focus of the narrative on members of one extended family alerts the reader to the importance of this family line for both the Abraham and Jacob narratives. This concentration on family affairs here provides a natural context for the theme of divinely chosen seed through a special line of descent. In virtually every passage, the main interest is in some aspect of the lines of descent — either the line chosen by God or one of those rejected by him.

One of the remarkable features of the patriarchal narratives, when compared with chs. 1–11, is the paucity of genealogical lists. This reflects the situation faced by Abraham, who, in spite of the promise of many descendants, has not even one son. Thus, in the Abraham narrative the only genealogy is a short list of the sons of Abraham's brother Nahor (22:20-23).

Sarah's childlessness is the backdrop against which all the promises of a multitude of descendants or seed are made to Abraham (11:30). A palpable tension is created in the narrative by juxtaposing these two incompatible elements — childlessness and many descendants. Thus, the promise of descendants in what seems to be an impossible situation provides the main focus of the theme of seed in the Abraham story.

Although the most detailed genealogical data are in the primeval narratives, a number of short genealogies do occur in the patriarchal narratives:

Nahor's sons (22:20-23)
Ishmael's sons (25:12-18)
Jacob's sons (35:23-26)
Esau's sons and a list of the kings of Edom (36:1-43)
Jacob's family line (46:8-27)

These genealogies, although brief, distinguish the family line with whom God made a covenant from the surrounding peoples. The genealogies provide a family tree for the people through whom God chose to channel his blessing to the world, and throughout Genesis they are woven into the narrative.

The "seed" in 3:15 is a hermeneutical crux.

The most significant and most enigmatic reference to the concept of seed in Genesis is the prophetic statement that the seed of the woman would bruise the head of the seed of the serpent (3:15). In order to understand the purpose and significance of the emphasis on seed in the book, it is necessary to assess how this verse should be interpreted.

The context of 3:15 is the appearance of the man, the woman, and the serpent before God following the disobedience of the first couple. The first pronouncement of judgment is on the serpent. Found guilty of leading the woman astray, the serpent is condemned to crawl in the dust (3:14). Furthermore, Yahweh will cause enmity or conflict to exist between woman and serpent that will be perpetuated through their respective descendants or seed (3:15).

The interpretation of this short pericope is crucial for our understanding of the rest of Genesis. It has been interpreted in ways that minimize its significance for the remainder of the book. For example, it may be understood as an etiological tale that explains why serpents crawl along the ground and why their relationship to humans is fraught with so much animosity compared with other animals. However, without denying an underlying etiological theme, Genesis has a strong thematic preference for the term "seed"; therefore it is important to investigate whether these references to the seed of the woman and the seed of the serpent have a significance beyond this passage that affects the entire message of the book. Rather than merely an etiological tale, could this possibly be a programmatic passage that prepares the reader for what is to come in the remainder of Genesis?

While some scholars have seen this passage as merely an etiological tale, others have seen it as nothing less than the first prophecy of the Messiah. At least as far back as Irenaeus (ca. A.D. 180) the seed of the woman has been understood as a prophecy of Christ, and this is still a very popular Christian reading of the text.

Although these two interpretations of 3:15 — the etiological interpretation and the messianic approach — seem totally incompatible, both have the same implications for the study of Genesis. Neither approach treats the remainder of Genesis as significant for understanding the passage. For the etiological approach, the meaning of the passage is to be found in humankind's fear of snakes, whereas in the messianic approach the terms of reference are in the Christ event, which lies outside Genesis. Although both approaches may shed helpful light on Genesis, in this section I want to explore the possibility that Genesis itself is the place where most helpful interpretative information may be found.

Let us consider the messianic approach which takes the reference to the seed that will bruise the serpent's head as a prophecy of Christ's victory over Satan on the cross. This involves the assumption that the first readers of Genesis would have only a vague idea of what was being prophesied. The messianic interpretation is a very viable and popular Christian reading because we understand it and can relate it to an event that has actually happened.

However, to jump from 3:15 to Calvary is analogous to beginning to read a novel at the back page. Without denying the value of a Christian reading, it is worthwhile reading Genesis as a book in its own right. If the first readers were curious about the reference to the seed who would bruise the serpent's head, surely they would expect the book to shed some light on this enigmatic reference. Where would the earliest readers look for the identity of this victorious seed if not in Genesis itself? Presumably, the narrator intended the readers to follow through the promise of seed in Genesis. This verse alerts the reader that one of the key themes of the book is the identification of the seed of the woman who would bruise the serpent's head. In other words, Genesis may be read as a search for the promised seed. This quest for the promised seed in Genesis is particularly pertinent, since the book highlights the special status of one line of descent.

In seeking to show that 3:15 has implications for the remainder of the book, we face a problem: Genesis does not identify the serpent,[7] and this makes it very difficult to ascertain what is meant by his seed in the context of the book. However, since Genesis is a strongly monotheistic book which is opposed to even a hint of dualism, it is not surprising that the serpent and his seed are overshadowed by the power of Yahweh and the seed that he has chosen. It is probable that the seed of the serpent is to be observed in "anything that represented the forces of evil."[8] Wenham regards the serpent as an anti-God symbol that "symbolizes sin, death, and the power of evil."[9]

Cain and Abel are the first characters in Genesis who would qualify as the seed of the woman. However, neither of them is referred to in this way; but with the death of Abel and the expulsion of Cain, it is Seth who is described by Eve as "another seed instead of Abel" (4:25). Taking this verse in isolation, it could be argued that the reference is just to the joy of Eve at bearing another child after the tragic death of Abel. However, in the light of 3:15 and the expectation that it raises in the reader's mind, it seems likely that 4:25 deliberately recalls the warning to the serpent that the woman's seed would bruise the head of his seed.

---

7. Von Rad argues that the failure to identify the serpent clearly is deliberate because "the narrator is obviously anxious to shift the responsibility as little as possible from man. It is a question only of man and *his* guilt; therefore the narrator has carefully guarded against objectifying evil in any way, and therefore he has personified it as little as possible as a power coming from without. That he transferred the impulse to temptation outside man was almost more a necessity for the story than an attempt at making evil something existing outside man. . . . Throughout the entire story this antagonist of man remains in a scarcely definable incognito, which is not cleared up"; *Genesis,* 87.

8. This is the view of Ross, *Creation and Blessing,* 145.

9. Wenham, *Genesis 1–15,* 80.

This line of seed in Genesis is followed from Eve through Seth, Shem, Noah, Abraham, Isaac, Jacob, and his sons. While Christians will undoubtedly see Christ as the most perfect fulfillment of this prophecy, the early readers of Genesis probably thought of this as a prophecy of the nation of Israel and perhaps of the Davidic line of kings. These are not mutually exclusive views, since Christians worship Jesus as the "Lion of the Tribe of Judah."

However, we turn now to examine the rivalry that existed between characters and how the key people in the Genesis family tree are identified and set apart from all others.

Contrasts, comparisons, and rivalry among the main characters highlight the chosen seed.

One of the ways that the theme of seed helps to shape the material in Genesis is the use of tragic foils to highlight the chosen seed. These foils are people whose career is described alongside the main character in such a way that the failure of the foil highlights the success of the main character and of his line of descendants. Almost all the main characters in the line of descent from Seth to the 12 sons of Jacob have a "foil"; they are shadowed by secondary characters whose main function is to show the main character in a favorable light. These secondary characters provide the counterpart to the one who is chosen for special blessing, and through their shortcomings or even through their position of not being chosen they serve to highlight or, to use another metaphor, to turn the spotlight on the chosen one. Thus, it is Cain's reaction to being rejected by God that draws attention to the privilege afforded to Abel by God's acceptance.

In the early chapters of Genesis, two of Seth's descendants have foils with the same name. There are two Lamechs and two Enochs. The Lamech who descends from Cain continues to exhibit the same bloodthirsty tendencies as his ancestor, but the Lamech whose lineage is traced back to Seth expresses hope for the future, just as his forefather, Seth, had brought hope to Eve (4:25; cf. 3:15). Furthermore, the Cainite Lamech refers to the number seven when speaking about revenge, but the length of his life is not given. For the Sethite Lamech, seven is also significant since he lives for 777 years. A comparison of the two people named Enoch links one with Cain's attempt to build a city (which was considered to be a negative venture), while the other is said to "walk with God."

A similar contrast is found in the story of Noah. Although Noah does not have a personal foil, the entire population of the world serves as his foil.

He is the only righteous one in his lifetime, in contrast to the wickedness of all those around him (6:5-12). Moreover, Noah is the recipient of God's grace at a time when the rest of the world has incurred his wrath. Thus, the wickedness of the world accentuates Noah's righteousness, just as the destruction of the world highlights his survival and the significance of his close relationship with God (6:13; 8:1). In the cryptic story of the cursing of Canaan, the opportunity for Shem and Japheth's righteous act is brought about by the sin of their brother: their reverent act stands in sharp contrast to his disrespect (9:22-23).

Although it is not immediately obvious, there are also interesting contrasts and comparisons between Adam and the patriarch Abraham:

Both originate in Mesopotamia.
The land on which they live is chosen by God for them.
Both are given positions of authority and dominion by God.
Personal obedience to God's direct orders is required from both: a prohibition for Adam and a positive command for Abraham.
God causes a deep sleep to fall upon each of them; the same rare word is used on both occasions.
God punishes and rewards them respectively in relation to land: Adam is driven from the good land, but Abraham is promised land for him and for his descendants.
Neither recognizes his offspring through the firstborn.

Thus Adam's failure becomes the backdrop to display Abraham's success more effectively. But it is not just the story of Adam that is reflected in the Abraham narrative; like Enoch, Abraham walks with God; like Noah he is a righteous man, and in contrast to the tower-builders he receives a "great name."

Abraham is also contrasted with his nephew Lot. Thus, Abraham leaves his homeland in obedience to the command of God (12:1); the text simply records that "Lot went with him" (12:4). Promises of numerous descendants, land, and a relationship with God are generously afforded to Abraham, but Lot can only benefit from these while he remains an associate of Abraham. When Lot chooses to go his own way he loses his wealth and his chance of posterity (13:8-12). Further contrast between Abraham and Lot shows in the development of their careers; Lot is portrayed as a city-dweller, surrounded and influenced by heinous sinners (13:13), while Abraham continues in the land that God has promised to give him, growing more prosperous by the day (13:14-18). As the story progresses, Lot's situation worsens until eventually he is taken captive by foreign raiders. However, the captivity of Lot is just another opportunity for the influence of Abraham to be displayed (14:12-16). Both Abraham and Lot are visited by divinely appointed messengers. Abraham is visited by three messengers who come to announce that he and Sarah will have a child who will be their heir (18:1-15). In contrast, Lot is visited by two messengers who rescue him from Sodom, but in his case his rescue takes place "for Abraham's sake" (19:1-29). Even the level of hospitality that Abraham gives to the visiting representatives of God is superior and lavish in contrast to the hospitality that Lot offers two of the same visitors. Furthermore, the visitors seem much more at home in Abraham's presence than they do in Lot's, since at first they even refuse to stay in Lot's house. Poignantly, Lot's posterity originates through incestuous relationships with his two daughters (19:30-38), in contrast to Abraham's heir, who owes his existence to special divine intervention in the lives of an elderly couple who everyone thought were too old to have children naturally (21:6).

As Lot departs ignominiously from view, the contrast between two characters changes to Ishmael and Isaac. Both of these lads are sons of Abraham and are described as his seed, but Ishmael is the son of Hagar, the Egyptian slave, and Isaac is the son of Sarah, Abraham's first wife. Ishmael is born through Sarah and Abraham's desperate efforts to have children, but Isaac is born as one promised by God in circumstances that seemed humanly impossible. The contrast between Isaac and Ishmael is also obvious in the record of their marriages; Ishmael's marriage is exogamous, but Isaac marries a member of his own clan, safeguarding the special line of descendants.

One of the most developed examples of contrast between characters in Genesis is found in the story of Jacob and Esau, who are contrasted from the moment they are born; Jacob has smooth skin and Esau is hairy. As the boys grow the contrast between them develops, with Jacob choosing to stay within the tent and its surroundings while Esau prefers the life of the open field. However, it is in their relationship with God that the narrator draws the sharpest contrasts between Jacob and Esau. Jacob recognizes the most important values in life and pursues the benefits of the birthright, whereas Esau despises his birthright, selling it as the price of a meal (25:29-34).

Although in many ways Jacob is the less likeable and more devious of the two characters, it is with him that God develops a close relationship in spite of his rather dubious ways of pursuing blessing. No record is given of Esau ever having an encounter with God or even seeking one, and he seems quite oblivious to the sort of values that his father and mother hold dear. Thus, he marries Canaanites, and when he hears that this doesn't please his parents he seeks to marry a daughter of Ishmael as well. Yet the contrast between Jacob and Esau is not simply a black-and-white contrast that makes Jacob look good and Esau look bad; throughout the stories the weaknesses of Jacob are given more prominence than the weaknesses of Esau. When Jacob is blessed by God, after deceiving his father, the blessing assures him that he shall dominate his brothers and that they will bow down to him. Significantly, Genesis records that Jacob bows down to Esau seven times rather than vice versa. Jacob as the chosen one of God does not always behave in the right way and does not always get everything that he wants.

In addition to the primary contrast between Jacob and Esau, when Jacob leaves home a new contrast begins between him and Laban. Laban and Jacob are similar in many ways; they are both devious, they both have a desire to accumulate wealth, and they both have dreams in which God speaks to them. As Jacob's foil, Laban shows how his reliance on household gods and on his own deviousness is no match for Jacob with his relationship with Yahweh. It is Jacob who gains the upper hand, not because of his own ingenuity, but because God is with him, protects him, and gives him promises that he does not give to Laban.

The narrator's fondness of contrasts between characters is also evident in the Joseph stories. Judah's daughter-in-law Tamar and Potiphar's wife both seduce a man. However, their motives are different, since the Egyptian is motivated by lust while Tamar is anxious to continue her husband's line of descent (seed).

Contrasts and comparisons are also made between Jacob's sons. Reuben, the firstborn, is shown to have lost his special position among the brothers by a sin that he committed in his early years, but he also is given credit for wanting to rescue Joseph from his brothers; nevertheless, Reuben fails in his rescue attempt and then joins the other brothers in their conspiracy. But in contrast to Reuben, Judah succeeds in preventing the death of Joseph, and it is at his suggestion that Joseph is sold. Reuben and Judah both figure prominently in the attempt to persuade Jacob to send Benjamin to Egypt. Reuben's suggestion achieves nothing, but Judah's reassurance that he personally will guarantee the lad's safety is accepted by Jacob.

However, the most extended comparison in the text is between Joseph and Judah. Their lives and attitudes are juxtaposed in the text in such a way that the reader is invited to compare them. This comparison is pertinent for the theme of "seed," because since Reuben and the eldest two of his brothers apparently forfeited the birthright it was important for the replacement to be identified.

> *"Seed" is an integral and important theme*
> *in the stories of Abraham and Sarah.*

The role played by this theme is particularly prominent in the Abraham narrative. The function of the theme of seed in the story of Abraham and Sarah is in some ways analogous to the role played by the virgin birth story in the Gospels. The doctrine of the virgin birth highlights the uniqueness of Jesus and establishes that his appearance on earth was an act of God and not part of the normal human reproductive process. The theme of seed in the Abraham narrative makes the same point, though in a different way. Isaac's birth was not possible except by divine intervention.

The sequence of events leading up to the birth of Isaac heightens the suspense in the narrative and leads the reader to the point where he or she must concede that a natural birth is impossible and that all alternatives are untenable. The first stage in this sequence is the announcement that Sarah has no children (11:30). This negative statement coming just before the promise of multiple descendants raises the question whether Abraham can have seed without Sarah. His callousness in abandoning his wife to the whim of the pharaoh suggests that even Abraham thought that Sarah was expendable (12:11-15). However, the idea of an alternative to having a child through Sarah was fraught with difficulties. How would this seed be recognized, and how could the promises be fulfilled through someone who was not Abraham's seed?

The most obvious alternative to Sarah and Abraham having a child of their own is that the nephew of Abraham, Lot, could be recognized as Abraham's heir. This view has been argued in detail by Helyer, who argues that the question of an heir for Abraham is a dominant theme running through not only the Abraham narratives but also the stories about Lot.[10] Wenham describes Lot as Abraham's presumptive heir.[11] Certainly, someone reading Genesis for the first time and unaware of the later episodes in the story would be led to the conclusion that, without any other descendants, Lot is the obvious choice. In a sense, the text teases the reader with this possibility; Lot goes everywhere with Abraham, and Abraham is his official guardian since his father, Haran, is dead. In a very subtle way, the text also begins to plant doubts in the reader's mind about the possibility and suitability of Lot as the recipient of the promises made by God to Abraham. There is no sign of a personal call to Lot; it is Abraham who is called by God, and Lot goes with him. Also, whereas Abraham builds altars to God in the land of Canaan, there is no sug-

---

10. Helyer, "The Separation of Abraham and Lot," 82-86.
11. Wenham, *Genesis 1–15*, 272.

gestion or hint that Lot does likewise. Furthermore, when Lot is given the choice of land, he raises further doubts about his suitability as Abraham's heir since the land he chooses is, at the very least, on the borders of the promised land if not altogether outside them. In the story of Lot's capture and subsequent rescue by Abraham, Lot does not appear to have any real part in the story except to make Abraham look brave and successful. The damning indictment on Lot that removes any possibility that he could be Abraham's heir is his failure to provide suitable husbands for his daughters, forcing them into an incestuous relationship. This contrasts with the care that Abraham would later take to provide a wife for his son. The description of Lot lying drunk in his cave, totally oblivious to what is happening around him, finally removes any possibility of his being the heir of the promises to Abraham.

Lot is not the only contender as heir of Abraham; there is an oblique reference to a person known as Eliezer of Damascus (15:2). Apart from the fact that Eliezer was Abraham's chief steward, we know nothing about him. However, even contemplating Eliezer as the one who would inherit his wealth means that Abraham was beginning to doubt the promises. This situation becomes the context for both a reiteration of the promises of God and a more detailed development of those promises (15:4-21). Abraham is promised that his seed will be as numerous as the stars, so as to make counting impossible. God gives the patriarch an outline of the future history of the promised seed, making it clear that God's future plans are based on Abraham personally.

Although the promises of seed are detailed and unequivocal, they stand in contrast and, indeed, in contradiction to the reality that Abraham and Sarah did not have seed and seemed unlikely to ever have seed.

We must credit the theme of seed with one of the most powerful messages in Genesis: when the promises seem far-fetched and are no more convincing than the promise of "pie in the sky," we should not underestimate the power of God to overrule human limitations and do what he has promised.

One of the tensest moments in the narrative is created by Sarah's decision to give her handmaiden to Abraham. Faced with a situation in which God has promised much but has not said how or when the promises would be fulfilled, Abraham and Sarah decided to expedite the promises by the only means open to them, in spite of all the assurances given in the theophany of ch. 15. Sarah expresses the belief that it is Yahweh who has prevented her from having children (16:2). She now feels that this is a situation in which she can do nothing except have a child through the surrogacy of another woman. We can see once again what a powerful theme seed is in heightening the tension in the narrative to breaking point. The result of the Hagar incident is that Abraham now has seed, but the sensitive reader is aware that all is not well.

211

This unhappy incident is followed by a most comprehensive confirmation of the covenant, replete with promised blessing for Ishmael and also the assurance that Abraham will have another line of descendants through Sarah. God makes clear to Abraham that, in spite of all the uncertainty, Ishmael will not be his official heir. The seed through whom God's promises will be fulfilled has not been born yet, and when he is, he will be the son of Sarah and Abraham. Although Ishmael is clearly Abraham's seed, he is not the seed through whom the covenant promises will be fulfilled.

Following the confirmation of the covenant, further reassurance is given about the promised seed to Abraham while Sarah listens in the background (18:1-15). This is probably the most outstanding example of a divine appearance in the OT. God appears to Abraham as a human being accompanied by two messengers. This unusual presentation of God as a human is one of the high points of Genesis, and the purpose of this appearance of the messengers must be deemed extremely important for the book's message. An appearance of God in human form, with all its implications, draws the reader's attention to the importance of the message that is carried by these messengers. The key phrase or question in the story is "Is anything too hard for the LORD?" The story presents the message that the promised seed will, indeed, be not a natural occurrence but a miracle child provided by God himself as a sign of the special nature of this line of descent. Thus, Genesis wants the readers to reevaluate and reassess the tremendous privileges that they have as the chosen ones of God. This passage suggests that the theme of seed is as central to the message of Genesis as the virgin birth is to the Gospels. Just as angelic witnesses foretold the birth of Jesus to establish beyond doubt the miraculous nature and the historic significance of his birth, these visitors establish the credentials of Isaac, not as a divine child but as the promised seed whose birth would have been impossible without special divine intervention.

With the birth of Isaac, the Abraham narrative has reached a point at which the tension created by the childlessness of the couple has been resolved (21:1-7; 22:1-19). The promised seed has been identified and born; through this person, Isaac, God's promises to Abraham will be fulfilled. However, as soon as this tension is resolved, further tension is created in two ways. First, there is conflict between Isaac and Ishmael, who represent two lines of Abraham's seed. Second, Abraham is commanded to go and sacrifice Isaac. In other words, he is told to sacrifice the seed through whom the promises should be fulfilled. The unique recognition given to Isaac is emphasized in the description of him as "your only son" (22:2, 12, 16). This is very significant, since the reader knows that Isaac is not Abraham's only son (16:16). The point being made is that Isaac is Abraham's son in a way that Ishmael is not; Isaac is his only son in terms of the promises; he is the seed through whom the blessing must come (12:1-3; 13:16; 17:19). The incident ends not only with the provision of a ram in Isaac's stead, but with a repetition of the promise of descendants and blessing.

Preparations for the marriage of Isaac develop the theme that he and his line of descent are the special provision of God. In the choice of a bride for Isaac, there is a tremendous emphasis on divine guidance and divine approval and, indeed, divine intervention. The servant whom Abraham sends to choose a bride for Isaac is clearly a person with a close relationship with God who seeks and receives guidance continually. Rebekah is not the choice of Abraham's servant but the choice of God himself.

This emphasis on the crucial role played by God is further promoted by the statement that at first Rebekah is not able to bear a child. Isaac's birth had been made possible by divine intervention, and now God must intervene to enable the line of descent to continue through Rebekah and Isaac. Once again, the future of the promised seed is in the hands of God himself. God's choice of Rebekah as the wife of Isaac and his intervention to enable her to have children provide a sense of cohesion between the stories of Sarah and Rebekah; but more importantly, it highlights the transition of the line of seed from Abraham and Sarah to Isaac and Rebekah.

Thus, we have seen the significance of the theme of seed in the Abraham narrative; the theme isolates the line of seed that God has chosen and shows that it could only exist through divine providence. The emphasis on lines of descent also helps to show the history of the other nations that eventually surrounded Israel, showing that although they may receive blessing, they have not been chosen in the same sense that the descendants of Abraham through Isaac have. Thus, the Ammonites, Moabites, and Ishmaelites are all accounted for, and the Ishmaelites especially are said to be the recipients of special divine blessing through Abraham. However, the chosen seed is only through Isaac.

"Seed" is an integral and important theme
in the Jacob and Esau narratives.

The theme of seed is also prominent in the Jacob stories. Before she gives birth, Rebekah is informed that the twins in her womb will be the progenitors of two nations. The younger of the two boys would become the ancestor of the stronger of two nations. A sense of suspense is created in these stories, because Jacob shows himself unworthy of the honor that he has been given and

"events zig-zag wildly, keeping tension high and the conclusion unpredictable."[12] However, in spite of all Jacob's mistakes, he is clearly privileged by
God; God meets him at Bethel, God promises to give him the land of his father Isaac and his grandfather Abraham, and furthermore, God promises that
all nations will be blessed through his descendants.

So Jacob continues the theme of the special line of descent through
which God will bring renewed blessing to the nations. However, Esau, the firstborn son of Isaac and Rebekah, becomes the ancestor of the Edomites. Thus
both Edomites and Israelites are descended from Abraham and Isaac, but there
is no doubt which nation has the more privileged relationship with God.

The theme of seed is developed on another level in the stories of Jacob
in relation to the struggles between his wives, Rachel and Leah. Their struggles to produce seed result in Jacob having 12 sons who become the eponymous ancestors of Israel. The birth of Jacob's children and their family history introduce a new phase into the Genesis story. In previous narratives, the
tension has been focused on one person who gains supremacy; but with the
birth of Jacob's 12 sons, we switch from a linear line of descent and now are
dealing with a segmented (i.e., horizontal) genealogy.

The long-term issues raised in the accounts
of Joseph and his brothers relate to "seed."

Although all 12 of Jacob's sons become the ancestors of Israel, there still is a
theme running through the narrative in which one son is chosen above the
others for blessing. Reuben is Jacob's firstborn, and normally he should have
received the preferential blessing in the family. However, Reuben is guilty of
immorality; consequently, his father refuses to recognize him as the firstborn.
The next two sons in order of birth were Simeon and Levi, but they also forfeit the benefits of primogeniture because of their bloodthirsty attack on the
Shechemites.

Since his three older brothers are disqualified, Judah is next in line to
receive the blessing and recognition due to the firstborn. It may seem irrelevant to us who should be regarded as firstborn, but it was an important issue
to ancient readers since, as we shall see, it is mentioned again in the book of
Chronicles. The text signals that a comparison is taking place between Joseph and Judah, not only by the prominence of the two characters, but also
by the structure of the Joseph narrative. The narrative begins in ch. 37, in

12. Cohn, "Narrative Structure and Canonical Perspective in Genesis," 8.

which Joseph's dreams and his sale to the Egyptians (proposed by Judah) are recorded. Then, while the reader expects to learn about Joseph's fate in Egypt in ch. 38, instead this chapter does not mention Joseph but gives an account of Judah's life. This strange location for the story of Judah should not be regarded as dislocation or faulty structure. Rather, it is a way of juxtaposing the story of Judah and the story of Joseph. Several points in the story of Judah invite comparison with Joseph. Both men marry foreign wives, but Joseph may not have had much choice. Both men are seduced: Joseph by Potiphar's wife and Judah by Tamar, his daughter-in-law. Joseph, in contrast to Judah, refuses the seductress and suffers for his morality. Judah succumbs to his seductress, unaware that she is his daughter-in-law. Both men have two children: Joseph's sons are Ephraim and Manasseh, and Judah's sons by his daughter-in-law are Perez and Zerah. Thus, a good case is made here for the firstborn's blessing to pass to Ephraim and Manasseh rather than Perez and Zerah (39:6-20; cf. 38:1-30).

One of the best opportunities that the reader has to compare Joseph and Judah is when they converse face to face (44:14-34). In this instance, Joseph hides his identity from his brothers and Judah thinks that he is dealing with a stranger, while in reality he is dealing with his own kith and kin. In this situation, it is Judah who comes across as the more honorable; Judah endeavors to keep the family unit together, and he represents the interests of his father. Judah has known what it was to fear the loss of his own youngest son (38:11), and now, with kindred feeling, he protects his father's youngest son, Benjamin, even offering himself as Joseph's servant in place of Benjamin (44:16-34). Joseph, on the other hand, seems to be willing to break up the family; he wants to keep Benjamin with him and send the others back to Canaan, paying no regard to the consequences of such action on the health of his elderly father.

Nevertheless, Joseph plays a very significant role. He has early aspirations to greatness, which are interpreted as conceit (37:5-11). These aspirations, however, prove to be prophetic, and Joseph is promoted to high office by the Egyptian monarch (41:39-44). His wise behavior is seen as evidence that God is with him, demonstrated when he provides food for Egypt and for the surrounding nations during a time of severe famine (41:46-57). Joseph's role in the famine relief leads to the deliverance of Jacob and his entourage from hunger and also, more importantly, leads to their emigration to Egypt (47:11-12). This is very significant in the overall theme of the Pentateuch, since the entire exodus story depends on Israel being in Egypt. Therefore, Joseph has a central role to play in setting the context for the fulfillment of the promises given to Abraham (e.g., in ch. 15).

The rivalry between Joseph and Judah is highlighted in the story of Jacob's bestowing blessing on his sons on his deathbed.

> "Judah, your brothers shall praise you; your hand shall be on the neck of your enemies; your father's sons shall bow down before you. Judah is a lion's cub; from the prey, my son, you have gone up. He stooped down; he crouched as a lion and as a lioness; who dares rouse him? The scepter shall not depart from Judah, nor the ruler's staff from between his feet, until tribute comes to him; and to him shall be the obedience of the peoples." (49:8-10 ESV)

Jacob's blessing on Judah begins on a laudatory note with a wordplay emphasizing that Judah will be praised by his brothers and that they will bow before him. The reason why Judah's brothers will praise him is not given, but it seems that they will recognize him as a hero. There are difficulties in translating these verses, especially 49:10, but it seems likely that the blessing refers to the dominance of the tribe of Judah, and the reference to the scepter anticipates Judah's later status as a royal tribe. There can be little doubt that one of the goals of the book of Genesis is to anticipate the Davidic kingdom. Much of what happened in David's own career is foreshadowed in Genesis. Like most of the prominent characters in Genesis, David was not the firstborn son, and there are references to rivalry between him and his brothers. He and Abraham share the same promise that God will make their name great. Furthermore, just as Jacob had to leave Canaan because of his altercation with Esau, David had to vacate Jerusalem because of Absalom. Therefore, it is not surprising that David's ancestor Judah should receive prophetic words of blessing from Jacob that point to his famous offspring.

However, it is Joseph who receives the preferential blessing due to the firstborn. This is achieved by Jacob's adopting Joseph's two children, Manasseh and Ephraim. The circumstances of the adoption are interesting because Jacob crosses over his hands putting his right hand, not on the firstborn Manasseh as Joseph intended but on Ephraim. Joseph's protests are ignored because Jacob believes that the firstborn would be bypassed by his younger sibling as had happened in his own experience (48:13-20). Thus both Judah and Joseph have an important role to play, not only in the stories of Genesis, but in terms of the future of the nation of Israel.

The significance of the contrast between Joseph and Judah is highlighted by the Chronicler, who relates that Joseph received the blessing forfeited by Reuben but Judah's descendants became the stronger of the two tribes (1 Chr 5:1-2). Thus this intricate matrix of comparisons concludes with the progenitors of the main tribes of Israel: Judah in the south and the Joseph tribes (Ephraim and Manasseh) in the north.

This emphasis on the future tribes may be the main goal of the theme of seed in Genesis, but Alexander argues that the purpose of Genesis is even more complex and detailed. He argues that it is not just the importance of the tribes themselves that is significant but their future leadership roles. He proposes that Genesis is not only identifying Israel as God's chosen people but is also identifying a royal line of descent and tracing its early history. He suggests that the family histories in Genesis reflect the early history of Israel in which first Ephraim and then Judah produced Israel's leaders.[12]

> Whereas the tribe of Ephraim is initially presented as the one from which Israel's leader will come, as reflected for example in the important role played by Joshua, 'the first-born' line of Ephraim is rejected in the time of Samuel and replaced by the line of David, from the tribe of Judah.[13]

Alexander highlights the reference to Judah's son Perez at his birth as very significant (38:29). Although Perez was expected to be born second, at the last moment he is described as having "broken out" before his brother. Alexander proposes that this reference to Perez anticipates the change in the early leadership from Ephraim to Judah:

> While this royal line is clearly linked to Joseph and Ephraim, Genesis anticipates that the line of Judah through Perez will replace this 'first-born' lineage. In this way Genesis focuses both on the birth of the nation of Israel and the early ancestry of a future monarchy.[14]

Alexander's theory is an interesting one and provides a coherent explanation about why there is such a concentrated focus on one line of descent. However, it is also possible that the narrative is anticipating not just the early leadership of Ephraim but the later divided monarchy. The early rivalry that provides much of the interest in Genesis may look forward to the rivalry between the northern and southern kingdoms of Israel. Although one of the main purposes of Genesis may be to trace a royal line, it may have been more important for the readers of Genesis during national decline to be able to trace their ancestry back to the man whom God promised to bless. For those from the northern kingdom, destroyed in 721 B.C., and those from the south,

---

12. Joshua was from the tribe of Ephraim.
13. Alexander, *From Paradise to the Promised Land*, 106.
14. Alexander, *From Paradise to the Promised Land*, 111.

destroyed in 587, Genesis provides a link back to Abraham and the blessings promised through him.

Summary and Conclusion: The Theme of Seed

The concept of seed is introduced, as we have seen, first of all in the creation story. It is emphasized that the existence of plants and trees is perpetuated through their seed (1:11, 12, 29). The seed of each plant bears further plants of the same kind as its parent. This emphasis provides a basis for the introduction of seed in the sense of human lines of descent in which those concerned bear the same characteristics. Ultimately Genesis focuses on the line of descent that leads to Israel. The first readers were reminded of their privilege as Abraham's seed and as God's chosen race.

As the story develops, the superiority of the line of seed is highlighted by clear indications that they have been chosen by God as an act of his divine prerogative. This choice does not always suggest that the person chosen is morally superior to others, but it emphasizes that God often chooses the most unexpected people, such as Jacob, who tried to deceive his father and steal his brother's birthright.

The line of seed leads to the 12 eponymous ancestors of Israel. However, of these 12 sons, two receive special prominence, Joseph and Judah. Although Judah lost the status of "firstborn" to Joseph, the blessing bestowed by Jacob recognized the special role of Judah in leadership among his brothers, and the future role of Judah as a royal tribe is anticipated. More importantly, Genesis also provides encouragement for Israelites throughout their history to renew their faith in the promises of God.

The continuity provided by the theme of seed is evident in the opening verses of Exodus, which repeat the names of the 12 sons of Jacob, providing the transition from these names being used to identify people to their use as the names of the 12 tribes of Israel. The genealogical information given in Genesis is not only important because it gives us the names and origins of the tribes, but because it roots these names in the purpose and plan of God. Genesis shows that the people of Israel owe their very existence to God, since Isaac would not have been born without divine intervention and Jacob would not have returned from Aram without divine protection. Furthermore, without the provision made by Joseph, the family of Jacob would have died in the famine, but Joseph would not have been in this high office without the intervention of God. Thus the story of early Israel and of their election by God can be seen in the context of God's intervention in Genesis. The theme of seed may be described as a unifying theme because of the way in which it provides a rationale for the disparate elements in Genesis, such as genealogical data and narratives, while providing an essential foundation for the message of the remainder of the Pentateuch. Moreover, since Genesis develops the theme of seed in the context of the creation of the world (chs. 1–11), it provides a universal dimension to God's choice of Israel. Other nations are promised God's blessing as well as Israel, and the call of Abraham envisages blessing to all the nations of the earth (12:1-3).

Blessing

Terminology and Meaning of Blessing and Cursing

The Hebrew root related to the concept of blessing is בּרך/*brk*. It occurs frequently in the Pentateuch (more than 160 times), and approximately half of these occurrences are in Genesis. The theme is very prominent in the creation narratives, where God blesses the birds and fish (1:22), the human beings (1:28), and the seventh day (2:3). This prominence of blessing at the very beginning of Genesis sets the agenda for the rest of the book and shows that God's purpose is to bless all creation and not just one nation. The theme is also found in every major narrative of Genesis, and all the heroes of the book are recipients of its benefits. One of the reasons for the large number of occurrences in Genesis is the idiomatic practice of repeating a root to highlight its importance. In English the repetition of a word can draw attention to it, but in Hebrew this is much more pronounced because the root of a word can be repeated in nouns, verbs, and participles. Thus, in the call of Abraham the root *brk* is repeated five times (12:1-3). This fivefold repetition of the root in the programmatic passage describing the call of Abraham is highly significant and alerts the reader to the significance of blessing in God's plan for Abraham.

References to cursing are much less frequent in Genesis than references to blessing. However, cursing plays a significant role in the book by providing the dark background against which the benefits of blessing are clearly recognized. The root ארר/*'rr* occurs more than 30 times in the Pentateuch and nine times in Genesis. It occurs in the early chapters of Genesis, where something or someone is declared as "cursed." Thus, the serpent (3:14), the ground (3:17), and Cain (4:11) are all pronounced "cursed."

Another root associated with cursing is קלל/*qll*, which means "to be light or slight" and thus "to treat someone with disdain," "to despise," or "to deprecate" (27:12; Deut 11:26; 23:5; 30:1, 19).

Hebrew concepts of blessing and cursing should not be confused with modern English usage, where the terms may merely refer to wishing someone good or ill. Biblical benedictions and imprecations are powerful and effect real change in the circumstances of the recipients. The content and the end result of the blessing or cursing vary from one situation to another, but generally blessing is the power to succeed and cursing is a harmful power that prevents or hinders success.

Blessing as a Unifying Theme

We have already discussed the significance of a special line of seed in Genesis that would lead from Adam through Noah and Abraham to Israel. No doubt Israelites reading Genesis, especially during the dark exilic and postexilic days, needed reassurance, not just that they were descended from Abraham, but also that they were the people whom God had promised to bless. Tracing one's ancestry back to Abraham would be cold comfort unless this connection carried promises of future blessing.

The significance of the special line of seed was that they were heirs to the relationship established between God and Abraham; the corollary of this relationship was that Abraham would receive God's blessing. It was crucial for the readers of Genesis that the blessing of God did not stop with Abraham but continued through his line of seed to the 12 patriarchs and through them to Israel, establishing the nation as one that was not only chosen by God but blessed by him.

The importance of the theme of blessing lies in its significance as an indicator of a person's relationship with God. Genesis shows that the world had got out of harmony with God and provoked his curse, but its main focus is that harmonious relations can be restored through Abraham and his offspring. Blessing was therefore a significant way of identifying the promised line of descent. God's chosen ones, while living in harmony with him, would be recipients of his blessing.

Genesis provides the link between the special line of seed and blessing by keeping blessing uppermost on the agenda of the lives of the main characters. It is significant that this "blessing" theme is particularly prominent at each main transition point in Genesis, showing the continuity of God's plan to bless the world from one generation to the next. These transitions at which blessing is emphasized include: the call of Abraham, the marriage of Isaac, the departure of Jacob from Canaan on his journey to Aram (where he would meet his wives), and finally, the deathbed blessing that Jacob bestowed on his sons, the eponymous ancestors of Israel. This passing of blessing from one generation to the next provides both unity and a sense of movement in the book.

Thus the themes of seed and blessing are closely linked and interwoven throughout the book of Genesis to point to Israel as the offspring of Abraham and heirs to the promises of God.

The Context of Cursing and Blessing

The precise meaning of blessing and cursing is often contingent on the context in which they occur. Blessing and cursing operate within the interrelationship between two people or parties, and the depth and quality of the benediction, or conversely of the imprecation, reflect the nature of the relationship between those involved. Blessing is bestowed when there is harmony, but disharmony results in cursing rather than blessing.

Creation week occasioned the first pronouncements of blessing. God pronounces blessing three times, on the birds and fish, on human beings, and on the seventh day. These pronouncements are made in a harmonious atmosphere in which everything God had made is "very good."

Noah's obedience (6:22) and sacrifice (8:20) provide the harmonious context in which the Creator blesses the postflood world (8:21–9:17), and the blessing of Abraham is contingent on his obedience to the divine call. Thus, the context for each pronouncement of blessing is harmony between God, who bestows the benediction, and the recipient. Even in human relationships harmony is the appropriate context for blessing. In Isaac's patriarchal blessing, Esau is the firstborn, and in normal circumstances this places him in a relationship with his father that provides the basis for blessing. Esau must prepare the sort of meal that Isaac appreciates as a prelude to the blessing so that the benediction is bestowed in the context of approval (27:1-4). Jacob disrupts the harmony and betrays his father's trust by purloining the blessing from his brother.

In contrast to blessing, curses reflect a breakdown in relationships. The curses announced in the primeval narratives on the serpent (3:14-15) and on the ground (3:17-19) are symptomatic of the alienation that has occurred between God and his created order. Further alienation leads to more cursing (4:11-12), culminating in the flood, which destroys every evidence of blessing on earth (7:21-23). The first curse uttered by a human being is the cursing of Canaan by Noah, where the intention is clearly to show disapproval (9:25). Similarly, when Jacob is encouraged to deceive Isaac, he is reluctant because the consequences of discovery would be strong disapproval leading to the pronouncement of a curse (27:12).

Relationships vary in depth and quality, and this affects the way in which the blessing is bestowed as well as its content. This is illustrated in the blessings bestowed by the creator on the fish and birds (1:22) and the blessing of the human beings (1:28). These blessings are pronounced in a way that indicates two different levels of relationship. The blessing on the human beings is communicated "to them," whereas the blessing on the fish and birds is simply pronounced and the words "to them" are missing. Although God blesses other creatures, it is the blessing on the humans that reflects the more intimate relations. Conversely, the fratricide committed by Cain represents a retrograde step in the relationship between human beings and their creator. Consequently, the imprecation is more personal and direct than the curses pronounced in Eden: Cain's parents have not been cursed themselves, but Cain is cursed personally (4:11).

The most profound and significant relationship in the Pentateuch is the one established with Abraham. Blessing provides both the context and the framework for this relationship. The programmatic passage in 12:1-3, in which the Hebrew root *brk,* "to bless," occurs five times, is all the more salient and noteworthy because of the dark canvas of the primeval narratives against which the new divine human relationship is portrayed (chs. 1–11). The blessing of Abraham is strategically positioned between the primeval narrative and the patriarchal narratives so that it marks a turning point in the book of Genesis — a turning point from an agenda dominated by cursing to one that is dominated by blessing. It represents a new phase in God's relationship with his world, since through Abraham all nations will be blessed. God initiates a covenant relationship with Abraham, making him both the recipient of blessing and its channel to others (15:18-21; 17:1-14). The promises of blessing are linked to Abraham's obedience and are finally confirmed by an oath after the great test of loyalty which shows that he is willing even to sacrifice his son in order to obey God (22:15-18).

God's covenant relationship with the patriarchs is manifest, not only in Abraham's life but also in the lives of Isaac (26:2-5) and Jacob (28:14-21). Ishmael also is blessed, but a distinction is made between his blessing and the blessing of Isaac within the covenant relationship (17:20-21). A similar distinction exists with Jacob, who receives blessing, not because of his deception but as a result of God choosing him for a closer relationship (25:23; 28:13-15).

This emphasis on blessing as the corollary of a close relationship with God is developed in the remainder of the Pentateuch. As we saw in the case of the theme of "seed," the themes of Genesis lay a foundation that is built upon in the books that follow.

In Deuteronomy, the implications of the covenant relationship are explicated and developed in more detail. God relates to Israel through a covenant of love, which is completely unmerited by the nation (Deut 7:7-8). To continue to enjoy the blessings of this deep relationship they must live in obedience to the covenant stipulations (Deut 7:11-15; 11:8-15; 28:1-14). Disobedience, however, causes the covenant relationship to break up, and the blessings are replaced by curses (Deut 28:15-68).

The importance of the concept of blessing and cursing is highlighted in the symbolism of the two mountains: Mount Ebal symbolizes the curses and Mount Gerizim, the blessings (Deut 11:26-32; 27:1-10). This area is probably chosen because of its traditional connection with the life of Abraham (Gen 12:6-7). The ceremony on the mountains demonstrates the imperative incumbent on the heirs of the covenant to emulate Abraham's obedience and, like him, to live in a close relationship with each other and with God (Deut 27:9-10; cf. Gen 12:1-3).

Through the cult Israel has the opportunity to live in harmony with God and to enjoy his blessing. One way that this is mediated to them is through the priestly blessing (Num 6:22-27). This pericope relates to blessing, not in terms of particular benefits such as fertility or prosperity, but to a continuing harmonious relationship with the Lord in which he protects them (Num 6:24), is gracious to them (Num 6:25), endows them with his presence and favor, and grants them peace (Num 6:26). By pronouncing this blessing, the priests place the Lord's name upon the Israelites with the assurance of continued divine blessing (Num 6:27).

The Significance of Cursing in Genesis

The pronouncement of curses in the garden of Eden (3:1-24)

We have already seen that cursing is the corollary of a broken relationship. A more detailed discussion of the passages where cursing occurs will help to elucidate this subject, since it is quite alien to Western thinking.

The blessings pronounced in ch. 1 are in the context of good relationships between the donor, God, and the recipients. In ch. 3 the one pronouncing the curses is the same person as previously pronounced the blessings; it is not the person who has changed but the circumstances and the context. The context has changed from harmonious relationships to alienation. The human beings seduced by the serpent disobey the creator's command and consequently incur his displeasure, and it is this displeasure that is expressed in the pronouncement of curses. Thus the curses are really the counterpart of

223

the pronouncement of the blessings. Like blessing, cursing is regarded as the bestowal of power; but whereas the power of blessing is for the advantage of the recipients, cursing places them at a disadvantage. To be blessed is to receive tremendous privileges and advantages, but to be cursed is to encounter a force that limits and debilitates.

The first curse is directed towards the snake as the one responsible for initiating the sequence of events leading to the disobedience of the human beings (3:14). The effect of cursing is clearly enmity and alienation. This is reflected in the new relationship between serpent and woman and also between the human beings themselves. The man and woman are not personally cursed, but their lives will be blemished and adversely affected by the effects of the cursing and of the new relationship with God and with their environment. The cursing affects especially the fertility of the womb and of the field. God declares that the woman will experience pain in childbirth and the man will experience pain as he seeks to till the recalcitrant ground. For both genders of the human race, the future would no longer be the unblemished satisfaction of having children and of producing food from the ground, because the satisfaction would now be tarnished by a sense of hard labor and by various problems such as thorns and thistles. The narrator recognizes here that there are two aspects to work of any kind. On the one hand, it can bring a great deal of fulfillment and blessing to a person; but on the other hand, duties and work are not always fully satisfying, and sometimes they do not yield adequate returns for the amount of effort expended. It is this unhealthy aspect of work that the narrator explains in terms of God's curse.

It is surely significant that the areas of human life that are affected by the cursing of the serpent and of the ground are similar to those targeted earlier for blessing. Procreation is an important element in the blessings of 1:22 and 1:28, and the woman's punishment also relates to procreation. This blessing is not destroyed completely, since procreation is still possible, but it now involves pain and alienation (3:15-16). The blessing on the human beings in terms of procreation and of their dominion over the animals creates a picture of well-structured, clearly defined relationships between the human couple themselves and between them and the animal kingdom (1:22-30; cf. 2:18-25). Not only is the blessing associated with relationships on the horizontal plane, but there is also the special relationship between human beings and God identified as the "image of God" (1:26-28). These relationships, which had all been cemented by blessing, are all also affected by cursing. At the same time, while these tensions have been introduced into the world and all the created order must live with the effects of cursing as well as blessing, the latter is not abrogated and human beings are still considered to be in the image of God (9:6 cf. Jas 3:9). Even the third blessing on the seventh day is affected by the curse. The blessing on the seventh day was related to cessation from work and satisfaction with the results of a job completed successfully. However, as a result of the divine curse, the work of human beings is increased and their satisfaction from their work is greatly impaired. Although they can still rest on the seventh day, human beings will no longer have the satisfaction that the Creator had in a fully finished task, because following the curse on the ground the work of human beings will involve an endless struggle with the cursed earth.

The Cursing of Cain

We have already seen that Adam and Eve were not directly cursed by God. The first human being to be directly cursed is the first murderer, and this is probably not a coincidence; murder attracts the cursing of God because it destroys another human being made in his image and also because in the ancient world it was considered to contaminate the ground with the shed blood of an innocent person.

As a result of his misdemeanor, Cain is cursed from the ground. This means either that he was cursed more than the ground or that the curse would separate him from the ground, which in the past had been his source of food. The latter explanation seems the more likely and is supported by most modern commentators. If this is correct, then the severity of the punishment lies in the fact that Cain is now separated from the agent through which the blessing of Yahweh, expressed in the fertility of the soil, is channeled to him.

Thus, Cain's life will be adversely affected in those areas that have previously been singled out for blessing: fertility (1:28), relationships (1:28-29), and rest from labor (2:3). Cain's crime of murder means that he will be singled out as someone whose life reflects a curse and not a blessing. The ground will not be fertile when he tries to cultivate it (4:12). Nor would he experience the rest and satisfaction from work experienced under the original blessing; instead he is doomed to be a "restless wanderer" (4:12). Relationships will also suffer. Cain is driven away, not just from the garden as Adam and Eve were, but from the land outside the garden of Eden as well; and although we cannot be sure how the curse will manifest itself, Cain feels threatened by all other human beings (4:14). However, in spite of the seriousness of Cain's crime, God still shows him mercy and provides protection even in judgment (4:15).

The Cursing of Ham

The enigmatic story of the cursing of Canaan introduces a new phase in the theme of blessing and cursing in Genesis. For the first time in the book, a curse is pronounced by one human being on another. The wording of this curse is interesting because it brings together the concepts of blessing, cursing, and slavery.[1] Following the cursing of Canaan, the blessing of Shem is introduced, but in a rather surprising way; it is not Shem who is said to be blessed, but his God (9:26 NIV). Clearly the narrator is using Shem as a link between the primeval world and the world of Abraham. Since his name, Shem, actually means "name" and God tells Abraham that his name will be great, this story of Shem relates to Abraham being the one who worships the God of Shem.

The Significance and Effect of Blessing

Pronouncements of blessing in the Pentateuch are powerful and efficacious. Such pronouncements are actions rather than simply speeches. They have the power to change situations and to alter circumstances. Their meaning and their effect vary from one situation to another, though generally blessing leads to success and cursing brings disaster. The effects of blessing include fertility, prosperity, authority, and security. A second and less frequent use of blessing occurs in which one person acknowledges the status of another. This may include an expression of gratitude or praise. Greetings belong to the same category.

Blessing brings fertility and success.

In the creation narrative the bestowal of fertility is prominent in the three commands addressed to the fish and birds and also to the human beings — be fruitful, multiply, and fill the earth (1:22; 1:28). Each of these verbs may be used on its own to express fertility and numerical increase. In this context they are used together to give maximum prominence to the concept that the creator's blessing would lead to a world teeming with life. Blessing in terms of fertility is prominent throughout the Pentateuch: Abraham's descendants will be as numerous as the stars or grains of sand (15:5; 22:16-18), Sarah will be the mother of nations (17:16), Ishmael will be the father of 12 rulers (17:20), Ja-

1. Cf. Miscall, *The Workings of Old Testament Narrative*, 44.

cob's descendants will be "a community of peoples" (48:4), Joseph is described as "a fruitful vine" and receives blessings of "the breast and womb" (49:22-26). This theme is continued in the theology of Deuteronomy, where as the result of God's blessing, Israel's children, animals, and crops will be fertile and numerous (Deut 7:13-14).

When land is blessed it is fertile and productive (26:12). Cursing, however, leads to infertility. When the ground is cursed (3:17-19), thorns and thistles make it more difficult to cultivate and less productive (cf. 5:29). The human beings must still work the soil, but the benefits they receive are greatly reduced (3:19, 23). Famines in the Pentateuch are not explicitly described as punishment from God, but they clearly imply the absence of blessing and suggest that the lands so afflicted are not blessed with divine favor (12:10; 26:1). Fertile soil and secure boundaries, however, are evidence of divine favor and blessing, as the following statement about Isaac makes clear:

> And Isaac sowed in that land and reaped in the same year a hundredfold. The LORD blessed him. (26:12 ESV)

Because blessing was linked with fertility, it also was associated with success and wealth. While this aspect of blessing is not uppermost in Genesis, it comes to the surface in stories where an outsider or outsiders are observing the people that have been blessed. For the patriarchs themselves, blessing meant more than success and wealth, but for those looking on it was different. For example, when Abraham's servant explains that the Lord has blessed his master, he couches it in terms of wealth (24:35).

The loss of fertility brought about by cursing affects not just the crops, but also the people themselves and their animals; this is emphasized not only in Genesis, but also in the other books of the Pentateuch (Deut 28:16-18).

Blessing brings authority and dominance.

God's blessing gave the humans authority over the rest of creation: they must subdue (כָּבַשׁ/*kābaš*) the earth and rule (רָדָה/*rādâ*) over its creatures. It seems that the human beings are empowered to exercise dictatorial rule over the rest of creation. This is the view taken by Vawter, who argues that the combined force of these two Hebrew words is "absolute subjugation."[2] This understanding of the first divine blessing bestowed on human beings has led some to criticize Genesis and to blame it for the ecological problems of the

---

2. Vawter, *On Genesis*, 60.

modern world, since it seems to give humans absolute rights over the entire created order.

Lohfink, however, argues that the authority given to humans does not refer to harsh and exploitative rule. He suggests that *kābaš* connotes "to place one's feet on something," in the sense of "take possession of."[3] In a similar vein, he argues that *rādâ* indicates "a shepherding and guiding function of man in respect of animals."[4] Thus, although the verbs used in God's blessing of humans are also used in contexts where harsh treatment is involved, this does not necessarily imply that harsh and exploitative behavior are demanded by the use of these words in the harmonious context of creation and blessing. These words would be out of harmony with the context in which we find them if they were unequivocally harsh and uncaring. Creation is clearly subservient to those whom God has blessed; but they are not given license to abuse and mistreat creation, which would be clearly inappropriate in the light of their creation in the image of God. Human beings are given responsibility for creation and authority over it, but the exercise of this supremacy should be harmonious and mutually beneficial. This idea of harmonious rule is also underlined by the indication that the animals are not a source of food at this stage, but they and the human beings eat the green plants and the produce of the trees (1:29).

A relationship in which the dominant person exploits others is always associated with cursing rather than with blessing. As a result of the curse the man will "rule over" the woman, which probably means that their previous harmonious relationship would be lost, leaving the woman vulnerable to exploitation (3:16).

Dominance is evident in the Abraham narrative. God's call to the patriarch to leave his country includes the promise "I will make your name great" (12:2). A great name probably means that Abraham will become famous and dominant as a result of the blessing; there are, indeed, several allusions in the text where it is implied that Abraham's name is taking on something of the promised greatness. Abraham's treatment in Egypt suggests that he is a person of considerable influence and importance. One might have expected the pharaoh simply to ignore Abraham's rights and imprison him, but instead he treats Abraham with much respect. Abraham has deceived Pharaoh, and yet Pharaoh rewards him by giving him many presents and letting him and his wife leave Egypt safely and unharmed. As D. J. Wiseman comments,

3. Lohfink, *Great Themes from the Old Testament*, 177.
4. Lohfink, *Great Themes from the Old Testament*, 179.

Abraham's rank and dignity were . . . acknowledged by the Egyptian king (Gn. 12:10-20) who would otherwise have dismissed an insignificant foreigner, especially if he were a suppliant for relief or a mere herdsman-nomad, whose action had affronted the court.[5]

Wiseman's argument is supported by the story of the visit of Jacob's sons to Egypt (42:1–44:34). Joseph's brothers do not have a great name in Egypt, and they are treated with suspicion and risk imprisonment (42:17). Not knowing that Joseph is their brother, they are greatly afraid in his presence because he has power over them. Abraham, in contrast, is treated with courtesy and generosity in Egypt (12:16). Further evidence that Abraham is an influential figure may be deduced from his rescue of Lot. In this story, Abraham is acknowledged as leader by a number of Hittites. The aftermath of the battle in ch. 14, from which Abraham emerges victorious, does much to enhance his fame. He is afforded the honor of an audience with Melchizedek, and he even appears superior to the king of Sodom. Melchizedek blesses Abraham and blesses his God. Not only does Abraham appear in this passage as one who is blessed of God, but he is also one who has been enabled to be a blessing to others, especially those whom he rescues. Further evidence of Abraham's influence and rank can be found in the story of his negotiations with the Philistines (21:22-34). There is no hint that Abraham is the inferior partner in the treaty that he makes with these people. Indeed, the fact that Abraham is encouraged to make a peace treaty with them shows that he is powerful enough to be a threat. The Philistine commander makes Abraham swear an oath that he will not harm him or his descendants, showing that Abraham is indeed a powerful figure. Furthermore, in his negotiations about a burial site with the Hittites, Abraham is treated with considerable deference and the Hittites refer to him as "a mighty prince among us" (23:6). Even if "prince" is not an official title, it nevertheless suggests that Abraham was well known and respected among the Hittites.

Authority is also present in the blessing of Jacob, where the struggle between the brothers is a struggle for dominance. Isaac's patriarchal blessing that he intended to bestow on Esau was mostly about dominance and prosperity.

> Then his father Isaac said to him, "Come near and kiss me, my son." So he came near and kissed him. And Isaac smelled the smell of his garments and blessed him and said, "See, the smell of my son is as the smell of a field that the LORD has blessed! May God give you of the dew of heaven and of the fatness of the earth and plenty of grain and wine. Let peoples

5. D. J. Wiseman, "Abraham Reassessed," 145.

serve you, and nations bow down to you. Be lord over your brothers, and may your mother's sons bow down to you. Cursed be everyone who curses you, and blessed be everyone who blesses you!" (27:26-29 ESV)

Ironically, although this blessing promises that Jacob's brothers will bow down to him, Esau does not bow to Jacob but Jacob bows seven times to Esau (33:3). Perhaps the dominance is not just a reference to Jacob's relationship with Esau but a reference to Israel's superiority over Edom. Jacob's struggle for dominance is reflected also in his struggle with the mysterious person who meets him before his encounter with Esau. Following this nocturnal wrestling bout, Jacob is informed that he has been struggling with God and has prevailed. The ultimate outcome of this declaration of dominance is that Jacob is blessed by God in that place. Perhaps the meaning of this enigmatic incident is that, whereas Jacob's life was characterized by struggles, the ultimate struggle was with God since true blessing comes from him (32:22-32).

Jacob's struggle passes to his sons, who even sell one of their number into slavery because of his dreams of dominance. Eventually, God's blessing on Joseph becomes evident by his promotion to high office. He not only rules over Egypt but has the satisfaction of seeing all his older brothers bowing down to him.

Dominance is an important theme in the patriarchal blessings bestowed by Jacob on his sons (49:1-28). Reuben loses the usual prominence given to the firstborn, and Judah is given dominance so that his "hand would be on the neck" of his enemies while his brothers would bow down to him. This authority has royal implications, since "the scepter will not depart from Judah, nor the ruler's staff from between his feet" (49:10 NIV). Joseph, however, is the one who receives the preferential blessing due to the firstborn. He has authority over all his brothers to the extent that after the death of Jacob they fear for their lives. But Joseph is merciful towards them, and his position of dominance does not lead him to treachery.

This idea that dominance is one of the outcomes of blessing is continued in the Pentateuch and applies to Israel as a nation. If Israel's relationship with God breaks down, the curses will result in subjugation by their enemies (Deut 28:36-37, 43). This is symbolized by the saying that they would be the tail and not the head in their relationships with others (Deut 28:44). If, however, Israel is given dominance over other nations, this is evidence of blessing and Israel can be described as the "head and not the tail" (Deut 28:7, 13). Blessing and cursing are also prominent in international relations. Before Israel's entrance into Canaan, the king of Moab, in an attempt to subdue Israel, summons a prophet to curse them (Num 22:5-6). Yahweh, because of his covenant relationship with Israel, thwarts all attempts to curse them and turns the cursing into blessing (Num 24:10). This reflects the promise to Abraham: "I will bless those who bless you, and whoever curses you I will curse" (12:3 NIV).

Blessing brings protection.

Closely associated with dominance is the idea that Yahweh protects those who have been blessed. God's blessing on Abraham includes the promise that "whoever curses you I will curse" (12:3). In other words, Yahweh promises to bless Abraham by taking his side against anyone who would despise him or wish him ill. Sometimes Abraham does not seem to value or appreciate Yahweh's protection. In Egypt, fear leads him to deceive the Egyptians and betray his wife, in an attempt to save his own life. This represents a virtual rejection of God's ability to protect him. As a result, he loses Sarah and jeopardizes the future of God's promises to him (12:14-16). However, Abraham's re-entry into Canaan heralds a restoration of his relations with both his wife and his God. He returns to the site of the altar that he had built earlier and calls on the name of Yahweh (13:1-4).

We have already seen that Abraham's victory in ch. 14 is presented as a blessing. This is made clear in the description of Abraham's encounter with Melchizedek (14:19-20). In this brief passage the Hebrew root representing blessing occurs three times. This emphasizes that Abraham's victory is to be seen as a direct result of the blessing given by "God Most High." Furthermore, in Abraham's uneasy confrontation with the king of Sodom it is implied that Abraham consulted God and accepted certain conditions before battle (14:22-23). The entire venture, then, was carried out under God's protective blessing in the context of a close relationship between God and Abraham.

The subject of Yahweh's protective blessing is taken up again in ch. 15. God's relationship with the patriarch is confirmed at a time when he seems to be in considerable danger, if the background provided in ch. 14 is taken as the immediate context. God declares himself to be Abraham's shield and his reward; both these terms are frequently used in a military context, the shield as part of a soldier's armor (2 Sam 1:21; Prov 6:11) and the reward referring to a soldier's wages (2 Kgs 7:6; 1 Chr 19:6). Yahweh presents himself to Abraham in terms of personal protection and reward. Yahweh has given him victory and will continue to protect him. In ch. 20, we have a further example of Abraham resorting to deceit to protect himself. Once again he claims, this time to the Philistines, that his wife is his sister and she is taken into the harem of Abimelech (20:2). This deceit places Sarah in danger once more, and it jeopardizes the future of the promised blessings. However, God protects Abraham and Sarah by appearing to Abimelech in a dream and by inflicting the ladies of his harem with childlessness (20:3-18). What a deep and effective relationship between God and Abraham is envisaged in this passage, where God will even use a dream to stop someone from harming his servant. This is one aspect of what Genesis means by being blessed by God. In other words, even where Abraham is to blame, God takes his part and supports and protects him.

The link between blessing and protection is developed in 22:16-18. In this brief but very important blessing passage, Abraham is assured that his descendants will "take possession of the cities of their enemies." So, just as God has blessed Abraham by protecting him and by giving him victory, the same blessing will be afforded to his descendants. In order to understand the importance of this, we should remember that the first readers of Genesis were the descendants of Abraham and were probably reading these words at a time when they felt vulnerable and surrounded by enemies, very much in need of the presence and protection of Abraham's God. Thus, throughout the Abraham cycle, the reader is given the clear impression that God is protecting the patriarch and also, indirectly, protecting the future of the descendants of Abraham and fulfilling the promise of blessing.

Jacob's life involves several struggles, and it is evident that as one who enjoys God's blessing he is protected from his enemies. During his encounter with God at Bethel, Jacob is reassured that wherever he goes God will protect (keep) him (28:15). This promise is realized in Jacob's confrontations with Laban (31:24) and Esau (32:9-32).

Blessing brings peace and rest.

Blessing is associated with "rest," both in Genesis and in the remainder of the Pentateuch (Exod 33:14; Deut 3:20; 12:9-10; 25:19). Eden represents a place of blessing where the inhabitants have work to do, but it is meaningful work and Eden is a place of rest and protection. The expulsion from Eden exposes the human beings to hard labor and to work without fulfillment (3:17-19). This sense of restlessness is particularly evident in Cain's complaint that God has forced him to be "a restless wanderer on the earth" (4:14). This desire for rest is reflected in the naming of Noah; although the etymology of the name is uncertain, it may be linked to a word meaning "to rest" (5:29). Yet, God frustrates the efforts of the people who attempted to build the tower of Babel, scattering them "over the face of the whole earth" (11:9 NIV).

Even though the promises to the patriarchs included land, it was not they but their descendants who settled there. So, throughout Genesis the quality of rest and peace originally enjoyed in the garden of Eden is not restored but remains a future goal. It is important therefore that Genesis is not understood in isolation but as part of the Pentateuch. The possession of Canaan is never explicitly described in the Pentateuch as a return to Eden, but the most significant aspects of Eden are to be replicated in the blessings promised to those entering Canaan. It is to be a place of fertility where God's laws are respected and his presence is manifest. The priestly blessing promises "peace" (Num 6). Expulsion from the land, though, would lead to "no repose," "no resting place for the sole of your foot," "an anxious mind, eyes weary with longing, and a despairing heart" (Deut 28:65 NIV).

Thus, although the patriarchs do not receive the blessing of rest in their own land but remain wanderers, the goal of the promises they receive is rest for their offspring.

Abraham and Blessing

The name of Abraham is inextricably linked with the theme of blessing in the short account of how God called him to leave his homeland. In just three verses the Hebrew root related to blessing is repeated five times (12:1-3). Since this is the first divine speech in the Abraham story, this pronouncement of blessing is extremely important. It gives the passage special significance, underscoring the importance of blessing since it is reiterated and emphasized by God himself. Because the earlier blessings on creation were also bestowed by God, these promises of blessing provide a link between the Abraham story and the theme of blessing in the first creation account.

Five main benefits are promised to Abraham on condition that he obey the divine imperative. First, he will become a great nation. Just as the fish, birds, and human beings were blessed at creation so that they would "be fruitful and increase in number and fill the earth," so Abraham is promised that his seed will be numerous. However, the Hebrew word used for "nation" implies national identity and territorial rights as well as numerous progeny. Second, Abraham will be blessed. This means that he will receive power from God to enable him to succeed in the role for which God has chosen him. Third, God promises to make his name great so that he will be a blessing to others (12:2). To have a name means "to be famous," usually in relation to mighty acts performed (1 Chr 5:24; 12:30). The description "great name" is used frequently in the OT as a description of God's name (Josh 7:9; 1 Sam 12:22; Ezek 36:23; Mal 1:11). There are only two references to men having a great name: Abraham (12:2) and David (2 Sam 7:9).[6] In both cases their "great name" is given by God.

Fourth, Abraham is promised that God will bless those who bless him and curse those who curse him. This means that God will vindicate him and protect him against any who would despise him.

Finally, the promises culminate in the assurance that all nations will be blessed through Abraham. Exactly how Abraham's descendants will be a blessing to the nations is not explicit. Probably their role is not to do things for other nations but to "model a way for the other nations also to receive a blessing from this God."[7]

Abraham mediates blessing to others.

The promise that all nations would be blessed through Abraham leads us to expect that the book of Genesis will include evidence of others being blessed through Abraham. At first, this promise seems to be in doubt when Abraham actually brings cursing to others instead of blessing. This is particularly the case with the way in which he brings trouble to the king of Egypt through his deceit. However, a number of passages do suggest that those who accompany Abraham receive blessing because of him. We have already seen that Lot is an example of this. Through his association with Abraham, Lot becomes extremely wealthy (13:5). But when he separates and goes his own way, his fortunes begin to take a steady downward turn: he is captured (14:12), despised (19:9), evacuated from a doomed city (19:16-22); his wife is turned into salt (19:26); and finally, while living in a cave in the wilderness, his daughters have an incestuous relationship with him (19:30-38). The fact that Lot survives at all is credited to God's relationship with Abraham (19:29).

There are other examples of people being blessed through their association with Abraham. Hagar, the Egyptian maid, is promised that she will become the mother of many descendants because of her relationship with Abraham (16:10; 17:20). Although the son of Hagar, Ishmael, cannot have any part of the covenant relationship that God establishes with Isaac, because he is Abraham's son God promises blessing to him. Abraham also brings blessing to others through his prayers; he prays that Abimelech's wives and concubines will be able to have children again, and God answers his prayers (20:17). Even Abraham's servant who carries out the commission to find a wife for Isaac knows that he has been blessed with success on account of his master (24:12, 27).

6. Wenham, *Genesis 1–15*, 275.
7. Brueggemann, *Genesis*, 120.

However, the promise to Abraham was not only that he would be a blessing to individuals but that he would be a blessing to nations. Abraham's role as a blessing to the nations is portrayed in ch. 18, where Yahweh asks whether he should hide from Abraham the news of the impending doom of Sodom. The reason God gives for sharing his decision to destroy the city with Abraham is that "Abraham shall become a great and mighty nation, and all the nations of the earth shall be blessed in him" (18:18). Thus, the reason for informing Abraham about the destruction before it happens is linked directly with his role of bringing blessing to the nations. Abraham is viewed as having influence with the highest possible authority; face-to-face with Yahweh, he is seen as bargaining about the safety of his nephew in terms that might possibly have led to a reprieve for a doomed city (18:23-33). This description of the patriarch bargaining with God is one of the most daring portrayals of human-divine relations in the entire OT. Although his interception is not successful in saving Sodom, the point being made is that Abraham and his descendants (Israel) have a relationship with God that gives them a special role as mediators of divine blessing.

Two passages in the Abraham cycle merit special consideration since blessing is particularly prominent. The first of these is 22:16-18, which comes at the conclusion of the passage that records Abraham's willingness to offer Isaac. The second passage is ch. 24, which is important because it provides a transition from the Abraham cycle to the Jacob cycle, and the theme of blessing is very prominent.

The promise of blessing in 22:16-18

In this passage, God responds to Abraham's act of obedience in being willing to sacrifice his son. In the first main account of blessing in ch. 12, the blessing is given on condition that Abraham is obedient; but this second promise occurs after Abraham's great expression of obedience to the command to offer up Isaac. Just as Abraham's life of faith began with the promise of blessing, so it reaches its climax with another promise of blessing. This passage is also important because it forms a bridge between the past and the future. It represents Yahweh's final confirmation of the blessings to Abraham before his death. This is why, when compared with 12:1-3, there is less emphasis in 22:16-18 on Abraham personally being the source of blessing. In 12:1-3, all the blessings relate to and depend on Abraham, but here the emphasis has changed. Although the narrative looks back to what Abraham has done as far as the blessing of the future is concerned, it looks beyond Abraham to his descendants.

Let us now compare the main statements in these two blessing passages:

12:1-3
1. I will make of you a great nation.
2. I will bless you.
3. I will make your name great.
4. You shall be a blessing.
5. I will bless those who bless you.
6. The one who curses you I will curse.
7. In you all the families of the earth shall be blessed.

Now in 22:16-18 note how the emphasis has changed. Although the narrative looks back to what Abraham has done, as far as the blessing of the future is concerned, it looks beyond him to his descendants.

22:16-18
1. By myself I have sworn says the Lord.
2. Because you have done this and have not withheld your son, your only son,
3. I will, indeed, bless you.
4. I will make your offspring as numerous as the stars of heaven and as the sand that is on the seashore.
5. Your offspring shall possess the gate of their enemies.
6. By your offspring shall all the nations of the earth gain blessing for themselves
7. Because you have obeyed my voice.

Thus, the first passage reaches its climax through "in you shall all nations be blessed," but now in the second passage it is "through your offspring that they will be blessed." In this way, the passage prepares for the spotlight to be taken off Abraham and focused on those who will follow him. It is no accident that the only person sharing this incident with Abraham is Isaac. This accentuates even further the idea that this is a bridge passage representing the transition from father to son.

Another important element in 22:16-18 is that its promises are given in the form of an oath. Since covenants are usually ratified by oaths (cf. 21:31), it may be argued that this oath represents the ratifying of the covenant of circumcision (17:1-27). This view is put forward by Alexander:

Abraham is tested by God in order to ascertain whether or not he truly fulfils the conditions laid upon him in 17:1. Does Abraham walk before God? Is he blameless? Clearly the events of chapter 22 show beyond doubt the deep loyalty of Abraham to God. Obedience to God over-rides paternal affection. As a result Abraham not only receives back his son but he also merits the divine ratification of the earlier promised covenant of circumcision.[8]

The theme of blessing in chapter 24

This is a transition passage in which the focus of attention moves from Abraham and Sarah to Isaac and Rebekah. We have already seen that the chapter is particularly significant for the theme of seed because it emphasizes that the divine intervention that brought about the birth of Isaac is still operating on his behalf. Interwoven in the chapter with the theme of seed is a strong emphasis on the theme of blessing. The function of the blessing theme here is to show that God's favor which rested on Abraham was now being passed to his offspring who would inherit the promises.

In this long chapter, the subject of blessing is never far from the surface; it includes five specific references to blessing, in which the Hebrew root occurs seven times. Abraham is now old and Yahweh has blessed him in every way. Having enjoyed the full benefits of blessing himself (24:1), it is now Abraham's responsibility to ensure that it is perpetuated through arranging a suitable wife for his son.

When Abraham's servant discovers that God has led him to the family of Abraham's brother, he is tremendously grateful to God and says, "Blessed be the Lord, the God of my master Abraham, who has not forsaken his steadfast love and his faithfulness toward my master" (24:27). Thus, by describing Yahweh as the blessed one, the servant is declaring that Yahweh is the source of his success and the source of his master's success.

The servant explains that Yahweh has blessed his master with wealth and with a son who has been made heir of all his father's possessions (24:35). The son, of course, is the main evidence of blessing, since no other acquisition could ever compensate for the lack of an heir. The servant, however, presents the fact that Abraham is very wealthy as the evidence of blessing. Indeed, he mentions Abraham's abundance of "sheep and cattle, silver and gold, menservants and maidservants, and camels and donkeys" before he refers to Isaac. The readers of Genesis know that these material blessings are not the main evidence of the fact that God has blessed Abraham; but the servant is addressing material-minded people who know nothing of Abraham's struggle of faith, and therefore it is Abraham's wealth that is the most convincing proof to them that Abraham has been blessed.

8. Alexander, "Genesis 22 and the Covenant of Circumcision," 21.

The fifth occurrence of the subject of blessing in ch. 24 is the farewell blessing pronounced by Rebekah's relatives. This may have been a traditional blessing pronounced on those leaving home to get married. The content of the blessing is a twofold wish for fertility and victory over enemies. It is quite strange that this blessing contains just these two elements, but it probably reflects the position of a woman in the ancient world for whom numerous children were seen as a tremendous blessing and for whom vulnerability was the main problem.

The theme of blessing in the Jacob cycle

In the Jacob cycle, the theme of blessing develops in a very different manner from that witnessed in chs. 1–25. Blessing in the Jacob stories becomes a kind of competition to see who can achieve it. At first this competition is between Jacob and Esau, but later, as the story develops, the struggle is between his wives.

Before studying this theme in the Jacob cycle in detail, it is necessary to take an overview, since this will be invaluable as we seek to assess how blessing fits into the complete picture. Significant work has been done on this material by Fishbane, who draws attention to the careful way that the Jacob material is structured. He argues that a "technique of symmetry" is used to integrate the contents of the cycle. Fishbane outlines his conclusions in the following table:[9]

Table A

A	oracle sought; Rebekah struggles in childbirth; *bekhorah*-birthright; birth; themes of strife, deception, fertility	25:19-34
B	interlude; strife; deception; *berakhah*-blessing; covenant with foreigner	26
C	deception; *berakhah*-stolen; fear of Esau; flight from land	27:1–28:9
D	encounter (verb; *paga‘*) with the divine at sacred site, near border; *berakhah*	28:10-22
E	internal cycle opens; arrival; Laban at border; deception; wages Rachel barren; Leah fertile	29
F	Rachel fertile; Jacob increases the herds	30

9. Fishbane, *Text and Texture*, 42.

E¹	internal cycle closes; departure; Laban at border; deception; wages	31
D¹	encounters (verb *paga*ʿ) with divine beings at sacred sites; near border; *berakhah* sites; near border; *berakhah*	32
C¹	deception planned; fear of Esau, *berakhah*-gift returned; return to land	33
B¹	interlude; strife; deception; covenant with foreigner	34
A¹	oracle fulfilled; Rachel struggles in childbirth; *berakhah;* death resolutions	35:1-22

I have reproduced Fishbane's table because it is very helpful in highlighting the important role played by the theme of blessing in this cycle. Fishbane describes blessing as "a primary driving power" of the Jacob cycle. He argues that the counterpoint of blessing is also prominent in the cycle and "can be characterized as *curse*" (cf. 27:12, 29). Fishbane concludes that "the hope for a blessing and fear of a curse clearly charge the actions of this cycle."[10] The development of the early Jacob story unfolds, as Goldingay observes, "in a rather jerky way."[11] The narrative will, indeed, seem to be erratic and lack coherence if we read it as the story of Jacob. Thus, first we have the birthright stories, and then, just when we would be expecting more detail about Jacob and Esau growing up, there is a chapter in which they are not mentioned (26:1-34). Chapters 34 and 36 also seem to hinder the smooth development of the Jacob stories. However, if instead of viewing the narrative as a story about Jacob we see it as a development of the themes of blessing, cursing, and childbirth, then the diverse strands of the story are interwoven well together and the narrative reads much more coherently. In other words, the theme that most credibly accounts for the material in the Jacob cycle as we have it is the theme of blessing and, in particular, the transmission of blessing. The cycle shows how the blessing passed on by Abraham becomes the legacy of Jacob and his sons, rather than that of Esau and his descendants. This still raises the question about why the birth and birthright stories should precede the story of Isaac (ch. 26). It is simply a measure of the importance placed on the birthright question by the narrator, an importance that lies in the significance of the transmission of blessing to a new generation. Because the narrator wants the main emphasis of the cycle to be on the transmission of blessing from Abraham to Jacob and his sons, the story of how Isaac is blessed must take second place to the stories of the birth and birthright.

10. Fishbane, *Text and Texture*, 61.
11. Goldingay, "The Patriarchs in Scripture and History," 17.

Joseph and Blessing

Although God promised Abraham that through him blessing would flow to the nations, there was little evidence of this in the Abraham narrative. However, this promise comes into clear focus with the story of Joseph. Joseph's brothers consider him to be a nuisance rather than a blessing and as a result they sell him. However, Joseph's first master in Egypt learns that Joseph is a very trustworthy and successful servant (39:5).

> From the time that he made him overseer in his house and over all that he had, the LORD blessed the Egyptian's house for Joseph's sake; the blessing of the LORD was on all that he had, in house and field. (NRSV)

Although Joseph's service to Potiphar is cut short, his ability to bring blessing to those he serves is evident even in prison, where he finds favor in the eyes of the jailor. Both Potiphar and the prison warden discover that anything that they make Joseph responsible for prospers. When Joseph is released from prison, as Alter points out, even Pharaoh benefits from his presence.[12] The denouement of the story finds not only Egypt but people from all the countries of the earth being blessed through the provision of food made available through Joseph's wise counsel and administrative ability.

A clear contrast exists between Abraham's first visit to Egypt, when he caused trouble, and this role played by Joseph. As a result of Abraham's visit the Pharaoh is cursed (12:17). But through Joseph Pharaoh, the Egyptians, and the surrounding nations are blessed. As Westermann aptly comments,

> The narrator simply presupposes that the blessing can flow over from the one whom Yahweh assists to a foreign people and adherents of a foreign religion precisely because of the one whom Yahweh assists. The power inherent in the blessing is expansive: the God of the fathers is further at work in Joseph's experience of servitude in a foreign land.[13]

Although Genesis' main focus is on the benefits that Joseph eventually brings to his family, it is quite remarkable to see this very clear message to Israelite readers, that God can use those whom he chooses to bring blessing to the world.

---

12. Alter, *The Art of Biblical Narrative*, 107-8.
13. Westermann, *Genesis 37-50*, 63.

Conclusions

Genesis begins with declaration of universal blessing (1:22; 1:28; 2:3) and explains how the blessing is renewed through Noah for all mankind (9:1-3), how it is narrowed down to one chosen family through Abraham (12:1-3), Isaac (26:1-5), and Jacob (28:12-15), and then how that same blessing is channeled through that family to other nations by Joseph (41:57). The book ends with Jacob blessing the eponymous ancestors of the 12 tribes of Israel (48:1–49:28). The Joseph cycle shows that the blessings can continue to flow through Israel to the rest of world, Joseph's accomplishments being no more than an example of what God could do through those whom he has chosen to bless. Blessing in Genesis is intended for all the world, not just one nation, but this divine intention to bless is hindered because of the sin of human beings. Nevertheless, the blessing pronounced upon Abraham clearly includes the goal that all nations will be blessed through him and his descendants. Although we have seen that this promise is undoubtedly partially fulfilled through Joseph, this is no more than an example of what God can do if his people accept the challenge that he has given them to channel his knowledge and his blessing to others all around them.

Throughout Genesis, blessing is the bestowal of divine favor. It manifests itself in many ways, but especially in fertility and success. The special relationship with Abraham and his seed does not exclude other nations from entering into a harmonious relationship with God and experiencing the blessing promised through Abraham.

Land

Closely related to the themes of descendants and blessing is the theme of land.

Vocabulary Related to Land Issues

The main Hebrew words denoting "land" in Genesis are אֶרֶץ/*'ereṣ*, אֲדָמָה/*'ădāmâ*, and שָׂדֶה/*śādēh*. Although the terms are often used synonymously, each has its own particular emphasis. *'ereṣ* occurs most frequently. It occasionally denotes "ground" (18:2; cf. Exod 4:3; Deut 15:23), but usually refers to large stretches of territory such as a particular region or country (12:1, 5; 17:8; cf. Exod 2:15; Lev 11:45; Num 13:2) or to the earth as a whole (1:1; 2:1; 6:4; 11:1; cf.

Deut 28:25); *'ădāmâ* may denote the habitable earth (12:3) or a particular country (47:20), but most occurrences refer to the "soil" or the "ground" (2:5, 7, 19; 3:17, 19, 23; 4:2, 3, 10; cf. Exod 3:5; Lev 20:25; Deut 4:18). Occasionally *śādēh* denotes a particular country (14:7), but usually it refers to cultivated land (37:7; cf. Exod 9:22; 10:5; Num 16:14; Deut 11:15) or to the open countryside (2:19, 20; 3:1, 14; 25:27, 29; cf. Exod 23:11; Deut 22:25). *śādēh* is used, for example, in relation to the land that Abraham bought from the Hittites (23:8-20).

Discussions about land in Genesis usually fall into two main categories. First, land in chs. 1–11 is approached with an emphasis on creation and ecological issues. Second, studies of land in chs. 12–50 usually concentrate on the promise of land to the patriarchs. However, since we are considering land as a unifying theme in Genesis, we need to evaluate whether there are principles about land developed in chs. 1–11 that have relevance for the understanding of land in the patriarchal narratives. We shall see that there are issues raised in chs. 1–11 that are of fundamental importance for the understanding of the theme of land in chs. 12–50 and indeed in the entire Pentateuch. In other words, the approach taken in this work suggests that the theme of land in chs. 1–11 is an interpretative key for understanding the theme of land, not only in Genesis, but in the rest of the Pentateuch.

We shall now consider the theme of land under three main headings to highlight the principles enunciated and to show how they provide an interpretative key for the patriarchal narratives, for the Pentateuch as a whole, and indeed for OT theology: the divine dimension of land ownership; relationships between people and land; significance of the garden of Eden.

Divine Dimension of Land Ownership

Genesis 1–11 establishes God's sovereignty over land. He is cast in the roles of "creator" and "supreme landlord." The land owes its existence to him, and he creates its inhabitants, continually monitoring and supervising their behavior. Land is the raw material for the formation of the first human, and it is also the medium through which divine rewards or punishments are administered. God allocates land to people and gives them work to do, making them responsible for cultivating the ground and keeping it under control (2:8). Far from being a local deity with interests in one nation, God is portrayed in Genesis as the ruler of the entire universe with a personal interest in the welfare and behavior of all its citizens (6:5-8; 11:1-9). His judgments and decisions have repercussions for plants, animals, and human beings alike, and in particular he makes decisions about where people live (11:1-9).

The clear emphasis on the sovereignty of God over land in the primeval narrative provides a good foundation for the development of this theme in Genesis, the rest of the Pentateuch, and indeed throughout the OT. Just as Eden was chosen and allocated to Adam and Eve, Canaan is promised to the Israelites (15:18-21), but God reserves the right to decide when and how this should happen (15:16). This idea of God's control of land is continued especially in the book of Deuteronomy, which contains references to the allocation of land to the Edomites (Deut 2:5), Moabites (Deut 2:9), and Ammonites (Deut 2:19).

Habel's characterization of Yahweh in Deuteronomy applies also to chs. 1–11:

> The image of YHWH promoted in Deuteronomy is that of a universal monarch who controls vast domains, of which Canaan happens to be one. YHWH is said to control more extensive domains than great rulers such as Nebuchadnezzar, Darius II, and their corresponding patron deities. YHWH, in fact, claims to be ruler over the heavens above and the earth below. YHWH is portrayed as ruler of all lands and God over all nations. YHWH is God of gods, controlling the world from on high (Deut. 4:39; 10:14, 17).[1]

This echoes the message of chs. 1–11 and carries a similar rejoinder against the Israelite tendency to an exclusive claim on God's patronage. The rebuff of Amos to Israelite nationalism is fully compatible with the message of chs. 1–11 (Amos 9:7).

Relationships between People and Land

Genesis 1–11 shows the close interdependent relationship between human beings and the land they inhabit. This is initiated when God, having already commanded the ground to bring forth vegetation, uses the soil *('ădāmâ)* as the material for the creation of humankind *('ādām)*.

Although there is probably no etymological link between *'ādām* and *'ădāmâ*, the close relationship between human beings and the ground is emphasized by this wordplay. This assertion, that humankind are made from clay, elevates the ground while reminding the human beings of their innate vulnerability; not only do they come from the ground, but when they die they return to it as mere dust (3:19). The close relationship that humans have with the ground means that they are obliged to care for it and enabled to reap its

---

1. Habel, *The Land Is Mine*, 37.

benefits (2:16), but it also means that anything adverse that affects the ground/land strikes deeply at the very basis of their existence. At the same time, the land would not survive without humans to care for it (Exodus 23).

In the primeval narrative, when humans become alienated from God it affects their relationship with the land. Infractions as diverse as eating "forbidden" fruit (3:17-19), murdering a brother (4:10-16), and building a tower (11:5-9) are all punished in relation to land. We shall look in more detail at these early crimes and how they were punished.

The punishment of Adam

When Adam rebels against God he adversely affects his relationship with the ground, since it is cursed because of his rebellion (3:17-19). Although there is no indication that Adam himself is cursed, a curse on the ground comes close to being a curse on him since, as we have already seen, he originated from the ground (2:7; cf. 3:19). In practical terms, the cursing of the ground means a loss of fertility and the growth of thorns and thistles.[2] The human beings will be forced to eat "the plants of the field" until they return to the dust (3:18-19). The ground from which Adam is formed will eventually claim him again, but until then he will experience life as a "dogged struggle" with the soil.[3] Adam must still work the soil, but the benefits he receives are greatly reduced (3:19, 23).

Following the cursing of the ground is one further consequence of sin, the expulsion of human beings from the garden of Eden. This is presented as a necessary precaution to prevent them from eating fruit from the tree of life. The significance of the expulsion is that the security provided by the garden of Eden has been removed. God exercises his authority as landlord and expels humans from the very secure and fertile piece of land in which he had placed them earlier. God, "like a landlord dissatisfied with his tenants, evicts them, not from the earth completely but from the particular parcel of land on which they rebelled."[4]

The punishment of Cain

The second punishment that relates to land is directed towards Cain (4:1-16). Like Adam, Cain is "a tiller of the ground" (4:2). When Cain's offering of pro-

---

2. Wenham comments, "Land blessed by God is well-watered and fertile (Deut 33:13-16; cf. Gen 2:8-14), so that when cursed it lacks such benefits"; *Genesis 1–15*, 82.

3. Von Rad, *Genesis*, 94.

4. McKeown, "Unifying Themes," 256.

duce from the ground fails to gain him favor with God (4:5), he reacts violently against his brother and kills him (4:8).

Although we would not normally link this crime with the ground, this connection is made in the Cain-Abel narrative; the ground opens its mouth to receive the victim's blood (4:10). The shedding of innocent blood defiles the ground and brings appropriate punishment upon the perpetrator of the crime. Cain is punished accordingly (4:11-12).

Cain is cursed מִן-הָאֲדָמָה/*min-hā'ǎdāmâ* (4:11). Literally, this means "he was cursed from the ground." However, this may be interpreted in two ways — either that he was cursed more than the ground or that he would be cursed "away from the ground." The latter translation seems the more likely and is supported by most modern commentators. This raises the question about what is meant by being cursed "away from the ground."

> "When you till the ground, it shall *no longer* yield to you its strength; you shall be a fugitive and a wanderer on the earth." (Gen 4:12 RSV)

Cain's punishment is not only that he will be driven off the fertile land but that the ground that he once tilled successfully would now become infertile, forcing him to wander in search of food. His direction is east, representing a move further away from Eden. As R. P. Gordon observes, this "marks a further step away from the divine presence as originally experienced in the garden."[5] Cain's sin had threatened and destroyed the tripartite relationship of humanity, land, and God.

The flood as punishment

It is quite remarkable that throughout the flood narrative a close connection is maintained between the land/ground and sin. This connection is emphasized by the frequent use of the word "land," אֶרֶץ/*'ereṣ*, which occurs precisely 40 times in the passage, commencing with the announcement of the *tôlĕdôt* of Noah and ending with the declaration that the earth would not be destroyed again by a flood (6:9–9:11). It would be precarious to postulate that this is deliberate without a clear indication of what the number 40 is intended to symbolize in this context. However, this large number of occurrences of land is significant in that it underlines the importance of this theme for the author. It is true, of course, that a story dealing with a flood will necessitate some mention of the earth/land. However, comparisons between the Genesis

---

5. Gordon, *Holy Land, Holy City,* 21.

narrative and the Atrahasis flood story show that the earth/land motif is much more prominent in Genesis than the story of a flood normally warrants. In Atrahasis 3:1:1–3:6:50, earth/land is mentioned only three times, against 40 times in the Genesis flood story.

The close connection between sin, the land, and the flood is emphasized by a very powerful wordplay using the root שחת/*šḥt* (6:11-13).

> Now the earth was corrupt *(wattiššāḥēt)* in God's sight, and the earth was filled with violence. And God saw the earth, and behold, it was corrupt *(nišḥātâ)*, for all flesh had corrupted *(hišḥît)* their way on the earth. And God said to Noah, "I have determined to make an end of all flesh, for the earth is filled with violence through them. Behold, I will destroy them *(mašḥîtām)* with the earth." (6:11-13 ESV)

Thus the root *šḥt* is used in three ways in 6:11-13; it describes the action of the human beings, the state of the earth as a result of sin, and the action which God takes against humankind. Human beings have brought God's earth into a state of *šḥt,* and now God brings judgment in terms of *šḥt* upon them. In other words, the punishment fits the crime.

Frymer-Kensky argues that the contamination of the ground has been caused by the shedding of innocent blood.

> The most serious contaminant of the land is the blood of those who have been murdered: the concept of "bloodguilt" is well-known in Israelite law. Because of the seriousness of the crime of murder, and perhaps also because of the mystical conception of blood in Israelite thought, the blood of the slain physically pollutes the land.[6]

This interpretation links the flood story very closely with the Cain-Abel story, suggesting that in both stories the main crime is the shedding of blood with the consequent contamination of the ground. In 6:11 the crimes of the human beings are all grouped under the general heading of "violence," which includes murder together with other forms of violence. The behavior of the human beings, as in the earlier stories of Adam and Cain, affects the ground on which they live and contaminates it. God decides to destroy humankind (6:17), but as a result the earth loses its value as a life-supporting medium and is itself destroyed.

6. Frymer-Kensky, "Atrahasis," 154.

The punishment of the tower-builders

God's role as creator and guardian of the earth is apparent again in the Babel narrative (11:1-9). The reader is alerted to the importance of the theme of *'ereṣ* (land/earth) in this passage by the sixfold repetition of the word in 11:1, 2, 4, 8, 9 (twice).

This repetition suggests that the attitude of human beings to the earth that God has given them is one of the main issues in the Babel story. The crime of the builders is to seek self-determination and to find security through land without acknowledging the Creator or his rights over the land. They seek the advantages of Eden (security) without having the prerequisite harmonious relationship with the Creator. Consequently, they are scattered over all the earth, a sharp contrast to all that Eden symbolized (11:8).

So a breakdown in relationship with God in the primeval narrative leads to:

Loss of fertility of land
Expulsion from land
Destruction of land
Dispersion away from the land

These four consequences of disobedience are important, not just for understanding Genesis, but also the entire biblical history of Israel and much of the prophetic literature. By giving us an introduction to the subject of exile, Genesis 1–11 is highlighting a subject that is highly significant for the history of Israel and one that is prominent in much of the literature of the OT.

Loss of Fertility of Land When Abraham enters Canaan the land is languishing in the grip of a severe famine. Lack of fertility is an indicator that the nation's relationship with God is not healthy. The Canaanites are not at the expulsion stage in Yahweh's judgment, but the lack of fertility is a sign that all is not well and that the land is showing symptoms of divine disfavor. This is an important theme in the prophets, where the infertile land is regarded as the victim of Israel's faithlessness (Amos 1:2; 4:7-9; Hos 4:2-3; Isa 24:4ff.; Jer 12:4).[7]

Expulsion from Land The theme of expulsion is prominent in chs. 12–50. Just as Adam, Cain, and the tower-builders were forced to leave the land they

---

7. Cf. Habel, *The Land Is Mine*, 84.

preferred, Abraham, Lot, Jacob, and Joseph all experience periods in exile. These experiences of exile are not always the result of personal sin. In Abraham's case, he is forced to leave Canaan and go to Egypt even though he has obeyed God in leaving his own country. Jacob, on the other hand, is forced into exile because of his deceitful act in connection with his father's blessing. Joseph's exile is the result of his brothers' envy rather than his own personal sin. However, Genesis anticipates the eventual expulsion of the Canaanites, and there is no doubt that this will happen in response to their increasing sinfulness (15:16).

This theme of expulsion that is introduced in Genesis is developed in the other books of the Pentateuch. In preparation for taking possession of the promised land, the Israelites are warned that the behavior of its inhabitants will affect the land. The Israelites must treat the land with respect and not defile it with vile practices as the previous inhabitants had done (Lev 18:25). In their pursuit of good harvests, the Canaanites have practiced promiscuous fertility rites. This brings the inhabitants into confrontation with God, and it also alienates them from their land. The land is portrayed as having been nauseated by its inhabitants, and, like a person who has eaten something disagreeable, it vomits them out (Lev 18:28). See Num 35:33-34; 2 Sam 1:21-22; 21:1-14.

Israel's teaching on land provides a rationale for the expulsion of the Canaanites and the possession of their land. On the one hand, Israel acknowledges driving out the Canaanites, but on the other there is a strong conviction that it was Yahweh who expels them (Exod 23:29; 34:11, 24; Lev 18:24; Deut 4:38; 6:19; 7:1, 22, 23; 8:20; 9:3, 5; 11:23; 31:3, 4). Indeed, Yahweh is actively involved:

> "I sent the hornet ahead of you, which drove them out before you. . . . So I gave you a land on which you did not toil and cities you did not build." (Josh 24:12-13 NIV)

So the way in which these expulsions is presented further emphasizes the tripartite relationship between human beings (in this case, Israel), God, and the land, since all three are involved in the expulsion.

Before leaving this theme of expulsion it is worth mentioning the experience of King David. The story of David's sin and consequent punishment reflects the teaching of chs. 1–11. The king not only perpetuated the sin of Adam in taking that which was forbidden, but he also emulated Cain by committing murder. Just as Adam was driven from the garden, David is forced to leave the palace and the sanctuary. Like Cain driven further east, he is forced to leave Jerusalem, and as he does so he is cursed. Although the imprecation comes from Shimei and not from God, David recognizes that God is permitting it to happen. David's experience epitomizes that of the nation. If the king stands the risk of being driven out of Jerusalem and out of the promised land, the same vulnerability characterizes the entire nation.

Destruction of Land   The flood demonstrates that in certain extreme circumstances God may choose to destroy his creation, including the human beings. While it may not solve all our ethical and theological problems, the flood story provides a rhetorical and literary context in which to study the Hebrew understanding of destruction by divine decree, whether we are thinking of the overthrow of Sodom and Gomorrah, the incident where the ground swallows the dissident priests (Num 16:27-33), or the destruction of the indigenous population of Canaan by the Israelites. According to the flood narrative, God destroys only those who have destroyed themselves and the destruction is accompanied with divine regret and pain (6:6).

Dispersion   During Israel's history others would appear to scatter other peoples and transplant them in foreign countries. Israel would always recognize that the only one who had this prerogative was Yahweh, and when the Assyrians seemed to claim this right they were doing it as tools of Yahweh. The Assyrian policy of removing people from their own country and dispersing them among other peoples had a similar effect to God's action resulting in the scattering of the tower-builders.

Significance of the garden of Eden

The garden of Eden story sets the scene in Genesis by describing the ideal place to live, and it has significance for not only Genesis but the theology of the OT. The garden of Eden story reflects the recognition that not all land is the same. This is obvious in terms of fertility and productivity, but the garden of Eden is also unique because the divine presence is encountered there in a most intimate way. The concept of a special piece of land whose inhabitants live in harmony with God and enjoy his protection and blessing is evident in much of Israel's thinking on the subject.

Eden represents a place of blessing where the inhabitants have work to do, but it is meaningful work and Eden is a place of rest and protection (Exod 33:14; Deut 3:20; 12:9-10; 25:19). The expulsion from Eden exposes the human beings to hard labor and to work without fulfillment (3:17-19). As the narrative in the Pentateuch moves towards the promised land, there are several indications that this is in some respects a return to the ideal conditions of the garden of Eden. As McConville observes, "it is not only Genesis that holds out an Edenic ideal; it lies behind much of the Old Testament."[8] While possession of the promised land is not explicitly described as a return to Eden, the most significant aspects of Eden are to be replicated in the blessings promised to those entering Canaan. It is to be a place of fertility and a place where God's laws are respected and where his presence is manifest. Expulsion from the land, by contrast, would lead to "no repose," "no resting place for the sole of your foot," "an anxious mind, eyes weary with longing, and a despairing heart" (Deut 28:65 NIV). As Wenham argues,

> The Garden of Eden is not viewed by the author of Genesis simply as a piece of Mesopotamian farmland but as an archetypal sanctuary, that is a place where God dwells and where man should worship him. Many of the features of the garden may also be found in later sanctuaries, particularly the tabernacle or Jerusalem temple. These parallels suggest that the garden itself is understood as a sort of sanctuary.[9]

To support his claim that Genesis 2–3 is using sanctuary symbolism, Wenham lists the large number of items in the garden that find parallels in later sanctuaries. These include the Kerubim, the entrance to the garden from the east, the tree of life, the river that flows out of Eden to water the garden, the mention of "pure gold," and the "tree of knowledge of good and evil." He points out that the verb הִתְהַלֵּךְ/*hithallēk*, "to walk to and fro" (3:8), is also used to describe the divine presence in the later tent sanctuaries in Lev 26:12; Deut 23:15; 2 Sam 7:6-7. Wenham observes that, "the Lord walked in Eden as he subsequently walked in the tabernacle."[10]

In a similar vein, Stager argues that the garden of Eden story provides the background to Solomon's temple. In the Jerusalem of Solomon's time "topography, hydrology, architecture, iconography, parks and gardens were all part of the sacred centre patterned after celestial archetypes."[11] Stager argues that the temple on Mount Zion, where the invisible deity dwelt, clearly replicated paradise. He argues this from the iconography of flowers and trees. Like Wenham, he also recalls the Kerubim, who guarded the way to the path of life and who were also associated with the tabernacle.

Stager argues that on the mountain of Yahweh, Mount Zion, "the indissoluble triad of creation, kingship and temple find their most profound visual

8. McConville, "The Old Testament and the Enjoyment of Wealth," 35.
9. Wenham, "Sanctuary Symbolism," 19.
10. Wenham, "Sanctuary Symbolism," 20.
11. Stager, "Jerusalem and the Garden of Eden," 189.

and literary expression."[12] Stager is suggesting that, when the Jerusalem temple was being built, Solomon believed that he was creating a cosmic center where he would rule according to God's command. Thus, he envisaged the city of Jerusalem as a garden where heaven and earth would meet, and as such he was replicating the garden of Eden (Ps 52:8; 92:12-13; Ezek 31:8-9).

The Connection between Land in the Primeval Narrative and in the Patriarchal Narratives

We shall now look in more detail at how the theme of land in the patriarchal narratives reflects the foundation laid in Genesis 1–11. The pattern that emerges in relation to land in the Abraham narrative is virtually a mirror image of that found in the primeval history. Instead of provision of land → stipulations to be obeyed → disobedience-expulsion, we have now lack of land → obedience → promise of land → land. The movement in chs. 1–11 is from possession of land to expulsion; but the reverse is the case in the Abraham narrative, where the movement is towards possession. Abraham is not expelled from his homeland; rather, he is commanded by God to leave it. He responds in obedience, which contrasts with the reaction of Adam and Cain, who although given land by God responded by rebelling. In chs. 1–11 those who possessed the land were warned that they could lose it, but in reverse Abraham receives promises that he will possess land. As Brueggemann comments,

> The book of Genesis presents two histories, both concerned with land. One, presented in Genesis 1–11, is about people fully rooted in land living toward expulsion and loss of land. Successively, Adam and Eve, Cain and Abel, Noah and his family, and finally the folks at Babel do everything they can to lose the land and they eventually do. That history is about presuming upon the land and as a result losing it. The Bible ponders the folly and carelessness that cause people securely landed to give it up. The other history of Genesis is in chapters 12-50. It features Abraham and his family, and is about not having land but being on the way toward it and living in confident expectation of it.[13]

The promise of the land to Abraham and the consequent expulsion of the previous inhabitants is a continuation of the principle enunciated by the primeval narrative; the earth belongs to God, and if its inhabitants fail in

12. Stager, "Jerusalem and the Garden of Eden," 188.
13. Brueggemann, *The Land*, 15.

their responsibilities, God himself reserves the right to remove them (cf. Sodom and Gomorrah).

Until the call of Abraham there is a progressive deterioration in the relationship between God and human beings, with the concomitant repercussions in relation to land. However, the call of Abraham represents a turning point. Beginning with the Abraham narratives the movement is towards a harmonious relationship with God in the promised land. Adam is expelled from Eden because of his disobedience; Abraham must be obedient in order to receive the land of promise. At first the promise of land is fairly vague and is introduced to Abraham as "the land I will show you" (12:1). However, the promises become more explicit as the narrative develops. Each stage in this development is preceded by a reference to Abraham's faith and obedience:

12:1	Initial command with an implicit promise of land
12:4	Response in obedience; Abraham leaves Haran
12:7	The Land is promised to Abraham's descendants
13:9	Act of faith in allowing Lot to choose his land
13:15	The Land is promised to Abraham and his descendants
15:6	Abraham believes God
15:12-21	The Land is promised under oath
22:1-24	Act of faith and obedience shown in the sacrifice of Isaac
23:1-20	Ownership of a plot of land

It can be seen from this table that major developments regarding land are closely associated with acts of obedience and faith on Abraham's part. The pathway to possession is, however, not without problems. When this land is revealed, Abraham discovers that it is already occupied and is in the grips of a severe famine, and his faith is severely tested (12:6). Eventually, God makes a clear unequivocal oath to give the land of Canaan to Abraham and to his descendants (15:12-21). These promises go hand in hand with a harmonious relationship between God and Abraham: God speaks to him and he listens and obeys (12:1-6; 22:1-3); he builds altars and calls on the name of the Lord (12:7-8); he is God-fearing (22:12) and walks before the Lord (24:40).

Following Abraham's death, the promise of land passes to Isaac (26:2-3) and then to Jacob (28:13-15). Eventually Jacob and his family leave Canaan during a famine and live in Egypt, but they leave with the assurance that their descendants shall return and take possession of it (46:1-4). The theme of land in Genesis continues into Exodus, where through the leadership of Moses the return towards the promised land begins (Exod 12:31-39). The movement towards land is accompanied by divine revelations and legislation that would facilitate harmonious relations between Israel and God (Exod 20ff.; Lev 1ff.; Num 5–10; 15; 18–19; 28–30; Deut 4–30). Thus, in the primeval narrative humankind has moved away from God and, consequently, from secure land. The reverse happens in the remainder of the Pentateuch as first the patriarchs and then their descendants move closer to the promised land.

The Interrelationship of the Themes of Blessing, Seed, and Land in Genesis

This study has dealt with these three themes, blessing, seed, and land, separately so that the distinctiveness of each one may be clearly seen. However, the intent is not to give the impression that the three themes run through Genesis like three parallel threads. The present chapter now highlights the interdependence of the themes, rather than their distinctiveness. We shall approach this task by examining briefly the three themes in Genesis as they occur together. This will enable us to see the interrelationship of the themes, and it will also highlight what the themes have in common with each other. In particular, it is important to note the way in which all three themes are linked with the idea of a close relationship between God and the recipient.

The theme of blessing is introduced in the creation narrative as the initiative of the Creator himself to ensure the proliferation of life on earth (1:22, 28). The good relations in which the blessing is originally given are destroyed by the rebellion of humans against the Creator. This brings cursing instead of blessing (3:14-19). While the initial creation blessing is not completely revoked, it is now accompanied by the opposing power of cursing. At this point we can observe the interrelationship between blessing and seed. The pronouncement of the cursing is accompanied by the first promise of seed (3:15). This means that the promise of seed is a message of hope closely related to the blessing/cursing tension. The cursing is directed against the aspects of human activity and life that received the benefits of the blessing originally. The promise of seed represents the Creator's concern that the blessing will prevail in the world rather than the cursing.

Surprisingly, although the third theme, land, is most prominent in the patriarchal narratives, it is also introduced in the primeval narrative and is clearly linked with the themes of blessing and seed. When Adam enjoys close communion with God in a relationship dominated by blessing, he is also in harmony with the ground/land from which God formed him (2:7). Cursing, however, not only alienates him from God, but it also adversely affects his relationship with the land (3:17-19). This estrangement from land is manifest in

253

two main ways. First, cursing results in the land being less productive and more difficult to cultivate; and second, humanity's new relationship with both God and the land leads to his expulsion from the piece of land where the blessing had been so much in evidence (3:24). Land and blessing are thus closely related; both are introduced in the context of harmony between God and human beings, but both are adversely affected by humanity's alienation from God. The only hint of hope in this situation is provided by the third theme, seed (3:15). The seed of the woman will bruise the serpent's head and, presumably, limit the adverse effects of the disobedience that the serpent has encouraged (cf. 3:1-6).

The theme of seed is introduced in a similar way. Just as both blessing and land are portrayed in a context of harmony between people and God and also in a context of hostility, seed also relates to both contexts. Eve has descendants (seed) through Cain, and these are listed in the appropriate genealogy (4:17-22). However, this line of descent is characterized by continued rebellion against God (cf. 4:23-24). The promise in 3:15 and Eve's expression of hope after the birth of Seth (4:25) represent the theme of seed and, indeed, a line of descent through which peaceful relations with God may be restored.

Both land and blessing are linked with the concept of seed by the important pericope in 5:29. The naming of Noah is linked with the line of chosen seed who would alleviate the suffering caused by the curse on the ground. Lamech's yearning for "comfort" gives the reader an insight into the desperate plight of mankind now struggling to eke out an existence from the recalcitrant earth in a situation where cursing seems to be more evident than blessing.

The flood witnesses the virtual extinction of every evidence of blessing from the earth (7:21-23). Only inside the ark is there hope of future blessing. The potential for procreation remains possible through the male and female members of the animals, birds, and humans (8:1). The human occupants not only make future blessing possible, but they also keep alive the hope of the seed expressed in 3:15. The interrelationship between seed and land is also prominent. The corruption of the earth/land has been the cause of the cursing manifest in the flood (6:11-13). Those leaving the ark step onto land that has been cleansed and purified through the judgment of the floodwaters (8:18-22). The rescue of those in the ark is clearly linked to the fact that Noah found favor in God's eyes (cf. 6:8). Indeed, the central statement in the flood narrative is that "God remembered Noah" (8:1). This personal relationship stands in contrast to God's relationship with the rest of the world (cf. 6:12), and it is within this peaceful relationship that God rescues Noah and his family. Indeed, after the flood, in the context of a covenantal relationship God restores to them the potential for blessing, land, and future seed (9:1-17). In this covenant, blessing is renewed in terns reminiscent of the creation blessings, and the earth is restored to mankind with a promise that it will not be destroyed again by a deluge.

The establishment of the covenant is followed by the story of Noah's success in viticulture (9:20-21). This story relates to a new beginning for the earth and its inhabitants. The concluding part of this story draws attention to the third theme, seed (9:22-29). An important contrast is made between the son (seed) who merits and enjoys a harmonious relationship with his father, resulting in blessing, and the son who dishonors his father and experiences the consequential cursing. The relationship of these sons reflects the relationship of mankind to God. Ham and his son Canaan represent those who are out of harmony with God, and their relationship is characterized by cursing. Shem, on the other hand, represents the line of promised seed who enjoy God's blessing within a harmonious relationship.

The themes of blessing, land, and seed are inextricably woven together in the Table of Nations in ch. 10. In common with all genealogical material, the list of nations is evidence of the effectiveness of the initial creatorial blessing (1:22, 28). Prominence is given to the line of Shem, and this emphasizes the theme of seed (10:21-31). The table also devotes attention to the subject of land (10:5, 10, 30), with particular emphasis on delineating the land belonging to the Canaanites (10:19). This brings together at this important juncture all three of these major themes.

The interrelationship of the themes of blessing, land, and seed is very obvious in the patriarchal narratives. The blessing is to be channeled through one family line with which God has a close relationship. This emphasis on one family line focuses attention on the theme of seed. Furthermore, the line of chosen seed will become a great nation *(goy)* and, by definition, will require land. Therefore, all three themes are on the agenda for the remainder of Genesis and are related to each other. The blessing will be lost if there is no chosen line through which it can be channeled to the world, and the chosen seed will have no influence in the world and will not appear blessed until they have land to occupy. Other nations will also have a share in blessing, seed, and land in a general sense, but this does not include a special relationship with God.

The importance of the divine promise speeches in the patriarchal narratives cannot be overemphasized. In these speeches the interrelationship of blessing, seed, and land is clearly seen. Genesis 12:1-3, with its fivefold repetition of the root for blessing, is a good example. Although the *Leitwort* establishes the importance of blessing in this pericope, the theme does not stand alone. The blessing is to be directed to the peoples of the world through Abraham and his seed (12:3). Although the details are not given, there is also the implicit promise of land; Abraham must leave his homeland, but he goes to the land that God will show him (12:1). Furthermore, the promise that his descendants will become a great "nation" includes the implicit promise that they will occupy territory (12:2). The important concept that links land, blessing, and seed here is that they are promised in the context of a close harmonious relationship with God. This is emphasized by the high profile given to God's personal involvement in the fulfillment of the promises. Six times in 12:1-3 God uses verbs in the first person singular:

> Now the LORD said to Abram, "Go from your country and your kindred and your father's house to the land that I will show you. And I will make of you a great nation, and I will bless you and make your name great, so that you will be a blessing. I will bless those who bless you, and him who dishonors you I will curse, and in you all the families of the earth shall be blessed." (ESV)

This approach from God requires a response in obedience from Abraham for the continuance of the relationship (12:4).

The separation from Lot is the context for a more developed divine promise passage (13:14-17). Abraham and Lot have been forced to separate because the land could not accommodate them both, together with the original inhabitants. Therefore, it is not surprising that the main emphasis of the promise is on land. The promises in this pericope commence and conclude with the subject of land (13:15, 17). The interdependence of the themes means, however, that land cannot stand on its own. The land is for the promised seed, and the promise of seed is given along with that of land (13:15). The theme of blessing is also present because Abraham's descendants will require the divine blessing if they are to become as numerous as the grains of dust (13:16). Again, the promises are backed up by God's personal commitment to fulfill them (13:15-17).

The divine speech in ch. 15 begins with a promise of protection and of a great reward — promises that belong to the category of blessing. The intensely personal element in this promise is very significant. This is not blessing in a general sense. God specifically emphasizes that he himself will be Abraham's shield and reward. Thus, the blessing promised here includes the idea of close personal communion with God in a harmonious relationship. As we observed earlier, it was this communal aspect of the blessing that was disrupted by humankind's disobedience. Abraham's reply to God's generous offer immediately links blessing to the theme of seed (15:2). Promises of blessing are not much comfort to Abraham since the question of an heir has not been settled, and God confirms the promise of the heir and the related promise of numerous descendants (15:4-5). The third main theme, land, is dealt with in the remainder of the chapter (15:7-21), where the theme of seed is also reiterated (15:18-21). The emphasis on God's personal involvement in the promises that we observed in the opening words of the dialogue (15:1) is intensified in the establishment of the covenant between God and Abraham. God is personally and actively involved in the covenant, and his dealings with Abraham are reminiscent of his dealings with Adam before the harmony between them was destroyed (15:12; cf. 2:21).

The covenant that God establishes with Abraham in ch. 17 begins with an emphasis on blessing, which will be given to Abraham if he lives in close communion with God. If Abraham behaves himself blamelessly before God, his numbers will increase greatly and he shall become the father of a multitude of nations (17:1). The divine blessing on Abraham means that many nations will trace their ancestry back to him (17:4). This is part of what is meant by the promise that God will greatly bless Abraham. However, it is not the whole story, because there is also emphasis on a specially chosen line of seed that will enjoy blessing within a close relationship with God (17:21). This involves a clear distinction between the multitude of Abraham's offspring and the specially chosen line of seed. It is this line of seed that is included under the benefits of the covenant. It is to them that the land of Canaan is promised (17:8), and they must bear the mark of circumcision (17:10-14). It is already clear in ch. 17 that, although Ishmael is the son of Abraham and is circumcised by his father (17:25), he does not enjoy a close relationship with God (17:18). Though God promises to bless Ishmael (17:20), it is blessing bestowed outside the covenant relationship.

The pronouncement of blessing on Sarah (17:15-16) brings together the themes of blessing and seed. Like Abraham, Sarah will be the mother of many nations, and this will be evidence that she has been blessed by God (17:16). However, this is only part of the promise; there will be a specific line of seed with which God will establish his covenant (17:19). This nation will worship him (cf. 17:7). The offspring of Abraham in general is evidence of God's promised blessing and is represented by Ishmael (17:20), while the promise of a special line of seed is represented by the prophecy of the birth of Isaac (17:21). Both sons may be called the seed of Abraham, both are promised blessing, and both will become great nations, which includes the idea of occupying territory (17:20-21). The difference between Ishmael and Isaac is that the concepts of blessing, seed, and land apply to Ishmael only in a very general sense, but they apply to Isaac within the terms of the covenant. Blessing, seed, and land are promised to Isaac within the context of a harmonious relationship with God.

The final pronouncement of divine promises to Abraham is located at the conclusion of Abraham's expression of obedience in the offering of Isaac (22:16-18). This significant pericope, presented as the divine response to Abraham's obedience, reiterates the divine promises. These promises confirm that Abraham will be greatly blessed and will have a multitude of descendants, presumably through both Ishmael and Isaac. More specifically, Abraham's descendants will gain possession of the gates of their enemies (22:17). This more specific reference is probably to the special line of seed and includes the implicit promise of land (possession of the gates of their enemies). Thus, blessing, seed, and land are all included in God's response to Abraham's obedience. Furthermore, the implicit promise of land is followed in the next incident by Abraham's acquisition of Machpelah (23:1-18).

Significantly, this same emphasis on blessing, seed, and land is found in the Jacob cycle. There is only one divine pronouncement to Isaac in the context of a famine (26:1-6). The divine speech encourages Isaac not to travel to Egypt but to stay in Canaan (26:2). This command leads naturally to a promise that if Isaac is obedient, he will be greatly blessed and the land will become the possession of his descendants (26:3). These descendants, who will occupy Canaan, are, of course, the special line of descent. This means that the promise of seed and land are once again combined in the promise of land for Isaac's descendants. Furthermore, the final outcome of these promises is that all nations will receive blessing through Isaac's seed (26:4).

The first divine pronouncement of blessing to Jacob (28:12-15) is in contrast to that received by Isaac. Isaac stays in the land of Canaan and receives blessing as a result, but Jacob receives blessing by deceit and is forced to leave Canaan. The divine pronouncement made as he prepares to leave the promised land emphasizes that this aspect of the promise still stands. Thus, the land on which Jacob lies during his last night before departing from Canaan will belong to him and to his seed (28:13). The link between land, seed, and blessing here is unmistakable: one promise cannot stand independent of the others; the land cannot belong to Jacob in perpetuity unless he has descendants, and the promised descendants will not be prosperous without land to dwell in. The fact that the seed of Jacob will be blessed is emphasized by the reference to the seed being as numerous as grains of dust (28:14). Once again the blessing is channeled through the promised seed to the nations of the world. The divine speech concludes, as it began, on the theme of land; God will be with Jacob and will restore him to the land that he is now leaving (28:15).

Although Jacob has a number of encounters with God, particularly on his return to Canaan, it is not until he returns to Bethel that there is a further comprehensive rehearsal of the promises in a divine speech (35:9-15). The divine speech commences with confirmation of the patriarch's change of name from Jacob to Israel (35:10). This change of name is actually part of the blessing and includes the idea of a close relationship between Jacob and God (cf. 12:2; 32:28). The blessing continues with an imperative reminiscent of the creation blessings (35:11; cf. 1:22, 28). The blessing is not just a command to "be fruitful and multiply" but includes the bestowal of power to fulfill these functions and to become "a nation and a company of nations."

Blessing, however, represents not only increased quantity but also increased quality and thus the assurance that kings will be among Jacob's descendants (35:11). The bestowal of blessing leads on to the promise of land and seed. The land that had previously been given to Abraham and Isaac is now being given to Jacob and to his seed (35:12). This links all three themes together; as a result of blessing Jacob will have numerous seed who will require land to inhabit, and this will be given to them in accordance with the promises made to Abraham and Isaac.

The final divine speech in Genesis is made to Jacob as he prepares to leave Canaan on his way to Egypt (46:2-4). This short passage does not use the terminology associated with blessing, seed, or land; nevertheless, there are allusions to all three themes. They are all included in the promise that God will multiply Jacob's descendants in Egypt and they shall return to Canaan as a great nation.

We have seen that the important divine speeches in 12:1-3; 13:14-17; 15:1-21; 17:1-27; 22:15-18; 26:2-5; 28:12-15; 35:9-15; and 46:2-4 all emphasize the themes of blessing, seed, and land. By repeating the same three themes in such important passages as these divine promises, the narrator provides structural and thematic cohesion to the book and clearly emphasizes the importance of blessing, seed, and land. These three themes must undoubtedly be seen as a major element in the message of the book.

KEY THEOLOGICAL TEACHING OF GENESIS

The Theology of Land

We have already argued that land is a unifying theme in the book of Genesis. In this section we shall consider the theological significance of land. Land is an important theme, not only in Genesis but in the Pentateuch as a whole. It has even been described as "*the central theme* of biblical faith."[1] Habel suggests that land is such an important and comprehensive symbol in the OT that "it could be ranked next to God in importance."[2]

Modern readers are at a disadvantage when approaching this subject, since our perception of land is greatly colored by our scientific approach to life and the mystery of how things grow has been dispelled. However, the perspective that the Israelites had on land was very different from the way modern suburbanites think about land. Today, land is often valued as a place to build rather than for its productive qualities. Productive land can be bought for a fraction of the cost of building lots. When the developer and builder finish, the new tenants do not think of themselves as owners of ¼ acre of land but as owners of the property built on it. Things are very different for people who eke out their subsistence from the land, such as, for example, Aboriginal Australians, for whom, as Habel points out,

> the land is sacred, filled with ancestral dreamings that determine kinship, sacred site, and ceremony. All species of life, including humans, are bound to the land. Land does not belong to people; people belong to land.[3]

While the Aboriginal view of land has more in common with the biblical ideology of land than the view of the modern city-dweller, there are still important differences. Genesis shows that land and human beings do not own each other but are placed in a symbiotic relationship by the Creator. In order to understand this relationship, we need to explore more closely the way that God used both humans and land in the creative process.

There are elements in the creation process and in the continuance of the created order that God delegated to people and, indeed, to "land." Fretheim, helpfully, uses the term "power-sharing" to describe God's method of creating.[4] There is no suggestion that God could not have worked alone as creator, but it is clear that he did not do so. Significant aspects of the creative process are delegated to selected partners in God's power-sharing arrangement. One of the key roles belongs to land, which receives the commission to "bring forth living creatures" (1:24 NRSV). Thus God addresses land directly and gives it a creative role to play. Land also provides the raw material for making the human being. In contrast to land, a lesser role is afforded to water, which

1. Brueggemann, *The Land*, 3.
2. Habel, *The Land Is Mine*, 6.
3. Habel, *The Land Is Mine*, 2.
4. Fretheim, *The Suffering of God*, 73-74.

simply must provide the medium for living creatures to swarm, crawl, and swim (1:20).

Human beings are key members of this power-sharing arrangement. God reserves the most comprehensive and influential role for them and affords them a primary status in partnership with him. Without them the garden will not reach its potential (2:5, 15). However, the role played by land is also significant, and the humans could not have fulfilled their role without the provision of the land. Furthermore, the human could not name the animals until the land had brought them forth (2:19).

God, of course, was not compelled to work in partnership. It was part of his own plan to involve members of the created order in the process of filling the earth and making it productive. God's own role was, undoubtedly, the key role, because without his personal creative power none of the other members in the process would have existed. Furthermore, the part that God played was fulfilled to perfection and was pronounced "good" and "very good" (1:12, 18, 31). Indeed, when land fulfills the role given to it by the Creator, the result is also described as "good" (1:25). It is among the living creatures that discord and rebellion arise. The serpent convinces the human beings that the roles and status they have been given are too narrow and limited (3:1-5). Ditching their original roles and status, they accept the new ones offered by the serpent which increase the jurisdiction of the humans and give God a role subservient to their newly found cravings and desires (3:6-8). This change in their relationship with God affects their relationship to the land. Indeed, the land itself, although it played no part in the rebellion, is affected by it and is cursed by God (3:17). Land suffers further when Cain forces it to drink his brother's blood (4:11).

This means that in Genesis land is not merely a passive onlooker in the created order, nor is it simply the material that God uses; it is actively involved in the process of creation, while other components of the universe, such as air and sea, remain passive. Furthermore, land has a unique relationship with the human beings and even provides the raw material from which the first man is made. The possession of land with clearly defined boundaries is the symbol of security and blessing, while lack of a fertile piece of land is equated with insecurity and danger. The human beings are dependent on land for their continued existence, since it is their source of food. However, the dependence of humankind on land is just one side of the picture; the land is not self-sufficient and, without human beings to till and maintain it, cannot reach its full potential of fruitfulness. Thus, humans and land were partners, and the welfare of each depended on the other. A close relationship with God was necessary for this relationship to work properly, and any alienation between the humans and God affected their relationship with the land.

As a corollary of the tripartite relationship connecting humans and land and God, Genesis shows that no one has prior claim to land apart from sanction received from Yahweh and that continuation in that land is in his gift alone. This understanding of God's role as "supreme landlord" forms the basis of Israel's land ideology and gives it unique nuances. Genesis elucidates how the possession of land could have both ethical and religious ramifications. It is recognized that human beings will receive the best benefits from land while they are living in harmony with God. Israel is not simply chosen in order to receive a special promise of land, but it is chosen to have a special relationship with God within the secure boundaries of Canaan. This is why there is an emphasis in Genesis on building altars, whereas when the patriarchs are in other countries such as Egypt the building of altars is never mentioned. Relationships with land and God were, therefore, interdependent.

While this emphasis on the allocation of land on the basis of divine justice enabled Israel to defend the occupation of Canaan as "an act of God," it was a two-edged sword. By accepting this theology, Israel was forced to acknowledge that when the nation lost a battle or lost control of its land this also was an act of God perpetrated because of Israel's failure (Ps 78:56-64; Lam 1:3-5).

During the exile Israel had to come to terms with the exile as a further example of Yahweh's right to expel those from their land who did not maintain harmonious relations with him. The effect of this process is reflected in the change in postexilic Israel from an emphasis on physical land boundaries to a prioritized sanctuary (Hag 1:9-14). This change of direction in Israel's thinking manifests itself in the lack of triumphalism and the emphasis on rebuilding the temple.

As a result of the exile, Israel's approach to the land issue was revolutionized in a way that reflected the teaching of Genesis 1–11 and acknowledged that the primary concern was the nation's relationship with God. It meant that the starting point to reclaim territorial rights was a humble acknowledgment of failure and spiritual inadequacy. To emulate the tower-builders and appropriate land arbitrarily would lead to the loss of land, but to accept land as a gracious gift would lead to the enjoyment of its produce. This is the direction that a careful reading of Israel's history points, and it is also the overall message of Genesis 1–11.

In situations where land is contested today there is often a tendency to quote the Bible for support. The idea that God takes sides in struggles for territorial supremacy is endemic to many ethnically motivated conflicts. In such conflicts, naturally, all parties want to claim that God is on their side. However, great care needs to be exercised in such claims, and we need to be particularly careful about how we apply the statements in the OT to territorial disputes today. Clare Amos, in her commentary on Genesis, relates the following disturbing incident:

> I will never forget my incredulity at being told by a Palestinian friend of mine, an educated woman from Ramallah, a town on the West Bank, how on a visit to Jerusalem she had had a conversation with a Western tourist. On discovering that she was a Christian living on the West Bank this person had informed her, quite categorically, that "she couldn't be a real Christian, because if she were a real Christian she would of course have been willing to leave her hometown, since she would know that God had given the land to the descendants of Abraham, Isaac and Jacob."[5]

A refusal to acknowledge another person's rights to his or her own land flies in the face of the teaching of Genesis.[6] In conflict situations it is all too easy to claim God's patronage for the cause without giving due consideration to what this means. Genesis encourages a humble attitude to land that recognizes the responsibility of humans to treat land well and acknowledge God as the giver. Humble dependence on God and submission to his will are parts of the biblical tradition.

The Doctrine of Creation

Von Rad wrote an influential article in 1938 in which he argued that the most significant OT theological emphasis is on the history of redemption. He regarded creation as a secondary theme that is much less significant than the doctrine of redemption. He argued that the most serious threat to Israel's conception of nature, as evidenced in Hosea and Deuteronomy, came from Canaanite Baalism, but that in these works Baalism is opposed not, as we might expect, by arguments based on God as creator but "in terms of Israel's redemptive history."[1] In support of his view, Von Rad referred to the prayer that accompanied the offering of firstfruits in Deut 26:5ff.

> The worshipper does not give thanks for the fruits which the Creator has provided for him, but simply acknowledges that he is a member of the

---

5. Amos, *The Book of Genesis*, xvii.

6. See, e.g., 20:15, where Abimelech speaks about the land promised to Abraham as "my land" and neither Abraham nor God dispute this claim. Genesis recognizes the rights of others to own the "promised land" until the right time comes for it to be given to Abraham's descendants.

1. Von Rad, "Theological Problem," 132.

nation which God brought into the promised land by a historical saving act, thus making him heir to the blessings of this land.[2]

Von Rad was not arguing that the doctrine of creation was entirely absent from Israel's faith, but his main thesis was that it was not formulated as an independent doctrine but was "invariably related, and indeed subordinated, to soteriological considerations."[3] In other words, von Rad believed that Israel's earliest expressions of faith and most significant theological concerns were about God's saving acts in Israel's history rather than about God as creator.

Von Rad's influential views "generated a great deal of expository literature."[4] Recently, however, scholars have become more positive about the role played by the doctrine of creation in the OT. Brueggemann writes about the "enormous shift now taking place . . . with reference to testimony about a God who creates."[5]

It is now acknowledged that, while Israel's early faith concentrated on "Yahweh's redemptive acts in history," it did not ignore "Yahweh's lordship over nature."[6] An integral element of the story of Israel's redemption from Egypt is the power of Yahweh over nature demonstrated in the plagues and in the crossing of the Reed Sea.

In spite of this renewed enthusiasm for the doctrine of creation in the OT, some scholars still play down its significance in the book of Genesis: Sarna speaks of an imbalance in Genesis because of the comparatively little space allocated to the creation accounts. He observes,

> This imbalance is there by design. The theme of Creation, important as it is, serves merely as an introduction to the book's central motif: God's role in history. The opening chapters are a prologue to the historical drama that begins in chapter 12.[7]

Sarna's reference to the theme of creation as "merely an introduction" could be misleading. It is more accurate to describe the role of the creation theme as foundational to the historical drama rather than merely introductory. Set in the context of polytheistic societies, the entire message of Genesis

---

2. Von Rad, "Theological Problem," 132.
3. Von Rad, "Theological Problem," 142.
4. Brueggemann, *Theology of the Old Testament,* 160.
5. Brueggemann, *Theology of the Old Testament,* 159.
6. Anderson, *From Creation to New Creation,* 5.
7. Sarna, *Genesis,* xiv.

rests on the programmatic truths established in the first two chapters, that one supreme God made everything that exists and exercises his prerogative as supreme ruler of the earth and its inhabitants. Nevertheless, the point that Sarna is making is important, that in Genesis creation is part of a much bigger picture; it is not a self-contained doctrine that stands independent of the rest of the book. Theological studies of the creation accounts in Genesis sometimes treat them as sources of all sorts of doctrinal minutiae that have no bearing on the overall message of the book. However, the early chapters of Genesis should not be approached as a self-contained unit but should be viewed as both a preface and an introduction to the rest of the book, since they provide a context for what follows. Often the reason for so much controversy in theological discussions is that texts are being used to source answers to questions that are outside the parameters of the original purpose of the text. It is good to bear this in mind as we study the theological discussions on creation in Genesis.

Creatio ex Nihilo

A frequently asked question is "Did God create the world out of nothing, or did he use preexistent material?" This question has been the subject of a protracted debate among scholars. The difference between God creating the cosmos out of preexisting material or out of nothing may seem unimportant, but some argue that it has significant implications for our view of God: is he the God who simply works with the material to hand and subdues or orders it, as other deities were understood to do, or was he master of everything, creating even the very materials that he would use? The view that God created the universe out of nothing excludes any possible hint of dualism and means that there was no preexisting recalcitrant matter that God had to reckon with. Copan and Craig describe the doctrine of *creatio ex nihilo* as "biblically grounded" and "theologically illuminating."[1] They argue that the doctrine "reinforces the idea of God's *aseity* or necessary existence," "underlines the doctrine of divine *freedom*," and "exhibits God's *omnipotence*."[2]

Others argue that whether the world was created out of preexisting material or not was irrelevant to the original writer and readers and is an example of modern issues writing the agenda for the ancient text. Many would

1. Copan and Craig, *Creation out of Nothing*, 25.
2. Copan and Craig, *Creation out of Nothing*, 25.

agree with Atwell that the concept of creation out of nothing "was not yet a significant theological idea" for the peoples of the ancient Near East.[3]

One of the main issues in the debate is the translation of the first verse of Genesis. The traditional translation seems to settle the matter very clearly:

> In the beginning God created the heavens and the earth.

This statement appears to leave no room for doubt that, before God began to create, apart from him nothing else existed. However, a problem arises because it is possible to translate the verse as a temporal clause:

> When in the beginning God created the heaven and the earth, the earth was without form and void.

This alternative translation allows the possibility that when God began to create there was already preexistent material from which he created the universe. According to this view, God brought order out of chaos and may have used preexisting material to create a functioning universe.

The controversy cannot be resolved by a discussion of Hebrew grammar since both views have support from competent Hebraists.[4] As Westermann observes, the discussion about these alternate translations has been "almost endless,"[5] and Wenham refers to "a complex and protracted debate."[6] The details of the debate about grammar can be found in the main technical commentaries, but since a study of syntax is not conclusive it is not included here.

Another main argument marshaled in favor of *creatio ex nihilo* is the meaning of the verb "to create." Moltmann concludes that *creatio ex nihilo* "is an apt paraphrase of what the Bible means by 'creation.'"[7] He places significant weight on the meaning of the verb "to create," בָּרָא/*bārā'*, which, he observes, "is used exclusively as a term for the divine bringing forth, for which there is no corresponding human analogy." He also points out that it is never used with "the accusative of a material out of which something is to be made."[8] Similarly, McIntosh argues that *bārā'* "is reserved for God's creation out of nothing."[9]

However, it is misleading to argue that the meaning of the verb *bārā'* is

---

3. Atwell, *The Sources of the Old Testament*, 4.
4. Brueggemann is correct that "The evidence of the grammar is not decisive, and either rendering is possible"; *Genesis*, 29.
5. Westermann, *Genesis 1-11*, 95.
6. Wenham, *Genesis 1–15*, 11.
7. Moltmann, *God in Creation*, 74.
8. Moltmann, *God in Creation*, 73.
9. McIntosh, *Genesis for Today*, 39.

conclusive in this debate. As Wenham points out, it "is not a term exclusively reserved for creation out of nothing."[10] It is used, for example, of the Lord creating "over the whole site of Mount Zion and over her assemblies a cloud by day, and smoke and the shining of a flaming fire by night" (Isa 4:5 ESV). Although the cloud and fire are created, there is no hint that they are created out of nothing. Another example relates to the city of Jerusalem:

> But be glad and rejoice forever in that which I create; for behold, I *create* Jerusalem to be a joy, and her people to be a gladness. I will rejoice in Jerusalem and be glad in my people; no more shall be heard in it the sound of weeping and the cry of distress. (Isa 65:18-19 ESV)

Obviously there is no suggestion that Jerusalem was created out of nothing, and it is not an issue in this passage. Although the verb *bārā'* is used exclusively with God as the subject, we have no grounds to suggest that the verb essentially means "to create out of nothing." Rather, as Middleton suggests, it may refer rather to "creative acts of radical newness."[11] There is little doubt that, as Van Leeuwen argues, "Biblical theologians, eager to discover theological significance in individual words, have overloaded" this verb "with semantic freight."[12]

Nevertheless, we should not underestimate the importance of *bārā'*. Copan and Craig accept that, while "we must be careful not to overload it [the word *bārā'*] with more freight than it was meant to carry, we must not overlook its significance either."[13] They agree that the verb *bārā'* "does not *always* speak of an *ex nihilo* creation, but can be used more widely than this," but they argue that, nevertheless, it "is never linguistically connected to any preexisting matter."[14]

Thus the verb *bārā'* is always predicated of God and the material with which he works is never mentioned. However, to claim that the verb always means "to create out of nothing" is to go beyond the evidence. This does not alter the fact that the verb *bārā'* is a highly significant word that evokes the majestic imagery of God bringing the world into existence effortlessly and unopposed.

Another area to consider in relation to *creatio ex nihilo* is the history of the concept. One important argument in favor of the traditional translation

---

10. Wenham, *Genesis 1–15,* 14.
11. Middleton, *The Liberating Image,* 73.
12. Van Leeuwen, "בָּרָא," 731.
13. Copan and Craig, *Creation out of Nothing,* 49.
14. Copan and Craig, *Creation out of Nothing,* 49, 53.

is the antiquity of this interpretation. As Wenham observes, the "versions and Masoretic pointing imply this was the standard view from the third century B.C. (LXX) through to the tenth century A.D. (MT)."[15] A number of biblical and extrabiblical texts are often quoted in support of the antiquity of the *creatio ex nihilo* concept.

For example, in the Apocrypha a mother encourages her son to accept martyrdom rather than deny his faith, and she exhorts him to

> Look upon the heaven and the earth, and all that is therein, and consider that God made them of things that were not; and so was mankind made likewise. (2 Macc 7:28)

In the NT, Paul refers to God as the one "who gives life to the dead and calls into existence the things that do not exist" (Rom 4:17 NRSV). The author of Hebrews is even more explicit:

> By faith we understand that the universe was created by the word of God, so that what is seen was not made out of things that are visible (Heb 11:3 ESV).[16]

One of the difficulties involved in finding references from antiquity is that many of the texts that apparently support this concept are ambiguous. As Pannenberg points out, the reference in Maccabees does not explicitly state that there was no preexisting material but "simply means that the world was not previously there."[17] The same could be said in relation to Paul's reference to creation, but the author to Hebrews seems closer to *creatio ex nihilo* with his assertion that the visible creation was made from what was invisible.

Since much of the linguistic and historical evidence in support of the doctrine of *creatio ex nihilo* is inconclusive and circumstantial, our verdict on the subject should be based on the text of Genesis and on a study of the purpose for which it was written. It may be argued that the idea of "creation out of nothing" is too complex and sophisticated to be in the mind of the writer and readers of Genesis.[18] However, the most important consideration is that the main issues facing the writer and his earliest readers were about the control of chaos and about God's sovereignty over chaos. Genesis 1 was written to expunge any suggestion that creation was a struggle between God and the

---

15. Wenham, *Genesis 1–15*, 13.
16. See also John 1.
17. Pannenberg, *Systematic Theology*, 2:13.
18. Cf. Anderson, *From Creation to New Creation*, 8.

gods and demons of chaos that featured so prominently in the creation myths that were current at that time. Unlike the other stories of creation such as *Enuma Elish,* Genesis shows that creation was not the result of strife among a number of deities but was an awesome and powerful act of a deity who had neither equal nor rival. So, while theologians today use philosophical concepts and vocabulary unknown to the author of Genesis, the purpose was the same: to exalt Israel's God as the one and only supreme divine being responsible for everything that exists and in total control. Genesis does not contain a fully developed doctrine of *creatio ex nihilo* since this was not the main issue at the time, but since the Genesis account does not exclude *creatio ex nihilo* it provides the foundation that later writers and theologians built on.

The developed form of the doctrine of *creatio ex nihilo* came as a response to Gnosticism. The Gnostics explained the existence of evil in the world as the result of the preexistent deficient material. As McGrath points out, in opposition to Gnosticism, "Christian theologians gradually came to the conclusion that creation was best understood as an action *ex nihilo.*"[19] Pannenberg credits Theophilus of Antioch and Irenaeus of Lyons with playing "a decisive role in establishing the doctrine of creation out of nothing." He observes that

> Theophilus in particular expressly opposed the Platonic idea of matter that was as uncreated as God (*Ad Autol.* 2.4). He argued that the greatness of God and his creative act may be seen only if he does not bring forth out of existing matter like human artists, but brings forth out of nothing whatever he wills. Irenaeus, too, emphasized that of his own free will God brought forth all things (*Adv. haer.* 2.1.1), including matter (2.10.4).[20]

For these early theologians as for their modern counterparts, the doctrine of *creatio ex nihilo* establishes that the world was "created neither out of preexistent matter, nor out of the divine Being itself."[21] This means that the world is not, as the Gnostics claimed, an emanation from God but is a determined act of his free will. As Tillich puts it, the "doctrine of *creatio ex nihilo* is Christianity's protection against any type of ultimate dualism."[22] This modern jargon is not the way that the author of Genesis would have phrased it, but he would have agreed with the end result that the God of Israel made everything that existed in an effortless sovereign display of creative power.

19. A. McGrath, *The Science of God,* 50.
20. Pannenberg, *Systematic Theology,* 2:14.
21. Moltmann, *God in Creation,* 75.
22. Tillich, *Systematic Theology,* 1:253.

The Fall

The doctrine of the Fall is highly significant in systematic theology. Tillich describes it as "a decisive part of the Christian tradition."[1] It asserts that Adam and Eve were created as perfect and sinless but with the freedom to sin. As Tillich observes, "Creaturely freedom is the point at which creation and the fall coincide."[2] When the first humans exercised their freedom and disobeyed God, sin entered the world and affected all humanity. Moreover, it is also argued that the natural world was perfect until the Fall, which somehow threw nature off balance and made the earth vulnerable to disasters such as earthquakes and floods (cf. Rom 8:20-21). The OT, however, does not specifically describe the sin of Adam and Eve as a Fall, and it does not link natural disasters to their first sin. Because of this, some OT scholars regard the doctrine of the Fall as alien not only to the book of Genesis particularly but to the OT as a whole. We have already seen how a Christian interpretation that ignores the context of an OT passage can obscure the original meaning. We must ask whether the doctrine of the Fall comes into the same category. Brueggemann is in no doubt that it does. Referring to the idea of a Fall, Brueggemann remarks, "Nothing could be more remote from the narrative [of Genesis] itself."[3] Of course, not all scholars take this view, and some such as Shuster complain about "the contemporary predilection of many biblical scholars and theologians to give short shrift to the Fall."[4]

In favor of the doctrine of the Fall, we may argue that the events of Genesis 3 are given such prominence that they cannot be regarded as a one-off occurrence. Genesis teaches that the disobedience in the garden of Eden was the first in a series of events that altered irrevocably the relationship between human beings and God. Whatever terminology we use, the events that took place in Eden were responsible for the transference of human beings from the idyllic conditions of paradise to a world of thorns, thistles, pain, and death. As Blocher argues,

> It is obvious that the Eden story is no peripheral anecdote or marginal addition; it belongs decisively to the structure of Genesis and to that of the Torah. It has a major etiological intention, with the following chapters showing the results of the inaugural tragedy.[5]

1. Tillich, *Systematic Theology,* 2:29.
2. Tillich, *Systematic Theology,* 1:256.
3. Brueggemann, *Genesis,* 41.
4. Shuster, *The Fall and Sin,* 4.
5. Blocher, *Original Sin,* 32.

This still leaves the question unanswered about the appropriateness of the term *"the Fall"* as a description of what happened in Eden. One objection against describing Genesis 3 as the Fall is that this is Christian but not biblical terminology. In the Gospels, the term "Fall" is used by Jesus, but the reference is to the fall of Satan and not humans (Luke 10:18). Thus, rather than impose a name that is alien to the Bible, some scholars prefer to use other terms to describe what happened in Genesis. Gow argues that "it is better to describe the disobedience of Eve and Adam as one of defection, deviation or transgression."[6] As Gow points out, "the so-called classic view of the Fall did not receive adumbration until the time of Augustine."[7]

Closely linked with the idea of the Fall of humanity is the concept of original sin, the doctrine that when Adam sinned, his sin affected all humanity, and every human being after Adam inherited sinful nature. This teaching arose not from Genesis itself but from the teaching of St. Paul (Romans 5; 1 Corinthians 15). The apostle spoke of two Adams. Through the first Adam human beings became sinners, but through the second Adam (Christ) they became righteous. This idea of inheriting sin through Adam has always been controversial, even in the time of Augustine, who observed that "Nothing is so easy to denounce, nothing is so difficult to understand."[8] Augustine's observation is still pertinent since scholars often reserve their most scathing comments for this doctrine. Thus Ricoeur caricatures the doctrine as "an old peculiar gentleman, all alone with his wife in a garden, who is supposed to have transmitted by means of physical generation his own most private nastiness."[9]

Brueggemann rejects the idea that Genesis teaches the concept of original sin or explains *"how evil came into the world."* This concept, he argues, is too abstract for the OT, and there "is no hint that the serpent is the embodiment of (sic) principle of evil."[10] Since no one actually dies in Genesis 3, Brueggemann also rejects the idea that the narrative is "an account of the *origin of death* in the world." The passage, he argues, "is not a reflection on death but on troubled, anxiety-ridden life," which "is a greater problem than death, both in our own context and in the world of this narrative."[11]

One of the main arguments of those who deny that Genesis contains a doctrine of original sin is that the concept is absent from the rest of the OT. It

6. Gow, "Fall," 285.
7. Gow, "Fall," 291.
8. Quoted from Blocher, *Original Sin,* 15.
9. Quoted from Blocher, *Original Sin,* 38-39.
10. Brueggemann, *Genesis,* 41.
11. Brueggemann, *Genesis,* 42.

is argued that if this passage taught such a programmatic doctrine as inherited sin, then this would be mentioned elsewhere in the OT. But in references to creation such as Ps 19:1, there is not even a hint of a cosmic fall.[12] Blocher, however, argues that there are more "echoes" of the account of Adam throughout Scripture than is generally recognized. For example, he claims that there are allusions to Genesis in Isaiah, and he draws attention to many echoes of the garden of Eden in Isaiah.

> But when we turn to Isaiah, with its thematic context of creation and its 'Paradise regained' atmosphere (*cf.* 11:5ff.), the promise that the serpent shall eat dust (65:25) distinctly recalls the verdict of Genesis 3:14. Implicitly, all the evils that shall at last be forgotten in the newly created Jerusalem (vv. 16ff.) are traced back to the original serpent's manoeuvre, for which he was sentenced to dust.[13]

Blocher also finds allusions to Genesis in Hosea, Ezekiel, Psalms, Job, Proverbs, and Ecclesiastes, and although there is debate about whether some of these really are alluding to Genesis, he concludes that "the cumulative force of plausibilities enables us to resist the pessimistic assessment of some regarding Old Testament echoes of the Genesis narrative of Eden."[14]

It is clear, then, that when we use a term such as "fall" or "original sin" we are not using a biblical term but are referring to an attempt by scholars to understand what happened in Eden in the light of the NT and in the light of the formulations of later theologians. Nevertheless, although Genesis does not use these terms, it teaches that the act of disobedience of the first parents led to an altered relationship between them and God, and it also meant that they were separated from the "tree of life." While this is not the fully formulated doctrine of original sin, it is the foundation on which others built.

The Character of God

A feature of Genesis that makes it stand out from the other books of the OT is its characterization of God. As Humphreys points out, "God is again and again focal in the sequence of events that comprise the narrative and in the lives of the other characters."[1] His presence is dramatically introduced in the

---

12. Cf. Santmire, "The Genesis Creation Narratives Revisited," 373.
13. Blocher, *Original Sin*, 44.
14. Blocher, *Original Sin*, 46.
1. Humphreys, *The Character of God*, 2.

opening sentence of the book, and he is the only character whose presence pervades every narrative. God's relationship to the other characters and his interaction with them are crucial to the plot and story line throughout Genesis. This in itself is not unique, and in stories such as *Enuma Elish* there is also continual interaction between divine and human. Even the type of activity that the God of Genesis carries out is not unique; he saves and blesses people, but so do the gods in other ancient Near Eastern stories. Fretheim observes that "it is not enough to say that God is the one who saves and blesses in these stories."[2] Since other gods are also credited with blessing and saving their people, we need to inquire about what kind of God is portrayed in Genesis. As Fretheim argues, "A capricious God can save and bless. Even an impersonal God could engage in such activities."[3] Genesis opens up God's character to the reader showing not only how God acts, but why he acts in a particular way. While some of the actions attributed to God are shrouded in mystery, many of his acts in Genesis are related in the context of a clear moral rationale. Thus, the Amorites will not lose their land until their sins merit this judgment (15:16), and if there are 10 righteous in Sodom the city will be spared because "the Judge of all the earth" must do what is right (18:32).

God reveals himself in various ways in Genesis; he appears in dreams, he walks and converses like a human being, and he is sometimes represented by an angel. His character is also revealed through divine speeches that add further detail to the characterization of God and reveal his thoughts to the reader.

The God Who Is Transcendent and Immanent

Sometimes the characterization of God seems contradictory because God is presented, on the one hand, as transcendent and above creation but, on the other hand, as closely involved in the created order and even emotionally affected by events on earth (cf. 6:6). Nowhere is this more apparent than in the first two chapters of the book. Two accounts of creation are presented side by side that give contrasting portrayals of the Creator. The first creation account (1:1–2:3) is a wonderful and majestic portrayal of God as the transcendent creator. Within a carefully structured framework of seven days, the creator God speaks and creation comes into being. God's awesome power and universal authority are revealed in the way that the world and all its components come

---

2. Fretheim, *The Suffering of God*, 24.
3. Fretheim, *The Suffering of God*, 24.

into being when he utters a word. The uniqueness of the divine activity is conveyed by the use of the verb "to create." This verb is never used in the OT with human beings as the subject; only God creates.[4] This portrayal of God emphasizes his distinctiveness from the things he created. He does not touch things in order to create them; he just speaks and they appear. This maintains a distance and a clear distinction between the Creator and the created. In contrast to religions that deified natural objects and phenomena, God creates everything but is not part of creation himself. God's existence is not explained or queried, and his uniqueness as the creator of all things is unassailable.

From 2:4 the atmosphere in Genesis changes and we are given a second creation account from a different perspective. We can identify that a new account is beginning because in the first account (1–2:3) creation is completed, including male and female, yet in ch. 2 nothing has grown yet, and Adam is formed first and then Eve. But the idea that there are two accounts can be misleading and needs qualification. These are not two contradictory accounts that require reconciliation since they do not cover exactly the same material, nor are they related to the same period of time. The accounts are complementary, and the second balances the first rather than contradicting it.

While the second account of creation is, like the first, unequivocally monotheistic and God is clearly separate from the natural order, there is a difference of emphasis and atmosphere. The different vocabulary used in the two accounts is particularly significant. Whereas in the first account the verbs employed to describe divine activity are laden with theological significance and emphasize God's uniqueness and transcendence, in the second account the verbs of everyday human activity are utilized. God "forms" the human beings as a potter would form a pot; God "plants" a garden, he "breathes" the breath of life, and he "walks" in the garden as a human would do in the cooler part of the day.

Thus at the very beginning of the book of Genesis the reader is presented with a "synoptic problem." Yet it would be irrelevant to ask which of these accounts is better or more accurate, since they complement each other and portray two aspects of the character of God. On the one hand, he is majestic and sovereign, but on the other hand, while God is distinct from creation and from human beings he does not remain at a distance from them.

God's immanence is most clearly revealed in his relationships with human beings. An emphasis that occurs in both creation accounts is that God

---

4. Another word is spelled the same and is used, e.g., of human beings clearing a forest, but there is probably no etymological link. Similarly in English we have, e.g., two words spelled "lead" but one of them is used to control a dog and the other to seal a roof.

involves the human beings in his creation and provides a role for them as his partners in caring for and controlling the created order. He commands that they have "dominion," and he involves them in the work of tilling the ground and caring for its produce.

However, for God to work in partnership with humans and have communion with them, he must make himself available to them. Obviously, if God remains transcendent and unapproachably awesome, it will be impossible for humans to have a meaningful relationship with him. Communication with humans and a personal relationship with them will involve God in self-limitation. Fretheim describes this self-limitation as "a divine *kenosis*" and observes that God's act of creation "might be called the beginning of the passion of God."[5] God has a price to pay for a partnership with fallible and sinful humans.[6]

The readers of Genesis are not treated to a philosophical discussion of God's character and intentions. God is disclosed mainly in his relationships with people, and the most revealing is his relationship with Abraham. The episode in which the Lord appears to the patriarch as one of three visitors is an outstanding example of interaction between deity and humanity. Although the main point of the visit is to announce the forthcoming birth of Isaac, its high point is the discussion between the Lord and Abraham about the future of Sodom and Gomorrah. This is remarkable because in a face-to-face encounter with a human being, God allows Abraham to debate with him about the future of the city of Sodom. The passage seems strange from the standpoint of modern Western culture, but even today the practice of bargaining is endemic to life in many parts of the Middle East. Abraham's encounter with God was characteristic of the sort of encounter that one human being might have with another. The amazing aspect of the story is not that Abraham bargains but that he does so with God. The incident shows God's willingness to become vulnerable to negotiation and subject to human bartering techniques.

Fretheim argues that the debate between Abraham and God left open the possibility of God reprieving the city.

> For this conversation to have any integrity, it thus seems necessary for the destruction of Sodom to be only a probability or a possibility, waiting upon the God/Abraham discussion before the final "go ahead" in the exe-

---

5. Fretheim, *The Suffering of God*, 58.
6. This theme is developed in the NT, where it is emphasized that Jesus accepted the role of servanthood and eventually death. Interaction with humans cost God dearly.

cution of the decision is given. Thus, human thought is taken into consideration by God in the shaping of the future.[7]

In a similar way God responds to appeals for mercy on behalf of others in a number of OT passages. For example, Moses debates the divine decision to destroy Israel in the wilderness (Num 14:11-20), and Moses and Aaron question God's decision in words that re-echo those of Abraham when they ask, "Shall one man sin, and will you be angry with all the congregation?" (Num 16:22).[8] These passages present God as not just desiring a relationship with human beings but desiring a partnership in which he takes them seriously and treats their views as worth considering.

While Abraham's relationship with God is the high point of human-divine relationships in the patriarchal narratives, there are other less dramatic ways in which God reveals himself. He associates his presence with particular places such as Bethel. However, Jacob's perception that the place where he met God was "the House of God" and "the Gate of Heaven" was not intended to limit God to one place. God's association with a place is part of his self-limitation for the sake of humans. Bethel is the place to which Jacob returns in troubled times, but he later acknowledges that God is actually with him wherever he goes and not just at Bethel (48:15). The place is not a limit to God's presence but a concession to the human need for something tangible to which they can relate. This point is clearly made by Fretheim, who refers to the later construction of the tabernacle as "a gracious condescension to the need of the human for that which is concrete and focused."[9] Such condescension is evident in the story of Naaman, who asks for Israelite earth on which to worship Israel's God (2 Kgs 5:17). However, associating God with a particular place became counterproductive for Israel's faith and distorted their perception of God. This distortion involved limiting God to actions associated with spatial location; a corollary of this was that the importance of the place increased at the expense of the deity it represented (cf. Jer 7:1-15). Ezekiel saw the divine presence leaving the temple as a prelude to its destruction (Ezek 10:18), while he witnessed a theophany in a place not considered sacred or special (Ezekiel 1).

In conclusion, Genesis presents God as unassailable and utterly transcendent, but it also shows that for the sake of humans God is willing to make himself known. In this self-revelation God becomes vulnerable to suffering

7. Fretheim, *The Suffering of God*, 50.
8. Cf. Fretheim, *The Suffering of God*, 51.
9. Fretheim, *The Suffering of God*, 63.

and disappointment. Long before the NT was written, Genesis reveals a God who is able to share our sorrows.

The Image of God

Although the concept of the image of God figures prominently in Christian theology, the concept is found in only three passages in the OT, and these are all in Genesis. The first occurrence is in 1:26:

> Then God said, "Let us make man in our image, after our likeness." (ESV)

The completion of this act is confirmed in the following verse (1:27):

> So God created man in his own image, in the image of God he created him; male and female he created them. (ESV)

The second passage is in 5:1, which recalls the status of human beings as having been made in God's image.

> This is the book of the generations of Adam. When God created man, he made him in the likeness of God. (ESV)

The third occasion on which the image and likeness of God is mentioned is in the context of the laws of Noah. The context is the sanction announced against murder (9:6).

> Whoever sheds the blood of man, by man shall his blood be shed, for God made man in his own image. (ESV)

These are all the references to the "image of God" in the OT, but there is also a significant reference to Adam bearing a son "in his own image" (5:3). As Barr points out, in other passages where we might expect the image to be mentioned, such as Ps 8:5-6, the concept is surprisingly absent.[1] This paucity of biblical references suggests that, as Curtis puts it, "the statement of humanity's creation in the image of God appears to have had less importance in the biblical tradition than it assumed in later theological discussion."[2] Yet, we may argue that the concept has received a great deal of attention from scholars because "the importance of the doctrine is out of all proportion to the laconic treatment it receives in the Old Testament."[3] As Bray observes,

1. James Barr, "The Image of God in the Book of Genesis," 11-12.
2. Curtis, "Image of God (OT)," 389.
3. Clines, "The Image of God in Man," 53.

The image of God in man does not occur often, but it comes at significant moments — the crowning of creation, the beginning of the genealogies and the prohibition of murder, which clearly distinguishes human from merely animal life. It also reappears in the New Testament, having been the object of considerable speculation during the intertestamental period. We might also add that the vast amount of attention paid to it both by Christian tradition and by modern scholarship (sometimes in the interests of demonstrating its insignificance!) shows that the concept cannot simply be dismissed as a matter of little or no real importance.[4]

The lack of explanatory information in the OT about the nature of the "image of God" has inevitably led to a plethora of interpretations beginning, as Bray points out above, as early as the intertestamental period. Some of the interpretations go so far beyond the evidence that Barr refers to it as "the blood-out-of-a-stone process."[5]

The first issue is whether the "image" and "likeness" are both the same thing or a distinction should be made between them. Jónsson points out that "the distinction between image *(imago)* and likeness *(similitudo)* . . . is first found in Ireneus and some of the Church Fathers" and it became especially common within Scholasticism.[6]

Most modern scholars regard "image" and "likeness" as two ways of saying the same thing, in other words, a duplication of synonyms. The words do, however, have slightly different nuances. "Image" is the more concrete term and refers, for example, to images of mice made from gold (1 Sam 6:11) or to images of Baal (2 Chr 23:17). "Likeness" is a more general term for resemblance and is a favorite term of Ezekiel as he describes his esoteric visions in terms of how the things he saw appeared (Ezek 1:5, 10, 13, 16, 22, 28). However, the word "likeness" is not always abstract, since it is used for the "sketch" (NIV) or "model" (NRSV) of an altar that King Ahaz sent to Jerusalem to have it constructed (2 Kgs 16:10).[7] Barr suggests that "image" is the more important of the two words, but "it is also the more novel and the more ambiguous." The second word, "likeness," was "added in order to define and limit its meaning, by indicating that the sense intended for ṣelem must lie within that part of its range which overlaps with the range of dᵉmut."[8] Thus, according to Barr the use of the two words avoids the possible confusion that the use of "image" alone could have caused.

4. Bray, "The Significance of God's Image in Man," 201.
5. Barr, "The Image of God," 12.
6. Jónsson, *The Image of God,* 30.
7. Cf. Bray, "The Significance of God's Image in Man," 197.
8. Barr, "The Image of God," 24.

Assuming that there is no major distinction between image and likeness still leaves us with the question about what this means. Is the image and likeness about the appearance of human beings, about their nature, about their relationship to God, or about their function within the created order?

Although it is difficult to ascertain the meaning of the "image," it is closely associated with the special status given to human beings over the rest of creation and "sets man and woman apart from everything else that God made,"[9] giving them a unique place in creation and a unique relationship with God. One popular explanation is to link the concept of "image" to royalty. In Mesopotamia and Egypt the kings were referred to as the image or likeness of particular gods; but in Genesis, it is argued, all human beings have this distinction, which clearly sets them apart from the rest of creation. As Sarna observes,

> Without doubt, the terminology employed in Genesis 2:26 is derived from regal vocabulary, which serves to elevate the king above the ordinary run of men. In the Bible this idea has become democratized. All human beings are created "in the image of God"; each person bears the stamp of royalty.[10]

While this theory may be correct, it cannot be proved or disproved from the text because it relies on the author and his readers having access to knowledge about the regal language of the ancient Near East. Certainly, if the image is intended as a royal idiom, Genesis gives little hint of it. As Bray correctly observes,

> At most there may be faint echoes of a royal ideology which would strike the hearer as an enormous contrast to the Israelite conception of God. That there was such a contrast is agreed by everyone; whether it was deliberately intended or not remains unknown, and probably unknowable.[11]

Others are much less reticent about the possibility of Egyptian royal ideology being reflected in Genesis. Curtis argues,

> It seems likely that the image of God idea was introduced into Israel through her contacts with Egypt, and the idea was emptied of content that was incompatible with Israelite theology and used to express the ap-

9. Curtis, "Image of God (OT)," 390.
10. Sarna, *Genesis*, 12.
11. Bray, "The Significance of God's Image in Man," 197.

parently uniquely Israelite idea that all persons, not just the king, occupy a preeminent place in the created order.[12]

Middleton, though, believes that we should look to Mesopotamian ideology rather than Egyptian to understand the concept of the image of God. While he agrees that the preponderance of references to the concept of the image of God is in Egyptian texts, Middleton argues that it is more likely that the Mesopotamian ideology of sacral kingship provides the background to the *imago Dei* in Genesis. He seeks to show that Genesis articulates a worldview in opposition to that of Mesopotamian literature. He argues that in Mesopotamian literature all significant events and actions, such as the founding of the first city, are attributed to gods or kings. The Mesopotamian worldview devalues humanity, but Genesis elevates it. In particular, the concept of the image of God was applied in Mesopotamia to idols, priests, and kings. Genesis, in contrast, democratizes the concept of *imago Dei* with the declaration that all human beings are made in the image of God. This affords humanity a dignity and status that are well beyond anything contemplated in the Mesopotamian writings.[13]

Others have sought for the meaning of the image of God neither in Egypt or Mesopotamia but in the text of Genesis itself. For a number of scholars such as August Dillmann (1823-1894), the starting point for interpreting the *imago Dei* is the emphasis in Genesis on the preeminence of human beings over the animals. The divine image according to this approach consists mainly in the spiritual and moral qualities that distinguish humans from animals.[14]

While this identification of the image with the spiritual and moral superiority of human beings is attractive, its main drawback is that it creates a dichotomy between the spiritual and physical aspects of human spirituality that is inconsistent with the OT view of humanity.[15] It was not human spirituality that was in the image of God but human beings in their totality. Therefore, any explanation of the image of God must show what is meant by humans being made like God in a sense that embraces their entire being. As Barr argues,

> The point was not that man had a likeness to God through acting as God's representative towards the rest of created nature, but that he him-

---

12. Curtis, "Image of God (OT)," 391.
13. Middleton, *The Liberating Image.*
14. For more detail, see Jónsson, *The Image of God,* 39.
15. Cf. Curtis, "Image of God (OT)," 390.

self was like God. In what way he was like God is not stated: probably it was essential to the writer's position that it could not be stated. There is of course a connection between the image and the dominion over nature, but this is not such that the image consisted in the dominion. It is likely rather to be a consequential relation: *since* man is in the image of God, let him have dominion, etc. Negatively, we may note one additional point. The idea that the image consists in dominion over nature does not fit with the other two places at which the image terminology is used.[16]

Discussions on the image of God have become quite complicated, but presumably the concept was clear to the writer and to the first readers. We may assume that the writer expected the readers to know what the image of God meant or to understand its meaning by reading the book. Therefore, we should look for the meaning of the image of God in Genesis itself. It is very likely that, if Genesis is making an important point through the concept of the image of God, this point will not only be compatible with the overall message of Genesis but also will be made and emphasized in other ways in the book. In particular, the passage that mentions the image of God (Genesis 1) also provides a strong defense against the deification of nature in general and the animal kingdom in particular. In the world of the writer it was common to deify the natural order; anything, it seems, could be deified, including astral bodies, animals, and humans themselves, especially rulers. Therefore, Genesis was teaching something quite alien to the popular religious ideas of the time. Plants, animals, birds, and fish, much less the astral bodies, were not in the image of God and they were not like God. The concept of the image of God showed that the only creature who was like God in some ways was the human being.

One question that we should ponder carefully is why the writer of Genesis does not spell out exactly how humans resemble God or what is meant by the "image of God." Perhaps when Genesis was written the question of the image of God would have been much more sensitive than it is today because of the danger of idolatry. As Sherlock observes, "God cannot be defined, and any endeavor on our part to do so constitutes idolatry."[17] Since defining God is a sensitive issue, Barr may be correct that

> There is no reason to believe that this writer had in his mind any definite idea about the content or the location of the image of God.[18]

16. Barr, "Man and Nature," 20.
17. Sherlock, *The Doctrine of Humanity*, 32.
18. Barr, "The Image of God," 13.

Perhaps the idea of the image is just one way of expressing the truth that is affirmed elsewhere in the OT, that human beings are unique in God's creation and are closer in their relation to him than any other creature. If the concept of the image is missing from Genesis 1, as Barr observes, "the effect would be that man was only a dominant animal."[19] However, if the superiority of the humans compared with the other creatures is not found in their superior intellect or ability but in their likeness to God, this reduces the right of humans to feel proud about their own status. They are only superior to other creatures insofar as God has given them a likeness to himself. To ask, then, "In what way humans are like God?" is to miss the point entirely. It is the fact itself that humans alone in creation bear a likeness to God that is important. This likeness to God opens up a relationship between humans and God that would be impossible for animals to have. Perhaps the best way to sum up what is meant by the image of God is to say that if God came to earth, he would come as a human person, because humanity is related to him and he would have relationships with humans at a deeper level than with any other aspect of the created order.

Thus the image of God teaches that human beings are more like God than other aspects of the created order, but yet they are not deities and cannot become gods. However, their creation in the image of God means that the human form corresponds with deity. Creation in the image of God means that it is not surprising that God can appear to Abraham in the form of a human being. Since God has made human beings in his image, their form and appearance are so closely related to deity that God can appear as a human being, whereas in the context of Genesis it would be absurd to think of God appearing in any other form. No other creature or aspect of creation can be appropriate for a divine appearance because only the human is in the image of God. In other religions it was acceptable to represent the deity with the image of an animal or bird, but in Israel all such images were forbidden since animals and birds were not created in the image of God.

The implications of this for biblical theology are significant. In the NT Jesus is "the image of the invisible God." This fits well with the emphasis in Genesis that there is nothing unusual about deity appearing in human form. However, by emphasizing that Jesus is the image of God, the NT writers are indicating not just that he is like God, but that he is God and bears that image uniquely.

Before leaving this discussion of the image of God, we need to discuss the common theological assertion that because of the Fall the image of God

19. Barr, "The Image of God," 14.

was somehow distorted. This significant theological proposition links the idea of God's image to moral perfection. If the possession of God's image rendered humans morally perfect, then the image must surely have been diminished or lost during the Fall. Although this theory has strong support among theologians and its logic seems unassailable, it is not mentioned in Genesis. After the Fall and after the flood God declares that human life is sanctified on the basis that humans are created in "the image of God" (9:6). As Bray points out, the teaching that the image was somehow lost or distorted was first developed in the intertestamental period and became very popular in the time of the Reformation.[20] However, it arises out of theological reflection on Genesis and is not mentioned in the book itself, which does not limit the idea of the image of God to moral perfection alone.

When God created human beings in his image, he did not permit them to eat of the tree of the knowledge of good and evil lest they would become like God, knowing good and evil (3:22). So the image of God is not linked to the moral distinction between right and wrong, but it is related to the ontological relationship between God and humanity that renders them on the same wavelength and makes them compatible beings. The image of God in humankind is not a reference to human morality or spirituality but means that in all creation humans are uniquely like God; and although metaphorically God may be described as an eagle, a lion, or a lamb, in terms of appearance, it is only the human form that is compatible with his being.

The Life of Faith

One corollary of God's willingness to reveal himself to human beings and of the creation of humans in the "divine image" is the possibility of living in a close relationship with God. Genesis records the encounters of a number of characters who, at one level or another, experience such a relationship: Abel, Enoch, Noah, Abraham, Sarah, Hagar, Isaac, Jacob, Joseph. Who are these people whom God chooses, and what is it that sets them apart from others?

The People Whom God Chooses

In Genesis God chooses people to be the recipients of his blessing. Sometimes his choices are based on a person's past record or on some action that they

20. Bray, "The Significance of God's Image in Man," 204.

have done. Abel is accepted and Cain is rejected because of their offerings, but God tells Cain that he will be accepted if he changes his ways. Enoch and Noah both walk with God, and Noah gains favor in God's eyes as an upright man. The sons of Judah, though, are slain by God because of their wickedness.

However, God often chooses people with no reference to their behavior as the reason for his choice. We are not told what sort of person Abraham was before God calls him, nor are we told why God chooses him instead of Nahor. Nothing derogatory is recorded about Nahor, and there is no indication that Abraham attracted God's attention because of his merits.

Jacob is chosen even though his brother is the firstborn and some of Jacob's behavior is far from exemplary. In Jacob's family God chooses Joseph, the pampered favorite of his father but the figure of hate for his brothers, to bring blessing to the world during a time of famine. Also, Judah emerges as God's choice as leader.

While some people are chosen or rejected on the basis of their behavior, the main characters in the family tree of Israel are all chosen without reference to their merits or the lack of them. In some cases, such as Jacob and Joseph, they are chosen in spite of flaws in their characters. Thus, Abraham and Sarah, Isaac and Rebekah, Jacob and his wives are chosen by God and no reason is given. The significance of this is developed in the book of Deuteronomy, with its emphasis that God chose Israel, not because of their merits but because he loved them (Deut 7:6-8; 9:4-6).

God's choice of Abraham and his descendants culminates in covenant. Unlike the covenant at Sinai, this covenant does not focus on what the recipient, Abraham, must do but on what God is doing for him and for his descendants. The record of the covenant makes it clear that Abraham's role is passive since he is in a deep sleep during most of the proceedings. Abraham's blamelessness is not the reason for the covenant; but the covenant becomes the reason and the motivation for a blameless walk before Yahweh. Furthermore, the covenant-making is presented in two separate accounts. In the first the covenant is made ("cut") by God (ch. 15), while in the second account the covenant is established or confirmed (ch. 17).

Although God takes the initiative in establishing relationships with people such as Abraham, the continuance of the relationship is based on their response to God in obedience and upright behavior. Abraham is chosen and called by God without reference to his merits, but he immediately responds by obedience. When the covenant promises are made to him, he responds in faith by believing the promises.

God's choice of the patriarchs is not based on his assessment that they are more righteous than others. They are shown as vulnerable, scheming, and deceptive. Abraham and Isaac deceive others about their wives. Jacob deceives his father and cheats his brother. Jacob's behavior, before and after Bethel, does not set him apart as a person who deserves God's blessing. God chooses and blesses the patriarch in spite of Jacob's shortcomings. Jacob's experience of God at Bethel highlights God's initiation of the relationship: Jacob actually sleeps while God establishes a relationship with him.

Jacob's 12 sons, the eponymous ancestors of the tribes of Israel, are certainly not chosen for their personal merits. Reuben apparently loses his rights as the firstborn because of an act of incest, while Simeon and Levi carry out a bloodthirsty slaughter of unsuspecting people. Yet these are the people God chooses, and no attempt is made to cover up their shortcomings. Obviously there is very strong emphasis in Genesis that God chooses the ancestors of Israel for reasons known to himself but not because they merit this choice.

The Demands of Faith

Yet although God does not choose the patriarchs because they are perfect, when he makes a relationship with them he requires high standards of conduct. God does not make a covenant with Abraham because he is blameless, but it is enough that Abraham believes God. When the relationship has been formed, God calls on Abraham to be blameless.

The first requirement made of Abraham is to obey God and leave his homeland. The deep pathos of Abraham's decision is conveyed by the slowly unfolding details of what obedience will involve.

> "Go from your country and your kindred and your father's house to the land that I will show you." (12:1 NRSV)

In this way the text conveys something of the enormity of the decision that God asks Abraham to make, a decision made no easier by the vague description of "the land that I will show you." Abraham must leave without knowing where he is going. Furthermore, his decision affects others also — those who go with him and also those who are left behind. Faith's demands are more apparent when Abraham reaches Canaan. This land that he has forsaken all to come to is in the grips of a very severe famine. This obstacle to faith is just one of a number of recurring obstacles that make the life of faith very difficult.

In Egypt the man of faith is gripped by fear that leads him to jeopardize his wife and with her the promise of descendants. When Abraham returns from Egypt, further problems arise when strife breaks out between Abraham's herdsmen and Lot's. The struggle of faith is also apparent in the story of Hagar. We can picture the intense struggle going on in Abraham's mind; he wants to believe God, but far from helping him, God is silent about the matter for a long period of time. He has made the most generous promises about Abraham's seed but allows the patriarch to be on the edge of despair with uncertainty until he is forced to make his own plans. Rather than making it easy for Abraham and Sarah, God allows them to struggle without any indication of how the promise of offspring will be fulfilled. God seems to work on a different plane, promising them offspring as numerous as the grains of sand while what they want and cannot get is a baby. The great promises of God can seem quite irrelevant when a pressing personal need limits our vision and makes us doubt him.

This waiting time between promise and fulfillment is a recurring theme in Genesis. It even appears in the primeval narrative, where Noah must wait for the flood to assuage with no better guide than whether or not birds return to the ark. It also affects Jacob, who, having received the divine mandate to return to Canaan, must anxiously wait while his brother draws near, the anxiety depriving him of sleep. He also faces the sad, apparent bereavement of Joseph followed by a ruinous famine. None of this bothers the readers greatly because they know that Joseph is not dead and is sorting out the famine. Why does no one tell Jacob? Why must he suffer the uncertainty and endure the long wait until, eventually, he is told that Joseph is not dead at all? Instead, Jacob has waited so long for this news that he is near death himself when he receives it.[1] The same necessity of waiting also plagues the life of Joseph. He waits down in the pit while the brothers eat a meal and casually decide his future. Joseph also waits in prison, hoping that Pharaoh's butler will fulfill his promise and bring his case to Pharaoh. For two years the butler forgets about Joseph, and he must wait until Pharaoh himself has a dream.

Less central characters also learn the difficulty of waiting: Tamar waits for Judah to give her his son Shelah, but Judah does not intend to reward her patience. Simeon waits in prison in Egypt while his father refuses to allow his other sons to return with Benjamin.

Thus, one of the main demands of faith is waiting, and this is made particularly difficult because it is usually accompanied by uncertainty. These

1. Jacob's situation was like that of Job. In both stories the events are happening in two places. In Job's case this is heaven and earth, and in Jacob's situation it is Canaan and Egypt. Job cannot see the drama being unfolded on the heavenly stage, and this makes his situation very frustrating and inexplicable. Likewise, Jacob's suffering is deepened because he does not know what is happening in Egypt. God is at work in ways that both men do not realize. Both have to wait until God reveals the bigger picture to them.

stories in Genesis about people waiting would have been pertinent to those in exile who also had to endure an uncertain future while waiting for promises to be fulfilled that must have seemed too good to be true. Waiting and uncertainty provide a challenge to the faith of people even today, and this theme and its denouement in Genesis provide a source of strength and hope for modern readers as it did for those in exile, some five centuries before Christ.

The Benefits of Faith

Divine protection

Fear figures high in the reasons Abraham gives for denying that Sarah is his wife. Fear also features in the story of Jacob meeting Esau, and it is the main reason for Jacob's return to Bethel after the massacre carried out by Simeon and Levi. Fear figures prominently in the interaction between Joseph and his brothers in Egypt.

Yet one of the prominent themes in Genesis is that, in spite of their fears, the patriarchs and their families are constantly under divine protection. The enemies they fear cannot harm them without Yahweh's permission. This is particularly evident in the story of Laban's pursuit of Jacob when Yahweh warns him in a dream not to harm his son-in-law.

In the story of Joseph the concept of divine protection is carefully developed. In the early stages of the story, as Joseph is thrown into a pit, sold into slavery, and unjustly imprisoned, there is little evidence of divine protection. It is with hindsight that Joseph can look back on his checkered career and confess that, in spite of all the appearances to the contrary, God had indeed been protecting him and planning not only for his future good but for the good of all those around him. Thus, after the death of Jacob, Joseph reassures his brothers,

> "Do not fear, for am I in the place of God? As for you, you meant evil against me, but *God meant it for good,* to bring it about that many people should be kept alive, as they are today." (50:19-20 ESV)

This faith in the ultimate purposes of God is a pertinent theme in times of exile and disaster. It is reflected particularly in a number of Psalms where the pain of exile and rejection is replaced with the realization that God is still protecting and blessing the nation (Pss. 121, 124, 125, 126, 136). The faith Joseph expresses is an example of Israel's conviction that even when things go badly wrong, God is still planning for their future blessing.

Covenant

The concept of covenant refers to binding agreements and was a term used in everyday life in the ancient Near East. Any kind of agreement could be referred to as a covenant, which had a variety of forms and applications:

- A covenant could be between individuals.
- It could be corporate as in a treaty between nations.
- It could be between an individual and a group as in a covenant between a king and his people.
- A covenant could be made between equals or between a superior and his subordinates.

The Hebrew word for covenant, בְּרִית/*běrît*, occurs 27 times in Genesis, 16 in Exodus, 8 in Leviticus, 5 in Numbers, and 27 in Deuteronomy.

A brief summary will show how the word *běrît* is used in Genesis. After giving Noah the instructions for building the ark, God promises to establish his "covenant" with him; this is the first occurrence of the word in the Bible (6:18). Chapter 9 contains seven occurrences relating to the covenant that God makes with Noah after the flood, including an introduction to the rainbow as the symbol of the everlasting covenant (9:9, 11, 12, 13, 15, 16, 17). In ch. 14 *běrît* refers to Abraham's allies (14:13). In the following chapter, while Abraham is in a deep sleep, God makes a covenant with him (15:18). The most concentrated use of *běrît* in Genesis is in ch. 17, where the word occurs 13 times in relation to God's covenant with Abraham and his offspring (17:2, 4, 7 [twice], 9, 10, 11, 13 [twice], 14, 19 [twice], 21). The two occurrences in ch. 21 relate to the covenant between Abraham and the "Philistines" (21:27, 32), and in ch. 26 the same group makes a covenant with Isaac (26:28). The final use of *běrît* in Genesis is occasioned by the separation between Jacob and Laban (31:44).

Covenant with Noah   The covenant with Noah is introduced in the context of the postflood sacrifice. When God smells the "pleasing aroma" of Noah's sacrifice, he resolves that he will "never again curse the ground by sending a flood" and that "while the earth remains, seedtime and harvest, cold and heat, summer and winter, day and night, shall not cease" (8:20-22). Following this statement of God's intention is a pronouncement of blessing on Noah and his sons. It is reminiscent of the blessing pronounced in the garden of Eden with its emphasis that the humans should "be fruitful and multiply and fill the earth." However, here the injunction is followed by sinister overtones:

> "The fear of you and the dread of you shall be upon every beast of the earth and upon every bird of the heavens, upon everything that creeps on the ground and all the fish of the sea. Into your hands they are delivered. Every moving thing that lives shall be food for you. And as I gave you the green plants, I give you everything." (9:2-3 ESV)

The new beginning after the flood will not be a return to the harmonious situation that prevailed in the garden of Eden. Humans will now eat animals as well as plants for food. The death of human beings is not to be taken lightly since they are made in the image of God. When murders do occur, whether committed by animals or other humans, they must be dealt with justly. Shedding human blood contaminates the ground on which it is shed. Even animal blood must be treated with respect, and all blood must be drained from animals prior to eating them. These laws are given to humans because they are made in God's image and they are God's representatives with authority and responsibility for the created order.

Following these stipulations, the covenant with Noah is summarized. Thus the stipulations are sandwiched between an announcement of God's benevolent intention and an account of the covenant itself. Essentially the covenant is unconditional, but at the same time it is closely associated with the stipulations for divine blessing. Repetition of the word for covenant seven times underlines the importance of this covenant pronouncement. Covenant and not destruction is on the divine agenda. In a special way, the covenant represents God drawing a line under the flood incident and labelling it as a one-off event that would never be repeated. Von Rad points out that the Hebrew word for "bow" in 9:13 is the same word that refers to a "battle bow." Accordingly, the bow in the sky according to von Rad represents God setting aside his battle bow.

> The Hebrew word that we translate "rainbow" usually means in the Old Testament "the bow of war." The beauty of the ancient conception thus becomes apparent: God shows the world that he has put aside his bow.[2]

Clearly the role of Noah is important, but the covenant is not just with him but with all the human beings, all the living creatures and indeed with

---

2. Von Rad, *Genesis*, 134.

the earth itself. The covenant is described as "an everlasting covenant." It represents God taking upon himself obligations and responsibilities that cannot be abrogated while the earth exists. The flood had threatened to return the world to the chaos that existed before the six days of creation. Now God vouchsafes his commitment to the continuance of the created order with no further threats to destroy what he had made.

Covenant with Abraham   The word "covenant" is not mentioned in the initial call to Abraham, but the goal of the relationship that begins when God calls and Abraham obeys is the covenant relationship. The covenant with Noah addresses the entire created order and assumes the continued rebellion of the human race (8:21). There is no expectation of mutual trust and respect between God and the beneficiaries of the Noahic covenant.

The covenant with Abraham, by contrast, arises out of a relationship that begins when God takes the initiative and calls Abraham to leave his homeland (12:1). Unlike the Noahic covenant, Abraham's participation is required. When Abraham obeys, he has very few details of what God plans to do for him and therefore he displays trust and confidence in God's agenda for him and his family. However, Abraham's faith is severely tested. The promise of land is placed in doubt because of famine, drought, and the presence of other inhabitants with a prior claim on the territory. The promise of descendants is also in doubt because the prediction of millions of offspring is cold comfort to someone who has not even one child. These concerns raise the question in Abraham's mind about how can he be sure that God would indeed fulfill his promises.

Abraham's need of reassurance is an important issue, not only for him but for future generations of Israelites, especially those in exile, whose faith in God's future agenda for Abraham's offspring was tested to the breaking point. God gives the reassurance required by entering a covenant relationship with Abraham and by taking an oath to fulfill its obligations.

The role of the covenant in providing reassurance is highlighted by the context in which it is made in both chs. 15 and 17. In ch. 15 Abraham asks two questions: first, in relation to offspring he asks, "O Lord GOD, what will you give me, for I continue childless, and the heir of my house is Eliezer of Damascus?"; second, in relation to land he asks, "how am I to know that I shall possess it?" (15:2, 8 NRSV). In response to Abraham, God carries out a covenant ceremony. Abraham has a role to play, but it is a clearly the minor role. He must provide animals, cut them in pieces, and ward off the birds of prey. During the ceremony itself a blazing torch passes between the pieces, presumably representing the presence of God. Abraham does not take an active role since he has passed into a very deep sleep, but he hears God's voice. The divine speech emphasizes that the purpose of the ceremony is reassurance of God's commitment to the fulfillment of his promises. Now Abraham can

> "*know for certain* that your offspring will be sojourners in a land that is not theirs and will be servants there, and they will be afflicted for four hundred years. But I will bring judgment on the nation that they serve, and afterward they shall come out with great possessions." (15:13-14 ESV)

This reassures the patriarch that he will have offspring and that after a period of oppression they will inherit the land in which he now sojourns. It also explains that the promise of land will not be realized in his lifetime. This message is reasserted in the covenant itself:

> On that day the LORD made a covenant with Abram, saying, "To your offspring I give this land, from the river of Egypt to the great river, the river Euphrates, the land of the Kenites, the Kenizzites, the Kadmonites, the Hittites, the Perizzites, the Rephaim, the Amorites, the Canaanites, the Girgashites and the Jebusites." (15:18-21 ESV)

The reassurance of land could not be clearer, and the identification of the land promised with the land of Canaan is unequivocal. However, the promise of offspring is still vague since the identification of the mother is not given, and this leaves room for the Hagar incident in ch. 16.

The confirmation of the covenant in ch. 17 develops and clarifies the main elements and highlights the role that Abraham must play. He is called to a blameless walk before God and is commanded to observe the rite of circumcision as the sign of the covenant. Abraham's name is changed to Abraham, and Sarai's name becomes Sarah. These changes are not etymologically significant but signify a new stage in the relationship between Abraham and God, while at the same time showing that Sarah is part of the covenant relationship and Abraham's offspring will be through Isaac and not Ishmael. The latter will enjoy God's blessing, but not within the terms of the covenant, even though he is circumcised.

The final episode in relation to the covenant with Abraham is in ch. 22 following the patriarch's act of obedience in his willingness to sacrifice Isaac. The Lord confirms the promises to Abraham by an oath. This oath is the final act of assurance that God's covenant promises will be fulfilled.

The Sinai covenant and its relation to the Abrahamic covenant Scholars have often regarded the Abrahamic covenant and the Sinaitic covenant as "different covenantal traditions."[3] Fretheim argues that, within the present canonical arrangement of the Hebrew Bible, these two covenants are "integrally related, with the Abrahamic covenant providing the framework within which the Sinaitic covenant is developed."[4] Evidence that the Sinai covenant does not supersede the Abrahamic covenant is found in the appeal that Moses makes to the earlier covenant when God threatens to overthrow the nation as a consequence of the golden calf incident (Exod 32:13). Moses reminds God that he has made promises on oath to Abraham, Isaac, and Israel to give them numerous offspring who will inherit the land of promise "forever." God does not deny that he has bound himself by an oath, which suggests strongly that the covenant with Abraham establishes the relationship between God and Israel and that the Sinai covenant is building on this rather than replacing it. Fretheim takes this one stage further, suggesting that the Sinai covenant is a "*vocational covenant* with those who are already God's people."[5] According to this view, the covenant with Abraham establishes the relationship between God and Abraham's offspring, but the covenant at Sinai provides "*a closer specification* of what is entailed in that relationship."[6] In other words, the covenant with Abraham establishes the status of God's relationship with Israel, but the Sinai covenant describes how this is worked out at a practical level for his descendants.

Davidic covenant   The covenant with David promises the continuation of God's close relationship with Israel through the Davidic dynasty. The context of the Davidic covenant is David's statement that he intends to build a house for Yahweh. Nathan's oracle utilizes the double meaning of the word "house" to move subtly from the subject of Yahweh's house to that of David's house. Yahweh informs David that he should not build the house for God but God would build a house for him (2 Sam 7:11). This passage is the initiation of the relationship between the house of David and Yahweh that would be both foundational and programmatic for OT history and theology. This oracle endows the Davidic dynasty with prophetic approval and divine sanction.

The covenant with David and that with Abraham are similar in content and focus. Abraham was promised that kings would be among his descendants, and now the promises made to Abraham are realized in King David. The promise to Abraham that his descendants would become a great nation

---

3. Fretheim points out that in the *Interpreters' Dictionary of the Bible* (*IDBSup*, 188-97), the two covenants are dealt with separately; "The Reclamation of Creation," 360.

4. Fretheim, "The Reclamation of Creation," 360.

5. Fretheim, "The Reclamation of Creation," 361.

6. Fretheim, "The Reclamation of Creation," 361.

are now evidenced in the Davidic kingdom, which would be "an everlasting kingdom." God promised Abraham a great name, and now he extends the same promise to David.

> "I will make for you a great name, like the name of the great ones of the earth." (2 Sam 7:9 NRSV)

Abraham's relationship afforded him protection from other nations and their leaders. In the Davidic covenant the blessing of divine protection and rest from enemies is very prominent. This "divine" rest is made possible by the establishment of David's kingdom in the land originally promised to Abraham.

> "And I will appoint a place for my people Israel and will plant them, so that they may dwell in their own place and be disturbed no more. And violent men shall afflict them no more, as formerly . . . and I will give you rest from all your enemies." (2 Sam 7:10-11)

Although Abraham is not mentioned by name in the Davidic covenant, the continuity of the promises made to the patriarch is unmistakable.

New covenant   The demise of the kingdom of Judah and its eventual fall, with the destruction of the temple, created an urgent need to reinterpret what had happened in a way that would rekindle faith in Yahweh's sovereign purposes. Jeremiah, Ezekiel, and Isaiah 40ff. express continued hope in the concept of an "everlasting covenant." Jeremiah also introduces the concept of a "new covenant."

Jeremiah is the only OT book to mention a new covenant, though it may be argued that the concept is present in passages such as Ezekiel 34 and Isaiah 40. The concept is inextricably linked to Israel's failure as a nation and to the hope that Yahweh has not totally abandoned them forever. It is argued that Israel had broken the covenant made at Sinai, even though it had distinguished them from all other nations and gave them great privileges as Yahweh's spouse (Jer 31:32). The concept of a new covenant embraces the hope that the relationship between God and his people could be restored. A new start and a renewed sense of purpose and mission are needed to resurrect national confidence and bring the nation out of its sense of defeat and rejection. The concept of new covenant offers the new beginning that the nation desperately needs. In the past they had not turned to him with all their hearts (e.g., Jer 17:1, 9), but now the new covenant will be written upon the hearts of God's people and not merely on stone. The emphasis will be on the individual's personal knowledge of Yahweh, and he will forgive all their sins (Jer 31:34).

Some scholars emphasize the continuity of the new covenant with the old. Thus, Rendtorff emphasizes that "it is the same Torah which is at the center of the new covenant as was at the center of the former one." He also argues that in both covenants (old and new) "the same promise is given to Israel and Judah: that the Lord will be their God and that they shall be his people."[7]

Williamson, however, argues that "the newness of the new covenant must not be underestimated" and refers to the "radical discontinuity with the past."[8] Obviously Jeremiah was introducing the concept to emphasize the continuity of Israel's relationship with God, and it is very unlikely that he would have expected part of the Bible to be called "New Covenant." However, the deliberate use of the word "new" indicates that Jeremiah was heralding a new beginning in Israel's relationship with God. At the same time, the relationship envisaged by Jeremiah is a continuance of the covenant made with Abraham.

GENESIS AND THEOLOGY TODAY

GENESIS AND SCIENCE

Christians approach the Bible, not just as an ancient literary artifact, but as God's word for our times. Ministers know that their sermons and Bible studies will not address the needs of the congregation if they are merely history lessons; the text must be applied and made relevant. However, while it is important to emphasize that the Bible is God's word for us, we must also remember that it was originally God's word for people over two thousand years ago and it answered the questions that they were facing in their own cultural, linguistic, and historical environment. This raises the issue about how far we should expect the Bible to relate to modern scientific language and theory.

Many come to Genesis expecting to receive answers to modern scientific questions about creation. Jews and Christians have for centuries believed that Genesis answers questions such as "How was the world made?" and "How long did it take God to create the world?" Even before the modern era this brought some people into conflict with scientific theory since, for exam-

7. Rendtorff, "What Is New in the New Covenant?", 197.
8. Williamson, "Covenant," 427.

ple, those who read Genesis literally found it difficult to believe that the moon reflected the light of the sun and does not produce light itself.

In the 17th century the archbishop of Armagh, James Ussher, used the genealogies in Genesis to determine that the date of creation was 4004 B.C. This very influential proposition was challenged in the 19th century by the declaration of geologists that the earth was many thousands and, indeed, millions of years older than this date suggested. A further challenge to the traditional interpretation of Genesis came when Charles Darwin published his *Origin of Species* in 1859.

The idea of evolution was particularly offensive to many Christians because they felt that it lessened the distinction between human beings and animals. A literal interpretation of Genesis was used to combat what many saw as a dangerous heresy. The literal interpretation of the creation accounts became a kind of touchstone for orthodoxy, with many believing that they could judge whether another person's doctrine was "sound" or not by the views that they held about these chapters. No room for maneuver exists and feelings run high, especially since many parents are deeply concerned about what their children are taught about these issues. If evolution is denied by the word of God, then it is wrong and should not be taught as if it is proven scientific fact.

We shall look briefly at some of the main approaches to Genesis to provide an overview of the various ways that the creation and flood accounts in Genesis are interpreted in our scientifically aware world.

Creationist Approach

"Creationists" are passionately convinced that the Genesis creation accounts are scientifically accurate accounts. These first chapters of Genesis are not poetry, parable, allegory, or myth; they are straightforward historical accounts that show how the world was made. If these accounts were written by human beings, then their accuracy could be questioned. After all, no human being witnessed creation, and therefore human creation accounts can never be anything other than speculative theories. But, it is argued, Genesis is the word of God and contains God's version of creation, which cannot possibly contain inaccuracies. On this basis, if scientific theory contradicts biblical truth, then, the word of God must be right and the scientists mistaken. The Bible itself warns that "in the last days" there will be attempts to divert people from the truth, and any suggestion that Genesis is not a scientifically accurate account is just part of the modern trend towards secularization and denigration of the word of God (cf. 2 Pet 2:1; 1 John 4:1). This, it is argued, is part of Satan's master plan to lead people away from the Bible and away from the truth. This helps to explain why this subject is often debated with passion and acrimony; it is not just the interpretation of Genesis that is at stake but the foundation of the Christian faith.

Adherents of this approach are united in their method of interpretation: Genesis must be understood literally with, for example, a real serpent who actually spoke and a real tree whose fruit could guarantee eternal life. As McIntosh explains,

> Without Genesis and a real Garden of Eden, a literal serpent, a genuine historical Fall, the whole account of redemption itself falls like a stack of dominoes.[1]

Concomitant with this literal approach is a belief that the days of creation in Genesis 1 were literal 24-hour days. This essential tenet of the creationist position rules out the possibility of vast periods of time during which evolution could take place. Arguments in favor of literal days include the observation that since the name "day" was given to a period of light followed by a period of darkness, the term "day" must refer to daylight hours. Whereas in poetry, it is argued, one might expect the term "day" to refer to an age, Genesis is not poetry but prose and must be taken literally. Furthermore, the Bible itself interprets creation as six literal days since the creation week is presented as a model for the working week of human beings (Exod 20:8-11). According to McIntosh, this paradigmatic use of the creation week is the "most conclusive of all arguments concerning the days of Genesis 1 being literal 24-hour periods."[2] Another argument is that the most important reason for taking the days literally is that this is the obvious meaning of the text, and probably no one would have thought of the days as being longer than 24 hours were it not for the problem of reconciling the Bible with geological discoveries. This view is explicated by Wright.

> For myself I believe in a six-day creation. A straightforward reading of Genesis by an intelligent man, not exposed to the evolutionary model, would suggest a literal six-day creation. The only way around this interpretation would be to suggest the account was allegorical or poetic. Nei-

---

1. McIntosh, *Genesis for Today*, 12.

2. McIntosh, *Genesis for Today*, 39. The argument is probably not as conclusive as McIntosh thinks, since it is the pattern of six days' work and one day's rest that is being emphasized in Genesis. If God's days are longer than ours, that does not detract from the effectiveness of the model.

ther in the opening chapters of Genesis nor elsewhere in the Bible is there a suggestion that the account is symbolic.[3]

Creationists still accept with minor adjustments the approach of Archbishop Ussher of Armagh (Ireland), who, using the genealogical material in the Bible, calculated that the earth was created in 4004 B.C. This date is arrived at by taking the genealogical data in Genesis literally and assumes that the genealogies provide a more or less unbroken record of descent from Adam to the time Genesis was written. While some are prepared to admit gaps in the genealogies, others are insistent that there are no significant gaps at all. Thus McIntosh admits only one minor gap:

> The Scriptures read straightforwardly, do not allow for any gaps in the Genesis genealogies, except in one minor instance where, at the very most, a few hundred years may be inserted. This point needs careful thought by all Christians. Our approach to this particular matter often reveals our true attitude to Scripture as a whole. Do we really believe the Scriptures as they stand or not?[4]

This uncompromising literal approach has important implications for the way that creationists interpret the genealogical data. If we read the postflood genealogical data without any gaps, Shem and Noah must have been alive during the time of Abraham, and Shem actually outlived Abraham. This means that Shem reached the age of 500 at a time when others like Abraham were dying before they reached 200, which is surprising, especially when the text declares that when Abraham died (at the age of 175) he was "a good old age, an old man, and full of years." Furthermore, if we do not allow gaps in the genealogies, the date of the tower of Babel incident must be just 200 years before the birth of Abraham, which does not allow enough time for the development of all the ethnic groups mentioned in the Abraham narratives. Some creationists recognize these difficulties, and Whitcomb and Morris outline the situation clearly:

> As we follow Abram in his wanderings, from Ur of the Chaldees to the land of Canaan, filled to overflowing with "the Kenite, and the Kenizzite, the Amorite, and the Canaanite, and the Girgashite, and the Jebusite" (Gen 15:19-21) and then follow him down into the land of Egypt with its Pharaoh and its princes (12:15); and then see him going to Lot's rescue in

3. Wright, "The Origin of Man," 126.
4. McIntosh, *Genesis for Today,* 41.

the vicinity of Damascus after Lot and other captives from the five Cities of the Plain had been deported by the kings of Shinar, Ellaser, Elam and Goiim (14:1-16); and then see him being met by a priest-king of Salem (14:18); and later see him coming into contact with a Philistine king (20:2) and Hittite landowners (23:2-20), we cannot help but feel that the judgment of God upon the Tower of Babel must have occurred many centuries before the time of Abraham.[5]

Whitcomb and Morris, then, although influential creationists, are forced to recognize that Genesis 11 should not be taken chronologically; they argue that "it seems Biblically possible, or even probable, that the Flood occurred several millennia before Abraham."[6] Their admission of gaps in ch. 11 and their admission that the genealogical data between the flood and Abraham should not be taken as "strictly chronological" seems to weaken the creationist case and is disputed by other creationists.

However, gaps in the genealogies of even a few thousand years are not really the issue, since geologists and astronomers believe that the evidence in their respective fields indicate that the earth is millions of years old. Advocates of a young earth, therefore, must explain the geological evidence, including the fossil record and the astronomical data that measures the age of some rocks in millions of years and the distance to some of the stars in many thousands of light-years. One explanation is that the dating techniques are wrong, but this is an inadequate answer because many rock formations have the appearance of great age to the trained eye. Therefore, creationists defend their position by the "Appearance of Age Theory," which postulates that if hypothetical observers had spied on the garden of Eden six thousand years ago they would have seen an adult person walking among the trees who in appearance was at least 20 years old. In reality, if their visit was on day six of creation, this person was only a few hours old. The same argument is applied to the trees of the garden, which would appear old and, presumably, would have growth rings. If the observers cut down a tree and counted the rings they would reach a highly inflated estimate of the age of the tree since it was created with the appearance of age. This theory is also used to explain the astronomical data: the stars were created recently but with the appearance of age and with their light already having reached the earth, even though it would normally take thousands of years to do so.

Creationists also defend the young earth theory by applying the princi-

5. Whitcomb and Morris, *The Genesis Flood,* 478-79.
6. Whitcomb and Morris, *The Genesis Flood,* 483.

ples of flood geology. Absolutely essential to this hypothesis is the universal extent of the flood. Some scholars who reject creationism have argued that the flood may not necessarily have been global. This suggestion seems to contradict the literal claim of Genesis that the whole earth, including every mountain, was covered. This argument is not as conclusive as it first appears since the Hebrew word for earth also means land and country. Furthermore, it may be argued that a comparison of the flood story with the Joseph story shows that terms that seem to imply the whole world really only apply to the world of the writer. The famine in the time of Joseph is said to have gripped the entire earth, and people from every country came to Joseph for food. Obviously, people did not come from Australia to buy food from Joseph, and the reference is to the known world at that time. However, creationists totally reject the suggestion that the flood could have been local. They believe that the flood was a global catastrophe that covered the entire world, including the highest mountains. This would require an enormous amount of water, since Everest is approximately 5 miles high. Ken Ham addresses the question about whether there is enough water to cover the earth's surface by the depth of 5 miles to cover Everest. He explains,

> When people say there wasn't enough water and therefore Noah's flood couldn't have happened as the Bible states — they're making some invalid assumptions. For instance, they're assuming that the mountains that exist today also existed at the time of the flood. However, this is not true. Did you know there are marine fossils on the top of Everest? Actually, as you look at the mountain ranges on the earth, it's obvious they were uplifted at some time. If you were to flatten out the mountains and the deep ocean basins, there would actually be enough water to cover it to a depth of nearly two miles. I believe that the way God ended the flood was to raise up the mountains and lower the ocean basins. This caused the water to run off the earth, to where it is today.[7]

Creationists believe that the flood was a powerful supernatural event accompanied by "great volcanic explosions and eruptions."[8] This catastrophe

7. Ham, *Did Adam Have a Bellybutton?*, 39.
8. Commenting on Gen 7:11 ("all the fountains of the great deep were broken up"), Whitcomb and Morris argue that this verse means "that great quantities of liquids, perhaps liquid rocks or magmas, as well as water (probably steam), had been confined under great pressure below the surface rock structure of the earth since the time of its formation and that this mass now burst forth through great fountains, probably both on the lands and under the seas." They argue that these eruptions would have brought about earthquakes and tidal waves that "would have augmented the Flood waters as well as accomplished great amounts of geologic work directly"; *The Genesis Flood*, 122.

brought about unprecedented geological changes to the earth's surface, forming the mountain ranges, changing the climate, forming sedimentary rocks, killing marine as well as land creatures, producing the fossil record, and causing the ice age. The enormous geological changes made by the flood are illustrated by Whitcomb in his explanation of the formation of mountain ranges during the flood:

> Enormously high, snow-capped mountain peaks could not have existed before the Flood. "The world that perished" had low-lying mountains which were probably less than six or seven thousand feet high, because they were completely covered by the waters of the Flood. . . . If the earth's surface had no irregularities at all, the oceans would cover it to a depth of about two miles. Therefore, if Mount Ararat, which is more than three miles high (or Mount Everest, which is more than five miles high), existed *before* the Flood at such altitudes, it could not have been covered by the Flood.[9]

Some creationists make no attempt to explain how such a cataclysm could have occurred, while others suggest a natural explanation. One proposal outlined by McIntosh is that

> the Flood was due to an impact with a large asteroid which catastrophically broke the Earth's mantle (possibly in the Pacific which would explain its great depth), tilted the earth off a "vertical" spin axis and caused earthquakes and volcanoes of cataclysmic proportions. Not only did water fall from above, but water originally beneath the earth was released with tidal waves of immense depths sweeping across the globe.[10]

Another effect of the flood, it is alleged, was the removal of a protective water canopy that sheltered the earth. Originally, it is argued, a water vapor canopy above the earth "provided a warm, pleasant, presumably healthful environment throughout the world."[11] This canopy sheltered the earth's inhabitants from the worst effects of radiation and allowed them to live longer, accounting for the longevity of the antediluvians.

Exponents of the universal theory of the flood are often asked about the distribution of the world's animals. One of the most popular questions is "After Noah's Ark, how did kangaroos ever get to Australia?" Ken Ham provides the following answer,

9. Whitcomb, *The World That Perished*, 40.
10. McIntosh, *Genesis for Today*, 36.
11. Whitcomb and Morris, *The Genesis Flood*, 399.

Well, the simplest answer is that they hopped! However, some would think they'd have to have an enormous hop to get across the ocean to Australia. But I believe there's actually a simple solution to this. Scientists have found lots of evidence that around one-third of the earth's surface has been covered by ice. There's evidence, for example, that large glaciers once carved the Great Lakes in North America. Creationists believe that this "ice age" occurred sometime after the flood — because of the flood. With warm water, cool land, and ash in the atmosphere blocking out sunlight at the end of the flood, there would be a lot of evaporation. The precipitation would come in the form of ice and snow. The build-up of ice and snow would lower oceans by around 600 feet — forming land bridges all over the earth. This would enable animals like kangaroos to migrate to different parts of the earth, and then eventually the ice would have receded to where it is today.[12]

Thus the advocates of the creationist approach have developed a system that allows them to read the Bible as a scientific account of how the world was created in six literal days, just a few thousand years ago. Not everyone is happy with this approach, though it is popular at present.[13] The main objections are that in order to take the Bible literally, the creationists are forced to add details that are not mentioned in the Genesis accounts. The idea that the mountains were raised up during the flood and that the ice age coincided with the patriarchal age are imaginative ways of accepting a literal interpretation, but it may be argued that if these events are essential to a true understanding of the text, they would have been mentioned somewhere in the creation and flood accounts. However, the Bible refers to the mountains as "ancient" and to the hills as "everlasting" (Deut 33:15). Furthermore, the shaping or forming of the mountains is associated with God's work as creator (Prov 8:25) rather than with the flood. The idea that the mountains were thrust up during the flood seems to have been unknown until modern creationist theories. This necessity to augment the biblical account with speculative additions has led many to conclude that the theory of flood geology "forces its holders into a series of increasingly unlikely scientific conclusions."[14]

---

12. Ham, *Did Adam Have a Bellybutton?* 52.

13. Pinnock observes that, "though this approach bears tremendous intellectual burdens and requires major leaps into speculation to deal with some of the problems, this is the approach presently enjoying considerable popularity"; "Climbing out of a Swamp," 144-45.

14. Burke, "Why Some Christians Believe in Evolution," 185.

Other Approaches

Many evangelicals have been unhappy with the assumption that Genesis and science conflict. They want to avoid repeating the mistakes of the church in the time of Galileo. Sincere defenders of the Bible believed that Galileo was guilty of heresy because his discoveries contradicted what people believed about the Bible. However, Galileo was not contradicting the Bible, just a literal interpretation of it. Before the first landing on the moon, some people said that this was impossible because the moon was a light and it was not possible to land on it without being burned up. Again this was a wrong interpretation that was easily disproved by the lunar landing.

Others raise questions, not because they do not believe that the Bible is true, but because they believe that it is not the Bible's role or purpose to teach us science. Often in the Bible, it is argued, scientific truth is subordinated to the theological message. One interesting example of this is the prayer of Joshua for the extension of daylight during a battle. We read that "the sun stopped in the midst of heaven and did not hurry to set for about a whole day" (Josh 10:13). No one suggests that this is a scientific account of what happened, but it is how the lengthening of the day appeared to observers; the sun and moon did not seem to be moving. The issue in the narrative is not whether the earth is stationary with sun and moon revolving around it; rather, the story is about God's miraculous intervention in a battle to ensure that his people were victorious. Similarly, in the book of Job when God speaks about the wonders of creation he does so poetically and not scientifically. Thus snow and hail are kept in large storehouses above the earth, and rain is stored in huge wineskins in the sky (Job 38:22, 37).

This principle, that the Bible's purpose is to convey theological truth rather than make us good scientists, is also evident in the teaching of Christ, who did not come to correct the scientific fallacies of his day but to preach spiritual truth. As Calvin suggests, Genesis is an accurate account of creation from the point of view of the observer. Calvin preceded the modern debate about evolution, but he had to explain the facts revealed by telescopes that contradicted Genesis. Calvin dealt with this information, not by denying the accuracy of the telescope, but by suggesting that Genesis 1 uses "the language of appearance" and presents creation as it would have been seen by the naked eye in the days of Moses and his contemporaries.[15] As Calvin himself put it, "The Holy Spirit had no intention to teach astronomy."[16]

15. Lucas, *Can We Believe Genesis Today?* 58.
16. Quoted from Lucas, *Can We Believe Genesis Today?* 59.

Gap Theory

Some have sought to show that Genesis can be interpreted in ways that do not conflict with science. These are known collectively as "concordist" positions. One of the most popular approaches, promoted by the famous preacher Thomas Chalmers, involves assuming that the Genesis record is an accurate scientific account but one that contains gaps. This approach became very popular because it was used in the Scofield Reference Bible and was espoused by well-known evangelical preachers such as Campbell Morgan.[17] This approach was based on the judgment that the words translated in the KJV "without form and void" could not describe the earth as God created it. An all-powerful creator would not make something that was without form and void; therefore, we should translate, "it became without form and void." It is argued that Gen 1:1 refers to an earlier creation of a perfect world in the dim, distant past. This was the age of the dinosaurs, and it also accounts for the ancient fossil record. This perfect world became without form and void as the result of a rebellion among the angels that resulted in Satan being cast down to earth. He reacted by destroying the created order, leaving it in a mess ("without form and void"); or in another version of the theory, the chaos was caused by God's judgment on his rebellious creatures. Thus the stories in Genesis are about a recreation of the original earth destroyed by Satan.

Many object to the "gap theory" because Genesis does not mention it and the narrator is apparently unaware of it. It implies that for about three millennia people have been misinterpreting Genesis. Only in the modern era has it been possible to read it correctly.

The Day/Age Theory

Another popular concordist approach regards the days of Genesis as ages rather than as 24-hour days. God is not limited to time and space, and we should not limit his working week to the same hours as finite humanity. If each day is an age of indeterminate length, this allows the creative process to extend over vast periods of time. Some advocates of this theory accept that one of the methods God used during these ages was evolution, though others strongly reject evolution but accept that the days need not necessarily be taken as 24 hours. Schaeffer, in his book *Genesis in Space and Time,* set out to

---

17. Morgan's espousal of the "gap theory" is mentioned by Wright, *The Origin of Man,* 126.

understand Genesis historically and literally but did not feel compelled to accept literal days. He deals with the question as follows:

> What does *day* mean in the days of creation? The answer must be held with some openness. In Genesis 5:2 we read: "Male and female created he them; and blessed them, and called their name Adam, in the *day* when they were created." As it is clear that Adam and Eve were not created simultaneously, *day* in Genesis 5:2 does not mean a period of twenty-four hours. In other places in the Old Testament the Hebrew word *day* refers to an era, just as it often does in English. See, for example, Isaiah 2:11, 12 and 17 for such a usage. The simple fact is that *day* in Hebrew (just as in English) is used in three separate senses: to mean (1) twenty-four hours, (2) the period of light during the twenty-four hours, and (3) an indeterminate period of time. Therefore, we must leave open the exact length of time indicated by *day* in Genesis. From the study of the word in Hebrew, it is not clear which way it is to be taken; it could be either way.[18]

Schaeffer also argues that before the time of Abraham "there is no possible way to date the history of what we find in Scripture."[19] Davis A. Young is a professional geologist and the son of the well-known conservative scholar, the late E. J. Young. In his book *Creation and the Flood,* he argues that the idea of a young earth is not required by Genesis 1. He observes that if the world was created in six literal days with the appearance of age (mature creation), scientific investigation is rendered impossible and illegitimate. The following passage illustrates his struggle to reconcile the teaching of Genesis with the evidence thrown up by his work as a geologist.

> The position of mature creationism, that is, the view that biblical creation took place in 144 hours, leads the practicing geologist into insoluble problems in actually dealing with rocks. The boundary between creation and history cannot be identified, and the geologist cannot know how he ought to interpret the rocks. This point is stressed for the benefit of those who are very insistent about the truth of mature creationism, for such individuals are often not sufficiently aware of the practical difficulties of that position. The existence of these difficulties, however, does not disprove the mature creationist interpretation of Genesis 1. In fact, given biblical evidence alone, mature creationism is an acceptable interpretation of Genesis 1. I will never argue with the Christian who wants to hold

18. Schaeffer, *Genesis in Space and Time,* 57.
19. Schaeffer, *Genesis in Space and Time,* 124.

the view, but I am fully persuaded that Scripture permits other legitimate interpretations. The *Christian* scientific investigator ought first, last, and always to be led into the truth, not by his theories or his feelings or his practical difficulties, but by the infallible Word of God.[20]

As a geologist Young is faced with a dilemma, because if Genesis really does teach about a young earth he must seek employment in some other field. Young, therefore, examines Genesis to check if there is only one possible interpretation — literal days. He shows how the creation week with six days' work and one day's rest is used as a model for human activity: human beings must replicate the divine pattern. However, he argues that in relation to the divine model we are still in day seven; there was no day eight or nine since God's period of rest following the creation of the world continues. In Genesis 1 the first six days conclude with the "evening and morning" formula, but this was not repeated in relation to day seven, suggesting that it was a continuing period. Genesis presents just one creation week with a day of rest that is not closed.[21] Young claims that the NT supports the view that we are still in the day of God's "rest," and in particular he quotes Hebrews with its invitation to enter into God's rest (Heb 4:9).

Having concluded that the seventh day has not ended, Young presses home the argument that if the seventh day is not a literal 24-hour day, then the other six days may also be understood as periods of time. Since the length of these periods cannot be determined, we cannot use Genesis to determine the age of the earth. Young believes that Genesis is historical and literal and that the events recorded there actually happened exactly as stated and in the same chronological order; but he argues that this literal interpretation of Genesis is not incompatible with the idea that the earth is 4.5 billion years old.

Days of Revelation

An interesting approach was proposed by P. J. Wiseman. Accepting the days as 24-hour days, Wiseman argued that they were days of revelation rather than days of creation. No human being witnessed creation, and therefore the accounts in Genesis are not eyewitness accounts of creation but a record of the revelation of creation. Creation is not brought into existence in six days, according to this view, but revealed in six 24-hour days. In other words, the

20. Young, *Creation and the Flood*, 79.
21. Young, *Creation and the Flood*, 84-85.

Genesis account is a literal account of what the author of Genesis saw during seven days of revelation in which God showed or reenacted how the world was made.

The Literary Approach

Creationists see a stark choice between scientific theory and biblical truth; either science is wrong or the Bible is wrong. However, others have pointed out that there is a third possibility, that our interpretation of the Bible may be wrong. Lucas writes,

> Just as scientists need humility, so do Christians! However traditional and cherished our particular understanding of a Bible passage may be, it is still only our interpretation of it and it might be mistaken. If scientists show us that it is mistaken, then we should be grateful to them for helping us to take a step nearer to a true understanding of God's Word.[22]

One of the main cruxes in the debate is about the type or genre of literature that we are dealing with. The Bible comprises documents written down over many centuries, and they represent a wide range of material extending from poetry and parable to legal documents and historical records. Elsewhere in the Bible figurative and poetic language is used in relation to creation, and no one, it is argued, suggests that it must be taken absolutely literally. There are several references in the Bible to apparently mythical creatures such as Rahab and Leviathan:

> By his power he stilled the sea; by his understanding he shattered Rahab. (Job 26:12 ESV)
> You crushed Rahab like a carcass. (Ps 89:10 NRSV)
> Was it not you who cut Rahab in pieces, that pierced the dragon? (Isa 51:9 ESV)
> In that day the LORD with his hard and great and strong sword will punish Leviathan the fleeing serpent, Leviathan the twisting serpent, and he will slay the dragon that is in the sea. (Isa 27:1 ESV)
> You divided the sea by your might; you broke the heads of the sea monsters on the waters. You crushed the heads of Leviathan; you gave him as food for the creatures of the wilderness. (Ps 74:13-14 ESV)

---

22. Lucas, *Can We Believe Genesis Today?* 27.

Who was Rahab, and how can we understand these references literally? Did Isaiah really mean that there is a dragon in the sea? Psalm 74 recalls an ancient story about a creature that had seven heads. The psalm alludes to this creature, asserting that God crushed its heads (Ps 74:13-14). Does this mean that we must accept that an animal with several heads actually lived, or is this simply a reminder that biblical authors referred to ancient myths in order to discredit them and ascribe all power and authority to Israel's God? Surely passages such as those quoted above show that the OT writers were interacting with the culture and language of their own time when these references to chaos and myth were well known. This does not mean that the Bible was relating mythical stories but it was using the language and vocabulary of myth as a literary genre to assure the readers that Israel's God was more powerful than the fearsome mythical beasts of the ancient world.

Readers interpret a text depending on the type of literature. Something that we read in a novel about the earth colliding with a comet will not alarm us, whereas the same information given in a scientific report will concern us greatly. When reading poetry, we make allowances for poetic license and literary devices. We also read parables and allegories from different perspectives. A literary approach begins by asking what type of literature is found in Genesis. Evidence for a nonliteral approach is found when a literal reading fails to make sense of the passage. An example quoted by Lucas is the statement by Origen that it is impossible for the first three days of creation to exist without sun and moon, while on the first day there was not even a heaven.[23] Pinnock claims that this is still a strong argument against reading Genesis 1 literally; he suggests that the "fact that God made the sun, moon, and stars on the fourth day, not on the first, ought to tell us that this is not a scientific statement (Gen. 1:14-19)."[24]

Problems of reading Genesis as a literal account have led many to think of ch. 1 as a wonderful anthropomorphism in which the Creator is pictured as the craftsman par excellence. A human builder would choose a site, assemble the materials, and set the boundaries of the project. Following the erection of the building he would provide the lights, divide the rooms, and bring in the furniture. Last of all, the inhabitants would be introduced to their new abode. It is argued that this is how creation is presented but on a much grander scale, as God himself is portrayed creating the universe within a framework that the readers would understand, thus making the most mysterious and complex processes intelligible to human beings. At the end of a week's work the hu-

23. Lucas, *Can We Believe Genesis Today?* 95.
24. Pinnock, "Climbing out of a Swamp," 148.

man builder would rest, but of course God does not need to rest. However, the human requirement of rest is predicated of God to give divine approval to the paradigm of six days' work and one day's rest.

According to this view, the days of creation are not intended literally but are a useful framework for organizing the details of creation. Pinnock draws attention to the "impressive parallelism" between the first set of three days and the second set and he concludes that

> The author is using the Hebrew week as a literary framework for display-ing the theology of creation. First God creates the spaces, and then he populates them with inhabitants. God deals with the challenge posed by the world being "without form and void" by providing first the form and then the fulness.[25]

Advocates of the literary approach regard the days of creation as a "mod-est example of anthropomorphism that is not to be taken literally."[26] Through-out the Bible actions and decisions of God are described in anthropomorphic terms to make them comprehensible to human beings, and this framework of days is considered as a further example of this practice. Blocher comments,

> The theological treasures of the framework of the Genesis days come most clearly to light by means of the 'literary' interpretation. The writer has given us a masterly elaboration of a fitting, restrained anthropomorphic vision, in order to convey a whole complex of deeply meditated ideas.[27]

One of the main arguments against a literary approach is that Genesis 1 is not poetry. Adherents of a literary approach argue that, although Genesis 1 is not poetry, it is structured poetically and should be read as a nonliteral account. This poetic character, it is argued, is evident in the prominence given to the numbers three, seven, and ten. Just how much a schematic approach based on these numbers dictates the structure of the chapter is highlighted in Lucas's helpful summary:[28]

Phrases that occur ten times
"God said" (three times concerning humans and seven times concerning other things)

---

25. Pinnock, "Climbing out of a Swamp," 149.
26. Blocher, *In the Beginning*, 50.
27. Blocher, *In the Beginning*, 59.
28. Lucas, *Can We Believe Genesis Today?* 97-98.

Creative commands (three times "Let there be . . ." and seven times
   "Let")
"to make"
"according to their kind"

Phrases that occur seven times
"and it was so"
"and God saw that it was good"

Three times it is said that:
"God blessed"
"God created"
"God created men and women"

Other numerical patterns
The introduction (1:1-2) contains 21 words in Hebrew (three times
   seven), and the conclusion (2:1-3) contains 35 words (five times
   seven);
"Earth" is mentioned 21 times and "God" 35 times.

Another argument for a nonliteral account is that the firmament and
the role it plays in the creation account are described in very nonscientific
terms. In the first day, God separated light from darkness, and in the second
day this work of separating continued with the division of the waters above
from the waters below. God effected this division by making a רָקִיעַ/*rāqîaʿ*,
which is something that has been stamped or hammered out — like a sheet of
metal. The Latin *firmamentum* has come to us through the KJV translation
"firmament" (i.e., something that is hard or firm). The NIV renders it as "expanse," and the NRSV as "dome." In Ps 19:1, the same word is translated "the
skies" (NIV). The word also occurs in Ezek 1:22-26 and 10:1, where it refers to
a platform above the heads of the living creatures, on which Yahweh's throne
rests. Thus the sky was probably thought of as a dome hammered out of
metal, relating to how people perceived the sky 2,500 years ago. This stands in
sharp contrast to Babylonian and Egyptian cosmologies that regarded the sky
as the body of a goddess. Lucas refers to Job 37:18, with its reference to the sky
that is "hard as a mirror of cast bronze" (NIV).[29]

Furthermore, the literary approach highlights the contrast between ch. 1
and chs. 2–3. Moving from ch. 1 into the stories of chs. 2–3, we enter an en-

29. Lucas, *Can We Believe Genesis Today?* 98.

tirely different literary world; style, vocabulary, and structure are all different. This is disturbing for people who want to read Genesis as a book and not as two different accounts brought together. But this is what happens in the NT, with the first three Gospels presenting a description of the same period and events from three different perspectives. To pursue this analogy, Genesis has its own synoptic problem!

Read together, the accounts do not contradict each other, providing we are reading them to discover their theological message. Taken absolutely literally, we do encounter problems: ch. 1 describes the creation of everything including human beings, but in ch. 2 the process begins again. There are no plants yet and no human beings. This is a new account from a different perspective. The differences are clearly highlighted by Pinnock.

> The focus is narrower, on the creation of man, not the cosmos. It asks the human, not the cosmological, question: How did we come to be? It begins by describing a very inhospitable earth without any vegetation or rainfall and then describes the creation of a man from the clay. The origin of woman is entirely unique. The whole ethos of the passage is pastoral. It describes the world of the shepherd, with its concerns about dry earth, abundant waters, fruited trees, and serpents.[30]

The claim that the garden of Eden stories are simply a detailed look at day six is difficult to defend unless the day is longer than 24 hours. The day begins with no plants or rainfall, and these are not produced miraculously but are watered by a mist. If this is so, the human being would spend his first day in a wilderness. Then, of course, this first day also includes the parade of animals before Adam to name them. If the garden was desolate, it would take some time to gather them; but since they were all made on day six, does this mean that all animals were created in the same place? The idea that none of the animals was a suitable mate for Adam would have taken time to discover, and then he required an operation during which he was in a deep sleep. Genesis 2 does not suggest that this all happened in one 24-hour day.

Whether chs. 2–3 should be read literally or figuratively is controversial. Not everyone who interprets ch. 1 literally does the same with chs. 2–4. It is not impossible to read them literally, but it raises issues, especially about Cain. Where did he get his wife? He complains that whoever finds him will kill him. Where did all these people come from? Cain builds a city, but how did he populate it? Presumably the first readers were not perplexed about

---

30. Pinnock, "Climbing out of a Swamp," 151-52.

these questions, or else the author would have clarified them. Perhaps they were accustomed to reading this sort of literature figuratively.

According to Lucas,

> To say that Genesis 2 and 3 give a figurative, symbolic account is not to say that it is unhistorical. Real historical events can be described in a symbolic way. To describe something symbolically can actually be a powerful way of bringing out its significance. Revelation 12:1-6 describes forcefully — and symbolically — how the Messiah came from the people of God in the face of Satan's opposition.[31]

How do we know when to read a passage symbolically? The imagery of Revelation certainly is so far outside our normal experience and so extraordinary that the reader knows that this type of literature is symbolical. Furthermore, since Revelation is dealing with events in the future, it is further evidence for symbolical reading; the events described have not happened yet and are therefore symbolical and not literal.

According to the literary approach, many of the events in Genesis 2–3 are of a similar extraordinary nature, so that the first readers would know that this was symbolic literature. The story of God coming down to earth and gathering together handfuls of dust to form it into the shape of a human being and then blowing the breath of life into it does seem like anthropomorphic language — language that explains the complex acts of God in human terms which present God's actions in language that human readers can understand.

The main strength of the literary approach is that it focuses on the message of Genesis and emphasizes that the material is theological rather than scientific. However, many will argue, particularly creationists, that if we treat one passage of Scripture as literary rather than historical, then what is to stop this same approach from being applied to other passages such as the NT story of the resurrection. The response that the poetic structure of Genesis 1 shows that this is not a historical narrative will not convince those who value a literal approach as the only valid way to interpret Scripture.

Cultural Perspectives

Cultural perspectives examine Genesis in the light of what we know about the ancient world. Cultural perspectives may be valued by those holding any of the preceding views. This approach focuses, not so much on the age of the

31. Lucas, *Can We Believe Genesis Today?* 134.

earth, but on the age of Genesis. Genesis was first read by people who lived more than two thousand years ago. What message did Genesis have for people of that time, and how would they have understood it? While we cannot hope to give complete answers to these questions, it is worth shifting the focus from our agenda to that of the writer and the first readers. We have spent so long studying Genesis according to a modern agenda, with its emphasis on the extent of the flood and evolution, while these subjects were alien to the original world for which Genesis was written. It is time to try to understand the context in which Genesis was written and read at the beginning of its history as a book. We know that it is dangerous to take even a single verse out of context, and yet many studies of Genesis totally ignore the historical context of its early readers. Genesis was not produced in a vacuum, and it was not the only account of creation in circulation.

When the text of Genesis is studied alongside other ancient Near Eastern literature of that time, it clearly combats the teaching of other creation and flood stories. Pinnock argues that Genesis

> demythologizes nature and sees it as the creation of the one true God. It presents the one God who created all things and who exists independently of nature. It says that there are no warring deities, and no monster goddess needing to be subdued and cut in half. It describes the separation of the primeval waters as a peaceful operation because the chaos is not a powerful force. Creation is by God's effortless word and requires no struggle at all. The text tells us that the heavenly bodies which the ancients worshipped and feared are just lights in the heavens (cf. Deut. 4:19) and that the great sea creatures are God's workmanship too and not mythical monsters. Most important of all, it teaches us that human beings are not a divine afterthought, created to do the dirty work of the gods. They were created to be lords of the world, because they are personal agents just like God is.[32]

We know that the sun and moon were worshipped, as were the stars. Those emphasizing a cultural approach draw attention to the way that Genesis does not use the names "sun" and "moon" and argue that this is because these names were used to refer to heathen gods. Avoidance of the names "sun" and "moon" helps to depersonalize these putative deities and show them as merely objects that God made and placed in the sky. In addition, the brief, almost incidental, mention of the creation of the stars is taken as further evidence of the intention of Genesis to oppose the worship of astral bodies. It is

32. Pinnock, "Climbing out of a Swamp," 149.

the Creator whom people must worship and not the things that he has made. Furthermore, the verb "to create" is used very sparingly in Genesis 1; it is used in the introductory formula "in the beginning God created," and it is used three times in the description of the creation of the human beings. It is also strangely used on one other occasion: to refer to the creation of the great sea monsters. Why are they so significant that they seem to merit special treatment? The usual answer is that this is a reference to the mythical monsters of the deep that in mythological stories battled with the gods and goddesses. In Babylonian creation stories, the gods had to battle against these monsters of chaos in order to create an ordered universe. However, in Genesis these creatures are clearly part of God's creation and as such pose no threat to his creation; like all his creatures, they are under God's control.

Criticisms of this approach are that it ties God's word to a specific cultural context, whereas Christians regard the Bible as God's word for them today. It may also be argued that truth is the clear issue, and only the literal truth can be expected from God himself. Moreover, it may be argued, a carefully structured and poetic approach does not rule out a literal interpretation. The Bible is not written just for scholars, and therefore it may be understood by a clear, straightforward reading. However, what may have been a clear, straightforward reading to someone two or three thousand years ago may be different from our perception today. It may be our scientific minds that are causing the complications.

Creation or Evolution

Evolution is still a very contentious issue among Christians, and the rejection of the creationist approach does not necessarily mean that the only alternative is to believe in evolution. Even if we do not take Genesis totally literally, people have other reasons for objecting to evolution.

Many who argue for seven ages rather than seven literal days accept the possibility of evolution, but others regard the idea of evolution as "utterly foreign to the Bible."[33] Those taking a literal approach to the text may have no difficulty accepting an ancient earth on the basis that the days of Genesis are not literal; but they may reject evolution because it is incompatible with many of the details of the creation story such as the creation of Eve from Adam, since the implication of the Genesis story is that there was a lapse of time between the appearance of Adam and that of Eve.

33. Young, *Creation and the Flood,* 138.

313

Evolution is also rejected by many on the basis that it is incompatible with human beings made in the "image of God." The statement that humans are in the image of God emphasizes the difference between them and animals, whereas evolution emphasizes continuity.

Many believe that evolution is not simply something that we can choose to take or leave: the choice is simple — you either believe that the Bible is the word of God or else you believe in evolution, but you can't have both. This is summed up by a well-known creationist author, Henry Morris:

> One can be a Christian and an evolutionist just as one can be a Christian thief, or a Christian adulterer, or a Christian liar. It is absolutely impossible for those who profess to believe the Bible and to follow Christ to embrace evolutionism.[34]

The concept of evolution still fills many Christians with revulsion because it does not make a clear distinction between human beings and animals and does not seem to do justice to the creation accounts in Genesis. According to Ham, the theory of evolution "is actually destructive to the very gospel message itself."[35] Ham argues that Christians who believe in evolution "probably haven't thought through the logical implications of their position." Ham argues that evolution contradicts the clear unequivocal statements in Genesis about Adam and Eve and the origins of sin and death.

> The Bible clearly teaches that when God created Adam and Eve, the world was perfect. There was no death and bloodshed. But because of the sin of Adam, God brought death as a judgment into the world. Of course, He provided a means by which man could be reconciled to his Creator. But if you believe in evolution, you believe that God used death and bloodshed over millions of years as a way to bring man into existence. This actually destroys the foundation of the Gospel message. The answer's in Genesis — there's no room for evolution in the Bible.[36]

A similar scathing attack is made on those who believe in evolution by Gish, who argues that anyone who believes in evolution does not believe the Bible.

34. Morris, *King of Creation* (San Diego: Christian Literature, 1980), quoted in Berry, "Response to V. Wright," 131.

35. McIntosh, in a similar vein, points out that "the very heart of the Gospel is put in question once one gives way on evolution." He argues that this "is hardly surprising, since evolution is really a religious philosophy. Consequently its worldview is bound to clash with that of Scripture, which revolves around man's fall and redemption"; *Genesis for Today*, 100.

36. Ham, *Did Adam Have a Bellybutton?* 91.

None of those who believe in evolution, atheist, theist, or otherwise, believes this biblical account of the creation of Eve. It is rejected as a false account for, they say, man and woman evolved together from some ape-like creature over a span of several million years. They simply do not *believe* the Scriptures at this point. However, the writers of the New Testament fully support the literal truth of the account of the creation of Eve.[37]

Gish makes a similar point about the historicity of Adam, claiming that since Paul referred to Adam when discussing the "literal bodily resurrection of Christ and of believers," if Adam is not a historical figure "then the Christian has no hope of the resurrection." Gish presses this point home, arguing that "if Adam is merely figurative, then our resurrection is merely figurative."[38]

However, in spite of the ferocious attacks on evolution, it is still accepted by many Christians who argue that God could use an evolutionary process as part of his method in creating the world, an approach known as "theistic evolution." Advocates of this approach are often scientists who see no conflict between their professional involvement in evolutionary theory and their Christian faith in the Creator God. Berry states his position clearly:

> As a scientist, I have no doubt whatsoever that evolutionary change has occurred and that its mechanism is along the lines described by neo-Darwinian theory; as a Christian, I am equally confident that God created the world and everything in it, and that all holds together in him. The Genesis account of creation is of a progress from nothing (or more strictly, God only) through geological and biological change to human-kind. Nowhere in the Bible are we told the mechanisms God used to carry out his work; indeed it is only by faith that we know that God is involved (Heb. 11:3).[39]

In support of this view that evolution and creation are not incompatible, Lucas uses the illustration of an engineer who makes a robot that makes a more complex robot, arguing that the engineer may legitimately claim to have made both robots.[40] In spite of the limitations of this illustration, it is relevant to the biblical teaching on creation, which includes the idea that God created the ground which then brought forth the grass. According to Lucas's analogy, this does not mean that God did not create grass.

37. Gish, "A Consistent Biblical and Scientific View," 140.
38. Gish, "A Consistent Biblical and Scientific View," 140.
39. Berry, *God and the Biologist*, 6.
40. Lucas, *Can We Believe Genesis Today?* 26.

Another issue that is closely related to questions about evolution concerns the identification of Adam in Genesis. Lucas summarizes the work of Canon E. K. V. Pearce, who identifies Adam and Eve with the appearance of Neolithic human beings. Advocates of this view point out that the first people of Genesis cultivated the ground, whereas Stone Age people were hunters and gatherers. The people of Genesis must have used stone tools because in Genesis 4 Tubal-Cain forges all kinds of tools out of bronze and iron. As Pearce points out, Neolithic culture arose in one of the areas identified from the evidence in Genesis as one of the possible sites of the garden of Eden.[41]

The argument made in support of theistic evolution is that at some stage God entered the stage and created the first human being in his image. Some see this as part of the ongoing process of evolution, while others envisage a special divine act. The first evidence of spiritual activity from archaeology is the discovery of ancient religious sanctuaries in the Neolithic city of Çatal Hüyük. If Adam and Eve were the first Neolithic human beings and the first to be truly human, this theory accepts that the earth at that time was inhabited by others who were like them physically. This would explain Cain's fears about being killed if he was forced away from his own society. It also explains how he had no problem finding a wife.

The theory of evolution will continue to be hotly debated, and the purpose of this work is to set out as clearly as possible the opposing views. All that we can hope for is that in the future the debate will be carried on with as much Christian grace as possible in the circumstances.

Concluding Comments on Genesis and Science

To summarize this complex debate succinctly risks oversimplifying the issues. Nevertheless, basically three categories of opinion may be identified, each with numerous variations.

First, the creationist approach claims to interpret the Bible in the most straightforward and literal way, while presenting a possible scientific framework and context that show how a literal reading is compatible with a scientific understanding of our world and its origins. The creationist approach takes the days of creation literally, with the corollary that creation was begun and completed within one literal week. Taking the genealogical data as literal with few if any gaps, creationists accept, with minor modifications, the general methodology applied by Ussher to date creation at 4004 B.C. The prob-

---

41. Lucas, *Can We Believe Genesis Today?* 135-36.

lem with the approach is that it raises a host of scientific questions that direct the reader away from Genesis itself and into a labyrinth of hypotheses, including the idea that mountains were not part of the original creation.

Second, concordists also claim to interpret the Bible literally and respect it as the word of God with just as much conviction as the creationists. However, this group believe that it is unnecessary to set up in opposition to scientific theory. In particular, this group accepts modern scientific claims about the date of the earth, and some concordists, but by no means all, also accept the possibility of evolution. Concordists do not want Christians to be thought of as obscurantist, like those who accused Galileo of heresy; therefore, they seek to reconcile science and the Bible. The main problem is that there is no agreement among them about how to achieve this goal, and furthermore, their views are incompatible with each other. Among the various concordist views the day/age theory is very popular because it allows a literal reading of the text. It is attractive to those who support the idea of a special creation but cannot accept a young earth.

The third group comprises those who think that it is a gross misunderstanding of an ancient text to treat Genesis as a scientific document. Whether we are convinced by scientists about the age of the earth or the evolutionary origins of the human race, this has nothing to do with Genesis, which was written in an entirely different cultural and religious environment and answers theological questions and not scientific ones. One of the main arguments against this approach is that it pays too much attention to Genesis as an ancient literary text and does not pay enough attention to the Bible as the word of God for today. Advocates of the approach reply that the theological message of Genesis is just as relevant today as it was some two or three thousand years ago.

It is hoped that the above discussion is fair to all sides in this debate and that the material will help the reader to understand the main issues and make an informed decision for themselves.

MISSION

Modern mission studies work to a very wide agenda, embracing a portfolio of disciplines as diverse as anthropology and negotiating with terrorists. Within this portfolio a place of honor is given to biblical studies, since they are considered as not just one subject of interest among others but as the foundation on which mission studies are based. Studies of the biblical basis of mission usually concentrate on the NT paradigms of the church's mission to the

317

world. Nothing, however, has been written on mission in the OT that compares with the depth of treatment given to the NT in Bosch's magnum opus, *Transforming Mission*.

Many textbooks include a chapter on the Bible and mission, but a more detailed treatment is *The Biblical Foundations for Mission* by Senior and Stuhlmueller, published in 1983 and still a widely used textbook for missiological studies.

The authors aim to provide a biblical approach for mission based on the whole Bible and not just the NT. However, their study of the OT includes the admission that, "at first glance, the movement of Israel's history and its Scriptures appears to be centripetal or inward."[1] They draw attention to the problem involved in using the OT as a foundation for international mission while its focus, they argue, is clearly on the national identity of Israel. Israel's focus on election and national exclusivism is seen as a problem for mission studies. Senior and Stuhlmueller recognize that the OT contains "signs of deep solidarity with the nonelect nations," but they acknowledge that such insights are not central to the OT but belong to Israel "at its best moments."[2] They characterize the main OT teaching as nationalistic, but argue that there are "flashes of a contrary movement" . . . "stirring beneath the surface."[3]

This approach of Senior and Stuhlmueller limits the OT's contribution to mission to universalistic passages and gives the impression that mission is certainly not central to the message of the OT. A good example of how they apply this approach is seen in their references to Genesis contrasting the centripetal thrust of passages such as the cursing of Canaan with the "radiation away from Israel toward Gentile nations" evident in the Table of Nations, which deals with Israel as one of a number of nations and shows that in origin they were no different from Gentile peoples.[4]

In their study of patriarchal religion, Senior and Stuhlmueller emphasize that the patriarchs "willingly accepted and interacted with Canaanite forms of worship and lifestyle," worshipping at traditional Canaanite sites. Furthermore, they did not initiate a separate priesthood and even accepted a blessing from the non-Israelite priest Melchizedek (14:18-20).[5] Evidence of patriarchal involvement in the secular and religious world of their time leads to the following conclusion:

---

1. Senior and Stuhlmueller, *The Biblical Foundations for Mission*, 315.
2. Senior and Stuhlmueller, *The Biblical Foundations for Mission*, 315.
3. Senior and Stuhlmueller, *The Biblical Foundations for Mission*, 10.
4. Senior and Stuhlmueller, *The Biblical Foundations for Mission*, 10-11.
5. Senior and Stuhlmueller, *The Biblical Foundations for Mission*, 17.

Even while God was calling the patriarchs away "from your country and your kindred" (Gen 12:1) to be the parents of a unique, elect people, it was being done in such a way as to show the *positive* contribution for a secular environment and pre-existing "pagan" religions. A message is being flashed to us that religion is never a pure creation by God but a synthesis of the best under a new inspiration from God. Secular movements, like the extraordinary migration of people across the fertile crescent of the ancient Near East during the twentieth and nineteenth centuries B.C.E., were to become key religious symbols because of the faith of Abraham.[6]

In a brief discussion on creation, Senior and Stuhlmueller argue that salvation rather than creation is the starting point for missiological thinking. This view is based on the judgment that the concept of creation portrays God as working alone, whereas salvation is about the more missiologically useful idea of God working with people in a world of political ideas and sociological problems, a world "deformed by its sin, weakness and prejudice."[7]

A full critique of the work of Senior and Stuhlmueller lies outside of the scope of this book, but in relation to Genesis it is important to point out that they tend to create false dichotomies. This is obvious in their contrast between God as the creator who works alone and God the savior who works in partnership. This will be dealt with in more detail below, in discussing God's partnership in creation. However, the most significant false dichotomy is evident in their juxtaposition between universalistic and particularistic passages. It is true that the book of Genesis moves from an international focus to a family focus; but there is also an international agenda involved, and the ultimate goal of God's choice of Abraham is blessing for all the families of the earth.[8] This universal goal is made possible through the offspring of the patriarch, since it is through Abraham that all nations will be blessed (12:1-3). The call of Abraham to be a blessing makes his call pivotal to the concept of mission, since, on the one hand, his genealogy is traced back to Noah through Shem (11:10-26) and, on the other hand, the impact of his calling and blessing will extend to "all the families of the earth" (12:3 NRSV).

This concept of blessing to the nations is discussed in detail by Carroll.[9] He commences his study with 12:1-3 and argues that "the mission of Abraham

---

6. Senior and Stuhlmueller, *The Biblical Foundations for Mission,* 18.

7. Senior and Stuhlmueller, *The Biblical Foundations for Mission,* 37.

8. Bauckham argues that the "singling out of Abraham from all the nations is not at all to be understood as God's giving up on the nations"; *Bible and Mission,* 28.

9. Carroll, "Blessing the Nations," 17-34.

and his descendants to the world is to be a blessing."[10] Within this mission, blessing embraces both the material and spiritual aspects of the patriarchs' lives while relating to promises of national greatness within a context of worldwide beneficence. Carroll acknowledges that the patriarchal narratives also highlight injustice, deceit, and even murder in the lives of those who were to channel blessing to the world; yet in spite of the failures of the patriarchs, "we must not avoid the benefits that will come from dealing honestly with this rich, yet intricate, narrative that is Genesis."[11]

Kaiser also begins with the call of Abraham in his search for mission in the OT, describing it as "the first Great Commission mandate of the Bible"[12] and the "grandest of all missionary texts."[13] He draws attention to God's promise to bless all the families of the earth through Abraham and deduces that "the blessing of God given to Abraham was intended to reach smaller people groups as well as the political groupings of nations."[14] Arguing that the niph'al of the verb "to bless" must be translated as a passive, he concludes that the blessing of Abraham stands in opposition to the curse on the "whole created order."

> The whole purpose of God was to bless one people so that they might be the channel through which all the nations on the earth might receive a blessing. Israel was to be God's missionaries to the world.[15]

Kaiser links this promised blessing with the promise that the seed of the woman would bruise the serpent's head (3:15).

Those who argue that social justice is a motive for mission find support in Genesis. For example, Du Preez points out that social justice is practiced by God himself, who refuses to permit Abraham's descendants to occupy Canaan until the behavior of the Canaanites merits expulsion (15:16).[16] Du Preez also observes that the judgment meted out against Sodom was not only for sexual sins but for injustice towards the vulnerable in the society. Thus God shares what he will do with Abraham because Abraham is righteous. Du Preez supports his argument by pointing out that Ezekiel understood the sin of the Sodomites as a failure to uphold social righteousness (Ezek 16:49-50). In support of this view we may also note that it is the absence of 10 righteous

10. Carroll, "Blessing the Nations," 30.
11. Carroll, "Blessing the Nations," 33.
12. Kaiser, *Mission in the Old Testament*, 13.
13. Kaiser, "Israel's Missionary Call," 27.
14. Kaiser, *Mission in the Old Testament*, 19.
15. Kaiser, *Mission in the Old Testament*, 20.
16. Du Preez, "Social Justice," 36-46.

people that seals the city's fate. Since God reveals himself as the champion of social justice, this concept must play an important role in preaching the gospel to the nations.

Much of what is written about mission in the OT can be described as "Christian readings." For example, Peters takes 3:15 as a key text for the understanding of the OT view of mission; he ignores the role that this programmatic verse plays in Genesis and gives it a christological interpretation without discussion.[17]

Taking 3:15 as protevangelium, Peters argues that it upholds at least six facts, which I summarize briefly:

1. Salvation comes from God.
2. Salvation will destroy Satan.
3. Mankind as a whole will be affected by salvation, and the human race as such will be saved.
4. Salvation will come through a Mediator who is organically related to mankind.
5. The suffering of the Redeemer is involved in bringing salvation.
6. Since the fall is part of history, salvation will be experienced within history.

Peters also highlights the universal aspects of the covenant with Noah. Since the covenant is with Noah and his sons, it "definitely concerns all nations."[18] Having indicated that the Table of Nations is universal, Peters argues that, although the call of Abraham was the beginning of a new epoch in salvation history which was "particularistic *in method*," that history was "universalistic in promise, design and effect."[19] He argues that "the call of Abraham is not personal favoritism of a particularistic god to establish a local religion in practice and design."[20] Thus, universality of salvation "pervades the entire Old Testament." According to Peters, the OT *"does not contain missions; it is itself 'missions' in the world"* (italics his).[21] Thus he applies to Genesis a universalistic approach based on a NT hermeneutic in order to portray its importance for Christian mission.

To summarize, discussions of mission in the OT tend to focus on passages usually termed universalistic. In Genesis, the first 11 chapters are consid-

17. Peters, *A Biblical Theology of Missions*, 83-130.
18. Peters, *A Biblical Theology of Missions*, 87.
19. Peters, *A Biblical Theology of Missions*, 89.
20. Peters, *A Biblical Theology of Missions*, 110.
21. Peters, *A Biblical Theology of Missions*, 129.

ered significant because they deal with the entire world rather than just Israel. However, it should be noted that these chapters that deal with the entire world have a clear agenda leading to Israel.

Abraham's call is the most popular missionary text in Genesis, in that it features a divine encounter with one individual but also includes all the peoples of the earth in its embrace. Other parts of Genesis are also mentioned by missiologists, with Abraham's rescue of Lot and his pleading for Sodom being described as "fine instances of missionary zeal, courage and devotion"; Joseph gains acclaim as "a great missionary, sent by God down to heathen Egypt, and used of Him for the physical salvation of the millions of the nation and the adjoining countries."[22]

While these approaches highlight missiological ideas and themes in Genesis, they are mainly isolated, and studying them does not lead to the conviction that the concept of mission is central and programmatic in the book of Genesis. Approaches that home in on chs. 1–11 as universalistic and therefore particularly significant for mission limit the concept of mission in the OT to the comparatively few universalistic passages. With this approach it is difficult to sustain the thesis which most missiologists want to uphold, that mission is at the heart of the OT. On the other hand, a Christian reading of the OT that reads NT concepts back into the OT is admitting that the OT message is not essentially missiological until it is viewed with hindsight, in the light of the church's mission.

Other problems arise when passages about bloodshed and war are described as mission. As mentioned above, Glover reads missiological principles into Abraham's rescue of Lot, and a similar approach is sometimes applied to the conquest. This is a risky line of reasoning because it suggests that colonization and empire-building may be excused as mission. Abraham's rescue bid was supported by his heathen neighbors; it certainly was an example of bravery but hardly qualifies as mission.

Abraham is every missiologist's favorite character. Even though not everyone would agree with Kaiser that it is the "grandest of all missionary texts," Abraham's call with its universal agenda is a very fertile planting medium for missiological concepts.[23] However, was Abraham really a missionary, and did he think of himself in those terms? Certainly, if his missionary call mandated him to bring blessing to the Gentiles he clearly failed in this respect. Abraham brought cursing to Egypt and to the Philistines, while in terms of morality the kings of both these nations outshone Abraham significantly.

22. Glover, *The Biblical Basis of Missions*, 17.
23. Kaiser, "Israel's Missionary Call," 27.

Perhaps a more convincing approach is to consider Genesis as an example of the failure of mission. Mission in the OT and, indeed in the Bible, begins with God. He creates the world with a view to blessing its inhabitants and filling the earth with them. While God could have done this as a project in which he worked alone, he chose partnership with the things and people he had made.

By sharing power in the created order, God became open to suffering because he chose a relationship that broke down. Thus, God is grieved because of what he has created, and the harmony and blessing of the original power-sharing arrangement is replaced by alienation and cursing (6:6). Eventually, a new relationship is formed with Abraham and his descendants. This relationship is launched successfully with Abraham's obedient response to the divine call to leave all that he has and start again (12:1-3). God's role is initiator and guarantor of the covenant, while Abraham responds by faith and obedience to the extent that he is willing to offer his son to God sacrificially. However, this initiative of God in choosing Abraham meant that God must make himself accessible to humans and vulnerable to suffering and disappointment. There could be no mission in the OT or in the NT without God's self-revelation. One of the most important events from a missiological perspective is the discussion that God holds with Abraham about the destruction of Sodom; God shares his concerns with the patriarch, treating him like a partner and confidant. God limits what he will do in accordance with an agreement made with the junior human partner whom he has permitted to express an opinion.

Abraham's relationship with God is reflected in good relations with other people. A high point in international relations is when Abraham rescues Lot and offers tithes to Melchizedek. Interestingly, it is Melchizedek who blesses Abraham rather than vice versa. Furthermore, when Abraham is purchasing the field in which to bury his wife, the Hittites acknowledge him as "a mighty prince among us" (23:6). So, Abraham was highly respected by those around him.

In spite of the success of the relationship between God and Abraham and his good reputation, the theme of failure is also woven into the narrative.[24] Bringing blessing to all nations is a tremendous commission, but not one that the patriarch fulfills with unqualified success. In his contacts with foreigners, he is more often a curse than a blessing. Abraham's first visit to Egypt brings cursing on the Egyptians. He builds no altars to Yahweh in Egypt and fails to impress the king with his moral cowardice that leads to his

---

24. Bauckham makes this point clearly; *Bible and Mission*, 30.

wife becoming a member of Pharaoh's harem. Abraham's distrust and fear of what foreigners will do to him because of the beauty of his wife leads also to confrontation with Abimelech, the Philistine ruler. Hagar, the Egyptian maidservant, is treated despicably by both Abraham and Sarah, who never even refer to her by her name. Missiologically, their treatment of a vulnerable foreigner leaves much to be desired and is certainly not a model for modern mission.

This theme of failure in relation to foreigners becomes much more obvious in the accounts of Jacob and his sons. Being a blessing to the nations is very low in the priorities of Jacob and his descendants. No sense of mission is apparent in Jacob's dealings with Laban, Esau, the Shechemites, or the Hittites. His sons also seem unaware of their mission as descendants of Abraham. Reuben, Simeon, and Levi all fail. Judah's marriage to a Canaanite and his unfair dealings with that family are not examples of someone trying to bring blessing to the nations. This brings us to Joseph, described by Glover as "that great missionary."[25] Serious problems arise in any attempt to view Joseph as a missionary. It is true that Joseph provided famine relief for many people including his own family; but this in itself does not make him a missionary, especially since he charged for the food, even buying the people's land and their very selves for Pharaoh (47:13-21). No suggestion is made that he influenced the Egyptians to worship Yahweh, and he himself married the daughter of a polytheistic priest (41:50-52).[26] He became so integrated into Egyptian society that his own family thought that he was an Egyptian, and his personal belongings included a divining cup which was associated with the Egyptian cult. Well might we ask which part of this makes him "a great missionary."

What we find in Genesis is the failure of human beings to fully participate in God's mission. The mission at the heart of Genesis is established by God as he prepares a perfect world and establishes a relationship with its creatures giving them responsibility as his partners. In sharing responsibility with others, God allows himself to suffer. The failure of the human beings brings pain and grief to the heart of God (6:6). Following the flood the new creation starts well with the human being worshipping God and cultivating the soil. However, an intoxicated Noah and pride-filled tower-builders who fail to accept the mission to fill the earth speak of the continued failure of human beings to fulfill God's mission. Thus God establishes a close personal relationship with Abraham and makes a covenant with him and his descen-

---

25. Glover, *The Biblical Basis of Missions*, 17.

26. However, as an Egyptian official directly responsible to Pharaoh he probably had no choice about whom he should marry.

dants. However, Abraham fails to bring blessing to the nations, and his descendants are even less successful. The message of Genesis about mission is that God desires to bless and not curse his creation; but he chooses human beings as his partners in this mission, and they fail to take their mission seriously. Israelites reading Genesis would see their own failure to fulfill their mission reflected in the experiences of their ancestors.

Genesis provides an important foundation for mission in portraying God as desiring to work in partnership with human beings to fulfill his mission for the world. The goal of mission is a relationship with God, the corollary of which is a harmonious relationship with nature and the environment. The most significant contribution to mission by Genesis is the focus on God's plan to share his mission with human beings. The significant corollary of this shared mission is God's willingness to make himself accessible to humans. This involves God in suffering and in accepting personally the consequences of human failure. By introducing us to a suffering God, Genesis provides the foundation for the Gospel message and for the concept of a mission to the world on the basis of God's sacrificial giving of himself in order to provide the context for harmonious relationships and universal blessing.

ECOLOGY

Dire and persistent warnings about impending ecological disasters have raised awareness that nature's resources are limited and need careful management. Many books have been written on the subject, and numerous epitaphs have been written for mother earth. Descriptions such as "apocalyptic" and "life-and-death struggle" heighten our awareness of the seriousness of the damage that has been and is now being done to our natural resources.[1] Schottroff describes the creation that was once declared "good" by God in the following bleak terms:

> Today's status of creation can be described in brief: agony is visible everywhere, the earth is being poisoned, forests are dying, clean water is disappearing. Everyone knows the cause: industrial production. Money is earned with products no one needs, above all with weapons.[2]

It is not just humans who are complaining. Mother Nature is expressing her displeasure in her own inimitable way: natural disasters and climate

1. Moltmann, *God in Creation*, xi.
2. Schottroff, "The Creation Narrative," 27.

problems are becoming increasingly frequent news items. While this section was being written, the tsunami in southeastern Asia claimed about 150,000 lives, and hurricanes, earthquakes, and fires take their toll almost daily. The finger of blame for climate change points directly to human beings, who, it is alleged, have become "the predominant destructive force on Earth."[3]

This subject is important in the present book because, as we have already seen, the theme of land is very prominent in Genesis. In this section we shall see that the theme has theological relevance for us today. But before we discuss the positive theological implications of land, we shall survey the negative approach that some have taken to the book of Genesis. Surprisingly, this 3,000-year-old book has been at the center of accusations and judgmental comments about the cause of the ecological crisis.

As Max Oelschlaeger observes,

> Environmentalists criticize the conservative creation story because of its anthropomorphism, anthropocentrism, and dualism. They charge that the conservative belief that God gave man dominion over the earth has led to its relentless humanization and exploitation.[4]

Probably, we should look on the bright side, since it is good to see that the relevance of Genesis to modern issues is recognized. The question we need to address is whether Genesis is really culpable or whether its message has been misunderstood. Ironically, the book that is blamed for the problem, upon closer examination, may be found to hold the key to providing a solution.

Since 1967 virtually every article and book on ecology and the Bible mentions Lynn White. In a short article he triggered controversy by pinning significant blame on the Western church for the ecological crisis, arguing that "Christianity bears a huge burden of guilt."[5] He argues that Christianity is "the most anthropocentric religion the world has seen," and this has resulted in the rest of creation being regarded as inferior and expendable.[6] White traces this alleged anthropocentrism to the Genesis creation stories.

> Christianity inherited from Judaism . . . a striking story of creation. By gradual stages a loving and all-powerful God had created light and darkness, the heavenly bodies, the earth and all its plants, animals, birds, and

---

3. De Witt, "Creation's Environmental Challenge," 61.
4. Oelschlaeger, *Caring for Creation*, 128.
5. White, "The Historical Roots of Our Ecologic Crisis," 40.
6. White, "The Historical Roots of Our Ecologic Crisis," 38.

fishes. Finally, God had created Adam and, as an afterthought, Eve to keep man from being lonely. Man named all the animals, thus establishing his dominance over them. God planned all this explicitly for man's benefit and rule: no item in the physical creation had any purpose save to serve man's purposes. And although man's body is made of clay, he is not simply part of nature: he is made in God's image.[7]

Pinning the blame on Christianity for the world's woes was popular with some who highly applauded White's sentiments. Oelschlaeger admitted that in the 1970s and early 80s he, like many others, was "worshiping at the altar of Lynn White's influential article."[8] Others objected to his views on various grounds; his criticisms were unfair because he was very selective in the texts of Scripture that he used; people of faiths other than Christianity had contributed to ecological problems. Furthermore, as Barr observes, the connection between the teaching of Genesis and what happens in modern science should not be exaggerated.

> If my arguments are correct, there is much less direct connection between biblical faith and modern science than has been recently believed in some theological currents. The Jewish-Christian doctrine of creation is therefore much less responsible for the ecological crisis than is suggested by arguments such as those of Lynn White. On the contrary, the biblical foundations of that doctrine would tend in the opposite direction, away from a licence to exploit and towards a duty to respect and to protect.[9]

Other Christian writers have approached White's accusations pragmatically and have sought to use them to raise Christian awareness about ecological issues, arguing that it "would be hasty to dismiss such criticisms out of hand."[10] Schaeffer argued that some of the criticism was well deserved because some Christian churches had not only failed in their duty to nature but even failed in their sociological duties to each other. According to Schaeffer, some of "our churches are a scandal; they are cruel not only to the man 'outside' but also to the man 'inside.'"[11]

There is general agreement that Christians must share the blame for the earth's ailments, but how does Genesis become implicated? White points to

---

7. White, "The Historical Roots of Our Ecologic Crisis," 37.
8. Oelschlaeger, *Caring for Creation*, 24-25.
9. Barr, "Man and Nature," 30.
10. Elsdon, *Greenhouse Theology*, 57.
11. Schaeffer, *Pollution and the Death of Man*, 68.

the creation stories in Genesis, which he believes teach that nothing in creation had any purpose other than to serve mankind.[12] He admits that human beings are linked with the rest of the created order in the Genesis accounts since they are made from clay; but this is outweighed in his view by the emphasis that humans are made in the image of God and are therefore distinct from and superior to everything else that God created. According to White, the Christian approach exalts human beings, allowing them to share God's transcendence of nature, thereby establishing a "dualism of man and nature" that led to the insistence that "it is God's will that man exploit nature for his proper ends."[13]

White is not anti-Christian in principle, and he points to the life of Saint Francis as providing "an alternate Christian view of nature and man's relation to it." White argues that Francis "tried to substitute the idea of the equality of all creatures, including man, for the idea of man's limitless rule of creation." He proposes Francis "as a patron saint for ecologists" and particularly highlights his emphasis on humility.[14]

> The key to an understanding of Francis is his belief in the virtue of humility — not merely for the individual but for man as a species. Francis tried to depose man from his monarchy over creation and set up a democracy of all God's creatures. With him the ant is no longer simply a homily for the lazy, flames a sign of the thrust of the soul toward union with God; now they are Brother Ant and Sister Fire, praising the Creator in their own ways as Brother Man does in his.[15]

While White's attack on the Christian approach to the ecological problem is probably the best known, others have made similar points. Van Zyl is critical of how missionaries in the past, believing that the first chapter of Genesis presents us with the perfect, eternal worldview, sought in their preaching to replace other worldviews, whether African or Asian. Van Zyl argues that, although missionaries acknowledged that God is the creator of everything and that he has given human beings the responsibility to rule over nature, this understanding has not seriously influenced their ecological outlook and conduct. Influenced by the Greek thinking of the West, missionaries, in Van Zyl's opinion, presented a "non-integrated understanding of reality, revealing a dichotomy between the spiritual and physical worlds,"

---

12. White, "The Historical Roots of Our Ecologic Crisis," 37.
13. White, "The Historical Roots of Our Ecologic Crisis," 38.
14. White, "The Historical Roots of Our Ecologic Crisis," 42.
15. White, "The Historical Roots of Our Ecologic Crisis," 41.

resulting in a failure to communicate ecological responsibility as part of the Christian message.[16]

Van Zyl argues that Genesis 1 is not an authoritative eternal worldview but shows how the early Israelites viewed creation. It is not a literal scientific account that answers the question "what happened." On the contrary, he argues, Genesis 1 is a confessional statement that asserts that Israel's God is the one who created the world. Arguing that various ages and historical contexts contribute to Genesis 1, Van Zyl concludes that the worldview presented in Genesis is "constantly on the move, being made relevant to and expressed in the terms of every new age."[17]

Because the church misunderstood the worldview presented in Genesis 1, it failed to communicate the ecological message of Genesis to the world. In particular, the church neglected to emphasize the Christian responsibility in relation to nature. Genesis spoke a prophetic word to the people within its worldview. It denied the divinity of nature and taught the Lordship of the Creator. According to Van Zyl, the church's duty is not to encourage everyone to accept the biblical worldview or try to solve modern problems by repeating "theological clichés," but to speak a prophetic word within the modern worldview. To be effective the church must come to grips with how modern people think and address them "in relevant terms within their own frames of reference."[18] In particular, Van Zyl argues that the most important contribution that the church can make to the ecological debate is to "address the problem of cosmology." By this he means that we must face our ecological responsibilities from the perspective "of a Christian understanding of the reality in which we live."[19]

A number of writers argue that it is not, as Van Zyl argues, an alternative Christian view that we need but a truly biblical one. Far from the biblical stories contributing to the problem, it is argued, they provide the best basis for understanding the predicament and point towards how it can be resolved. As Sider points out, the problems we have are not due to biblical teaching but to the "destructive, unbridled consumerism of modern society" which is rooted in the "narcissistic individualism and materialistic naturalism that flow from the Enlightenment."[20] In contrast to the anthropocentric focus of the Enlightenment, Sider argues that the Bible provides an effective approach to nature and to the ecological problems.

16. Van Zyl, "Cosmology, Ecology, and Missiology," 203.
17. Van Zyl, "Cosmology, Ecology, and Missiology," 207.
18. Van Zyl, "Cosmology, Ecology, and Missiology," 212.
19. Van Zyl, "Cosmology, Ecology, and Missiology," 213.
20. Sider, "Biblical Foundations," 48-49.

Biblical faith, on the other hand, provides a framework within which we can both enjoy material abundance and understand its limits. I believe biblical faith provides a solid foundation for caring for the creation entrusted to us by the Creator. Perhaps if more Christians engaged in environmental practices that were consistent with biblical teaching, more environmentalists would be ready to explore again the claim that a biblical framework would offer the best hope for a comprehensive Earth-healing.[21]

Thus, the criticism levelled against Christianity on the basis of the creation accounts needs to be taken seriously, but is it the interpretation of Genesis that is at fault rather than the creation accounts themselves? Christians have, together with everyone else, contributed to the ecological crisis, and defending them is not the way forward. Since Christians claim to have a special relationship with the Creator, it seems surprising that they have not been at the forefront of promoting ecological awareness. Many would agree with White that anthropocentrism is a major contributing factor to the ecological crisis, but the most important issues in relation to Genesis are whether the creation stories actually teach anthropocentrism and whether they give human beings a mandate to exploit and destroy the earth's natural resources.

By focusing exclusively on the dominion and uniqueness of human beings, we get a distorted picture of the teaching of Genesis. In the creation accounts the human being is "one creature among many," in what Moltmann describes as "a fellowship of creation."[22] The solidarity between humans and animals includes the concept of *nephesh* or soul, but not to be confused with the Greek concept. Both animals and humans are described as *nephesh*.

Because human beings were created last, it is easy to jump to the conclusion that they are therefore the crown of creation and that everything exists for their pleasure; but this is a caricature of the teaching of Genesis in which everything is created for the glory of God and not humanity. Moltmann argues convincingly that human beings are not the crown of creation in the Genesis accounts:

> Human beings are the last to be created. In so far they are the apex of created things. But they are not 'the crown of creation'. It is the sabbath with which God crowns the creation which he beholds as 'very good'. Moreover, as the last thing to be created the human being is also dependent on

21. Sider, "Biblical Foundations," 48.
22. Moltmann, *God in Creation,* 187.

all the others. Without them his existence would not be possible. So while they are a preparation for him, he is dependent on them.[23]

Undoubtedly, Genesis does emphasize the superiority and distinctiveness of human beings, and it does teach that they are to have dominion over the rest of creation. Their distinctiveness is maintained in a number of minor ways, but it is the concept of the "image of God" *(imago dei)* that leaves the distinctiveness and superiority of the human beyond doubt. However, this is only one aspect of the message of Genesis, since it also emphasizes the solidarity of humans with the rest of creation. Moltmann captures this emphasis by his insistence that humans are made not only in the "image of God" but also in the "image of the world" *(imago mundi).*

> As God's last creation before the sabbath, the human being himself is the embodiment of all other creatures. The complex system 'human being' contains within itself all simpler systems in the evolution of life, because it is out of these that the human being has been built up and has proceeded. In this sense they are present in him, just as he is dependent on them. He is *imago mundi*. As microcosm the human being represents the macrocosm. As 'image of the world' he stands before God as the representative of all other creatures. He lives, speaks and acts on their behalf.[24]

Like Moltmann, Schaeffer does not want to understate the emphasis in Genesis on the uniqueness of human beings "made in the image of God," since this establishes that the human "has personality" and "is unique in the creation." However, at the same time Schaeffer argues that the human is related to all the other creatures "as being *created.*" The point that he is making is that humans have affinity with God because they are made to relate to him in a way that other creatures cannot; but the human is also united to the rest of creation because he is a created being, whereas God is uncreated. The corollary of this is that only God is independent, and everything and everyone else is dependent on him; "man, the animal, the flower and the machine, in the biblical viewpoint, are equally separated from God, in that He created them all."[25]

Although Christians have been culpable in not taking ecology seriously enough, their belief in God the Creator should make them more, not less, conscious of our responsibility to care for the earth. Schaeffer highlights the

23. Moltmann, *God in Creation*, 187.
24. Moltmann, *God in Creation*, 189-90.
25. Schaeffer, *Pollution and the Death of Man*, 49-50.

331

implications of the Christian belief in the Creator God by affirming "that on the side of creation and on the side of God's infinity and our finiteness . . . we really *are* one with the tree!"[26]

> The man who believes things are only there by chance cannot give things a real value. But for the Christian the value of a thing is not in itself autonomously, but because God made it. It deserves this respect as something which was created by God, as man himself has been created by God.[27]

Thus, human beings relate to God who gives them dominion and authority over other creatures, but their solidarity with those creatures means that this dominion and authority are not synonymous with exploitation and oppression. The mandate for human beings to have dominion over the created order was given in the harmonious setting of the garden of Eden (1:28). Dominion in this context is the exercise of God-given authority for the ultimate good of all, including those under that authority. Adam exercised his dominion by giving the animals names, and they accepted his authority by coming to him. In this idyllic portrayal of authority and harmony Genesis portrays the human as a creature endowed with special blessing to control and care for his fellow creatures. Apart from naming the animals, the human exercised his dominion by tilling the ground so that "human mastery over the earth is intended to resemble the cultivating and protective work of a gardener. Nothing is said about predatory exploitation."[28]

As DeWitt explains,

> dominion as outright oppression is not advocated or condoned by the Scriptures. First, the Genesis 1:28 passage gives the blessing and mandate to people before the fall. Second, this passage must be understood in the context of the rest of the Bible. If this is done, one must come to the conclusion that dominion means responsible stewardship.[29]

DeWitt's argument that the creation accounts should not be studied in isolation from other Scriptures is echoed by several writers. Sider, for example, finds similar evidence in Matt 6:26-30, which affirms that God "feeds the birds and clothes the lilies."[30]

26. Schaeffer, *Pollution and the Death of Man*, 54.
27. Schaeffer, *Pollution and the Death of Man*, 58.
28. Moltmann, *God in Creation*, 30.
29. DeWitt, "Creation's Environmental Challenge," 70-71.
30. Sider, "Biblical Foundations," 47.

Human beings must not exaggerate their own status. No other member of the created order has the ability to write and discuss its own origins or to understand the issues relating to the use and abuse of natural resources. Our unique ability as humans should not fill us with a sense of arrogance and a feeling that we can treat the created order with contempt. Rather, humans should be filled with a sense of responsibility — a sense that the command to take control still applies to us, but not in the sense that we should be not destroyers or wasters but accountable stewards and wise conservationists. In performing this role we will show due concern for the other creatures who co-inhabit planet earth with us and will be taking the message of Genesis seriously.

The concept of the domination of other species that people such as White complain about is not advocated in Genesis but is explained in terms of the disobedience of humankind and their concomitant alienation from God, from one another, and from their environment. Only stewardship was required in Eden, where there were no thorns or thistles, vicious animals, or danger. The act of disobedience led to a struggle with the soil to produce crops and the constant danger from natural disasters and ruthless predators.

Several well-known passages claim that this will be reversed in a future age, but this should not prevent Christians from doing what they can here and now. As Schaeffer points out, it is not enough for Christians to say that at a future time healing will take place in the natural order. Rather, we should accept and teach that, as Schaeffer argues, "by God's grace substantially, upon the basis of the work of Christ, substantial healing can be a reality here and now."[31]

Why do the dire predictions of disaster not make more impact in the behavior of many individuals? No matter how dire the prediction or ominous the forecast, when ecological issues begin to affect our lifestyle, cause us inconvenience, or cost us money, it is tempting to feel that I as one person cannot make a difference; why should I be the one to try to save the world!? However, the message of Genesis is relevant here because it highlights the importance of individuals and shows what can be done when one person, be it Noah, Abraham, Rebekah, or Joseph, is open to God's influence. As we saw in the section on mission, God entered a partnership with human beings at creation and gave them responsibility to care for the land from which they were made (1:26; 2:7; 2:15). After the flood, Noah was made aware of his responsibilities (9:1-11). If we take the theme of land in Genesis seriously, we shall seek to play our part in the conservation of the land and environment that God has entrusted to us.

31. Schaeffer, *Pollution and the Death of Man*, 67.

FEMINIST APPROACHES

Modern readers of ancient texts will, obviously, feel quite differently about the material than the ancient readers. Indeed, we have no certain knowledge about how the texts were originally understood or what were the main issues that concerned the first readers. We come to the text with different issues in our minds, and we are more sensitive in some areas of our thinking because of what we know about how modern people will react. Undoubtedly, the ancient reader also had areas of extreme sensitivity, but they were different from ours. Feminist approaches have made us aware of an important area that some people today are very sensitive about, not necessarily only women. In the last few decades we have adjusted our thinking and our writing, sometimes without giving it much thought, to avoid giving offense. Thus, when I was a child in primary school there was no apparent problem in the teacher pointing out that "he" in some contexts meant "he" or it could mean "she." Now we know that we should be more careful in our writing to avoid the impression that we undervalue women. Similarly in relation to Genesis, centuries of readers did not realize just how much inferior the traditional interpretation of Genesis made some women feel. Now this has become an issue and must be addressed. Does the Genesis account of creation really present the woman as inferior? She is, after all, taken from the man and provided to be his "helper"; furthermore, it is the woman who sins first and not the man. Clearly these details could provide fuel for misogynist thinking. However, this does not necessarily mean that the text of Genesis or its message originally implied that women were inferior. We shall turn now to see how feminist writers have approached these texts.

Our first problem in tackling this subject is that there is no agreed feminist position on Genesis. As the title of this section suggests, there is a plurality of feminist approaches to the Bible in general and to Genesis in particular. Furthermore, some of these approaches are not only conflicting but mutually exclusive. Some reject Genesis as a hopelessly anti-feminine book, while others value Genesis but feel that it has been misinterpreted throughout history and that we are heirs to a tradition that distorts the intrinsic message of the book. Trible complains about the misogynist interpretation of the biblical text that over the centuries has "acquired a status of canonicity."[1] Schüngel-Straumann agrees that those who read Genesis today are unwittingly perpetuating a misogynist tradition.

---

1. Trible, *God and the Rhetoric of Sexuality*, 73.

There is a tradition of more than 2000 years and a history of the text's reception which foster anti-woman arguments from which we are still suffering today. These arguments were seldom inherent in the texts themselves; rather, and for various reasons, they were propagated through a long and complicated history of interpretation. That is why everybody reading or listening to these old texts, even a theologian, is to some extent, biased, as evidenced everywhere in handbooks, dictionaries, essays and so on.[2]

Feminist writers complain that readers of the Bible have worked in a cultural environment dominated by men and as a result have become blind to the discrimination endemic in their interpretation. The Bible, according to Aldredge-Clanton, "reflects the strong bias of a patriarchal (male-dominated) culture."[3] Moreover, the church today, it is argued, has failed to break free from the limits placed on God-language by the male society from which the Bible emerged. The accusation is a serious one, and Aldredge-Clanton equates it with idolatry:

Even at the beginning of the twenty-first century, the majority of churches continue to . . . limit God by exclusively masculine names and images. Speaking of deity only in masculine terms creates God in the image of a masculine being, giving powerful sanction to the dominance of men in church and society. Exclusively masculine God-language is oppressive and idolatrous. It undermines the human equality of women made in the divine image, resulting in social and economic injustice. We also create an idol when we worship only a masculine deity, breaking the commandment against idolatry (Ex 20:4).[4]

Feminists have not only highlighted alleged failures in past approaches, but many have sought to show how the Bible can be reinterpreted in a way that reflects the equality of the sexes. Numerous attempts have been made to provide a feminist hermeneutic, but the results have failed to produce a consensus of opinion. Nevertheless, a number of key areas have been identified that have produced new perspectives on the ancient text. Trible is probably the best-known scholar in this area, and she has done a great deal to show that Genesis may be interpreted in a way that highlights gender equality.

2. Schüngel-Straumann, "On the Creation of Man and Woman in Genesis 1–3," 53.
3. Aldredge-Clanton, *In Whose Image?*, 11.
4. Aldredge-Clanton, *In Whose Image?*, 1.

Gender Issues in the Garden of Eden

The main problems for a feminist hermeneutic arise not from the first chapter of Genesis but from chs. 2 and 3. These chapters relate that Adam was made first and then Eve was made from his rib. Trible investigates the way in which Genesis presents the creation of woman from Adam's rib; in particular she focuses on the phrase "taken from." Trible challenges the idea that because the woman is taken from Adam (whom she refers to as "the earth creature") she is therefore inferior; does derivation mean subordination? She points out that it is not the woman that is taken from earth creature but the raw material. The earth creature itself is taken from the earth, but this does not mean that the earth is superior. Indeed, the opposite is the case; the earth creature is superior to the earth from which it is taken. The dust of the earth and the rib of the earth man are just raw materials, and both the earth creature and the woman owe their existence as living creatures to God. "The relationship of the couple is one of mutuality and equality."[5]

Yet the order of creation, man first and then woman, seems to suggest the higher status of the man.[6] Feminist scholars, however, note that the sequence of creation was from the lower forms of life to the more sophisticated.[7] The order in which the humans were made, they argue, does not logically suggest that the one made first is dominant, because the ground and the animals were made before Adam and he is obviously superior to them.[8] If we develop this paradigm, Eve's later appearance would render her superior to Adam and not the reverse. Furthermore, feminist interpretations usually reject the idea that Adam was the first man and that Eve was created from him. It is argued that Adam was not actually the first man, because before the "rib" was taken from Adam he comprised both male and female genders. The modern feminine approach is to avoid referring to Adam as "man" before the creation of the woman and to use a nongender-specific word such as "Groundling" or "Earthman."[9]

Since Eve was Adam's helper (עֵזֶר/ '*ēzer*), it has been suggested that her role was subservient to the one she was helping. It is often assumed that "the person doing the helping puts himself in a subordinate role to the person who has primary responsibility for carrying out the activity."[10] Feminist theo-

---

5. Trible, *God and the Rhetoric of Sexuality*, 101.

6. Grudem makes this point; *Evangelical Feminism and Biblical Truth*, 30.

7. See, e.g., Bechtel, "Rethinking the Interpretation of Genesis 2:4b–3:24," 114.

8. However, the Apostle Paul argues for male leadership on the basis of Adam's prior existence before Eve (1 Tim 2:12-13).

9. See Trible, *God and the Rhetoric of Sexuality*, 80.

10. Grudem, *Evangelical Feminism and Biblical Truth*, 37.

logians counter this argument by showing that "there is no linguistic evidence whatsoever that the term [helper] is meant to designate an inferior."[11] Trible argues that "the English word *helper* suggests an assistant, a subordinate, indeed an inferior, while the Hebrew word *'ēzer* carries no such connotation."[12] Attention is often drawn to the role of God as Israel's helper.[13] In this case, it is the people whom God helps who have the lower status, and God "the helper" is superior. Although Eve was made to be Adam's helper, this does not denote an inferior role since the same term is used to describe God as "helper." Grudem, however, argues that even God is somehow subordinate in his role as "helper," because "when God helps us, He still holds us primarily responsible for the activity, and He holds us accountable for what we do."[14] Grudem denies that a subordinate role essentially makes a person inferior. He argues that men and women are equal, but that their roles are different and it is the woman's role to be subordinate to male leadership. Grudem concludes that

> Eve was created as a helper, but as a helper who was Adam's equal. She was created as one who differed from him, but who differed from him in ways that exactly complemented who Adam was.[15]

The position of Clines, on the other hand, is unequivocal: the helper is always not just subordinate but inferior:

> What I conclude, from reviewing all the occurrences in the Hebrew Bible, is that though superiors may help inferiors, strong may help weak, gods may help humans, in the act of helping they are being 'inferior'. That is to say, they are subjecting themselves to a secondary, subordinate position. Their help may be necessary or crucial, but they are *assisting* some task that is already someone else's responsibility.[16]

This leads to the all-important question that Clines' book highlights, "What does Eve *do* to help?" According to Clines, Genesis teaches that Eve has only one role in the creation narratives, "to produce children." Since this greatly limits the value of womanhood, Clines concludes that Genesis is irre-

11. Laffey, *An Introduction to the Old Testament,* 24.
12. Trible, *God and the Rhetoric of Sexuality,* 90.
13. See, e.g., Schüngel-Straumann, "On the Creation of Man and Woman in Genesis 1–3," 66.
14. Grudem, *Evangelical Feminism and Biblical Truth,* 37.
15. Grudem, *Evangelical Feminism and Biblical Truth,* 37.
16. Clines, *What Does Eve Do to Help?,* 30-31.

deemably androcentric and presents a distorted and limited view of the female gender. For Clines, the book of Genesis is not the solution but the problem.[17]

Clines argues that this androcentric bias is also evident in the way that Adam announces the name of his new partner. Two stages in the naming process are recorded. First, when the couple meet for the first time in Eden, Adam announces that she shall be called "Woman."

> Then the man said, "This at last is bone of my bones and flesh of my flesh; she shall be called Woman, because she was taken out of Man." (2:23 ESV)

Second, after the pronouncement of divine judgment, Adam calls his wife "Eve."

> The man called his wife's name Eve, because she was the mother of all living. (3:20 ESV)

What significance, then, should we place on this process of naming? Earlier God had brought the animals to Adam and he had named them in a procedure that leaves little doubt that the person pronouncing the names is superior to those receiving names. How then should we interpret the naming of Adam's female partner, first as "Woman" and later as "Eve"?

The second of these announcements certainly suggests the exercise of Adam's authority in announcing the personal name of his wife as "Eve." Just as parents exercise their authority to give names to their children, so Adam assumes authority over Eve. According to Trible, "the man reduces the woman to the status of an animal by calling her a name."[18] This does not necessarily mean that Adam was right to do so, since this may be a reflection of the strained relationships between human beings that emerged after their disobedience. Throughout Genesis there are a number of incidents where women are treated badly, but it is clear that the narrator is describing what happened as a result of the male-dominant society while not approving of it. The naming of Eve seems the first sign that after their disobedience the first couple have lost their earlier sense of harmony.

For this interpretation to be valid there must be a difference in the first naming pronouncement which takes place immediately after the couple are introduced. The most obvious difference is that whereas Adam calls her name "Eve," he does not call her name "Woman" but rather announces that "she shall be called Woman." This, it may be argued, is a statement of fact rather

17. Clines, *What Does Eve Do to Help?*, 35.
18. Trible, *God and the Rhetoric of Sexuality*, 133.

than the bestowal of a name, since the noun "name" is missing and Woman is not a personal name.

Clines sees no distinction between these two accounts of naming and argues that in both announcements the man is exercising his authority over the woman. He concludes that this is further evidence of the androcentric orientation of Genesis. Grudem also places the naming of "woman" in the same category as the naming of the animals. This leads him to conclude that

> When Adam says, "she shall be called Woman," he is giving a name to her. This is important because in the context of Genesis 1–2, the original readers would have recognized that the person doing the "naming" of created things is always the person who has authority over those things.[19]

Trible, however, shows that the naming of the animals that establishes the earth creature's power over them combines the verb "to call" with the noun "name," whereas in the announcement of the name Woman, the verb "to call" is not combined with the noun "name"; therefore, the naming of the woman is different from that of the animals and does not include the idea of male superiority or dominance. "The verb *call* by itself does not mean naming; only when joined to the noun *name* does it become part of a naming formula."[20]

Adam declares that her name will be "woman" (*'iššâ*). Trible argues that this is a reference to gender and sexuality; it is not a personal name.[21] It is a powerful wordplay to mark the creation of woman: the word for "man" is אִישׁ/*'îš* and the word for "woman" is אִשָּׁה/*'iššâ*. Furthermore, if Adam was using his authority to announce the name "woman," it would be a new name that he had invented; but this is not the case, since the word "woman" has already occurred in the text (2:22). However, when Adam announces the name "Eve," the noun "name" is present and the exercise of authority is implied. This means that the exercise of authority by man over woman comes after their disobedience and reflects the disrupted harmony of their previously perfect relationship. As Trible explains,

> When the transformed earth creature called the woman *'iššâ* (and himself *'îš*), he did not name her but rather rejoiced in the creation of sexuality (Gen 2:23). But when the disobedient man called his woman's *name (šēm)* Eve, he ruled over her to destroy their one flesh of equality (Gen 3:20).[22]

19. Grudem, *Evangelical Feminism and Biblical Truth*, 31.
20. Trible, *God and the Rhetoric of Sexuality*, 99.
21. Trible, *God and the Rhetoric of Sexuality*, 100.
22. Trible, *God and the Rhetoric of Sexuality*, 160.

We can conclude then, that the Genesis account of the garden of Eden raises issues about gender that have evoked different reactions, even from those who want to defend the equality of the genders. Clines is representative of those who argue that the Eden story is the product of a male-dominated patriarchal society and is to be condemned as irredeemably androcentric.[23] Others, such as Trible, accept that the text itself teaches the equality of the genders, but she argues that male interpreters have distorted the true meaning of the narrator. An entirely different approach is to accept that the Eden account teaches the subordinate role of women, but to argue with Grudem that this is not the product of human preference but is the will of God for human interrelationships.

Gender Issues in Genesis 1

Many feminist writers would agree with Clines that the story of Adam and Eve in the garden of Eden is androcentric. At the same time they would argue that the opening chapter of Genesis sets the scene for equality with the assertion that male and female are made in the image of God and are given dominion over the rest of the created order.

Most attempts to show that male and female are equal before God refer to 1:27:

> So God created man in his own image,
> in the image of God he created him;
> male and female he created them. (NIV)

This is an important verse for feminist hermeneutics: Trible describes it as the "topical clue" for her work and argues that the verse is the "first scriptural clue for the subject of God and the rhetoric of sexuality."[1]

The significance of the verse lies in its unequivocal declaration that "God's image includes the feminine gender as well as the masculine, and men and women stand in equal partnership."[2] In this verse the word translated "man" is אָדָם/*'ādām*, which is later used as the personal name of the first man. However, in this context the word refers to male and female and should probably be translated "humankind" since it embraces both genders. This means that both male and female represent the human race and do so on an equal footing.

23. Clines, *What Does Eve Do to Help?*, 37.
1. Trible, *God and the Rhetoric of Sexuality*, 12.
2. Aldredge-Clanton, *In Whose Image?*, 2.

This significant verse is followed by a blessing that God bestows on the first human beings. Included in the benediction is the command to have dominion over the earth.

"Be fruitful and multiply and fill the earth and subdue it and have dominion over the fish of the sea and over the birds of the heavens and over every living thing that moves on the earth." (1:28 ESV)

It is easy to associate this dominion with almost exclusively male activity, but God's command is addressed to both male and female humans. This joint dominion, according to Schüngel-Strauman, "implies only too clearly that one gender may not claim power over the other."[3] Male and female humans are called to exercise authority over the rest of creation, but not over each other. Thus, these concepts of equality in the image of God and joint dominion at the beginning of creation provide the lens through which the rest of the creation story may be understood. However, an increasing number of scholars do not accept this view and regard even the first chapter of Genesis as the product of a biased patriarchal society that regarded women as inferior. Clines, for example, argues that if we say that women as well as men are created in the image of God, we have moved "beyond the horizon of the text."[4]

Commenting on 1:27-28, he argues:

The text does not mean to say that women, every bit as much as men, are to have dominion over the animals — not so much because women are not equal with men, though we know in advance from the text's perspective they most probably are *not* — but because it is undifferentiated humanity that is being spoken of.[5]

In the same way, Clines argues that the text does not teach that women as well as men are made in the image of God but simply that undifferentiated humanity is in God's image. According to Clines, this does not imply that men and women are equal. He concludes that the first chapter of Genesis, like chs. 2–3, is "indefeasibly androcentric" and cannot be "redeemed" from its "patriarchal or sexist stance."[6] This view would seem to devalue the OT and render it irrelevant. However, while Clines argues that we should not approach the Bible to find dogmas, since some of its dogmas may be wrong, he

---

3. Schüngel-Straumann, "On the Creation of Man and Woman in Genesis 1–3," 75.
4. Clines, *What Does Eve Do to Help?*, 44.
5. Clines, *What Does Eve Do to Help?*, 42.
6. Clines, *What Does Eve Do to Help?*, 45.

also thinks that the Bible is "a resource for living which has no authority but which nevertheless manages to impose itself powerfully upon people."[7]

While this approach exemplified by Clines has become quite popular, there are also many scholars who confess and value the authority of Genesis and seek to understand its message, not as the product of an ancient patriarchal society but as a divine revelation of the origins of humanity. From this confessional viewpoint, the "image of God" and the command to subdue the earth addressed to both male and female provide the foundation for understanding male and female as equal in the sight of God. The responsibility of humankind to bring the earth under subjection may be understood as something that could not be done without the complementary relationship of male and female working together. According to the key verse (1:27), both male and female are given joint responsibility in their equal status as "created in the image" of God. Together, not singly, they are responsible for subduing the earth (1:28). Nothing in the creation stories rescinds this joint authority, and there is no indication that one gender was created subservient to the other. The focus of the account of the creation of Eve is on her unique suitability as Adam's partner rather than on questions about status. However, the complicating factor in this kind of confessional approach is that some scholars who accept the authority of the Bible believe that Genesis teaches that, while women are created equal to men, their role is to be subordinate to male authority. So from the same texts emerge conflicting interpretations both from confessional and nonconfessional methodologies.

No doubt this controversy is far from being resolved, but we have seen that the main approaches are:

1. An outright condemnation of the text as the product of a male-dominated society whose views were shared by the author of Genesis.
2. A belief that Genesis teaches the equality of the genders, but that through the centuries the true message has been distorted at the expense of the status of women.
3. A faith in Genesis as God's revealed truth and a belief that the traditional interpretation that gives dominance to the male is correct.
4. Acceptance of Genesis as God's word but a rejection of the traditional interpretation of female subordination. Genesis teaches the equality of the sexes, and neither gender is dominant until the catastrophic rebellion in the garden of Eden.

7. Clines, *What Does Eve Do to Help?*, 48.

Positions 2 and 4 are very similar, since both accept that Genesis may be interpreted to show that men and women have equal status and that male domination is a deviation from the original situation in the garden of Eden. However, the difference between these two approaches is that position 2 reaches this conclusion by scholarly analysis alone and holds no particular view about the authority of the text. Position 4, on the other hand, is a confessional approach that views the text not as the product of a human author, but as the word of God.

A Tale of Two Gardens

In a very interesting chapter of her book *God and the Rhetoric of Sexuality,* Trible uses the garden of Eden story as the hermeneutical key to the biblical book the Song of Songs. She regards the story of the garden of Eden as "a love story gone awry" and the Song of Songs as "love's lyrics redeemed."[1] This works rather well, because a garden figures prominently in both passages. In the Genesis story, the relationship between the human couple breaks down and the story ends tragically with expulsion from the garden. Although the garden in the Song of Songs is not perfect since anger and violence exist (Song 1:6; 5:7), the Song nevertheless reflects the idyllic setting of a garden in which the story is one of love rather than tragedy. The trees and plants are mentioned succinctly in Genesis as "every tree that is pleasant to the sight and good for food" (2:9 NRSV), but "what the storyteller in Genesis reported succinctly, the voices in the Song praise extensively."[2] Plants, flowers, and trees become the backdrop to harmonious yearnings for love. Even the thorns feature, but the woman of the story is described as a lily among thorns (Song 2:2). No snake interferes, no disobedience ruins the harmony, and one gender is not ruled over by the other. In this context, as Trible observes, "there is no male dominance, no female subordination, and no stereotyping of either sex."[3] The woman's role includes shepherding the flocks and tending the vineyards. Throughout the Song, argues Trible, "she is independent, fully the equal of the man."[4]

Although the creation account in Genesis and the Song of Songs were written independently of each other, Trible has shown how helpful it is to

1. Trible, *God and the Rhetoric of Sexuality,* 154.
2. Trible, *God and the Rhetoric of Sexuality,* 154.
3. Trible, *God and the Rhetoric of Sexuality,* 161.
4. Trible, *God and the Rhetoric of Sexuality,* 161.

compare biblical passages with each other, and it is particularly evocative to compare the garden of Eden with the garden in the Song of Songs. However, our conclusions must be held tentatively and not dogmatically given the different genres that we are dealing with. In spite of the helpful comparisons that Trible makes, the Song of Songs is not actually teaching anything either positive or negative about gender equality.

The Role and Status of Women in the Patriarchal Narratives

For feminist readers of Genesis it is not just the creation stories that are problematic. The patriarchal narratives seem to marginalize women, and it is difficult to interpret this marginalization out of the text because it seems to be intrinsic to the message of the book. Thus Abraham treats his wife badly to ensure his own personal safety, not once but twice. Hagar is treated badly, but God seems to concur, and so does Paul, for that matter! Furthermore, God's relationship is with Abraham, and when God appears and speaks to Abraham, Sarah has to listen from behind the tent flap. Even the sign of the covenant, circumcision, is a male sign. No amount of hermeneutical acrobatics can avoid the impression of male dominance in the patriarchal narratives.

Hagar's Story from a Feminist Perspective

In her book *Texts of Terror,* Trible draws attention to the plight of Sarah's maid Hagar. She and Sarah are torn apart by the circumstances that make them competitors for the approval of the patriarch. The scene opens with Sarah's plight:

> Now Sarai, Abram's wife, had borne him no children. She had a female Egyptian servant whose name was Hagar. (16:1)

Usually in Hebrew sentences the verb comes first and then the subject, but in this verse "Sarai" is placed as the first word in the sentence. Although this verse is two sentences in most English translations, in Hebrew it is one sentence, beginning with the name "Sarai" and ending with the name "Hagar." Trible catches the significance of this juxtaposition of the two women:

> Beginning with Sarai and ending with Hagar, the narrated introduction opposes two women around the man Abram. Sarai the Hebrew is mar-

ried, rich, and free; she is also old and barren. Hagar the Egyptian is single, poor, and bonded; she is also young and fertile. Power belongs to Sarai, the subject of action; powerlessness marks Hagar, the object.[1]

The narrative shows that in the eyes of Abram and Sarah Hagar is more an object to be used than a person to respected. They never refer to her by name, and she is not consulted by them. In contrast, the angel of the Lord does call Hagar by name: she is treated much more respectfully by God than by her master and mistress (16:8; 21:17). They treat her abusively, and she has no means of redress. Israelites would later be oppressed by the Egyptians, but they showed in the persons of the patriarch and matriarch of their nation that they could be pitiless and oppressive against the weak and vulnerable.

Sarah believes that Yahweh has prevented her from having children, and now she decides to overturn the will of the deity and obtain in her own way what she feels he has forbidden (16:2). In the midst of her misery and frustration she treats God as someone who can be manipulated and whose decisions may be overturned. Sarah takes charge of the situation and tells Abram what to do: he passively concurs (16:3-4).

Abraham takes Hagar as his wife, but the Egyptian has no choice in the matter and no one consults her. However, when she conceives and becomes pregnant there is a dramatic change. She is no longer just a mere slave; she has a child in her womb, and in her newfound status she despises Sarah (16:4). We are not told how this happens or how Sarah knows that her maid despises her. Succinctly, the narrator relates only the essential elements of the drama. We may assume that the ease with which Hagar becomes pregnant makes her feel superior to her mistress, who had tried for years to achieve what has come so readily to her slave. Sarah, having brought about this situation, now blames Abraham, but he continues his passive role. Hagar is now his wife, but he does not defend her but hands her over to Sarah, who afflicts her (16:6). As Trible points out, the word used is the same word that later describes how the Egyptians afflict the Israelites. Hagar makes her escape, not as later Israel would do, under direction from God, but on her own initiative (16:6).

The angel or messenger of the Lord meets Hagar, and now for the first time she is addressed by name (16:8). Although she is reassured by the angel, her trials are not over; she must return to Sarah and submit to whatever unjust treatment her mistress metes out (16:9). There is a difference though, because Hagar now has hope for the future. She shall have a son, and he will not be a slave like her but will be free like a wild ass (16:10-12).

---

1. Trible, *Texts of Terror*, 10.

When the child is born, he is called Ishmael, which means "God hears." In this case, it is Hagar whom he has heard; and contrary to Sarah's plan, the child is never known as hers: he is Abraham and Hagar's son (16:15). The eventual birth of Isaac leads to the expulsion of Hagar and her son with a particularly stingy farewell present from Abraham of bread and water (21:10-14). The story shows the dangers that arise when a person is regarded as dispensable and a life is treated as less than human because she is a slave girl. From a feminist perspective, the story demonstrates the dangers of a society that honors one gender more than another or that devalues certain people because of their ethnic identity.

Trible reads the story of Hagar in the light of contemporary issues and argues that it "depicts oppression in three familiar forms: nationality, class, and sex."[2] Hagar is "the innocent victim of use, abuse, and rejection."[3] Her obedience to God's messenger, who told her to return to her oppressive mistress, would have taken great courage. Trible believes that Hagar's story, if properly understood, can be an encouragement to oppressed people today:

> As a symbol of the oppressed, Hagar becomes many things to many people. Most especially, all sorts of rejected women find their stories in her. She is the faithful maid exploited, the black woman used by the male and abused by the female of the ruling class, the surrogate mother, the resident alien without legal recourse, the other woman, the runaway youth, the religious fleeing from affliction, the pregnant young woman alone, the expelled wife, the divorced mother with child, the shopping bag lady carrying bread and water, the homeless woman, the indigent relying upon handouts from the power structures, the welfare mother, and the self-effacing female whose own identity shrinks in service to others.[4]

Hagar's story is told with great pathos and sympathy by the narrator of Genesis. She was the victim of a patriarchal and nationalistic society that treated her dismally. However, in Genesis she is the first woman who is visited by the angel of the Lord, and the annunciation of the future birth of her child puts her in the company of several well-known mothers in the Bible, including Elizabeth and Mary.

2. Trible, *Texts of Terror*, 27.
3. Trible, *Texts of Terror*, 28.
4. Trible, *Texts of Terror*, 28.

The Sacrifice of Isaac from a Feminine Perspective

A story that is often highlighted as ignoring the rights of a mother is the episode on Mount Moriah. The main complaint is that the story is written from a male perspective and no feminine voice is heard. When God calls Abraham to sacrifice Isaac, Sarah is not even consulted, though, as Clare Amos asserts, "her voice surely deserves to be heard."[1] The story assumes that the child belongs to Abraham, but as Delaney argues,

> If God is omniscient, as most theologians and lay persons believe, then he would know that the child belonged to *both* parents. Could he or would he have asked only one of them?[2]

So although the story of Abraham's obedience is highly acclaimed in Jewish, Christian, and Muslim traditions, it is found wanting from a feminine perspective. Delaney argues that the story does not deserve to be presented as a model of faith:

> Why should the model of faith not be a person who passionately protects a child, rather than sacrificing or being willing to sacrifice it? What kind of religious/ethical system might develop from that? Why should love of God be in conflict with love of one's child? And why should love of God be demonstrated by suppressing compassion rather than through compassion?[3]

This story of the near sacrifice of Isaac has been regarded as a great example of faith, but it also raises moral and ethical issues, not only for feminists but for everyone who, like Brueggemann, experiences "the aversion immediately felt for a God who will command the murder of a son."[4] Nevertheless, the story is framed in the context of God's sovereignty; and in spite of the tension in the story, the reader is never in any doubt about the outcome. Although this does not remove all the difficulties, it does highlight the importance of the reader, who throughout the story is reassured that, even though God asks his people to endure the most severe tests, he has an ultimate purpose. Perhaps the story would be particularly relevant for those in exile who had seen sons and daughters sacrificed to the swords of Nebuchadnezzar's brutal regime. For readers in such a situation, the message that God cared and that they were

---

1. Amos, *The Book of Genesis,* 154.
2. Delaney, "Abraham and the Seeds of Patriarchy," 137.
3. Delaney, "Abraham and the Seeds of Patriarchy," 145.
4. Brueggemann, *Genesis,* 185.

heirs of Abraham's faith may have been more crucial at that particular time than issues about the role of women in society.

Sympathetic Treatment of Women in Genesis

In spite of the difficulties mentioned above, the narrator is evidently concerned about the treatment of women. The account draws sympathetic attention to the mistreatment of Hagar. Abraham and Sarah use her and then dismiss her, but the narrator seems sensitive to her plight. She may be merely a piece of property to Sarah, but she is a person with a future to God. Actually, Hagar receives more personal attention from God than Sarah receives. Sarah receives God's word through Abraham, but Hagar is addressed directly. (This is not because Sarah is married, since Rebekah, Isaac's wife, is privy to direct divine revelation.) Laban's daughters are also dealt with sympathetically in Genesis, and their innermost feelings are treated as important. God helps the unloved Leah, and both she and her sister are given the opportunity in the text to express their feelings about how their father has treated them.

Genesis does not ignore the difficulties that women face in a patriarchal society. Almost all the main female characters of the book face difficult situations that highlight their resourcefulness and resilience. While the text does not always condone their actions, the women of Genesis stand head and shoulders above the men in their ability to turn difficult situations to their advantage. Lot is prepared to treat his daughters like pawns, but in the end it is they who manipulate him and he becomes the pawn in their game plan. Rebekah shows how resourceful she could be by making her husband such a meal from domestic animals that he is deceived and thinks he is eating wild animals shot by his son. Rachel, having stolen her father's household gods, cleverly conceals them. Tamar, slighted by Judah, brings his secret treachery into the open by her dubious but clever scheme.

Genesis shows that women living in a patriarchal society face many challenges. Their lives seem to be a constant struggle for recognition. However, Genesis does not portray women as weak and defeated, but shows that, given the opportunity, they are not at all inferior and often outwit the men.

Concluding Thoughts on Feminist Interpretations

The diversity of feminist approaches and the extreme interpretations at which some of them arrive have given people the excuse to ignore them. However, there is a problem, particularly in evangelical circles, about the way that women are regarded in popular thinking. I am referring to the kind of problem highlighted by the confession of the missionary Gladys Aylward, who believed that, although she had been very successful as a missionary, she was not God's first choice.[1] This judgment was based on the belief that God would have chosen a man if one had been available. Although the various interpretations of Genesis may be confusing, the church needs to reaffirm that male and female are equal in God's sight. Aylward's sense of inferiority came from mistaken interpretations of the Bible and not from the Bible itself. The very idea that God would use a woman only as second choice is an indictment of the church's failure to separate cultural male dominance from the Bible's message that male and female are equal in God's sight. In spite of arguments to the contrary mentioned above, Genesis teaches that male and female are made in the image of God and given dominion together over the created order.

GENESIS AND BIBLICAL THEOLOGY

GENESIS IN CANONICAL CONTEXT

Whatever its context when it was originally written, Genesis now comes to us as part of the Pentateuch. These five books comprising Genesis to Deuteronomy have been associated together as Pentateuch or Torah from earliest times in Jewish and Christian canons. As the first of these five books, Genesis lays the foundation for the themes, theological teaching, and historical references that are developed in the remainder of the Pentateuch. Genesis also comes to us as the first book in the Hebrew Bible, and its main themes and characters are frequently mentioned in the other books of the Hebrew canon. Indeed, the promises and plans introduced in the Pentateuch do not reach their denouement until the book of Joshua. Furthermore, the themes and people encountered in Genesis are referred to frequently in the NT, and a theological study of Genesis in a Christian context is incomplete without a study of this wider context.

Genesis is just the first volume of Israel's story, and it anticipates the books that follow it. Its Greek title is an excellent description of its contents because it is about "Beginnings." Genesis is about the promises made to the patriarchs, embraced mainly in the themes of blessing, progeny, and land. Remark-

---

1. Thompson, *A Transparent Woman*, 182-83.

ably few of the promises made in Genesis are actually fulfilled in the book itself. In terms of progeny, the special line of seed with its promised nationhood is not even perceivable as a microcosm. In terms of blessing, progress has also been slow, since evidence of fertility and success is scarce, epitomized by the portrayal of Abraham's descendants scrounging for food in Egypt. The promised multitude of descendants, which would also be a sign of blessing, has reached only 70 people. Abraham had also been promised that he would possess land, but with his descendants in Egypt the only occupants of the land of Canaan descended from Abraham are those who lie dead in the cave of Machpelah.

Links between Genesis and Exodus

The book of Exodus provides continuity with Genesis and further develops the story. Detailed genealogical information ensures that the people whom Moses leads out of Egypt can trace their ancestry back to the patriarchs introduced in Genesis. Thus Exodus opens with a list of Jacob's 12 sons and notes how their numbers multiply in Egypt. This population explosion, which is so great that the Egyptians are alarmed, is evidence of blessing. The Israelites exemplify the creation blessing with its mandate to "multiply and fill the earth."

Continuity is also provided through the concepts of covenant and promise. In a key verse that is reminiscent of the turning point in the flood story when God remembered Noah, we now read that "God remembered his covenant" (Exod 2:24). Abraham's descendants in Egypt may appear like hapless slaves, but in this case appearances are deceptive: they are God's covenant people and deliverance is imminent.

Moses' encounter with God at the burning bush renews the promises made to Abraham and makes them relevant to the new generation. The person who addresses Moses at the burning bush is described as the "angel of the Lord." In this context, the angel of the Lord represents an appearance of God himself. He identifies himself as "the God of your father, the God of Abraham, the God of Isaac, and the God of Jacob" (Exod 3:6). Referring to the descendants of the patriarchs as "my people," God promises them a "land flowing with milk and honey" (Exod 3:8).

Thus, in the first three chapters of Exodus the themes of progeny, blessing, and land are introduced in a way that is reminiscent of Genesis; but they are also developed appropriately in preparation for the exodus. Also, these themes are set in the context of the continuation of the covenant relationship that began with the patriarchs.

Enns suggests that it is not just these main themes that link Genesis and

Exodus. He writes about the "explicit and repeated connection the author of Exodus makes between Exodus and Genesis."[1] Enns shows how the early chapters of Exodus abound with vocabulary and stories that reflect on the early chapters of Genesis. He mentions that the word used for "ark" in the Genesis flood story is not used elsewhere in the Bible except for the reference to baby Moses in the ark of bulrushes. He argues that the story of Noah and the story of Moses are linked theologically.

> Both Noah and Moses are specifically selected to escape a tragic, watery fate. Both are set on an 'ark' treated with bitumen and are carried to safety on the very water that brings destruction to others. Both Noah and Moses, in other words, are re-creation figures. They serve as the vehicles through whom God 'creates' a new people for his own purposes.[2]

The creation theme, according to Enns, clarifies the entire exodus story. He argues that Pharaoh should be understood as a force that is hostile, not just to the Israelites, but to God himself. God's creation mandate is for humans to multiply, but Pharaoh attempts to destroy Israelite children and to prevent them from multiplying. Thus Pharaoh represents an obstacle to God's creation purpose. Enns describes Pharaoh as "the false god Pharaoh who wishes to keep Yahweh's people under his own power."[3]

Enns also identifies creation language in the narratives of the plagues and the parting of the Red Sea. He describes the plagues as "an undoing of creation, a series of creation reversals, at Egypt's expense."[4] Whether the first readers would have identified the exodus as a reversal of creation we cannot be sure, but a number of features in the exodus story seem to be the opposite of what happened at creation. The most significant of these features is the darkness occurring during daylight hours. However, Enns identifies other reversals: "beasts harm rather than serve humanity . . . waters become a source of death rather than life; the climax of Genesis 1 is the creation of humans on the last day of creation, whereas the climax of the plagues is the destruction of humans in the last plague."[5]

If the plagues are a reversal of creation, then the parting of the Red Sea may be understood as an act of re-creation, because in both creation and the Red Sea incident the waters are controlled by God to allow dry land to appear.

1. Enns, "Exodus (Book)," 146.
2. Enns, "Exodus (Book)," 147.
3. Enns, "Exodus (Book)," 147.
4. Enns, "Exodus (Book)," 148.
5. Enns, "Exodus (Book)," 148.

According to Enns, "Yahweh has once again tamed the waters of chaos, this time for the purpose of creating a new people for himself."[6]

Thus the idea of continuation between Genesis and Exodus is not just provided by genealogical information and by the story line but also by the recurrence of creation and flood motifs in the exodus event itself. Although the strongest links are between Genesis and Exodus, the most significant themes in Genesis are also found in the remainder of the Pentateuch. In particular, we shall look at the continuity provided through the themes of blessing and land.

The Theme of Blessing in the Pentateuch

In Genesis the first blessings are pronounced in the garden of Eden, when relationships between God and human beings are completely harmonious. When Abraham obeys God, he enters a harmonious relationship that culminates in covenant, establishing a close link between covenant and blessing. At Sinai the descendants of Abraham become God's covenant people and receive his law. Continued blessing depends upon Israel living within the stipulations of this law.

While the covenant is initiated in Genesis and Exodus, it is in the book of Deuteronomy that the concept is explicated and its implications revealed. According to Deuteronomy, God relates to Israel through a covenant of love which is completely unmerited by the nation (Deut 7:7-8). To continue to enjoy the blessings of this deep relationship, they must live in obedience to the covenant stipulations (Deut 7:11-15; 11:8-15; 28:1-14). Disobedience, however, causes the covenant relationship to break up, and the blessings are replaced by curses (Deut 28:15-68). The importance of the concept of blessing and cursing is highlighted in the symbolism of the two mountains; Mount Ebal symbolizes the curses and Mount Gerizim, the blessings (Deut 11:26-32; 27:1-10). This area is probably chosen because of its traditional connection with the life of Abraham (Gen 12:6-7). The ceremony on the mountains demonstrates the imperative incumbent on the heirs of the covenant to emulate Abraham's obedience and, like him, to live in a close relationship with each other and with God (Deut 27:9-10; cf. Gen 12:1-3). Six tribes stand on each mountain, and the Levites pronounce 12 curses. The theme that runs through these curses is "relationships" (contra Craigie, who tentatively suggests "secrecy"[1]). The curses are directed against those who break their relationships

---

6. Enns, "Exodus (Book)," 148.
1. Craigie, *The Book of Deuteronomy,* 331.

with others: with God through worshipping idols (Deut 27:15), with their parents by dishonoring them (Deut 27:16), with their neighbors by encroaching on their land (Deut 27:17), with the vulnerable in society by deceiving a blind man and leading him astray or by denying justice to the foreigner, the orphan, or the widow (Deut 27:18-19), with others in society through sexual impropriety or murder (Deut 27:20-25). Thus any act that disrupts relationships is incompatible with divine blessing and must attract cursing.

Deuteronomy emphasizes that one of the implications of alienation from God would be a loss of national independence and subjugation by their enemies (Deut 28:36-37, 43). This is symbolized by an animal analogy: Israel would become the tail and not the head in their relationships with others (Deut 28:44). If, however, Israel maintains her relationship with God, she would be blessed with national independence and a relationship with others analogous to being the "head and not the tail" (Deut 28:7, 13).

The book of Numbers shows how Israel may live in harmony with God and enjoy his blessing. One way that this is mediated to them is through the priestly blessing (Num 6:22-27). This highly evocative passage relates to blessing, not in terms of particular benefits such as fertility or prosperity, but to a continuing harmonious relationship with the Lord in which he protects them (Num 6:24), is gracious to them (Num 6:25), endows them with his presence and favor, and grants them peace (Num 6:26). By pronouncing this blessing, the priests place the Lord's name upon the Israelites with the assurance of continued divine blessing (Num 6:27).

Numbers also highlights the significance of blessing and cursing in international relations. Before Israel's entrance into Canaan the king of Moab, in an attempt to subdue Israel, summons a prophet to curse them (Num 22:5-6). Yahweh, because of his covenant relationship with Israel, thwarts all attempts to curse them and turns the cursing into blessing (Num 24:10). This reflects the promise to Abraham: "I will bless those who bless you, and whoever curses you I will curse" (Gen 12:3 NIV).

The Theme of Land in the Pentateuch

The continuity between the promise of land to the patriarchs and the exodus from Egypt is often emphasized (Exod 3:8; 6:4, 8; 12:24-25; Deut 1:8, 21; 31:7, 21). The narrative describes the differences between the new land and the land of Egypt. Egypt is a land that is irrigated "by foot" (perhaps a reference to the way that water channels were regulated using mini mud dams built up or demolished by the feet of the farmer). However, the land of Canaan is a "land of hills and valleys, watered by rain from the sky, a land that the LORD your God looks after" (Deut 11:10-12). This contrast highlights Israel's need to rely on God, whether in the wilderness or in the promised land.

One of the main crises that threatens possession of the land is the Israelites' refusal to enter Canaan following the report of the spies. Returning to their camp with a huge cluster of grapes, the spies dramatically confirm that the depiction "flowing with milk and honey" aptly describes the land of Canaan (Num 13:27), but they also argue that it will be impossible for Israel to conquer the country (Num 13:28-33). They fail to give sufficient credence to the truth that this land is being given to them by God and instead they focus on their inability to conquer the country. Further ingratitude towards God is evidenced in the rebellion of Korah, Dathan, and Abiram. Ironically, they accuse Moses of bringing them "up out of a land flowing with milk and honey" into a wilderness (Num 16:13). Their punishment is apt: the earth/land swallows them (Num 16:31-33). Thus, the rebellion of Adam is punished by lack of fertility, that of Cain by banishment, and that of Dathan and company by swallowing. These incidents show the significant role that land plays in divine punishment.

Condemned to wander in the wilderness, the Israelites are dependent on the providential supplies of water and food. The wilderness cannot provide for them, and it serves as a foil for the fertile land. Just as the shortcomings of characters such as Cain and Lot highlight the roles played by Abel and Abraham respectively, the inadequacy of the wilderness enhances the attractiveness and desirability of the promised land. The wilderness is a negative and hostile place (Num. 20:4-5). It stands in sharp contrast to the fertile garden of Eden and to the promised land of Canaan. The promised land is characterized by its fertility. It is a "good land" (Deut 1:25) that is endowed with flourishing cities, houses, wells, vineyards, and olive groves (Deut 6:10-11). It is a land "where you may eat bread without scarcity, where you will lack nothing, a land whose stones are iron and from whose hills you may mine copper" (Deut 8:9-10 NRSV).

Israel's occupation of Canaan is portrayed as a divine gift to an unworthy people. They are the beneficiaries of the promises to Abraham and are granted the land because of God's relationship with the patriarchs. However, although Israel receives the land as a gift, paradoxically the land must be occupied and retained through obedience and conquest. These apparently contradictory aspects of Israel's occupation of Canaan are presented as two complementary aspects of Israel's relationship with God. Through the covenant relationship the gift of land is realized, but obedience and conquest are required for its acquisition and maintenance. Furthermore, Israel must maintain a good relationship with God without which the gift of land will be withheld or withdrawn.

The occupation of the land of Canaan is associated with "rest" (Exod 33:14; Deut 3:20; 12:9-10; 25:19; 28:65). From the time when God cursed the ground and expelled the human beings from Eden, they longed for rest (Gen 5:29). Egypt and Israel's sojourn there epitomized hard labor, and the wilderness was a place of restless wandering. The acquisition of the promised land, while not explicitly described as a return to Edenic bliss, would give Israel the "rest" and security that had been endemic to paradise. This rest is not just understood in the negative sense of no longer needing to wander but also denotes security and safety from one's enemies (Deut 25:19). In the NT this concept is developed and associated with a Sabbath rest (Heb 4:9).

Regulations concerning Land

In preparation for taking possession of the promised land the Israelites are warned that the behavior of its inhabitants will affect the land. The Israelites must treat the land with respect and not defile it with vile practices as the previous inhabitants had done (Lev 18:25). In their pursuit of good harvests the Canaanites had practiced promiscuous fertility rites. This brought the inhabitants into confrontation with God, and it also alienated them from their land. The land is portrayed as having been nauseated by its inhabitants, and, like a person who has eaten something disagreeable, it vomits them out (Lev 18:28).

The gift of the land to Israel is explained in terms calculated to engender a sense of respect and humility: it is not because Israel is righteous that they receive the good land, but because the previous inhabitants were wicked and because of God's close relationship with the patriarchs (Deut 9:4-6). To remain in the land and to enjoy longevity the Israelites must subject themselves to God's will as their forefathers had done (Deut 4:40; 5:33; 11:2; 32:47).

The tripartite relationship between God, humans, and land in the garden of Eden portrays the ideal for which Israel must aim. In Eden God's presence is openly manifest and there is communion with him. There are laws to be kept concerning the land, and the human beings have certain responsibilities in relation to caring for it and exercising control over it (Gen 2:15-17). Failure to obey God leads to expulsion from Eden, and failure to obey will also lead to the expulsion of Israel from Canaan. The land is a place of harmony and rest for Israel, but expulsion from the land will lead to "no repose, no resting place for the sole of your foot," "an anxious mind, eyes weary with longing, and a despairing heart" (Deut 28:65 NIV). Therefore, obedience is essential for continued possession of the land.

It is against this background that the laws and regulations are given in the Pentateuch. It is recognized that human beings will receive the best benefits from land while they are living in harmony with God. Israel is not simply chosen in order to receive a special promise of land, but it is chosen to have a special relationship with God within the secure boundaries of Canaan. Relationships with land and God are, therefore, interdependent. The promised land reflects the ideal conditions in Eden and replicates significant aspects of the primeval paradise. Like Eden, the promised land is a place of fertility where God's laws are respected and his presence is manifest. The erection of the tabernacle and the giving of the ceremonial laws which are so prominent in the Pentateuch are an essential part of the preparation for living in the promised land, since harmony with God is the paramount requirement for those desiring fertility from the ground. However, although Israel's settlement in Canaan is presented as reminiscent of Eden, it is not presented as equal with Eden. Canaan does not fully replicate the uninhibited communion with God or the harmony and fertility that are endemic in the primeval garden.

The laws regarding the Sabbatical Year that are given in the wilderness (Lev 25:1-55) would seem harsh if they were given to people already reaping the benefits of agricultural land. In the wilderness setting, however, the emphasis is not on how much God is taking from them, since they have no agricultural land, but on how much he is giving them. God is giving them fertile land for six years. In the seventh year they must leave it fallow. This recognizes that they have responsibility to treat the land well: the sabbath laws for human beings recognize their rights to rest, and now Israel must recognize that the land has the right to a sabbath rest, albeit not every seventh day but every seventh year. Furthermore, it reminds them that the land ultimately belongs to Yahweh.

When they are blessed with fertile land they are to avoid greediness and dishonesty. Their generosity should be apparent in the way they harvest their crops. They are commanded to leave some of their crops in the fields so that food would be available to the poor and needy who have no land of their own (Lev 19:9-10; cf. Ruth 2). Furthermore, when buying or selling, their weights and measures should be fair and accurate (Lev 19:35-36). They should always remember that the Lord who makes these stipulations is the one who brought them out of their poverty and slavery in Egypt (Lev 19:36). They should acknowledge the Lord's sovereign right to the land by the symbolic act of a priest presenting a sheaf of the first grain harvested (Lev 23:9-10).

The law also makes provision for the redemption of land so that if a person is forced to sell his land, it can be bought back (redeemed) for the family by one of his relatives (Lev 25:24). In cases where land is not redeemed, it is safeguarded by the prohibition of permanent land sales. The maximum lease is 49 years, since every 50th year the land is to return to its original owner. The Levites are not permitted an allocation of land (Deut 10:9). A consequence of this ruling is that they need suitable housing and pasture for their animals (Num 35:1-5). This is not regarded as a land grant but as the minimum provision for the flocks and herds. The laws about the Jubilee Year there contain special provisions to protect the rights of the Levites (Lev 25:32-34).

Since land and justice are clearly related, there are laws about bloodshed. In the event of accidental death, the perpetrator can escape the vengeance of the family of the deceased by taking refuge in certain cities nominated for this purpose (cf. Num 35:6-29). However, unpunished murder defiles and pollutes the land and requires atonement, which could only be provided by the blood of the murderer (Num 35:30-34). As Frymer-Kensky observes,

> The most serious contaminant of the land is the blood of those who have been murdered. . . . Because of the seriousness of the crime of murder, and perhaps also because of the mystical conception of blood in Israelite thought, the blood of the slain physically pollutes the land.[1]

Failure to obey God's laws within the covenant obligations and failure to treat the land properly will be severely punished: their rain will turn to dust and powder, they will be scattered over the earth, while their land will be burned out by sulphur and salt (Deut 28:24, 64; 29:19).

Thus the theme of land as introduced in the book of Genesis is greatly developed in the remainder of the Pentateuch. The main links between the developed teaching and the introduction to land in Genesis are the role of Eden as a paradigm and the promise of land to Abraham.

Problems Involved in Relating Genesis to the Rest of the Pentateuch

In spite of the thematic continuity linking Genesis with the other books of the Pentateuch, there is a problem relating to the character of God. Was the God of the patriarchs the same God as the God of the Exodus? Certainly the

---

1. Frymer-Kensky, "Atrahasis," 154.

names of God in the Pentateuch include the name "Yahweh," but other names are used such as the "Fear of Isaac" (Gen 31:53). Moreover, household images seem to have been valued in patriarchal society but are condemned in the Pentateuch, and even the hero Joseph owns a "divining cup," even though divining is later condemned (Deut 18:10-11).

In spite of these different names, the evidence suggests that the patriarchs worshipped the same God as later Israel. Like later Israel, the patriarchs built altars and offered sacrifices. Although the locations of their altars varied, they were always built inside Canaan. Some of these locations, such as Bethel, became traditional sites for the worship of Yahweh. However, Yahweh was not limited by location or nationality; he could act just as effectively in Egypt and Aram as in Canaan, and he could appear to a Philistine ruler (Gen 20:6) or an Aramean trickster (31:24).

Another traditional feature of Israelite faith already observed in patriarchal worship is the absence of images of Yahweh. Images of gods other than Yahweh are mentioned, and they seem to have been greatly valued. Thus when Laban pursues Jacob, one of his main complaints is that his household gods have been stolen. Laban's search for his gods highlights the pathetic nature of these deities who cannot defend their own images. What self-respecting deity would allow his images to be stolen and then sat upon by a woman while the worshipper seeks for them in vain? This story of powerless images is fully compatible with the views of Israel's prophets (cf. Jer 10:3-6; Isa 44:9-20). In contrast to Laban's stolen images, Yahweh is active in the story, protecting Jacob from his father-in-law (Gen 31:24). Images are mentioned again in Genesis in the account of Jacob's return to Bethel, but they seem to be a hindrance to the worship of Yahweh and so Jacob buries them under a tree.

> So Jacob said to his household and to all who were with him, "Put away the foreign gods that are among you and purify yourselves and change your garments. Then let us arise and go up to Bethel, so that I may make there an altar to the God who answers me in the day of my distress and has been with me wherever I have gone." So they gave to Jacob all the foreign gods that they had, and the rings that were in their ears. Jacob hid them under the terebinth tree that was near Shechem. (35:2-4 ESV)

Thus the exclusive demand of Yahweh that "You shall have no other gods before me" is an important feature of patriarchal worship.

Covenants and the practice of circumcision that would be important in Israel's cultus are also already evident in patriarchal religion. Some aspects of worship in Genesis provide the foundation for a close personal relationship with God such as that evident in the books of Jeremiah and Ezekiel. This is seen in the personal appearances of God, not only to patriarchs but also to the slave girl Hagar. Also, as in later Israel, personal tithes were made and vows taken.

The Name Yahweh

Although the name Yahweh is used throughout Genesis, it may be inferred from Exodus 6 that this name was revealed for the very first time to Moses.

> God spoke to Moses and said to him, "I am Yahweh. 3 To Abraham, Isaac and Jacob I appeared as El Shaddai, but I did not make my name Yahweh known to them." (Exod 6:2-3 NJB)

Exodus 6 is very important, but it is a difficult passage to interpret. At face value it appears that God is revealing a new name to Moses — a name that was not known to the patriarchs. However, the problem is that the name Yahweh is mentioned in the patriarchal narratives — indeed, it is even found in the Adam and Eve stories. Some of the possible interpretations are as follows:

a. Some find the solution in terms of the Documentary Hypothesis. Sources E and P teach that the patriarchs did not know the name Yahweh, and they do not use that name until after Exodus 6. Source J, however, uses the name Yahweh from the very beginning, even introducing it into the creation story (Gen 2:4ff.).

b. Some reject the literal meaning of Exodus 6 and argue that the name Yahweh was known to the patriarchs. It was not a new name which was revealed to Moses, but rather a new significance for a well-known name. Thus Motyer translates Exod 6:3 as follows: "And I showed myself to Abraham, to Isaac and to Jacob in the character of El Shaddai, but in the character expressed by my name Yahweh I did not make myself known to them."[1]

c. The use of the name Yahweh in the patriarchal narratives may be regarded as proleptic. The patriarchs themselves did not use the name Yahweh. However, later editors, realizing that the God whom the patriarchs worshipped was the God who was known in their day as Yahweh, put that name in their mouths. In support of c) it is worth noting that no personal names are found in the pre-Mosaic period compounded with Yahweh or with the abbreviated form Yah.

---

1. Motyer, *The Revelation of the Divine Name*, 12.

Genesis in the Historical Books

Genesis in Joshua

In Genesis the theme of rest is introduced in the first creation account when God rests on the seventh day. One of the consequences of sin is the loss of rest. Satisfying work in the garden of Eden is replaced with hard labor, so that Lamech names Noah with the hope that he would bring rest. This concept of rest reappears in Joshua 1, where the land that they enter and claim is described as a place of rest. Later in the book this is repeated with the note of satisfaction that the Lord has given them rest in fulfillment of the promises made to their ancestors. Not one of the Lord's promises has failed (Josh 21:43-45).

In Joshua, God's role is very similar to the one he plays in Genesis. He is the landowner who gives land to his people, and he is the Creator who is personally involved in causing the river to dry up and even causing the sun apparently to stand still (Josh 10:12-14).

Of course, the theme of descendants and land are unmistakable in Joshua. The land is allotted to the tribes named after the sons of Jacob, with the Joseph tribes split into two groups, Ephraim and Manasseh, as previously explained in Genesis. The order of birth of Joseph's sons was Manasseh and Ephraim, but the order was reversed by Jacob and this reversal is continued in Joshua (Joshua 16–17).

The word used to explain that Israel subdued the land is שָׁבַ֫שׁ/kābaš, the same word used by God in his creation ordinance (Gen 1:28). Among those subdued are the Anakim, who first appear in Genesis (Josh 11:21). However, identification of the Anakim in Joshua with the group in Genesis is problematic, since those mentioned in Genesis live before the flood which presumably destroyed them.

In Joshua's farewell speech, he traces these promises back to Abraham, whom God had called away from his homeland where he and his family worshipped other gods. At the end of his life, Joshua repeats a speech from Yahweh to Israel that mentions Isaac's two sons, Jacob and Esau. In Yahweh's role as land executive he declares that he gave Esau the hill country of Seir to possess, but to the sons of Jacob he gave the land of Canaan (Josh 24:8, 11).

Another episode from Genesis brings the book of Joshua to a close. Joseph's bones are buried at Shechem, fulfilling the oath that he made his relatives swear (Gen 50:25; Josh 24:32).

Genesis in Judges

When comparing Judges with the preceding books, it is the differences that are most obvious because the focus is on the struggle for territory by the individual tribes.

The concept of rest in the land gets a slightly different nuance in the book of Judges; indeed, an atmosphere of restlessness pervades the book. When Israel sins, Yahweh hands them over to their enemies, who pillage the land. When they repent and the enemies are defeated, the land has rest again (Judg 5:31).

Like Genesis, Judges offers an interpretation of history that sees Yahweh's involvement in every detail. He appears to individuals such as Gideon. Only Yahweh is powerful, and gods such as Baal cannot harm anyone. Just as Rachel dishonored Laban's gods and proved them powerless by sitting on them, Gideon destroys the image of Baal. The god cannot harm him, but Gideon is rightly concerned about the worshippers of the image (Judg 6:27-31).

Baal cannot harm Gideon, and with God's help he defeats the enemy with just 300 men (Judges 7). This story of a small army overcoming a huge one is reminiscent of the story of Abraham's rescue of Lot with his army of 318 men (Gen 14:13-24).

Depravity reaches its lowest level in the book with the story of the rape and murder of the Levite's concubine (Judges 19). The sordid tale awakens in the reader a sense of déjà vu, since the treatment of the Levite mirrors the treatment of Lot's angelic visitors by the men of Sodom (Gen 19:1-11). Having descended from Jacob's youngest son, one of his favorites, the Benjamites have stooped very low indeed, and Jacob's metaphor of the wolf applied to Benjamin (Gen 49:27) now seems grossly unfair to wolves.

Judges is a disturbing book, showing how far from the ideal rest and Edenic bliss Israel had become. It is a story of broken relationships between Israel and God, and in a negative sense shows what happens when the people forget the promises that God made with Abraham.

Genesis in Ruth

Abraham's first experience of Canaan was not to marvel at the abundance of milk and honey but to forsake the land and go to Egypt because of a severe famine. History repeats itself in the book of Ruth as Elimelech, Naomi, and their two children depart Canaan for Moab to escape famine.

No blame attaches to the couple for their decision; leaving the land was common practice in such circumstances. Both Abraham and Jacob had left

Canaan and had gone to Egypt during famines. However, Elimelech is never able to return to Canaan since he and both his sons die in Moab. Naomi returns to Canaan accompanied by her daughter-in-law, Ruth.

The most significant link between the themes of Genesis and Ruth concerns offspring. In Genesis the family tree of God's chosen line of offspring contains considerable surprises. For example, Perez, the offspring of Judah and his daughter-in-law Tamar, is the ancestor of King David (Gen 38:27; Ruth 4:18). The book of Ruth springs a similar surprise, since Ruth's marriage to Boaz and the birth of their baby Obed make the Moabite Ruth the great-grandmother of David (Ruth 3:17).

Genesis in Samuel and Kings

A number of motifs found in Genesis surface again in Samuel and Kings. Samuel's birth to a barren mother is clearly reminiscent of the birth of Isaac (Genesis 18; 21:1-7; 1 Samuel 1). Continuity with Genesis is provided by the theme of a special line of seed that is fulfilled in God's choice of David as king and in the covenant made with him (2 Samuel 7). God's choice of David provides significant points of comparison with the divine choice of people in Genesis. David was not the firstborn, a disadvantage he shared with Abel, Isaac, Jacob, and Judah. Like Abel, the shepherd, David finds favor in God's sight even though, like Joseph, he experiences the hostility of his brothers. It is interesting to see how this rejection of the firstborn in favor of the younger is repeated later in Israel's history. However, Jehoiakim, the firstborn son of Josiah, whom the Egyptian King Neco II put on the throne to replace his younger grother Jehoahaz, is not one of Yahweh's favorites (2 Kgs 23:37; cf. Jer 22:15-17).

Genesis assumes kingship. The genealogy of Esau refers to "the kings who reigned in the land of Edom, before any king reigned over the Israelites" (36:31 NRSV), and in Jacob's blessing on Judah the reference to the scepter seems to point to the reign of David (49:10). Furthermore, the promises to Abraham include the idea that he and Sarah would have kings among their descendants (17:6).

Linkage between the covenant with David and the promises to Abraham are made through vocabulary, thematic equivalence, and the development of key theological concepts. God's call to Abraham promised him a great name. David and Abraham alone in the OT receive this promise (12:2; 2 Sam 7:9). Others had sought for it, from the builders of the tower of Babel onward through Absalom, but the divine promise of a great name is made only to Abraham and David.

Characterization of God in the Davidic covenant harmonizes with that of the God who is personally involved in creation and in the life and activities of his people. The use of the verb "to plant" (2 Sam 7:10) conveys God's involvement with Israel, just as Genesis portrays him planting a garden and walking in it during the cool part of the day (Gen 2:8; 3:8). Furthermore, David's offer to make a house for Yahweh leads to the reciprocal promise that Yahweh will make him a house (2 Sam 7:10); again a verb that normally denotes human craftsmanship is applied to Yahweh. God's promises to Abraham had involved a divine land grant, and now land features prominently in the promises to David, with the land described as Israel's "own place." David is promised rest from enemies, and this picks up two themes from Genesis: creation rest and protection from enemies (2 Sam 7:11).

The promise of offspring to Abraham specifically referred to seed that would come from his body (Gen 12:4). These promises of a continued relationship with the special line of descendants is not merely repeated in 2 Samuel (2 Sam 7:12). They are developed to include a new dimension of relationship; David's seed, offspring, will be adopted by Yahweh into a father-son relationship (2 Sam 7:14).

We saw that in Genesis the shadow of exile is never far away. Even with a land as perfect as Eden, the threat of exile must be taken seriously. Cain too faced exile, and it was a punishment that he considered too great to bear (Gen 4:12-14). King David himself experiences exile, and the story of his forced flight from Jerusalem echoes with themes from Genesis (2 Sam 15:13-31). David is secure within the fortified city, but like Adam and Eve, he partakes of that which is forbidden. As a result, like them he should face the death penalty, but instead he is forced to leave the security of his favorite city. His departure gives opportunity for his enemies to curse him (2 Sam 16:5-14). The security of Jerusalem represents blessing and peace, but the disobedience of David brings forced cursing and alienation.

The dangers of disobedience are also highlighted in the account of the struggle against Baalism during Ahab's reign. Elijah explains a lengthy drought as God's punishment for the national apostasy (1 Kgs 17:1-7). Elijah's God has the power to give or withhold rain, whereas Baal does not. This struggle reaches its climax with the challenge to Baal on Mount Carmel (1 Kings 18). Elijah, in his attempt to bring the nation back to its traditional faith, addresses God as the "God of Abraham, Isaac, and Israel" (1 Kgs 18:36). More than just a way of identifying God, this calls the people back to the covenant relationship that began with Abraham. The covenant is mentioned later in Kings to explain God's active involvement in protecting Israel against her enemies in spite of her disobedience (2 Kgs 13:22-23).

This theme of being cast from God's presence pervades the entire story of Samuel and Kings, and the main plot moves inexorably towards its tragic denouement of the nation of Israel losing the land promised to Abraham.

Genesis in Chronicles, Ezra, and Nehemiah

Chronicles, like Ezra and Nehemiah, was written in the postexilic era. It surveys Israel's history from the perspective of the disasters that had befallen the nation. How could the promises that God made to Abraham have any validity in the light of the Assyrian overthrow of the northern kingdom and the Babylonian exile of the people of Judah? It is these questions that Chronicles seeks to answer through the medium of a historical overview of the nation's history. As Selman points out, Chronicles approaches Israel's history in the context of God's purposes for the world:

> The Chronicler combines material from Genesis on the themes of creation and election. He shows how the line of Abraham and Jacob grew out of the nations created by God and continued through the twelve tribes to the post-exilic community (1 Chr. 1:1–9:34). Thus the Chronicler's readers could see a direct connection between God's work in their own day and God's original creation of the human race.[1]

Accordingly, 1 Chronicles begins with a genealogy that traces the Israelites back through David, Jacob, Isaac, and Abraham to Adam. Concern with the past is reflected in lengthy genealogical tables that comprise the first nine chapters of the book. Ancestors of Israel are linked with Canaan; to claim territory and extend borders within Canaan, as Jabez desires, is regarded as commendable and receives divine approval (1 Chr 4:10).

Chronicles clarifies the question of which of Jacob's sons receives the privileges of the birthright. Clearly as Genesis indicates, Reuben forfeited this position (49:4; cf. 35:22), but it is unclear in Genesis to whom Jacob passed the birthright, though Joseph and Judah both received preferential blessings. Chronicles clarifies this, indicating that the blessing belonging to the firstborn went to Joseph. However, it also indicates that Judah became prominent among the brothers and that a ruler descended from him (1 Chr 5:1-2).

Chronicles echoes the theme so clearly demonstrated in Genesis that faithfulness to God is rewarded by land, while worship of other gods is apos-

---

1. Selman, "Chronicles," 189.

tasy causing alienation from God and punishable by loss of land. It therefore presents a clear focus on the importance of remembering God's covenant. This is highlighted in David's prayer when the ark of God is transferred to Jerusalem.

> Remember his covenant forever, the word that he commanded, for a thousand generations, the covenant that he made with Abraham, his sworn promise to Isaac, which he confirmed as a statute to Jacob, as an everlasting covenant to Israel, saying, "To you I will give the land of Canaan, as your portion for an inheritance." (1 Chr 16:15-18 ESV)

Chronicles emphasizes that in times of war and trouble Israel's best leaders appealed to God on the basis of the covenant with Abraham. When war is imminent, King Jehoshaphat in his prayer asks,

> "Did you not, our God, drive out the inhabitants of this land before your people Israel, and give it forever to the descendants of Abraham your friend?" (2 Chr 20:7 ESV)

Jehoshaphat's appeal is successful, and he is reminded that "the battle is not yours but God's" (2 Chr 20:15). In the reign of Hezekiah, after the destruction of the northern kingdom, the remaining inhabitants are exhorted to "return to the LORD, the God of Abraham, Isaac, and Israel" (2 Chr 30:6). This appeal is made on the basis that the Assyrian success was permitted by God because Israel had the covenant.

The book of Nehemiah provides this same emphasis on the land being promised by covenant.

> "You are the LORD, the God who chose Abram and brought him out of Ur of the Chaldeans and gave him the name Abraham. 8 You found his heart faithful before you, and made with him the covenant to give to his offspring the land of the Canaanite, the Hittite, the Amorite, the Perizzite, the Jebusite, and the Girgashite. And you have kept your promise, for you are righteous." (Neh 9:7-8 ESV)

A major theme, then, running through Chronicles and Ezra-Nehemiah is that God has made a covenant to give the land of Canaan to Israel forever. To avail themselves of the benefits of the covenant promises, Israel must return to God and remain faithful to the covenant stipulations that prohibit idolatry and polytheism. The foundation on which this theology is built is the covenant with Abraham as related in the book of Genesis.

Genesis in Esther

No direct allusions to Genesis occur in the book of Esther. However, the story shares a common plot with the story of Joseph. Both Joseph and Esther are insignificant exiles who attain positions of influence in royal households. In both cases they have an opportunity to influence the future of the descendants of Abraham. The theme of both stories is that God is at work fulfilling his plans for his people, even though circumstances such as Joseph's imprisonment or Haman's edict would suggest otherwise.

Wisdom Literature

Although Wisdom literature shares the same interests as other parts of the Bible, it does not usually reflect on Israel's history and there is no emphasis on the sacrificial system, legal stipulations, or prophetic pronouncements. It is concerned mainly with how to cope with life and how to succeed. Not surprisingly, there are no allusions to the patriarchs.

However, creation is an important theme in Proverbs. The book emphasizes that the world was created through perfect wisdom and, therefore, is an ordered, intelligible world that can be understood only through wisdom.

> The LORD by wisdom founded the earth; by understanding he established the heavens. (Prov 3:19 NRSV)

The psalm to wisdom in Prov 8:22-31 is an outstanding creation poem that virtually personifies Wisdom as God's helper when he was creating the world.

Although creation is a major theme in the final section of Job, the book contains no clear allusions to Genesis. The author uses the theme of creation to put Job's questions about God and suffering in the context of the complexity of God's creation. There are some things that Job cannot understand because he is a creature and not the creator.

The description of creation in Job 38 is a wonderful poetic composition that highlights the grandeur and magnificence of the creation event. It compares God's awesome and spectacular power displayed in creation to Job's limited knowledge and understanding. The poem thus calls for a humble appreciation of the complexity and profundity of life in the light of the overwhelming power and majesty of the creator God.

The underlying theology of this poem is compatible with Genesis. In this cosmogony there is no trace of a battle between the Creator and the forces of disorder. There is no dualism and no hint of preexistent evil. In the Mesopotamian creation epic Marduk, after slaying Tiamat (the sea dragon), creates the primeval seas and places a bar and guard to keep back the waters. Here, in Job as in Genesis, it is Yahweh who controls the waters and sets boundaries for the waves (Job 38:8-11; Gen 1:6-8). The poem describes the mysteries of land and sky and contrasts these with Job, who is limited and finite (Job 38:16-38). Snow, hail and, lightning are all under God's control and are used by him as weapons in battle (Job 38:22-24). He also controls rain, dew, and ice (Job 38:25-30).

The creation poem in Job is written in a different style and is composed in a different context than the creation story of Genesis. Yet the accounts are complementary and together present a noncombatant view of God's creative activity that contrasts with the other cosmogonies of the ancient world.

Psalms

Creation is also a recurring theme in the book of Psalms. Most of the references are to the grandeur of creation and to the greatness of God's power and majesty displayed in the beauty of the earth and the heavens (e.g., Psalm 19). Psalm 33 has a more specific link with Genesis through the concept of creation by God's powerful word.

> By the word of the LORD the heavens were made, and by the breath of his mouth all their host. He gathers the waters of the sea as a heap; he puts the deeps in storehouses. Let all the earth fear the LORD; let all the inhabitants of the world stand in awe of him! For he spoke, and it came to be; he commanded, and it stood firm. (Ps 33:6-9 ESV)

In this psalm, God's credentials as Creator demonstrate his faithfulness and show that his word is upright; the earth is full of his steadfast love (Ps 33:4-5).

Psalm 147 also mentions creation by divine speech, but this psalm links God's creative word with his covenant relationship with Israel.

> He sends out his command to the earth; his word runs swiftly. He gives snow like wool; he scatters hoarfrost like ashes. He hurls down his crystals of ice like crumbs; who can stand before his cold? He sends out his word, and melts them; he makes his wind blow and the waters flow. He declares his word to Jacob, his statutes and rules to Israel. He has not dealt thus with any other nation; they do not know his rules. Praise the LORD! (Ps 147:15-20 ESV)

Thus in Psalm 147 the God of creation is also the God of the covenant, and the divine word that brought creation into being has communicated God's special covenant relationship to Israel.

Specific references to the covenant with Abraham (Genesis 15) occur in a number of psalms. In Psalm 47 God is "a great king over all the earth" but he is also the "God of Abraham" (Ps 47:2, 9). Israel's failure to keep the covenant is mentioned particularly in historical psalms. In Psalm 78 the message of Genesis is repeated that God always fulfills his promises but Israel has invoked his wrath by disobedience (Ps 78:51-59). Psalm 105 presents a similar message, that God has made an everlasting covenant with Abraham but Israel has forsaken him and brought disaster (Ps 105:9-11; cf. 1 Chr 16:15-18). Thus the theological message of Genesis was firmly established in Israel's worship tradition. God had never forgotten his promise with Abraham; it was an everlasting covenant, but Israel must return to God in faith and humility.

THEMATIC CONTINUITY IN THE PROPHETS

In the Prophets the theme of a special line of descendants is foundational. An underlying presupposition of the prophetic tradition is that those who trace their origins back to the patriarchs are God's chosen people. Thus Isaiah reassures the people that they are the "offspring of Abraham," the friend of God (Isa 41:8). This theme of Israel's special relationship with God is closely linked, as it was in the Abraham narrative, with a belief that God had given Israel the land of Canaan and that he would bless them there. This theme did not need much emphasis, since the people firmly believed it.

Before the exile, the Israelites believed that their land and temple were inviolable because of their covenant relationship with God. The prophets, however, criticize this popular view that God had given the land to Israel unconditionally. Jeremiah argues that Israel had defiled the land that God gave them (Jer 2:7), and he explains the conditions that Israel must fulfill for continued possession.

> For if you truly amend your ways and your deeds, if you truly execute justice one with another, if you do not oppress the sojourner, the fatherless, or the widow, or shed innocent blood in this place, and if you do not go after other gods to your own harm, then I will let you dwell in this place, in the land that I gave of old to your fathers forever. (Jer 7:5-7 ESV)

Ezekiel refers to Israelites who place their confidence in God's promises but disobey his word. He warns against reliance on their links with Abraham since their sin has annulled their relationship with God and made the promises ineffective.

> Son of man, the inhabitants of these waste places in the land of Israel keep saying, "Abraham was only one man, yet he got possession of the land; but we are many; the land is surely given us to possess." Therefore say to them, Thus says the Lord God: You eat flesh with the blood and lift up your eyes to your idols and shed blood; shall you then possess the land? (Ezek 33:24-25 ESV)

A major prophetic task was to explain why Israel lost the land that had been promised to the patriarchs. The prophets argue that the promises were genuine and that God had not failed his people. The promises, however, had been conditional and Israel's sufferings were self-inflicted (Jer 7:7, 14; 11:10; 32:23; Zech 8:14). Isaiah reminds the people about what they had lost:

> Oh that you had paid attention to my commandments! Then your peace would have been like a river, and your righteousness like the waves of the sea; your offspring would have been like the sand, and your descendants like its grains; their name would never be cut off or destroyed from before me. (Isa 48:18 ESV)

Another facet of the prophetic explanation about what had happened to Israel utilizes the concepts of blessing and cursing in much the same way that these concepts are employed in Genesis. The disobedience of Adam and Eve affected their relationship with the ground, and this resulted in the growth of thorns and thistles and lack of fertility (Gen 3:17-18). Jeremiah takes up a similar theme and argues that because of Israel's disobedience and "because of the curse the land mourns, and the pastures of the wilderness are dried up" (Jer 23:10). This association of blessing with fertility and cursing with barrenness is further explicated in the contrast that Jeremiah makes between a blessed person and a cursed person. The former is likened to a tree planted beside water. Even in times of drought this tree continues to bear fruit (Jer 17:8). In contrast, the person who does not trust in God and attracts cursing is likened to a desert shrub that is withered, dry, and fruitless (Jer 17:5-6).

Prophetic hope for the future promised unparalleled blessing, including the promise that Israel would be the third greatest nation after Assyria and Egypt, and they would be "a blessing in the midst of the earth" (Isa 19:24). The future blessing heralded by the prophets includes fertility of both field and womb (Isa 44:1-3; Ezek 34:25-27). In their sense of insignificance and weakness following national disaster, Israel are reminded to look back to Abraham and

Sarah, whose lack of offspring was incongruous with the promises of numerous offspring. Just as God fulfilled his promises to Abraham and Sarah, he would also bless Israel and multiply their numbers (Isa 51:1-2; cf. Zech 8:13-14).

Theme of Creation in Genesis and the Prophets

Another thematic link between Genesis and the Prophets is provided by their use of the creation theme. The prophets do not refer to this theme frequently, but it does play an important role in their understanding of who God is and in their teaching about his special relationship to Israel. They use God's activity as sole creator to show Israel the futility of worshipping other gods. While the gods of the nations were the products of human workmanship, Israel's God created all things (Isa 40:19-22).

The prophets also employ Yahweh's unique status as sole creator as a theme of reassurance to help the Israelites cope with their sense of inferiority as a nation compared to the powerful empires that surround them. Israel is reminded that the nations that terrify them are no more significant than a drop from a bucket or dust on scales in the light of Yahweh's creatorial power (Isa 40:15).

The creation theme underscores that Israel herself is God's creation. Employing creation terminology, the prophets show that, just as God created the universe and formed human beings, in the same way he created a special nation for himself (Isa 49:1-5).

Just as in the flood, when almost all life had been wiped out, Israel has suffered similar devastation. However, after the flood God established a covenant of peace, and through his blessing the earth was repopulated. Israel will likewise experience a renewed relationship with Yahweh (Isa 54:9-10).

The prophetic view is that if Israel is faithful to Yahweh, the future will be bright, analogous to a return to the idyllic conditions that prevailed in the garden of Eden:

> For the LORD comforts Zion; he comforts all her waste places and makes her wilderness like Eden, her desert like the garden of the LORD; joy and gladness will be found in her, thanksgiving and the voice of song. (Isa 51:3 ESV)

The prophets were convinced that the land of Canaan belonged to God, and he would restore it to his people when they repented (Joel 2:18). Genesis teaches that the Canaanites would be expelled because of their sinfulness

(Gen 15:16), and the prophets preach that the Israelites themselves had suffered the same fate. However, because Israel is the offspring of Abraham, God would restore them if they turned to him (Isa 41:8-10; Joel 2:12-13).

New Testament

Clear thematic continuity may be discerned between Genesis and the NT. The important themes of blessing and offspring are clearly woven into the message of the Gospels and Epistles, particularly through the recognition that Abraham is the father of those who believe. The theme of land is less prominent, and it is no longer the land of Canaan that is the main focus.

Abraham

The NT writers make frequent reference to Abraham, employing his name in two main ways. First, Abraham links the faith of the early church with the faith of ancient Israel. Second, the international aspects of the promises made to Abraham assure that the Gentile believers may legitimately be referred to as "Abraham's children."

Abraham: A Link with the Past

Connection between Jesus and the past was fundamental to the early church, and this is reflected in the NT. Matthew's concern to show Jesus as the continuance of the past is reflected in the first verse of the Gospel, which links Jesus to both Abraham and David: "An account of the genealogy of Jesus the Messiah, the son of David, the son of Abraham" (Matt 1:1 NRSV). Luke's Gospel traces the ancestry of Jesus back through Abraham to Adam (Luke 3:23-38). Luke also emphasizes the continuing efficacy of the promises made to Abraham. For example, in the passage that has become known as the "Magnificat," Mary thanks God for "the remembrance of his mercy," and she links this with the promise that God made to "Abraham and to his offspring forever" (Luke 1:55 ESV). Later in the same chapter Zechariah, the father of John the Baptist, refers to

> "the oath that he [God] swore to our father Abraham, to grant us that we, being delivered from the hand of our enemies, might serve him without fear, in holiness and righteousness before him all our days." (Luke 1:73-75 ESV)

371

Probably the strongest connection between Abraham and Jesus is enshrined in Jesus' statement that claims preeminence over Abraham: "Before Abraham was, I am" (John 8:58). This clear linkage between Abraham and Jesus continues in the preaching of the apostles and in the Epistles (Acts 3:13, 25; 13:26). The Epistle to the Hebrews also deals with the subject of Jesus' preeminence. The author recalls the account of Abraham paying tithes to Melchizedek and identifies Jesus as a "priest forever after the order of Melchizedek," thus establishing Jesus' superiority not only to Abraham but also to the Aaronic priesthood (Heb 6:19–7:28).

It was important for the early Christians to show that they were not establishing a new religion but that they were heralding a new era of blessing in which the promises made to Abraham would be fulfilled through Jesus Christ.

Abraham's Offspring Not Limited to Israelites

Although Paul deals with this theme in detail, it is also foreshadowed in the Gospels. Jesus refers to those who would come "from the east and the west" to "recline at table with Abraham, Isaac, and Jacob in the kingdom of heaven" (Matt 8:11 ESV; cf. Luke 13:29).

Since Paul seeks to show that Abraham was the father of all who believed, he bases his argument on Gen 15:6: "And he [Abraham] believed the LORD, and he counted it to him as righteousness" (ESV). Paul points out that Abraham is referred to as righteous through faith before the rite of circumcision and that, therefore, he is the father of both the circumcised and the uncircumcised (Rom 4:11-12). The true children of Abraham are not those who are physically descended from him but those who share his faith and who are, therefore, "children of the promise" (Rom 9:8). This theme is developed in Galatians, where Paul argues that the "offspring" or "seed" promised to Abraham is Jesus Christ. All who are "in Christ" are, through this relationship, true offspring of Abraham (Gal 3:16-18). Paul develops his thoughts on Abraham by allegorically contrasting the offspring of Hagar and the offspring of Sarah (Gal 4:21–5:1); Hagar's child was born in slavery and represents Mount Sinai, the Jewish Law. Sarah's child, on the other hand, was born free. Paul then argues that those who are offspring of Abraham through faith are set free from the Law and are living under God's grace, as children of Jerusalem in a spiritual sense, because, he argues, "the Jerusalem above is free, and she is our mother" (Gal 4:26 ESV).

Thus Paul's understanding of the Abraham stories helps to establish that the promises made to Abraham were not just for Jews but for all who believe in Christ. This has the effect of transforming the promises from their focus on the physical land of Israel and giving them a new spiritual focus on the blessings available to those who trust in Christ.

The Theme of Land

Although the theme of land is not prominent in the NT as a promise of physical territory, the relational aspects of the theme are prominent.[1] In Genesis the theme of land is inextricably bound up with a close relationship with God. A failure to maintain this relationship leads to the loss of land for Adam, Cain, Noah's contemporaries, and the Canaanites.

The corollary of this is that the fulfillment of the promise of land to Abraham receives a spiritual interpretation in some NT passages. Note particularly Hebrews 11, where the focus of Abraham's faith is on something much greater than the physical land of Canaan.

> By faith Abraham obeyed when he was called to go out to a place that he was to receive as an inheritance. And he went out, not knowing where he was going. By faith he went to live in the land of promise, as in a foreign land, living in tents with Isaac and Jacob, heirs with him of the same promise. For he was looking forward to the city that has foundations, whose designer and builder is God. (Heb 11:8-10 ESV)

Earlier in this epistle, the settlement in the promised land is characterized as "rest" (Heb 3:11). The author develops this idea of rest and gives it a spiritual application. There is a "rest" for God's people that is much greater than the physical land of Canaan (Heb 4:8-11). It is for rest in this spiritual sense that the readers of Hebrews are encouraged to strive.

This same emphasis occurs in the Epistles of Paul. Christians, Jews, and Gentiles do have an inheritance, but it is not a particular land or country. When Paul writes about "the riches of his glorious inheritance in the saints," he is encouraging his hearers to believe that what God has in store for them is beyond anything they have ever experienced before (Eph 1:18; cf. Col 1:12). This is what Peter refers to as "an inheritance that is imperishable, undefiled, and unfading, kept in heaven for you" (1 Pet 1:4 NRSV).

Thus the emphasis on the land that dominates much of the OT is not the main concern of the NT, where the emphasis is on the spiritual and eter-

---

1. This point is made very clearly by Millar in "Land."

nal rather than on the political and physical benefits of a close relationship to God. No doubt part of the reason for this was that the church embraced people of many nations and not just Jews. Members of the Jewish community could focus on the promise of a national identity in a specific territory, but the Christian hope was of necessity international and nonpolitical. In many ways the goal was not dissimilar to the original garden of Eden, reminiscences of which appear in the book of Revelation (Rev 22:1-2).

Adam

Paul develops the Genesis story of Adam and Eve theologically. He argues that the first man, Adam, brought sin into the world through his disobedience and, as a consequence of sin, death spread to all people born after Adam (Rom 5:12). However, if all could become sinners through one man, Paul argues that all may become righteous through one person, Jesus Christ (Rom 5:17). Adam left humanity a legacy of death since death reigned as a consequence of his act of disobedience, but through the righteous act of Christ grace would now reign with its legacy of eternal life (Rom 5:21). Paul returns to this theme in 1 Corinthians in the context of the resurrection. He makes the same contrast as in Romans, that Adam represents death and Jesus Christ represents life. Paul divides humanity into two groups: in Adam and in Christ. Those in Adam inherit death, but those in Christ share in new life through him (1 Cor 15:22).

The Prologue to the Gospel of John

The opening words of John's Gospel recall Genesis 1: "In the beginning . . ." It is not just that John regards the coming of Jesus Christ as an event that heralds a new beginning as significant as the creation of the world. For John all creation owes its existence to Christ, since "all things were made through him, and without him was not any thing made that was made" (John 1:3 ESV). Jesus Christ is the true light that dispels the darkness of the world (John 1:5). As Moyise points out, John probably interprets the Genesis injunction "Let *us* make humankind in our image" as a reference to the role of Christ the Son of God in creation.[1]

---

1. Moyise, *The Old Testament in the New*, 71.

Hebrews 11

In the context of the importance of faith, the Epistle to the Hebrews cites several characters from Genesis as examples. Abel, Enoch, Noah, Abraham, and Sarah had faith in God in very difficult circumstances. In the story of Cain and Abel, Hebrews explains the reason for the rejection of Cain's sacrifice and the acceptance of Abel as a reflection of Abel's faith and Cain's lack of it (Heb 11:4). Note also the emphasis on the faith of Sarah, which is not highlighted in Genesis, where her cynical laughter is given more prominence than her faith (Heb 11:11).

CONCLUSION

The book of Genesis has many interrelated themes and characters. It is well suited to be a book of beginnings, since many of these themes and characters are found throughout both the Old and New Testaments. While some of its emphases, such as the theme of land, are subsequently reinterpreted, there is nevertheless a sense in which Genesis is in microcosm a sourcebook for biblical theology.

Bibliography

Aalders, G. Ch. *Genesis*. 2 vols. BSC. Grand Rapids: Zondervan, 1981.

Abraham, Joseph. *Eve: Accused or Acquitted? A Reconsideration of Feminist Readings of the Creation Narrative Texts in Genesis 1–3*. Paternoster Biblical and Theological Monographs. Carlisle: Paternoster, 2002.

Aldredge-Clanton, Jann. *In Whose Image? God and Gender*. Rev. ed. New York: Crossroad, 2000.

Alexander, T. Desmond. *From Paradise to the Promised Land: An Introduction to the Main Themes of the Pentateuch*. 2nd ed. Grand Rapids: Baker, 2002.

———. "Genealogies, Seed and the Compositional Unity of Genesis." *TynBul* 44 (1993) 255-70.

———. "Genesis 22 and the Covenant of Circumcision." *JSOT* 25 (1983) 17-22.

———. "Royal Expectations in Genesis to Kings: Their Importance for Biblical Theology." *TynBul* 49 (1998) 191-212.

———, and D. W. Baker, eds. *Dictionary of the Old Testament: Pentateuch*. Downers Grove: InterVarsity, 2002.

———, and B. S. Rosner, eds. *The New Dictionary of Biblical Theology*. Leicester: Inter-Varsity, 2000.

Allen, Christine Garside. "'On Me Be the Curse, My Son!'" In *Encounter with the Text: Form and History in the Hebrew Bible*, ed. Martin J. Buss, 159-72. Philadelphia: Fortress, 1979.

Alter, Robert. *The Art of Biblical Narrative*. New York: Basic Books, 1981.

———. *Genesis*. New York: W. W. Norton, 1996.

Amos, Clare. *The Book of Genesis*. Peterborough: Epworth, 2004.

Anderson, Bernhard W. "From Analysis to Synthesis: The Interpretation of Genesis 1–11." *JBL* 97 (1978) 23-39.

———. *From Creation to New Creation: Old Testament Perspectives*. OBT. Minneapolis: Fortress, 1994.

Andrews, E. H. "The Age of the Earth." In *Creation and Evolution*, ed. Derek Burke, 46-67.

Attfield, Robin. *The Ethics of Environmental Concern*. 2nd ed. Athens: University of Georgia Press, 1991.

Atwell, James E. *The Sources of the Old Testament: A Guide to the Religious Thought of the Hebrew Bible.* London: T&T Clark, 2004.

Bailey, John A. "Initiation and the Primal Woman in Gilgamesh and Genesis 2–3." *JBL* 89 (1970) 137-50.

Barbour, Ian G. *Religion in an Age of Science.* Gifford Lectures, 1989-1991. San Francisco: Harper & Row, 1990.

———, ed. *Western Man and Environmental Ethics: Attitudes Towards Nature and Technology.* Reading, MA: Addison-Wesley, 1973.

Barr, James. "The Image of God in the Book of Genesis — A Study of Terminology." *BJRL* 51 (1968/69) 11-26.

———. "Man and Nature — The Ecological Controversy and the Old Testament." *BJRL* 55 (1972) 9-32.

Barton, John. *Reading the Old Testament: Method in Biblical Study.* Philadelphia: Westminster, 1984.

Basset, Frederick W. "Noah's Nakedness and the Curse of Canaan: A Case of Incest?" *VT* 21 (1971) 232-37.

Bauckham, Richard. *Bible and Mission: Christian Witness in a Postmodern World.* Grand Rapids: Baker, 2003.

Beattie, D. R. G. "What Is Genesis 2–3 About?" *ExpTim* 92 (1980/81) 8-10.

Bechtel, Lyn M. "Rethinking the Interpretation of Genesis 2:4b–3:24." In *A Feminist Companion to Genesis,* ed. Athalya Brenner, 77-117.

Berry, R. J. *God and the Biologist.* Leicester: Apollos, 1996.

———. "I Believe in God . . . Maker of Heaven and Earth." In *Creation and Evolution,* ed. Derek Burke, 76-108.

———. "Response to V. Wright." In *Creation and Evolution,* ed. Derek Burke, 131-38.

———, ed. *The Care of Creation: Focusing Concern and Action.* Leicester: Inter-Varsity, 2000.

Blocher, Henri. *In the Beginning: The Opening Chapters of Genesis.* Downers Grove: Inter-Varsity, 1984.

———. *Original Sin: Illuminating the Riddle.* New Studies in Biblical Theology. Grand Rapids: Wm. B. Eerdmans, 1999.

Bosch, David J. *Transforming Mission: Paradigm Shifts in Theology of Mission.* Maryknoll: Orbis, 1991.

Bray, Gerald. "The Significance of God's Image in Man." *TynBul* 42 (1991) 195-225.

Brenner, Athalya, ed. *A Feminist Companion to Genesis.* The Feminist Companion to the Bible 2. Sheffield: Sheffield Academic, 1993.

———. *Genesis.* The Feminist Companion to the Bible (second series) 1. Sheffield: Sheffield Academic, 1998.

Brodie, Thomas L., *Genesis as Dialogue: A Literary, Historical & Theological Commentary.* Oxford: Oxford University Press, 2001.

Brueggemann, Walter, *Genesis.* Interpretation. Atlanta: John Knox, 1982.

———. *The Land: Place as Gift, Promise, and Challenge in Biblical Faith.* OBT. Philadelphia: Fortress, 1977.

———. *Theology of the Old Testament: Testimony, Dispute, Advocacy.* Minneapolis: Fortress, 1997.

Buchanan, George Wesley. "The Old Testament Meaning of the Knowledge of Good and Evil." *JBL* 75 (1956) 114-20.

Burke, Derek. "Why Some Christians Believe in Evolution." In *Creation and Evolution,* 169-89.

————, ed. *Creation and Evolution.* Leicester: Inter-Varsity, 1985.

Calvin, John. *Genesis.* Wheaton: Crossway, 2001.

Carmichael, Calum M. "Some Sayings in Genesis 49." *JBL* 88 (1969) 438-44.

Carroll R., M. Daniel. "Blessing the Nations: Toward a Biblical Theology of Mission from Genesis." *BBR* 10 (2000) 17-34.

Cassuto, Umberto. *A Commentary on the Book of Genesis.* 1: *From Adam to Noah.* 2: *From Noah to Abraham.* Jerusalem: Magnes, 1961-64.

Childs, Brevard S. "Eden, Garden of." *IDB,* 2:22-23.

Clarke, Ernest G. "Jacob's Dream at Bethel as Interpreted in the Targums and the New Testament." *SR* 4 (1974/75) 367-77.

Clines, David J. A. "The Image of God in Man." *TynBul* 19 (1968) 53-103.

————. "The Significance of the 'Sons of God' Episode (Genesis 6:1-4) in the Context of the 'Primeval History' (Genesis 1–11)." *JSOT* 13 (1979) 33-46.

————. "Theme in Genesis 1–11." *CBQ* 38 (1976) 483-507.

————. *The Theme of the Pentateuch.* 2nd ed. JSOTSup 10. Sheffield: Sheffield Academic, 1997.

————. *What Does Eve Do to Help? and Other Readerly Questions to the Old Testament.* JSOTSup 94. Sheffield: Sheffield Academic, 1990.

Coats, George W. *Genesis, with an Introduction to Narrative Literature.* FOTL. Grand Rapids: Wm. B. Eerdmans, 1983.

Cohn, Robert L. "Narrative Structure and Canonical Perspective in Genesis." *JSOT* 25 (1983) 3-16.

Copan, Paul, and William Lane Craig. *Creation out of Nothing: A Biblical, Philosophical, and Scientific Exploration.* Grand Rapids: Baker, 2004.

Craigie, Peter C. *The Book of Deuteronomy.* NICOT. Grand Rapids: Wm. B. Eerdmans, 1976.

Curtis, E. M. "The Image of God (OT)." *ABD,* 3:389-91.

Dalley, Stephanie. *Myths from Mesopotamia: Creation, the Flood, Gilgamesh, and Others.* New York: Oxford University Press, 1989.

Davies, Philip R., and David J. A. Clines, eds. *The World of Genesis: Persons, Places, Perspectives.* JSOTSup 257. Sheffield: Sheffield Academic, 1998.

Delaney, Carol. "Abraham and the Seeds of Patriarchy." In *Genesis,* ed. Athalya Brenner, 129-49.

DeWitt, Calvin B. "Creation's Environmental Challenge to Evangelical Christianity." In *The Care of Creation,* ed. R. J. Berry, 60-73.

Diamond, J. A. "The Deception of Jacob: A New Perspective on an Ancient Solution to a Problem." *VT* 34 (1984) 211-13.

Dillmann, August. *Genesis, Critically and Exegetically Expounded.* Edinburgh: T&T Clark, 1897.

Donaldson, Mara E. "Kinship Theory in the Patriarchal Narratives: The Case of the Barren Wife." *JAAR* 49 (1981) 77-87.

Dumbrell, Wiliam J. "The Covenant with Abraham." *RTR* 41 (1982) 42-50.

Du Preez, J. "Social Justice: Motive for the Mission of the Church." *JTSA* 53 (1985) 36-46.

Eichrodt, Walther. "In the Beginning." In *Israel's Prophetic Heritage: Essays in Honor of James Muilenburg,* ed. Bernhard W. Anderson and Walter Harrelson, 1-10. New York: Harper, 1962.

Ellis, Peter F. *The Yahwist: The Bible's First Theologian.* Notre Dame: Fides, 1968.

Elsdon, Ron. *Greenhouse Theology: Biblical Perspectives on Caring for Creation.* Tunbridge Wells: Monarch, 1992.

Emerton, J. A. "Some Difficult Words in Genesis 49." In *Words and Meanings: Essays Presented to David Winton Thomas,* ed. Peter R. Ackroyd and Barnabas Lindars, 81-93. Cambridge: Cambridge University Press, 1968.

Enns, Peter E. "Exodus (Book)." *NDBT,* 146-52.

Fishbane, Michael. *Text and Texture: Close Readings of Selected Biblical Texts.* New York: Schocken, 1979. Repr. as *Biblical Text and Texture.* Oxford: Oneworld, 1998.

Fisher, Eugene. "*Gilgamesh* and Genesis: The Flood Story in Context." *CBQ* 32 (1970) 392-403.

Fisher, Loren R. "Creation at Ugarit and in the Old Testament." *VT* 15 (1965) 313-24.

Fokkelman, J. P. *Narrative Art in Genesis: Specimens of Stylistic and Structural Analysis.* SSN. Assen: Van Gorcum, 1975.

Foster, Benjamin R., trans. "Gilgamesh." *COS* 1:458-60.

Fraser, A. G. "The Age of the Earth." In *Creation and Evolution,* ed. Derek Burke, 17-41.

Fretheim, Terence E. "The Reclamation of Creation." *Int* 45 (1991) 354-65.

———. *The Suffering of God: An Old Testament Perspective.* OBT. Philadelphia: Fortress, 1984.

Frishman, Judith, and Lucas von Rampay, eds. *The Book of Genesis in Jewish and Oriental Christian Interpretation: A Collection of Essays.* Traditio exegetica graeca 5. Louvain: Peeters, 1997.

Frymer-Kensky, Tikva. "The Atrahasis Epic and Its Significance for Our Understanding of Genesis 1–9." *BA* 40 (1977) 147-55.

———. "What the Babylonian Flood Stories Can and Cannot Teach Us about the Genesis Flood." *BAR* 4/4 (1978) 32-41.

Fung, Yiu-Wing. *Victim and Victimizer: Joseph's Interpretation of His Destiny.* JSOTSup 308 Sheffield: Sheffield Academic, 2000.

Geller, Stephen A. "The Struggle at the Jabbok: The Uses of Enigma in a Biblical Narrative." *JANES* 14 (1982) 37-60.

Gesenius, Friedrich Heinrich Wilhelm. *Gesenius' Hebrew Grammar.* Ed. E. Kautzsch. Trans. A. E. Cowley. 2nd ed. Oxford: Clarendon, 1910.

Gibson, John C. L. *Genesis.* Daily Study Bible. 2 vols. Philadelphia: Westminster, 1981-82.

Gish, D. T. "A Consistent Biblical and Scientific View of Origins." In *Creation and Evolution,* ed. Derek Burke, 139-63.

Glover, R. H. *The Biblical Basis of Missions.* Los Angeles: Bible House, 1946.

Goldingay, John. "The Patriarchs in Scripture and History." In A. R. Millard and D. J. Wiseman, *Essays on the Patriarchal Narratives,* 11-42.

Good, Edwin M. "The 'Blessing' on Judah, Gen 49:8-12." *JBL* 82 (1963) 427-32.

———. *Irony in the Old Testament.* Philadelphia: Westminister, 1965.

Gordon, Cyrus H. "The Story of Jacob and Laban in the Light of the Nuzi Tablets." *BASOR* 66 (1937) 25-27.

Gordon, R. P. *Holy Land, Holy City: Sacred Geography and the Interpretation of the Bible.* Carlisle: Paternoster, 2004.

Gow, M. D. "Fall." *DOTP,* 285-91.

Graves, Robert, and Raphael Patai. *Hebrew Myths: The Book of Genesis.* Garden City: Doubleday, 1964.

Greenburg, Moshe. "Another Look at Rachel's Theft of the Teraphim." *JBL* 81 (1962) 239-48.

Greengus, Samuel. "Sisterhood Adoption at Nuzi and the 'Wife-Sister' in Genesis." *HUCA* 46 (1975) 5-31.

Griffiths, J. Gwyn. "The Celestial Ladder and the Gate of Heaven ('Genesis xxviii. 12 and 17')." *ExpTim* 76 (1964/65) 229-30.

Gruber, Mayer I. "Was Cain Angry or Depressed? Background of a Biblical Murder." *BAR* 6/6 (1980) 35-36.

Grudem, Wayne. *Evangelical Feminism and Biblical Truth.* Sisters, OR: Multnomah, 2004.

Habel, Norman C. *The Land Is Mine: Six Biblical Land Ideologies.* OBT. Minneapolis: Fortress, 1995.

Hallo, William W., ed. *The Context of Scripture.* 1: *Canonical Compositions from the Biblical World.* Leiden: Brill, 1997.

Ham, Ken. *Did Adam Have a Bellybutton? And Other Tough Questions about the Bible.* Green Forest, AR: Masterbooks, 2000.

Hamilton, Victor P. *The Book of Genesis: Chapters 1-17.* NICOT. Grand Rapids: Wm. B. Eerdmans, 1990.

Helyer, Larry R. "The Separation of Abram and Lot: Its Significance in the Patriarchal Narratives." *JSOT* 26 (1983) 77-88.

Hirsch, Samson Raphael. *Commentary on the Torah.* 1: *Genesis.* London: Judaica, 1966.

Humphreys, W. Lee. *The Character of God in the Book of Genesis.* Louisville: Westminster John Knox, 2001.

Jónsson, Gunnlaugur A. *The Image of God: Genesis 1:26-28 in a Century of Old Testament Research.* ConBOT 26. Stockholm: Almqvist & Wiksell, 1988.

Kaiser, Walter C. "Israel's Missionary Call." In *Perspectives on the World Christian Movement: A Reader,* ed. Ralph D. Winter and Steven C. Hawthorne, 25-34. Pasadena: William Carey Library, 1981.

———. *Mission in the Old Testament: Israel as a Light to the Nations.* Grand Rapids: Baker, 2000.

Kidner, Derek. *Genesis.* TOTC. Downers Grove: InterVarsity, 1967.

Lacey, Robert, and Danny Danziger. *The Year 1000: What Life Was Like at the Turn of the First Millennium.* Boston: Little, Brown, 1999.

Laffey, Alice L. *An Introduction to the Old Testament: A Feminist Perspective.* Philadelphia: Fortress, 1988.

Lambert, W. G. "Trees, Snakes and Gods in Ancient Syria and Anatolia." *BSOAS* 48 (1985) 435-51.

———, and A. R. Millard. *Atrahasis: The Babylonian Story of the Flood.* Oxford: Clarendon, 1969.

Lohfink, Norbert. *Great Themes from the Old Testament*. Edinburgh: T&T Clark, 1982.

Longacre, Robert E. *Joseph: A Story of Divine Providence*. Winona Lake: Eisenbrauns, 1989.

Longman, Tremper, III. *How To Read Genesis*. Downers Grove: InterVarsity, 2005.

Lucas, Ernest C. *Can We Believe Genesis Today? The Bible and the Questions of Science*. Leicester: Inter-Varsity, 2001.

McCarthy, Dennis J. "Three Covenants in Genesis." *CBQ* 26 (1964) 179-89.

McConville, J. Gordon. *Grace in the End: A Study in Deuteronomic Theology*. Grand Rapids: Zondervan, 1993.

————. "The Old Testament and the Enjoyment of Wealth." In *Christ and Consumerism: A Critical Analysis of the Spirit of the Age,* ed. Craig Bartholomew and Thorsten Moritz, 34-53. Carlisle: Paternoster, 2000.

————. "The Shadow of the Curse: A 'Key' to Old Testament Theology." *Evangel* 3 (1985) 2-5.

McGrath, Alister E. *The Science of God: An Introduction to Scientific Theology*. London: T&T Clark, 2004.

McIntosh, Andy. *Genesis for Today: Showing the Relevance of the Creation/Evolution Debate to Today's Society*. Epsom: Day One, 1997.

McKeown, James. "Blessings and Curses." *DOTP*, 83-87.

————. "Land, Fertility, Famine." *DOTP*, 487-91.

————. "A Study of the Main Unifying Themes in the Hebrew Text of the Book of Genesis." Ph.D. diss., The Queen's University of Belfast, 1991.

Martens, Elmer A. *God's Design: A Focus on Old Testament Theology*. 2nd ed. Grand Rapids: Baker, 1994.

Martin, R. A. "The Earliest Messianic Interpretation of Genesis 3:15." *JBL* 84 (1965) 425-27.

Middleton, J. Richard. *The Liberating Image: The Imago Dei*. Grand Rapids: Brazos, 2005.

Millar, J. G. "Land." *NDBT*, 623-27.

Millard, A. R. "The Celestial Ladder and the Gate of Heaven (Genesis xxviii.12, 17)." *ExpTim* 78 (1966/67) 86-87.

————, and D. J. Wiseman, eds. *Essays on the Patriarchal Narratives*. Winona Lake: Eisenbrauns, 1983.

Miller, J. Maxwell. "The Descendants of Cain: Notes on Genesis 4." *ZAW* 86 (1974) 164-74.

————. "In the 'Image' and 'Likeness' of God." *JBL* 91 (1972) 289-304.

Miscall, Peter D. "The Jacob and Joseph Stories as Analogies." *JSOT* 6 (1978) 28-40.

————. *The Workings of Old Testament Narrative*. Philadelphia: Fortress, 1983.

Moltmann, Jürgen. *God in Creation: A New Theology of Creation and the Spirit of God*. Gifford Lectures, 1984-1985. San Francisco: Harper & Row, 1985.

Motyer, J. A. *The Revelation of the Divine Name*. London: Tyndale, 1959.

Moyise, Steve. *The Old Testament in the New*. Continuum Biblical Studies. New York: Continuum, 2001.

Oelschlaeger, Max. *Caring for Creation: An Ecumenical Approach to the Environmental Crisis*. New Haven: Yale University Press, 1994.

Pannenberg, Wolfhart. *Systematic Theology*. 3 vols. Grand Rapids: Wm. B. Eerdmans, 1991.

Passmore, John. *Man's Responsibility for Nature: Ecological Problems and Western Tradition*. 2nd ed. London: Duckworth, 1980.

Peters, George W. *A Biblical Theology of Missions*. Chicago: Moody, 1972.

Pinnock, Clark H. "Climbing out of a Swamp: The Evangelical Struggle to Understand the Creation Texts." *Int* 43 (1989) 143-55.

Pirson, Ron. *The Lord of the Dreams: A Semantic and Literary Analysis of Genesis 37–50.* JSOTSup 355. London: Sheffield Academic, 2002.

Polzin, Robert. "'The Ancestress of Israel' in Danger." *Semeia* 3 (1975) 81-98.

Porter, Ray. "Where Was the Garden of Eden?" *Origins* 1/3 (1987) 3-4.

Pritchard, James B., ed. *Ancient Near Eastern Texts Relating to the Old Testament.* 3rd ed. Princeton: Princeton University Press, 1969.

Rad, Gerhard von. *Genesis.* 2nd ed. OTL. Philadelphia: Westminster, 1972.

———. *Old Testament Theology.* Vol. 1. New York: Harper & Row, 1962.

———. "The Theological Problem of the Old Testament Doctrine of Creation." In *The Problem of the Hexateuch and Other Essays*, 131-43. Edinburgh: Oliver & Boyd, 1966.

Redford, Donald B. "The 'Land of the Hebrews' in Gen. XL 15." *VT* 15 (1965) 529-32.

———. *A Study of the Biblical Story of Joseph (Genesis 37–50).* VTSup 20. Leiden: Brill, 1970.

Rendsburg, Gary. "Janus Parallelism in Gen 49:26." *JBL* 99 (1980) 291-93.

Rendtorff, Rolf. *The Problem of the Process of Transmission in the Pentateuch.* JSOTSup 89. Sheffield: Sheffield Academic, 1990.

———. "What Is New in the New Covenant?" In *Canon and Theology: Overtures to an Old Testament Theology*, 196-206. OBT. Minneapolis: Fortress, 1993.

Ross, Allen P. *Creation and Blessing: A Guide to the Study and Exposition of the Book of Genesis.* Grand Rapids: Baker, 1988.

———. "The Curse of Canaan." *BSac* 137 (1980) 223-40.

———. "The Table of Nations in Genesis 10 — Its Content." *BSac* 138 (1981) 22-34.

Roth, Wolfgang M. W. "The Wooing of Rebekah." *CBQ* 34 (1972) 177-87.

Ruether, Rosemary. *Gaia and God: An Ecofeminist Theology of Earth Healing.* San Francisco: HarperSanFrancisco, 1992.

———. *Sexism and God-Talk: Toward a Feminist Theology.* Boston: Beacon, 1983.

Santmire, H. Paul. "The Genesis Creation Narratives Revisited." *Int* 45 (1991) 366-79.

Sarna, Nahum M. *Genesis.* JPS Torah Commentary. Philadelphia: Jewish Publication Society, 1989.

Sasson Jack M. "Word-Play in Gen 6:8-9." *CBQ* 37 (1975) 165-66.

Sawyer, John F. A. "The Meaning of בְּצֶלֶם אֱלֹהִים ('In the Image of God') in Genesis I–XI." *JTS* 25 (1974) 418-26.

Schaeffer, Francis A. *Genesis in Space and Time.* Downers Grove: InterVarsity, 1972.

———. *Pollution and the Death of Man.* Wheaton: Tyndale, 1970.

Schottroff, Luise. "The Creation Narrative: Genesis 1:1–2:4a." In *A Feminist Companion to Genesis*, ed. Athalya Brenner, 24-38.

Schüngel-Straumann, Helen. "On the Creation of Man and Woman in Genesis 1–3: The History and Reception of the Texts Reconsidered." In *A Feminist Companion to Genesis*, ed. Athalya Brenner, 53-76.

Selman, M. J. "Chronicles." *NDBT*, 188-95.

Senior, Donald, and Carroll Stuhlmueller. *The Biblical Foundations for Mission.* Maryknoll: Orbis, 1983.

Sherlock, Charles. *The Doctrine of Humanity.* Downers Grove: InterVarsity, 1996.

Shuster, Marguerite. *The Fall and Sin: What We Have Become as Sinners.* Grand Rapids: Wm. B. Eerdmans, 2004.

Sider, Ronald J. "Biblical Foundations for Creation Care." In *The Care of Creation,* ed. R. J. Berry, 43-49.

Skinner, John. *A Critical and Exegetical Commentary on the Book of Genesis.* 2nd ed. ICC. Edinburgh: T&T Clark, 1930.

Speiser, E. A. *Genesis.* 3rd ed. AB 1. Garden City: Doubleday, 1979.

Stager, Lawrence E. "Jerusalem and the Garden of Eden." *ErIsr* 26 (1999) 183-94.

Sternberg, Meir. *The Poetics of Biblical Narrative.* Bloomington: Indiana University Press, 1985.

Thomas, W. H. Griffith. *Genesis: A Devotional Commentary.* Grand Rapids: Wm. B. Eerdmans, 1946.

Thompson, Phyllis A. *A Transparent Woman: The Compelling Story of Gladys Aylward.* Grand Rapids: Zondervan, 1971.

Thurman, L. Duane. *How To Think about Evolution and Other Bible-Science Controversies.* 2nd ed. Downers Grove: InterVarsity, 1978.

Tillich, Paul. *Systematic Theology.* 3 vols. Chicago: University of Chicago Press, 1951-1963.

Trible, Phyllis. *God and the Rhetoric of Sexuality.* OBT. Philadelphia: Fortress, 1992.

—————. "The Other Woman: A Literary and Theological Study of the Hagar Narratives." In *Understanding the Word: Essays in Honour of Bernhard W. Anderson,* ed. James T. Butler, Edgar W. Conrad, and Ben C. Ollenburger, 221-46. JSOTSup 37. Sheffield: JSOT, 1985.

—————. *Texts of Terror.* OBT. Philadelphia: Fortress, 1984.

Turner, Laurence. A. *Announcements of Plot in Genesis.* JSOTSup 96. Sheffield: JSOT, 1990.

—————. *Genesis.* Readings. Sheffield: Sheffield Academic, 2000.

Van Leeuwen, Raymond C. "בָּרָא." *NIDOTTE,* 1:728-35.

Van Seters, John. *Abraham in History and Tradition.* New Haven: Yale University Press, 1975.

Van Zyl, D. C. "Cosmology, Ecology, and Missiology: A Perspective from Genesis 1." *Missionalia* 19 (1991) 203-14.

Vawter, Bruce. "The Canaanite Background of Genesis 49." *CBQ* 17 (1955) 1-18.

—————. *On Genesis: A New Reading.* Garden City: Doubleday, 1977.

Weinfeld, Moshe. "The Covenant of Grant in the Old Testament and in the Ancient Near East." *JAOS* 90 (1970): 184-203.

—————. The Promise of the Land: The Inheritance of the Land of Canaan by the Israelites. Berkeley: University of California Press, 1993.

Wenham, Gordon J. "The Coherence of the Flood Narrative." *VT* 28 (1978) 336-48.

—————. *Genesis 1–15.* WBC. Waco: Word, 1987.

—————. *Genesis 16–50.* WBC. Waco: Word, 1994.

—————. "Sanctuary Symbolism in the Garden of Eden Story." *PWCJS* 9 (1986) 19-25.

—————. "The Symbolism of the Animal Rite in Genesis 15: A Response to G. F. Hasel, *JSOT* 19 (1981) 61-78." *JSOT* 22 (1982) 134-37.

Westermann, Claus. *Genesis 1–11.* CC. Minneapolis: Augsburg, 1984.

—————. *Genesis 12–36.* CC. Minneapolis: Augsburg, 1985.

—————. *Genesis 37–50.* CC. Minneapolis: Augsburg, 1986.

————. *Joseph: Eleven Bible Studies on Genesis.* Minneapolis: Fortress, 1996.

Whitcomb, John C. *The World That Perished.* Grand Rapids: Baker, 1973.

————, and Henry M. Morris, *The Genesis Flood: The Biblical Record and Its Scientific Implications.* Philadelphia: Presbyterian and Reformed, 1961.

White, Lynn, Jr. "The Historical Roots of Our Ecologic Crisis." In *The Care of Creation,* ed. R. J. Berry, 31-42.

Whybray, R. N. "The Joseph Story and Pentateuchal Criticism." *VT* 18 (1968) 522-28.

Wifall, Walter. "Gen. 3:15 — A Protevangelium?" *CBQ* 36 (1974) 361-65.

Williamson, Paul R. *Abraham, Israel and the Nations: The Patriarchal Promise and Its Covenantal Development in Genesis.* JSOTSup 315. Sheffield: Sheffield Academic, 2000.

————. "Covenant." *NDBT,* 419-29.

Willis, John T. *Genesis.* Living Word Commentary. Austin: Sweet, 1979.

Wiseman, Donald J. "Abraham Reassessed." In A. R. Millard and D. J. Wiseman, *Essays on the Patriarchal Narratives,* 139-56.

Wiseman, P. J., *Ancient Records and the Structure of Genesis.* Nashville: Nelson, 1985.

————. *Clues to Creation in Genesis.* London: Marshall, Morgan & Scott, 1977.

Wolde, Ellen von. *Stories of the Beginning: Genesis 1–11 and Other Creation Stories.* Harrisburg: Morehouse, 1997.

Wright, Verna. "The Origin of Man." In *Creation and Evolution,* ed. Derek Burke, 116-30.

Young, Davis A. *The Biblical Flood: A Case Study of the Church's Response to Extrabiblical Evidence.* Grand Rapids: Wm. B. Eerdmans, 1995.

————. *Creation and the Flood,* Grand Rapids: Baker Book House, 1977.

Index of Names

Index of Scripture and Other Ancient Writings

3:1-5	261	4:10-16	244	6:9-10	52-53
3:1-6	254	4:10	41, 55, 105, 242,	6:9—9:11	61, 62, 245
3:1-24	223		245	6:9	2, 29, 200
3:1	242	4:11-12	41, 221, 245	6:11-13	53-55, 246, 254
3:6-8	261	4:11-14	42	6:11	246
3:6-19	42	4:11	41, 74, 219, 222,	6:12	54, 254
3:8	46, 250, 363		245, 261	6:13	54, 207
3:14-15	221	4:12-14	363	6:14-22	55-56
3:14-19	253	4:12	93, 225, 245	6:14	55
3:14	36, 73, 204, 219,	4:14	225, 232	6:15	55
	224, 242, 272	4:15	225	6:17	54, 55, 246
3:15-16	224	4:17-22	43, 254	6:18	288
3:15-17	46	4:17-24	43-44	6:18-22	56
3:15	10, 36, 37, 38, 39,	4:17-26	201	6:22	56, 221
	44, 90, 198, 203,	4:17	46	7:1-5	56-57
	204, 205, 206, 253,	4:18-19	46	7:3	198
	254, 320, 321	4:18-22	201	7:5	57
3:16	36, 37, 47, 228	4:20	44	7:6-16	57-58
3:17-18	369	4:21	44	7:11	299
3:17-19	36, 42, 221, 227,	4:22	44	7:13-16	62
	232, 244, 249, 253	4:23-24	201, 254	7:13	62
3:17	47, 73, 95, 219,	4:23-26	43	7:17-24	58-59
	242, 261	4:25-26	44-45, 201	7:17	62
3:18-19	41, 244	4:25	90, 198, 205, 206,	7:18	62
3:19	38, 227, 242, 243,		254	7:19	58
	244	5	201	7:20-22	62
3:20	338, 339	5:1-3	45	7:20	58
3:21	66	5:1-32	45-47	7:21-23	221, 254
3:22-24	37	5:1	3, 19, 29, 200, 277	7:21—8:1	141
3:22	283	5:2	304	7:23	62
3:23	38, 54, 227, 242,	5:3	46, 277	7:24	58, 62
	244	5:22	46	8:1-14	59-60
3:24	93, 254	5:24	46, 52	8:1	59, 62, 109, 146,
4	182, 201, 316	5:25-31	46		207, 254
4:1-7	39-41	5:28-29	53	8:3	62
4:1-16	244	5:29	46, 47, 65, 74, 227,	8:4-6	62
4:1	39, 90		232, 254, 355	8:5	59
4:2	242, 244	6:1-2	49	8:6	59
4:3-15	43	6:1-4	15, 48	8:8	59
4:3	242	6:3	49, 50	8:10-12	59
4:4	40	6:4	50, 74, 241	8:13	59, 62
4:5	40, 245	6:5-8	50-52, 242	8:14	59, 62
4:7	40	6:5-12	207	8:15-19	61
4:8-12	42	6:6	51, 249, 273, 323,	8:16-19	62
4:8-16	41-43		324	8:18-22	254
4:8	41, 245	6:7	51, 93	8:20-22	60, 288
4:10-12	42	6:8	52, 65, 254	8:20	221